Quentin W. Fleming

Put Earned Value (C/SCSC) Into Your Management Control System

HUMPHREYS & ASSOCIATES inc.

Management Consultants
1300 Quail Street
Newport Beach, California 92660
(714) 955-2981

© Copyright 1983, **PUBLISHING HORIZONS, INC.**
623 High Street
Worthington, Ohio 43085

Printed in the United States

34  54

Library of Congress Cataloging in Publication Data

Fleming Quentin W.
    Put earned value (C/SCSC) into your
management control system.

    Includes bibliographical references and index.
    1. Cost control. 2. Program budgeting.
3. Production control. 4. United States Dept. of
Defense—Procurement—Cost control. I. Title.
II. Title: Put earned value (C./S.C.S.C.) into your
management control system. III. Title: Management
control system.
HD47.3.F6 1983   658.1'552   83-3054
ISBN 0-942280-04-0
ISBN 0-942280-03-2 (pbk.)

CONTENTS

LIST OF FIGURES

PREFACE

This book is about the Department of Defense's (DOD) Cost/Schedule Control System Criteria -- C/SCSC. First introduced in 1967, these 35 criteria have resulted in the modification of well over 100 management control systems at firms and their operating divisions throughout the United States. This document is intended to provide both an executive type summary (unofficial) on the impact of these modifications, as well as a more comprehensive textbook on the subject in which the reader may go into as much depth as is personally desired.

Although the idea was first introduced and successfully implemented by the military procurement establishment, there is nothing inherent in the concept which limits its use to the management of DOD programs only. On the contrary, the C/SCSC technique has made its way over to other governmental agencies, as well as to some private firms which have incorporated the concept into their internal management control systems.

The C/SCS Criteria approach and the resulting modified management control systems have been referred to by many titles over the years. It has been termed simply "C-Spec," "C/S Squared," "Earned Value Budgeting," "Performance Measurement System," and so on. But whatever name is used, the resulting concept is always the same, and has three primary objectives:

One -- to merge the activities of planning, task definition, work authorization, budgeting, accounting, and scheduling into one all-inclusive management control system.

Two -- to require detailed, comprehensive planning which may be quantified and measured along the way.

Three -- to focus management's attention on "earned value," i.e., what work was actually accomplished from the detailed plan. Management looks at its gross schedule position as the difference between what it had planned to accomplish and what it actually accomplished (earned value), and at its cost position as the difference between what it actually spent and what it actually accomplished (earned value).

In this book we will use the term earned value in the title, but we will refer to the management control systems resulting from the Criteria as C/SCS, for that would seem to be the most widely accepted general name, and because it seems to best describe the management systems in a generic sense. But throughout most of these chapters we will focus on the Department of Defense's C/SCSC for the main thrust will be to review the systems and procedures that have had 15 years of hard-won experience in the defense industry. As every seasoned manager knows all too well, any management control system is only as good as its ability to accurately reflect the truth in an objective way, as well as its ability to not be subject to the manipulations or distortions by some manager wanting to portray a different story. The DOD and its private contractors have carefully worked out many of the bugs associated with the implementation of these modified systems over the past decade and a half. Hence, we will focus on the DOD C/SCS technique and the lessons learned as a way of describing a management control system with wide applications beyond this one industry.

This book was prepared to give those business people who may have heard of C/SCS, but who have not actually worked with it, an opportunity to review the concept. It is quite possible that C/SCS will have applications with their particular business or project. It is not that the subject has been ignored by writers. On the contrary, when I began this project I had a stack of government/private publications on C/SCSC over six inches high, which has since grown to over four feet in length, and this is likely only a small sample of what has been written. Unfortunately, as with most government and company publications, these documents are technically accurate and about as interesting as reading a local telephone directory. Of more importance, however, is the fact that nowhere does there seem to exist a concise summary dealing with the essential theory of an earned value management control system in a comprehensive way. Short of attending a three-to five-day seminar costing several hundred dollars -- and there are some excellent ones available -- there is little opportunity for the curious business person to obtain an introduction to the subject. Hence, this book was prepared.

***

My first formal exposure to C/SCS came in 1970 when my company, the Aircraft Division of Northrop Corporation, went through an initial Air Force validation of its modified management control system. The system was approved in 1971, and it has been used ever since on the F-5 fighter aircraft series to keep it within costs, on schedule, and to meet its technical performance objectives.

In that same year of 1971, I took a leave of absence from Northrop and went on a short-term (which lasted five years) overseas appointment with the U.S. government. During that period I had absolutely no contact with Northrop Corporation, my friends in the aerospace industry, or C/SCS. Upon my return from overseas I rejoined the company and, to my amazement, found C/SCS not only alive and well, but actually thriving. The Aircraft Division was using its basic C/SCS to manage all programs, even those under firm fixed price contracts where there was no governmental requirement to do so. In short, Northrop Aircraft had found the concept to be useful and had adopted it as its sole internal management control system. There can be no greater compliment to a governmental requirement than to have private industry, of its own accord, adopt such requirements for its own private use.

To set the record straight, it wasn't that I didn't believe that C/SCS had merit, which it certainly has. Rather, after having spent some dozen or so years in the industry at the time, I had seen many a new governmental system introduced, be "permanently" imposed, and later watched it fade away with the retirement of some general or admiral -- the system's sponsor. C/SCS seems to have transcended the efforts of any one officer or department or group. The C/SCS Criteria concept appears to be accepted and expanding in applications with the government and, to a lesser degree, with private industry. But the private industry applications of the C/SCS systems have barely started.

***

I mentioned earlier that my first formal exposure to C/SCS came in 1970; put an emphasis on the word "formal." Over the years I had worked with two aspects of program management: budgeting and scheduling. I had witnessed the two functions rarely working together as a team; more often each going off in a separate direction, each building their own loyalty bases. On some programs, the schedulers and budgeters rarely even talked. The implementation of C/SCS required that these two functions and others work within the same framework of one management control system.

But the point I want to stress here is that C/SCS is a management control approach that requires the integration of both the scheduling and the budgeting functions of management. To properly understand C/SCS, therefore, one should have some basic understanding of what the budgeting and the scheduling functions are all about. To understand only one, or worse, neither of these two functions, just what they do and why they are needed in business, would do an injustice to a full understanding of C/SCS (earned value) theory. Thus, this book will have the following four parts in an effort to provide a proper foundation of the subject:

Part I   The Basics of Budgeting

Part II   The Basics of Scheduling

Part III   The Cost/Schedule Control System Criteria Concept

Part IV   Further Applications & Executive Summary

ACKNOWLEDGEMENTS

There were several people who guided me through this project, and I would like to express my personal thanks to each of them.

From the beginning my sometimes boss, always spiritual advisor, Lee F. Wade, Controller of Northrop's Aircraft Division, helped me. It was Lee who played a major role in the 1970-71 validation effort, which had to reshape the existing management control system to meet the C/SCS Criteria. But probably of greater significance, it has been Lee who has had to defend the system against unnecessary changes from each new manager who comes on the scene. A small change here, a modification there, and soon the validated system becomes invalid. Lee has had the unpleasant task of saying "no" to each hard-nosed executive who arrives and wants to remake the approved system.

Two of Lee's closest lieutenants also contributed much to this work. Paul J. Jaromscak, a manager in Northrop's new Advanced Systems Division, reviewed every chapter and caused me many a rewrite when I failed to say what I had intended to say. Donald L. Rainey, also a manager in this same organization, was quick to point out when he felt I was off the main thrust. Of particular significance was the contribution of Jim Kinnu, Vice President and Program Manager, who by his temperament and management style will challenge every sacred cow that comes his way. We knew we were on solid ground when he accepted our earned value system.

Outside of Northrop, I have received special encouragement from two gentlemen from an organization which specializes in C/SCS applications, Humphreys & Associates, management consultants of Newport Beach, California. Gary Humphreys, whose firm has conducted seminars for over 10,000 people from 450 organizations in the United States and Europe, and who was the U.S. Army Team Director on the first Tri-Service demonstration review, made significant comments on every section of the manuscript. Also, Lloyd L. Carter, who joined Humphreys in 1981 after retiring from the Air Force Institute of Technology (AFIT) where he taught C/SCS applications to some 5,000 people, and who has been affiliated with C/SCS since 1967 and participated in over 20 validation reviews, was kind enough to read each chapter and supply me with valuable material on the subject.

In addition to those who helped me while the book was in preparation, certain individuals took time out from their busy schedules to read and comment on the preliminary draft. From Northrop my personal thanks to Ernest P. Salmon, Manager of Financial Planning and Overhead Control of the Aircraft Division; and to Don A. Tatman, Vice President of Financial Management in the Aircraft Services Division.

From the government, I must give very special thanks to Daniel Schild, Chief of the Cost Management Systems Division, Aeronautical Systems Division, Wright-Patterson Air Force Base, Ohio. Dan was on Northrop's original review team in 1970, has been Team Chief on some 14 demonstration reviews, and has participated in almost 40 other full and partial C/SCS reviews. Also from Dan's organization I must thank Judy Collins who has served as cost performance analyst and Team Chief on many important validation reviews. Also my thanks go to Seymour Uberman, now a management consultant, recently retired from the Defense Systems Management College, DSMC, Fort Belvoir, Virginia, where he taught their C/SCSC course for several years prior to his retirement in 1981. Also, to Robert R. Kemps, who, while he was with the Assistant Secretary of Defense (Comptroller) did much original presentation work which helped the C/SCSC concept to survive, and has now joined the Department of Energy where he is continuing his fine work with the technique, for the material he sent me, some of which you will see in the forthcoming pages.

I must give thanks to four people from the academic world: Dr. Edward V. Sedgwick, lecturer in management at the Graduate School of Management, University of California at Los Angeles; Dr. Arthur W. Gutenberg, professor of management and policy sciences, Graduate School of Business Administration, University of Southern California; Dr. Linn C. Stuckenbruck, lecturer in systems management with the Institute of Safety and Systems Management, University of Southern California, and author of The Implementation of Project Management, Addison-Wesley, 1981; and to John Badin recently a professor of management, Florida Atlantic University, who earlier retired from the Air Force Systems Command where he served as the Chairman of the AFSC cost accomplishment subgroup which developed the Cost/Schedule Planning Control system specification that was later adopted by the DOD as the C/SCSC. I am deeply honored to have their comments on the draft.

Lastly, I must give thanks to the Aircraft Division of Northrop Corporation for having developed perhaps the finest C/SCS management control system in the nation and, of equal importance, for using their system consistently over the past decade.

Quentin W. Fleming

PART I
THE BASICS OF BUDGETING

BUDGETS AND
SOME BUDGETING CONCEPTS

> *budg'et... 3 a : a statement of the financial position of a sovereign body (as of a nation) for a definite period of time based on detailed estimates of planned or expected expenditures during the period and proposals for financing them -- used orig. of such a statement presented annually by the chancellor of the exchequer to the British House of Commons b : a plan for the coordination of resources (as of money or manpower) and expenditures <a good family ~ keeps something in reserve for emergencies> ; esp : such a plan covering a definite period of time ...*

> *Webster's New International Dictionary*
> *of the English Language*
> *Third Edition 1981*

For nearly half a century Webster's Dictionary has offered definitions of a budget, only part of which seems to fit the modern business environment. They are cumbersome definitions which fail to reflect how budgets are used in industry today. Years later (1940), an accountant from the Midwest defined budgets in the following way in his popular book on the same subject: "A budget is a forecast, in detail, of the results of an officially recognized program of operations based on the highest reasonable expectation of operating efficiency."[1]

Well, this is certainly a more palatable definition of a budget than the earlier Webster version, but still it lacks the conciseness of a description recently published in a book by Herbert Spiro on finance for "non-financial" managers (which is probably why so many liked it). Dr. Spiro states simply that a budget is "a quantitative expression of management's plans."[2] In just six words this gentleman has managed to focus on the subject.

In addition to providing an excellent six-word definition of a budget, his full definition describes in detail what a budget is supposed to be and what it is supposed to do for an organization. There is much substance in his full definition, which should be reflected on in order to get a proper perspective on the subject of budgets:

> A budget is a quantitative expression of management's plans. Both explicitly and implicitly it presents the intentions and objectives of management to all echelons of the organization and provides a vehicle for monitoring the implementation of plans. In addition, it enables management to assess the adherence of individuals and organizational components to the goals stipulated in the plan and thereby to provide a quantitative basis for measuring and rewarding individual and departmental performance.[3]

First, he assumes that the organization has a plan for itself and that this plan is made available to all levels of an organization. Basic stuff -- certainly. But how many organizations exist today without going through the trouble of establishing a long-range strategy for themselves. Some firms do prepare such a document, called a long-range plan, but then limit its distribution to a selected few as if it were some closely guarded proprietary secret. Even worse, some organizations actually go through the effort of preparing a long-range planning document for the sole reason that the requirement to do so is imposed on them from above, but these organizations have no commitment to the implementation of such plans. They merely go through an annual exercise, then file it away for another year. Dr. Spiro's definition has assumed that management's goals are reflected in their strategic plan and that the plan is communicated to all levels of the organization through the use of operating budgets.

Second, management's plan, as reflected in the budget, provides the basis for monitoring results along the way. An organization does not have to wait until a time period is past in order to determine how well it is doing in relation to its goals. A well prepared budget is time-phased, so that status can be determined periodically and reviewed with management. Individual components of the budget can be examined so that those on track and, more importantly, those off track can be examined. A properly prepared budget allows management to know its status continuously, i.e., who is sticking to the plan, and allows for corrective action to be taken if deemed necessary by an informed management.

Lastly, a well-prepared budget allows a "quantitative basis for measuring and rewarding individual and departmental performance." It's an old-fashioned concept but one as basic as a pat-on-the-head when Johnnie's been good, and a kick in the -- when he's been bad. Why not? If management's goals are truly manifested in its budget, everyone knows what those goals are and what is expected of them in the way of performance, why not a reward/punishment system for good/bad performance?

TOP-DOWN, BOTTOM-UP, AND ROLLING-WAVE BUDGETS

There are a few budget terms that are used continuously in business settings and that should be completely understood. The term top-down budgets refers to gross, unsupported projections, often used to allow senior management to set out the goals or financial parameters for an organization. Such top-down budgets should be subsequently supported by detailed bottom-up budgets, which serve to reinforce that such goals of management can, in fact, be met. Bottom-up budgets are, as the term implies, a summation of the individual pieces. Both terms have definite utility in today's business setting.

Top-down budgets have their value in that they are easily prepared, easily analyzed, and easily modified to accommodate new tasks or redirections. They fit in well in long-range planning exercises, i.e., five- to ten-year projections. Their short-coming is that they are not always realistic, i.e., when the pieces are subsequently added up, the top-down values are sometimes found to be overambitious and unattainable. Another drawback is that since no detail exists for such projections, each organizational component (individual managers) doesn't know what their piece of the action is, because only the top summary is defined.

Bottom-up budgets have their value in that they provide maximum assurances that management's goals are reasonable and attainable because of the supporting detail and the fact that more thought process has gone into their preparation. Each of the managers should have had their say and, once approved, should know exactly what is expected of them. But bottom-up budgets are slower to prepare, cumbersome to modify, and take greater efforts to monitor.

Both top-down and bottom-up budgets have their own utility and both are incorporated in another technique called the rolling wave budget. In this approach, a full-period projection is made using a combination of top-down/unsupported budgets, with the nearest six-month segment fully supported by detailed bottom-up budgets. As time passes, the top-down budget is progressively definitized and replaced with bottom-up budgets (the rolling wave), which should extend three to six months into the near-term future, then projected to the end with only top-down budgets. Thus, each of these techniques -- top-down, bottom-up, and rolling wave budgets -- have their own value when used at the appropriate time in the budgeting cycle.

THE BUDGET WINDOW

Every organization has an opportunity to establish optimum performance goals for itself and such periods last but a short time. For simplicity, this brief time frame will be given a name: the budget window. Such windows occur prior to the start of the period to be budgeted, i.e., the next fiscal quarter, the next calendar year, etc., but late enough to be able to gain the interests of the performing managers. From a financial standpoint, it might seem desirable to have detailed bottom-up budgets a year in advance of the period to be measured. But try to get the attention of line/staff managers a year in advance. "Hell, I can't see next week, let alone next year" would likely be a common response.

The budget window when allowed to pass, forfeits an excellent opportunity to establish maximum performance goals from all performing organizations. Prior to the start of the new period, it is rather easy to obtain realistic but ambitious performance goals from all of the operating departments. However, once into the budget period, individual managers become painfully aware of some of the problems to be encountered, and they are then reluctant (no longer willing) to sign up for ambitious targets for themselves. True, top management can still impose ambitious goals for everyone. But once the period starts, it's not as effective as the pre-period individual commitments made by the very managers who will be making daily choices, and who can influence in a collective way the final outcome of their organization's direction.

The budget window is also critical to the success of an organization because it is during this short time frame that two set-asides must be made from the limited resources available, coming right off the top of the funds to be allocated: One -- a provision for profits, and Two -- a provision for a management reserve. The management reserve is intended to cover any and all contingencies that are certain to occur, and it is expected that the reserve will be used up during the period of performance. The management reserve is the buffer which gives assurances that the profit set-aside will, in fact, survive the future uncertainties facing all organizations.

WHO NEEDS A BUDGET

Leaving the world of theory for a moment, how many industry executives can truthfully say that their organization's budget is an accurate representation of the goals for their activities? Further, how many can say that each of their lieutenants are rewarded and/or punished with some type of bonus system for performance against these budgets. Unfortunately, far too many executives would have to answer in the negative. Those executives who do not bother with budgets, or who pay them lip service only leaving that activity for the "bean counters," are missing an opportunity to employ a proven management tool, one which can be used to maximize the performance of their organization.

Returning to the definition of budgets once again, two more are worth mentioning, more for what they do not say:

A budget is simply a financial plan.[4]

Budgets are formal statements of the financial resources set aside for carrying out specific activities in a given period of time.[5]

These definitions are certainly adequate and no financial person could or likely would quarrel with them. However, what is not included in these definitions of a budget is of greater importance, in a practical sense, than what is said. Inherent in any definition of a budget are these five basic assumptions:

1. A budget reflects a financial plan, which in turn truly represents the goals of management for their organization.
2. A budget will be expressed in time-phased quantifiable or measurable terms, so that status along the way can be determined.
3. All individual components of the organization will be made aware of their portion of the overall budget.
4. Performance against the budgets will be monitored and reviewed periodically with management.
5. Good and/or bad performance against the approved budgets will be rewarded and/or punished by management.

Who then needs a budget? Answer: Any and all organizations which intend to maximize their performance and minimize or reduce the chance factor in their firm's overall future direction.

ENDNOTES

1. John R. Bartizal, Budget Principles and Procedures (New York: Prentice-Hall, Inc., 1940), page 1.
2. Herbert T. Spiro, Finance for the Non-Financial Manager (New York: John Wiley & Sons, Inc., 1977), page 110.
3. Ibid.
4. J. Fred Weston and Eugene F. Brigham, Managerial Finance (Hinsdale, Illinois: The Dryden Press, 1978), page 112.
5. James A. F. Stoner, Management (Englewood Cliffs, New Jersey: Prentice-Hall, Inc., 1978), page 593.

MORE ON BUDGETS

On the battleship Missouri in Tokyo Harbor, September 2, 1945:

> The weather was so clear that Mount Fuji, the Fortunate
> Warrior, could be seen sixty miles away. The sun sparkled
> on the white uniforms of American sailors. Tokyo Bay
> overflowed with Allied vessels of war -- the greatest
> armada ever assembled. MacArthur delivered an oration and
> used five pens to sign the surrender instrument. The
> Japanese signatories walked and talked as stiffly as
> mechanical dolls. As soon as possible they climbed back
> down to the launch provided for them and made for shore.
> They went directly to the palace and reported to the
> Emperor. The next morning Hirohito and his closest
> advisors repaired to the Palace Shrine to announce officially
> the end of the war to his ancestors and the sun goddess.[1]

By the end of that day no one in Imperial Japan, no one in the
United States, practically no one in the entire world was unaware of
the fact that World War II had ended. There is truly something to be
said for some kind of formality.

Now what does any of this have to do with budgets? Well, with
somewhat less formality, (one pen instead of five; one battleship
instead of an armada) when a budget is issued, everyone affected by
the process should be absolutely aware of that fact.

Too often in the every day business setting there is confusion as
to whether or not a given budget has been issued. Even in those
instances where there is general agreement that a budget has in fact
been issued, often no one can agree on the value of the budget issued,
or on what modification to it they should be working. Not only does
this confusion frequently exist with the recipients of the budget, as

one might expect, but not infrequently the budget-issuing people are not sure, or cannot prove, exactly what budget they have issued. An ambiguous budget creates a worse environment than no budget at all. At least with a no-budget condition there can be an agreement as to the budget value -- nothing. It takes less effort to straighten out a no-budget situation than it does to unravel an environment of budgets of varying interpretations.

While no one would likely suggest that budgeting people reactivate the old Missouri battleship to create the proper atmosphere for the release of their budgets, nevertheless, some formality is needed. There is no excuse for allowing confusion or doubt to exist as to the exact value of all budgets. This is a controllable activity, and it should be controlled by the budgeting people. No exceptions.

TECHNIQUES USED BY MANAGERS TO AVOID BUDGETS

Some of the very smartest people in today's business environment are engineers. Engineers are by nature typically creative people who thrive on new ideas, pushing the state of the art. By their very nature and educational training, engineers make excellent managers. But engineers also love to avoid budgets.

It isn't that engineering managers are dishonest. On the contrary, once they make a definite commitment they take their commitment as seriously as anyone. But there is sort of an unspoken undercurrent that suggests: "OK business-school wise guy, if you can't do your job and pin me down, I'm not going to help you." Engineers consider themselves professionals, and rightly so, and they expect the budgeting people to be equally professional in doing their jobs. If budgeters can't define escape-proof budgets, they will get no help from the performing managers.

Over the years the ingenious methods used by some managers, engineering managers in particular, to escape from or to avoid their budgets has been impressive. It might be useful to relate just a few of these in an attempt to outline what takes place, and to suggest some possible remedies.

Manager's Position	Symptoms/Remarks	Remedy
1. "I'm confused."	"Whose numbers are these?" "Where did they come from?" "Who prepared them?"	Formality. Put the budget in writing, ask the recipient to initial it, give the person a copy.
2. "Things are different now."	"The effort has changed." "This isn't the same job I bargained for."	Formality. In addition to numbers, the budget must have a work statement and a time frame for performance, i.e., a schedule.

Manager's Position	Symptoms/Remarks	Remedy
3. "I don't have the time."	"I'm so busy doing the job I can't stop to fool around with budgets."	Define the budget and get a commitment before the period begins, i.e., in the budget window."
4. "That's not my commitment"	"I'm the new kid on the street -- that budget belongs to my predecessor."	Upper management when appointing the new person must get a commitment for all aspects of the new assignment, including that of budget performance.
5. "Other areas are making me overrun my budget."	"The late release of engineering drawings is causing me to overrun."	Upper management must impress upon all performing managers their duty to foresee delays which could affect them, in order to stay within their own budget commitment.

Formality in the budgeting process is the best way to pin down an evasive manager.

THE BUDGETING PROCESS

The process of budgeting was touched on briefly in the previous chapter. The activities typically found in the budgeting cycle are listed in five sequential steps as follows:

1. The Establishment of a Budget Baseline. Money resources are aligned to the work to be done and to the desired schedule; a profit goal is established, and funds set aside for it. A management reserve is provided to cover the unexpected. All values so allocated are realistic and attainable by the performing departments.
2. The Budget Release. Done in a formal manner so that there are no doubts in anyone's mind as to what their particular budget values are. If the full period budget is not released for any reason, the differences are set aside using the rolling-wave budget approach.
3. Monitoring of Performance and Variance Analysis. Taking the actual costs and comparing them to the planned budget for the same time period, any differences are analyzed by

category of cost to understand why such differences occurred, either above or below the planned budget. Performing managers are interviewed, shown their results, and are solicited for their reaction to all variances beyond a given acceptable tolerance.

4. Projection of Final Results. Taking the actuals to date and comparing them to the plan, make the best educated guess as to what the final financial results will be in the end.

5. Management Review and Corrective Actions. After management has been apprised of the status of their budget versus actuals to date (and hopefully there is some relationship between actual costs and earned value), does management want to take any corrective action, i.e., descoping of work, issuing management reserve, etc., to keep on an acceptable budget path.

In order to get the full cooperation and maximum performance by managers, budgets must be attainable by mortal men and women. It serves no purpose to issue budget goals which can not be achieved under any circumstances, although it is not too uncommon to do so in industry. There are legitimate changes in conditions which necessitate changes in budgets. When these changes occur, budgets must be modified to accommodate such changed conditions in order to make budgets reasonable and attainable.

THERE ARE "BUDGETS" AND THERE ARE "BUDGETS"

If one could somehow make a survey of all companies and departments within all firms, and ask them a common question --"Do you use budgets?" -- one would likely get a universal response -- "Yes." But the "yes" answer would have vastly different meanings for these organizations. For although few managers would likely admit to using no budgets, what constitutes their "budget" would certainly be colored by widely divergent management attitudes. Budgets come in all different types, some quite sophisticated in that they allow for a high degree of autonomy, and some -- unfortunately -- are quite archaic.

The most sophisticated budgets to be found would be expressed in purely monetary terms, dollars. Ultimate sophistication would be a dollar budget for the full period, not time-phased by quarter or month. The time phasing would be done by the performing manager. This approach would give the performing managers absolute flexibility in the manner in which they perform their operations. They could perform in any way they feel is best for their operation. For example, they could use their own people, hire outside people, rent or buy robots, and so on. The approach would be purely up to them. Rarely does industry ever achieve this level of budget sophistication, and by not doing so it misses an opportunity to achieve maximum performance from the ingenious methods of their operating managers. Budgets should stimulate the flow of new ideas, not inhibit them by unnecessary controls.

The other extreme of budgeting approaches, the opposite of sophistication, will be referred to as the archaic. Here a budget is issued, but it has little real significance. Each time a manager attempts to do something, he/she must go through additional approval cycles, as if there were no budget. If they want to hire someone, they must get upper management approval for a Personnel Requisition. If they want to buy something, they must get additional approval for a Purchase Requisition. The archaic budget approach keeps all organizations tightly in line because managers of all departments must go through a series of administrative hurdles each time they attempt to move out in their operation. The archaic approach frustrates and irritates the operating managers because they are, frankly, not treated as adults by the financial controllers.

Unfortunately, in industry today, one sees budget techniques more closely aligned to the archaic than the sophisticated. And by over controlling the operating managers with too restrictive, little-value budgets, industry loses the maximum benefits and flow of new ideas which can come when personnel are allowed to perform in a manner as they see fit while, of course, still staying within the overall confines of their dollar budgets.

A few years back the young people had an expression about "needing their own space." Too often, finance people when issuing budgets, forget that operating managers also need their "own space."

ENDNOTES

1. David Bergamini, <u>Japan's Imperial Conspiracy</u> (New York: William Morrow and Company, Inc., 1971), page 137.

PART II
THE BASICS OF SCHEDULING

SCHEDULES

sched'ule... 3 : a usu. written plan or proposal for future procedure typically indicating the objective proposed, the time and sequence of each operation, and the materials required <planned a new ~ of operations for the factory> <their ~ allowed for only 50 percent of last year's production> <laid out a ~ for building the new school> ...

Webster's New International Dictionary
of the English Language
Third Edition 1981

Returning once again to the same Webster's Dictionary that was used earlier to define a budget, part 3 of the above definition seems to fit quite well with schedules as they are currently used in today's industrial or business settings. But so that all will have the same understanding of the process, it might be useful to add a few additional definitions of scheduling, as contained in selected textbooks. Thus, scheduling has been defined as:

"...the process of fitting jobs into a logical time table"[1] and, "detailed planning of work with respect to time"[2] and,"...the determination of when each item of preparation and execution must be performed."[3]

These definitions all appear to be clear, adequate, and consistent with one another. A schedule is simply a plan for accomplishing certain work and focuses on the tasks to be done and the timing of each, in order to complete a job in a systematic manner.

16

Three more definitions are probably needed before a discussion of some of the specific scheduling techniques used in business today can be undertaken. They are:

1. <u>Event</u> is something that happens at a moment in time. It happens once, as when one "starts to read the book" or "stops reading the book."

2. <u>Activity</u> is something that happens over a period of time, as with "reading the book." An activity is always preceded by an event of "start," as with "start reading," and ended with an event of "stop," as with "stop reading."

3. <u>Milestone</u> is an event of particular importance. While a milestone might also be an activity, i.e., something which occurs over a period of time, in the scheduling sense, a milestone is normally thought of as an event, a point in time.

Marriage is a milestone of significance to everyone. While the marriage ceremony might last several hours and, therefore, be an activity, a milestone entitled "marriage" in the scheduling sense would be an event, a point in time, as with "marriage ceremony completed."

TYPES OF SCHEDULES

In today's business environment there are numerous types of schedules in use. But in the practical sense, and for purposes of illustration, only three types of schedules will be reviewed, for most of the variations in use today are really some form of derivative from the three. They are: (1) Gantt or bar charts, (2) milestone or event charts, and (3) network schedules.

Gantt or Bar Charts

Gantt or bar charts are probably the most widely used of all schedules in use today. They are the product of Henry L. Gantt who perfected them during World War I. A Gantt chart typically lists all activities vertically in the left column, then expresses a planned time frame for each of these activities on the right side, by use of a hollow bar symbol. As activities are completed, the bars are shaded in. Thus, as in the illustration in figure 3.1, line 1 is exactly on schedule; line 2 is ahead of schedule; and line 3 is behind schedule, with the completion date slipping to the end of April. Obviously, there can be many variations on the precise displays of these type schedules. Gantt charts are so simple to use, and so clear in what they are depicting, they have received wide acceptance in the business world. Rarely is there any discussion over what is meant by a Gantt chart display.

Figure 3.1 Gantt or Bar Chart

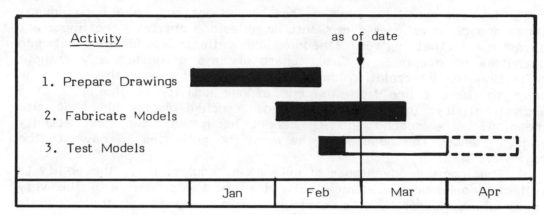

Milestone or Event Charts

Milestone or event charts are also very popular scheduling displays to reflect events over a time scale. The planned events are normally expressed using hollow triangles, and completed events are shown in solid. Rescheduled or slipped events are frequently displayed with a diamond symbol, as shown in figure 3.2, but the symbols can be of any type without changing the meaning. When the late milestones are completed, the diamond symbols are filled in to reflect what has occurred.

Figure 3.2 Milestone or Event Chart

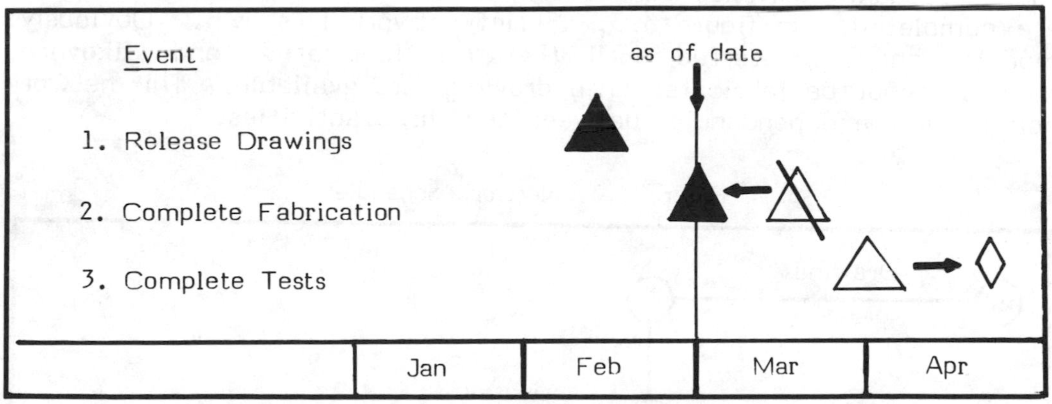

While for purposes of reviewing these two types of schedules they were described separately, in fact, many of the more common schedule displays in use today are a combination of both the Gantt and milestone schedules, reflecting a combination of activities with bars, and events with triangles, both on the same chart.

Network Schedules

Network schedules have several variations and have both advantages and disadvantages over Gantt or milestone charts. The important advantage is that network schedules can reflect dependencies between activities or events. A Gantt chart displays activities only without reflecting the interrelationships or dependencies between them. If one were to draw a line from the end of one activity to the start of a second activity, in the scheduling sense, such a display has a definite meaning: the second activity <u>cannot</u> begin until the first activity ends. Hence, the dependency between the activities is shown to the reviewer.

The inherent advantages of network schedules, i.e., the ability to reflect dependencies between activities or events, are also the very thing which makes them cumbersome as a management tool. While both Gantt and milestone schedules are simple to use, easy to understand, and practical as a display technique, networks are complicated and difficult to follow in a presentation. Senior management is always in a hurry and presentations to them must be clear, simple, and to the point. It isn't that upper management can't understand the network displays, they just don't have the time as a rule. Hence, the networks per se are not normally utilized as a presentation device. Most of the value of network schedules comes in their use as analytical tools with the first and intermediate levels of management. Networks are ideal devices to isolate and to analyze schedule problems, and then to present the summary results to senior management.

Back to what a network schedule looks like. Picture a Gantt chart, but with lines connecting the activities and in effect one has a network schedule. The dependencies between activities indicate that the subsequent activities cannot take place until the earlier activities are completed. In figure 3.3, a brief network is shown. Obviously, models cannot be tested until they are fabricated, and, likewise, models cannot be fabricated until drawings are available. This network points out the dependencies between the three activities.

Figure 3.3 Network Schedule

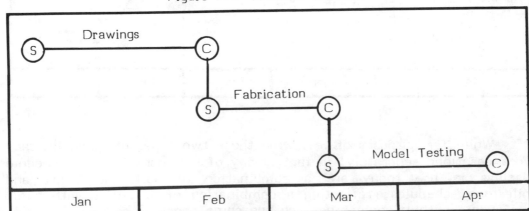

The same work effort has been shown in figures 3.1, 3.2, and 3.3, but only in figure 3.3, the network, is the full relationship and dependencies between the separate activities shown. These three illustrations are intentionally simple, and in real life situations such problems are not so neat and clear cut. Often, a given activity is dependent on multiple activities before it can start. Example, before one can break ground on a new building one ordinarily must have drawings, work crews, equipment, financing, a building permit, and so forth, to mention just a few of the conditions preceding the actual event. However, many buildings have been started with only verbal approval from a city official, partial or preliminary drawings, partial work crews, partial equipment, and initial funding only. Real business problems are complex, and networks necessarily become complex to display such real problems.

Network schedules go under a variety of titles. Perhaps the most common is PERT, an acronym which stands for Program Evaluation and Review Technique. Another frequently used name is CPM, Critical Path Method. Still other titles are flow diagrams, goes-into charts, set-back charts, to name a few. They all have a common denominator: to graphically illustrate the work to be done by pointing out the relationships between different events and/or activities.

Both PERT and CPM are important techniques in the management sense, and they will be discussed in greater detail in the next chapter. Both techniques have as their primary purpose the isolation of what is called the critical path, which is that sequence of work to be done which will take longest to occur in order to complete any given project. The basic assumption is that by knowing where the critical path is, steps can be taken by management to reduce the sequence, or to work around it by allocating additional resources. Lastly, network schedules help to expose the left outs which other techniques often overlook. Left outs are the things that spoil scheduling plans.

The material covered in this chapter has been made intentionally simple and basic. Anyone who has ever worked with schedules could have skipped it -- perhaps. But prior to working with C/SCSC, which combines budgets and schedules, it is important that these fundamentals be properly and fully understood, or else the implementation of C/SCSC will be on shaky ground.

The first two schedule types described above, Gantt or bar and event or milestone, are the types most frequently used to define the schedule portion of Work Packages, which are the lowest "bricks" in the C/SCS foundation. Each milestone or bar is given weighted values to reflect some portion of the total Work Package effort to be performed. Work Packages are used to define specific effort to be done, and in C/SCS progress must be measured against such detailed plans. Therefore, it is essential that everyone working with C/SCS fully understand the process of scheduling/planning and quantifying the work to be done, and then measuring the effort actually accomplished against the plan. Bar and milestone schedules are most frequently used to define the planned effort in C/SCS Work Packages.

20

At the very top level of most projects is a Master Schedule, against which all subordinate activity, e.g. Work Packages, must conform. Most Master Schedules are displayed as milestones or bar charts, for these are easiest to understand. However, behind the top milestone or bar chart displays is likely to be a master summary network or PERT chart. This is particularly true if the effort to be done is complex and/or there are potential schedule problems inherent with the effort. Networks work well at the top summary or master schedule level, and they also work well at various intermediate levels on larger projects. They are generally not used at the lowest or Work Package levels, simply because there the Gantt or milestone charts seem to provide the best and easiest display to use.

The next two chapters will cover two of the more sophisticated scheduling techniques used by the Defense establishment: PERT (Program Evaluation and Review Technique) and LOB (Line of Balance). Both have their definite merits -- when used properly. Unfortunately, they have probably been misused as often by industry as they have been successfully deployed. They have their importance, however, because they were the forerunners of C/SCSC.

ENDNOTES

1. Charles A. Koepke, Plant Production Control (New York: John Wiley & Sons, Inc., 1949), page 453.
2. Lawrance F. Bell, "Factory Systems & Procedures," in Industrial Engineering and Management, ed. Ireson & Grant (Englewood Cliffs, N.J.: Prentice-Hall, Inc., 1955), page 475.
3. Thomas M. Landy, "Production Planning and Control," in Industrial Engineering Handbook, ed. H. B. Maynard (New York: McGraw-Hill Inc., 1956), page 6-15.

4

PERT PROGRAM EVALUATION
AND REVIEW TECHNIQUE

The next two chapters will continue the theme of schedules and will discuss PERT -- Program Evaluation and Review Technique and LOB -- Line of Balance, two of the more advanced type scheduling methods used in military program management. In the case of PERT, costs were later added to the scheduling technique, and basic PERT was thus transformed into PERT/Cost. PERT/Cost will be covered in some detail both because it was an attempt to merge the two functions of budgeting and scheduling into one management control system, and, more importantly, because it was the first serious attempt to add the concept of earned value/performance measurement into a management control system. Later, to differentiate basic PERT from PERT/Cost, the former was referred to as PERT/Time, to indicate the scheduling technique only.

It was PERT which was referred to in the introduction of this book when it was stated "...after having spent some dozen or so years in the industry at the time, I had seen many a new Government system introduced, be 'permanently' imposed, only to see it later fade away with the retirement of some general or admiral, i.e., the system's sponsor." PERT was supposed to revolutionize all aspects of management and have a lasting impact on management techniques. A realistic assessment of PERT's contribution to management today is a far cry from its proponents' claims in the early 1960s. PERT was, and still is, an excellent tool for management. But at the time of its introduction it was oversold, made unduly complicated, and almost totally rejected by the old guard program managers. Yet facets of both PERT and LOB are in use today in some form or another and are important control techniques -- when used properly.

Although Line of Balance was developed in the early 1940s, some 15 or so years before PERT came on the scene, PERT/Time and PERT/Cost will be discussed before covering LOB. The reason is that

22

PERT is a tool used to manage developmental projects, whereas LOB is used on recurring, repetitive, or production type efforts. Since one must normally develop something before one produces it, discussing PERT and then LOB seems to be the most logical sequence.

PERT/TIME AND CPM

PERT was perfected and first employed in a major way by the Navy (assisted by the consulting firm of Booz, Allen, and Hamilton) in the 1957 time frame under its Fleet Ballistic Missile program, more commonly known as the Polaris Missile. The technique received instant success, and there was a rush by other services and private firms to adopt/modify/expand the applications. Many new variations came into use with a variety of exciting new acronyms such as: PEP, PAR, TOPS, TRACE, LESS, MAPS, SCANS, CPM, and others. Quite naturally, most of these so called variations were abandoned, and only PERT and CPM -- Critical Path Method, exist today.

CPM was perfected about the same time period as PERT, and it is not clear which technique came along first. For discussion purposes it doesn't matter. CPM was essentially used by the construction industry, whereas PERT was the product of the military establishment. Many people refer to the two techniques as if they were synonymous, which is incorrect. There are unique features of each, although some of the earlier differences have since disappeared. CPM as a technique seems to have received better acceptance in the construction industry than PERT did in the defense industry. Thus PERT may well be in existence today, more because of CPM, than because of its own merits.

PERT produces a milestone/event oriented network, whereas CPM employs an activity oriented network. In their simplest form, CPM is a Gantt chart with connecting lines, and PERT is an event chart with connecting lines. The connecting lines reflect dependencies between the activities or events, i.e., one cannot start a later event or activity until the earlier event or activity has been completed. Graphically, the two networks look quite different, as figure 4.1 illustrates. Note, both networks are reflecting the same sequence of effort.

Both CPM and PERT attempt to accomplish two things: (1) to display a future job in a network form to facilitate the analysis of the future work, and (2) to isolate the Critical Path, i.e., that sequence of the effort which will take longest to complete, and thereby pace the overall finish of the project. In theory, it is also useful to know where the Slack Paths lie, i.e., those sequences of effort that will be completed ahead of the scheduled need times and, therefore, have slack or positive times in their sequence. The theory is that by isolating both the Critical and Slack Paths, management can simply sit back and allocate resources from one path to the other. Wonderful in theory, difficult in practice. In practice, one often finds that resources are not always interchangeable.

Figure 4.1   PERT and CPM Networks

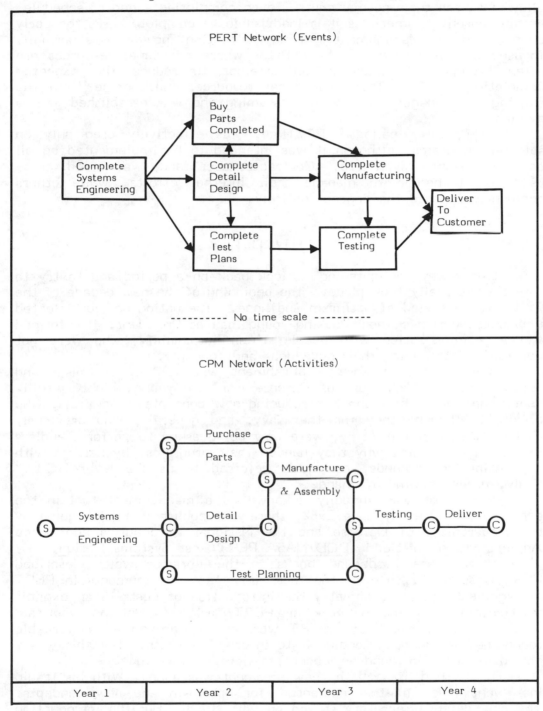

PERT Network (Events)

---------- No time scale ----------

CPM Network (Activities)

| Year 1 | Year 2 | Year 3 | Year 4 |

In the management of a program it is most helpful to know which sequences of the effort have positive, and which have negative flows (behind schedule), if for no other reason than to better understand just where management must focus its attention. Slack Paths are usually allowed to run their normal course, even completing ahead of schedule, within reason. Sometimes it is inadvisable to complete tasks too early on a program. Management's primary attention, however, is normally focused on the Critical Path or Paths where additional resources are often brought into play in an attempt to reduce the expected completion dates. These additional resources must come from the shifting of management reserve, assuming one was established and is available.

PERT, later called PERT/Time, was effectively used only on selected programs, although it was intended to be implemented on all contracts over a given size. Contractor acceptance was mixed, some used the technique to manage their internal efforts, while others adamantly opposed the concept entirely.

PERT/COST

It is always enlightening to look back on a period and to try to assess what really took place. The beginning of the new decade of the 1960s was a period of optimism and hope. The nation had just elected a bright, energetic, good-looking young man as President. He formed a new administration with people of similar beliefs, who were not bashful at introducing their new ideas and concepts.

Likewise the defense establishment was full of optimism and hope. The new Secretary of Defense was also young, highly intelligent, and not bashful about introducing new concepts. Admirals, who previously thought they ran the Navy, and generals, who previously thought they ran the Army, were now being asked to perform endless justifications on just why they needed their programs, by persons with accounting backgrounds, commonly referred to as the "Whiz Kids." Truly, it was a time of change.

PERT/Cost was virtually unknown as a management tool in the early 1960s. Yet by June 1962, there was published a joint guide by the Department of Defense and the National Aeronautics and Space Administration entitled: DOD/NASA PERT/Cost Systems Design. By 1963 there were hardbound books in the libraries which described PERT/Cost as "...one of the most important developments in PERT Management Systems, namely, the introduction of costs in an explicit relationship with the network or PERT/Cost."[1] Nothing was said which indicated that basic PERT was not yet proven as a workable technique, let alone extending it to incorporate costs. But this was a period of optimism, and new concepts were in the vogue.

By the end of 1963 the new president was gone. With his tragic loss went much of the momentum for optimism and new concepts. The new defense secretary stayed on until 1968. But the introduction of new techniques had slowed, and some of the previously introduced ideas and concepts were being discarded. One of these casualties was PERT/Cost. It never caught on as a useful tool. However, it is important to briefly review PERT/Cost, for conceptually, it was the

forerunner of C/SCS. Many of the tenets of C/SCS were first introduced in PERT/Cost. Thus, PERT/Cost is important today not for
what it was, but for what it led to.

***

In the beginning, the same group which developed PERT for the
Navy, later called PERT/Time, recognized that if one could express a
program's development schedule in a network and time it to completion, one could also add costs into the same framework. Quite
wisely, they felt that implementing any new management concept
would be met with resistance, and, therefore, they chose to focus
initially on the schedule/time aspects of the network only. Once
PERT/Time had received its acceptance, they then planned to add the
cost dimension to the network.

PERT/Cost builds on, or better, builds within the same network
as PERT/Time. Both require a definition of the tasks to be peformed,
i.e., the network, and both must use the same network, or else there
would be an inconsistency between schedule and costs. The cost
dimension may be added to either a PERT network (events) or a CPM
network (activities).

The objectives of those introducing PERT/Cost woro broadei than
tho initial objectives of PERT/Time. PERT/Cost hoped to:

- provide an improved means to obtain realistic cost
  estimates;
- provide a means of obtaining an accurate assessment of
  cost status, at any point in time;
- provide a means of measuring work performance, i.e.,
  earned value;
- provide a technique for accurately estimating the total
  end costs of a program, once started;
- provide a program management technique which combined
  both schedule and costs into one system.

Thus PERT/Cost had essentially the same objectives as did C/SCS
later in the decade. The most important aspect, and the thing which
made PERT/Cost and now makes C/SCS different from all other management control systems is the concept of earned value, or performance
measurement. If PERT/Cost had worked and been accepted, there
would be no C/SCS today.

By June of 1962 the DOD and NASA had jointly issued a
PERT/Cost Systems Design, as was mentioned above. Nine months
later, March 1963, the DOD and NASA issued supplement No. 1 to
their guide entitled PERT/Cost Output Reports. Whether by that
time PERT/Time had been sufficiently accepted and utilized by
program managers to take the next step of incorporating costs is deba-
table. Many would likely argue that it was not. True, contractors
were submitting PERT reports to their buying customers, but for the
most part PERT was still an after-the-fact compilation of what had
actually taken place. PERT/Time was not in the main stream of the

management process when PERT/Cost was introduced as a requirement on all major programs by both the DOD and NASA in 1963.

PERT/Cost Reporting (Forerunner of C/SCS Reporting)

The joint DOD/NASA guide issued in 1963 required that all contractors subject to PERT/Cost submit eleven (yes eleven!) reports each month, ten of which were specific tables/charts and one was a narrative problem analysis report. Of particular significance to anyone studying the subject of performance measurement is the fact that certain of these early PERT/Cost reports incorporated the concept of measuring earned value (i.e. what work was actually performed) as a way of determining status. The step was only partial, however, for most of these reports used the more conventional plan versus actuals displays.

It might be worth digressing for a moment to point out the differences between what will be called the conventional cost control approach and compare it to an earned value concept, which is best typified by the DOD's C/SCSC. Under the conventional approach there are only two points of reference: the plan of work to do, and the actual costs spent. Under a performance measurement or earned value (the two terms are synonymous) technique a third reference point is added: Earned Value. The earned value, or what work was actually performed of the effort budgeted, becomes the primary point of focus in a performance measurement/earned value management system.

It is not only the addition of earned value into the system that is of significance, it is what managment reviews each month as a way of assessing its status, which separates the earned value technique from the conventional. The following summary illustrates these differences:

Management's Focus:	Conventional Cost Control	PERT/Costs	C/SCSC (earned value)
• Plan (work to do)	yes	yes	yes
• Actuals (costs spent)	yes	yes	yes
• Earned Value (work performed)	no	yes	yes
Variance Displays:			
• Plan vs. Actuals (Plan Variance)	yes	yes	no
• Earned Value vs. Actuals (Cost Variance)	no	yes	yes
• Earned Value vs. Plan (Schedule Variance)	no	no	yes

Thus in a performance measurement management system it is the fact that management's attention is focused primarily on the earned value and variances from it (plan and actuals) which is key to the system. PERT/Cost reports took a small step in that direction. Later, C/SCS reports went the rest of the way.

One of the PERT/Cost reports which highlighted earned value was the Cost of Work Report, as shown in figure 4.2. This report was quite novel for its time, for it pointed out in clear graphic terms that management should watch not only its initial plan and actual costs, but also what it was accomplishing in the value of work performed, i.e., earned value. This type of display is probably the most commonly used chart in the C/SCS status review meetings today.

Two other PERT/Cost reports are worth mentioning because they have made their way into the present C/SCS reports. The Manpower Loading Report exists today as Format 4 of the C/SCS Cost Performance Report -- CPR, in a slightly different data display. Also, the Problem Analysis Report, which is a narrative describing why

Figure 4.2 PERT/Cost -- "Cost of Work Report"

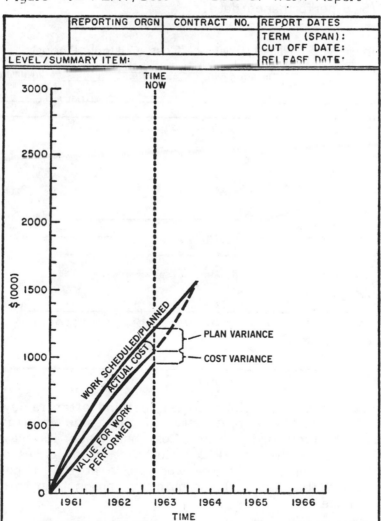

28

schedule/cost parameters have been penetrated, was a requirement under both PERT/Cost and C/SCS.

The tendency under PERT/Cost reporting was to ask for all the data available, and then some. As a result, there was a suspicion in the minds of most contractor personnel that the customer was merely placing these reports in some vault somewhere, never bothering to do anything with it. By contrast, the C/SCS CPR uses five rather simple formats of data, monitors fairly high level summaries, and only goes into greater detail when previously agreed to parameters of cost and schedule are exceeded.

Two PERT/Cost reports which have continued in use, but are not a requirement per se of C/SCS, are the Cost Outlook Report, shown in figure 4.3, and the Schedule Outlook Report, shown in figure 4.4. Both these reports are identical in technique, one reflects schedule status and the other cost status. While C/SCS does not require these displays, any contractors on top of their programs, and most customers monitoring C/SCS performance will use similar displays. Note -- these type reports will be covered in some detail in Chapter 14 on the monitoring of C/SCS performance data.

Figure 4.3 PERT/Cost -- Cost Outlook Report

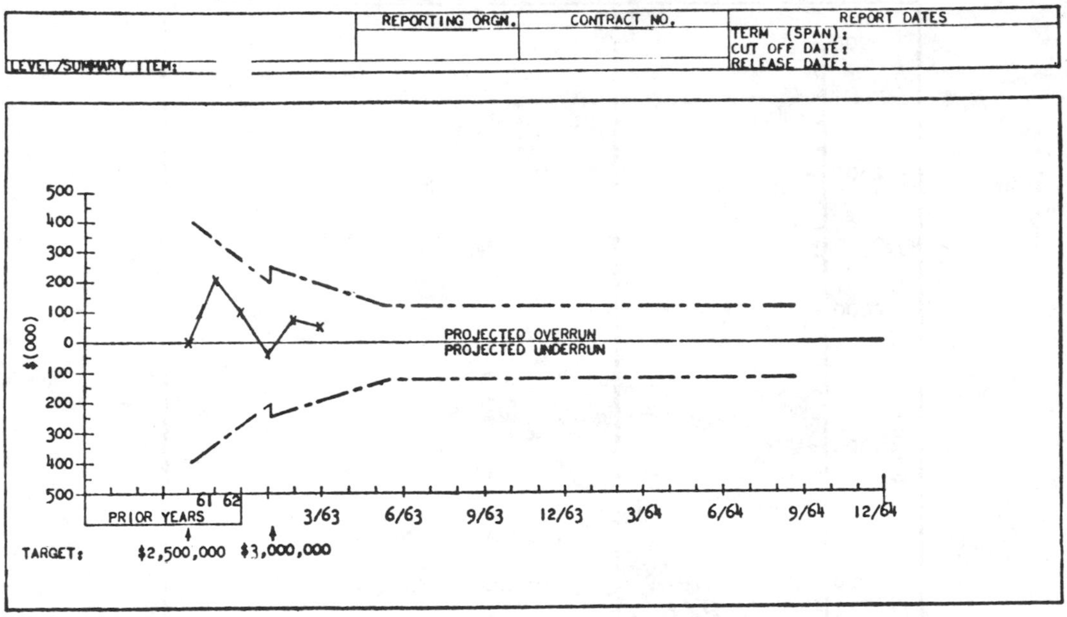

The obvious conclusion which comes to mind after reviewing these early PERT/Cost reports is that much of the same information that was previously required under PERT/Cost has made its way into the present C/SCS. Why then did PERT/Cost not catch on as a management technique? People not in the work force at that time would be wise to understand this issue, if for no other reason than to preclude a repeat performance.

Figure 4.4 PERT/Cost -- Schedule Outlook Report

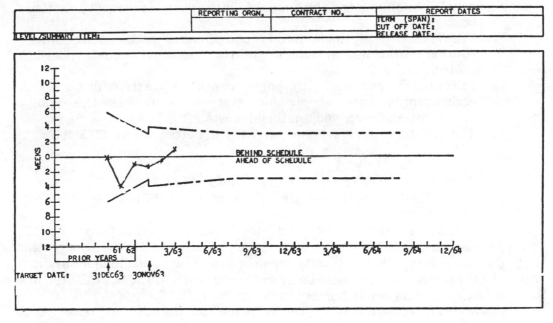

REQUIEM FOR PERT/COST

PERT/Cost as a management control system was "decreed" to be implemented in 1962. It lasted perhaps five years to 1967. Some feel it never caught on as a management tool -- was never used by program managers/upper management to aid in their decision-making process. Anyone who worked with it would likely want to be included in this group. Perhaps it was used somewhere by some program manager to manage some program -- perhaps.

Two gentlemen who wrote a book on PERT/CPM in 1967, summed it up nicely:

> Many firms doing business with the government resented the strong pressure to install a completely new cost accounting system. Not only was it costly and difficult to do so, but they felt it was an unnecessary duplication of their existing systems. Perhaps some of the initial resistance to the PERT/Cost system was due to the government's somewhat forceful method of introducing it. Not only did the coercion cause resentment, but also there was an implied criticism of existing cost accounting systems which firms had developed over a period of years.2

There are probably countless opinions of just why PERT/Cost failed, and it would serve no purpose to debate them here. Offered below are five reasons why PERT/Cost did not last:

1. PERT/Cost placed too much emphasis on schedule, over the cost aspects of management.

2. PERT/Cost was poorly planned, poorly introduced, and poorly implemented by people with poor (arrogant) attitudes.
3. PERT/Cost was made overly complicated and required more routine information than mortal persons could possibly absorb.
4. PERT/Cost required (in some cases) a restructuring of a contractor's cost accounting system to handle the application of indirect and material costs.
5. The military buyers came up with a better idea: C/SCSC.

PERT/TIME IS ALIVE AND WELL
(and living under the name of EZPERT)

It would be unfair to end the overall subject of PERT, PERT/Time, and PERT/Cost, and leave anyone with the impression that these concepts have totally vanished and are no longer in use. While PERT/Cost has in fact been replaced with C/SCS, PERT/Time has continued and is an important adjunct to C/SCS.

Many improvements have taken place in the 20 or more years since PERT was first developed. During this period there have been giant steps made in computer processing. Perhaps even more important, there have been improvements in end product objectives which have closed the gap between the needs of the users (management) and the capabilities of the improved computers. One of the most obvious improvements has been in the development of a computer software package called EZPERT. This package was obviously developed with the needs of the user kept clearly in mind.

EZPERT is capable of providing automatic printout displays of Gantt bar charts, tasks, and cumulative graphs drawn on an XY plotter, reflecting resources on the vertical scale and time on the horizontal. Network schedules may be automatically drawn on a time scale and are available to reflect either a CPM (activity) or PERT (event) network. Some 16 separate programs are available, many free from the government or for a price from commercial houses. These programs may be run on eight or more commercial computers that are presently available.

Thus the management technique of PERT, which got off to a somewhat bumpy start, has now evolved into a proven and useful tool for the efficient management of one-time, non-recurring programs.

ENDNOTES

1. Robert W. Miller, Schedule, Cost, and Profit Control with PERT (New York: McGraw-Hill Book Company, Inc., 1963), page 89.
2. Jerome D. Wiest and Ferdinand K. Levy, A Management Guide to Pert/CPM (Englewood Cliffs, N.J.: Prentice-Hall, Inc., 1967), page 87.

LINE OF BALANCE—LOB

The last subject which will be covered to provide a foundation on the basics of the budgeting and scheduling functions is that of Line of Balance -- LOB. This technique was conceived some 40 years ago to provide management with visibility on production or recurring type activities. During the 1970s, with slight modifications, it has been found to also be useful in the management of complex one-time only projects, in lieu of PERT.

The Line of Balance -- LOB technique is generally acknowledged to have been developed by or for the United States Navy in World War II, although some authors give direct credit to its development to the Goodyear Company and a man named George E. Fouch.[1] But no matter who is recognized as having been the actual creator or perfecter of LOB, a close examination of the technique will reveal the earlier contributions of some turn of the century management innovators, such as Frederick W. Taylor and Henry L. Gantt. Thus, if there were a paternity suit on LOB, the jury might have some difficulty deciding this one.

To gain an understanding of the concept and to best illustrate the evolution of LOB from a production only control device, to that of a management technique also used on developmental projects, two definitions of the method may be helpful. The earlier concept of LOB was as follows:

> Line of Balance is a technique for assembling, selecting, interpreting, and presenting in graphic form the essential factors involved in a production process from raw materials to completion of the end product, against a background of time. It is essentially a management-type tool, utilizing the principle of exception to show only the most important facts to its audience. It is a means of integrating the flow of materials and components into manufacture of end items in accordance with phased delivery requirements.[2]

A more recent description of LOB obviously expands its applications:

The LOB is a management tool akin to PERT except that it
presents only the current project status and has no predictive
features such as in PERT.   When applied to a project
involving a single unit or a small quantity, the LOB represents a status report, depicting the degree to which each of
the disciplines associated with a project meet the schedule
objectives that were established.   Originally, the LOB technique was designed for and used on production projects
involving large numbers of units.   The concept was later
modified and variations of the technique are now used for
projects involving the design and development of single or
small quantities of units ....[3]

As we trace through the four elements that make up the LOB
technique, we will attempt to point out where the modifications
occurred to expand its utility.

The Line of Balance -- LOB display chart has three distinct sections, as may be seen in figure 5.1.   They are The Objective; the
Progress Chart; and the Production Plan.   When the next step is
taken, and the Line of Balance is struck to reflect production status at
a point in time, these four parts make up the LOB technique.   Each
of the four parts will be reviewed below in some detail.

The first element of LOB is The Objective, which is displayed in
the upper left corner of figure 5.1.   In a production type job, the
objective is to manufacture units, and in this illustration 80 units are
to be produced.   In an expanded LOB use, the objective will display
something other than production units, and that approach will be
discussed with appropriate illustrations later.   In this initial discussion,
a production effort is assumed of some 80 units, as shown in figure
5.1.   In the Objective section, the display reflects cumulative Planned
Deliveries by month, versus cumulative Actual Deliveries.   As of the
time of this display, 1 May, 30 units should have been delivered, but
only 14 had actually been made as the chart reflects.

The second element of LOB is the Production Plan, and it is
shown across the bottom of figure 5.1.   In an expanded LOB role, this
element is simply referred to as the Plan.   Here, the Production Plan
is a network, which works backward from the point of delivery,
displayed as item 12.   The network is drawn on a time scale, again
backward from the point of delivery, herein reflecting a 24-day
working sequence.   Depending upon what is being produced, the time
scale in the Production Plan may be reflected in work days, work
weeks, work months, etc., but not tied to specific dates in the LOB.
In the manufacture of aircraft, such Production Plans often reflect 24,
36, or 48-month set-back displays.   The Production Plan element of
LOB is almost universally accepted as a display technique in the manufacturing world.

The third element of LOB is called the Progress Chart and is shown in the upper right corner of figure 5.1. The Progress Chart displays the 80 units to be produced on the vertical scale, (note that both the Objective and the Progress Chart use the same scale in this production application, but in other applications these two elements will use two different measurements), and across the bottom are listed the components of the Production Plan, specified by number. As these components are completed, working toward the 80 units, a barometer type display fills up vertically.

The fourth and last element of LOB is that of striking the Line of Balance, as of a point of time, e.g. 1 May. In figure 5.1, the illustration shows that components 1, 6, and 9 are ahead of the need date, while components 2, 3, 4, 5, 7, 8, 10, 11, and 12 are all behind schedule.

The Line of Balance as shown on the Progress Chart of figure 5.1 appears as a step-down or stairs type display because as of any reporting date (here 1 May) it is based on the set-back need dates of the Production Plan element. In every case, the components of

Figure 5.1 Line of Balance -- LOB -- Display Chart

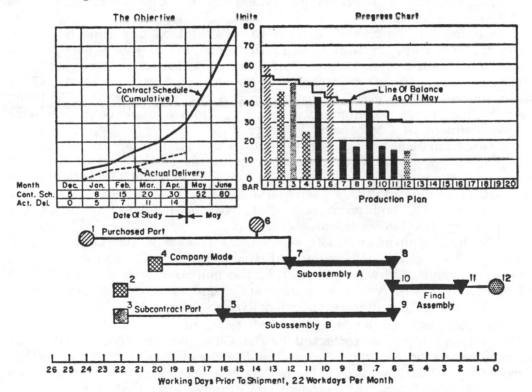

Source: From Schedule, Cost and Profit Control with PERT by Robert W. Miller. Copyright 1963 by McGraw-Hill Book Co., Inc. Used with the permission of McGraw-Hill Book Company.

item 1 will be needed earlier than say item 10, simply to support the assembly sequence of the Production Plan.

Thus, it may be seen that LOB is a management by exception tool, which integrates three types of displays to reflect status as of a point in time. As another person defined the technique in 1978:

> Line of Balance (LOB) is a management technique for collecting, measuring, interpreting, and presenting in graphic form information relating to time and accomplishment during production. It shows the progress, status, timing and phasing of interrelated project activities. Although it can be used on one-time projects like building a plant, LOB has proven most useful in production programs from the point when incoming or raw materials arrive to the shipment of the end product.[4]

EXPANDING LOB TO ONE-TIME ONLY PROJECTS

Although Line of Balance was originally created to aid in determining the status of production or recurring type jobs, recently there are those who feel that the technique may also be useful in the control of one-time only or nonrecurring type projects, the construction of a building for example.

In order for the LOB technique to be useful on one-time only type projects, however, certain modifications had to be made in the data being displayed. The second definition of LOB above described the technique for use on developmental or nonrecurring projects. That same source will be used to trace through two examples of LOB being used to monitor a developmental project, from a book on the subject of Management of Engineering Projects.[5]

Two examples are shown in figures 5.2 and 5.3, to monitor a scheduled 48-week project, reflecting its status at the end of the 30th week. Just as was done when LOB was covered earlier reflecting a production application, this example will trace through each of the four elements of LOB and point out what must be modified to adapt the technique to developmental projects.

The first element of LOB which must change is the Objective, as shown in the upper left corners of figures 5.1, 5.2, and 5.3. In a production mode, as with figure 5.1, the objective was to manufacture 80 units, so, therefore, the appropriate display was cumulative planned deliveries versus cumulative actual deliveries over a time scale.

By contrast, on a developmental type job, one unit only, some other activity must be reflected in the Objective section. That other activity as shown in figure 5.2 is the functional display of Engineering, Purchasing, Drafting, etc. Note that the vertical scale was changed from "80 units" in the production display, to that of "percent complete" in this developmental role.

In the other developmental display, shown in figure 5.3, all functions and effort are merged together to reflect "planned" versus "actual" curves, cumulative over a time scale. Again, the vertical scale reflects "percent complete" status as of a point in time.

The second element of LOB which must change when applying the tool to developmental projects is that of the Production Plan, now referred to as simply the Plan, shown across the bottom of figures 5.1, 5.2 and 5.3. In the production application the display reflected manufacturing activities, working backward on a time scale of days from the point of delivery. By comparison, in the developmental mode, as shown in figures 5.2 and 5.3, the Plan reflects the events of the developmental effort, moving from left to right on a time scale that reflects the 48-week effort.

Digressing for a moment to the last chapter when PERT/Time and CPM network schedules were reviewed, the Plan in figure 5.1 is an example of a CPM (activities) network, whereas, the Plans in figures 5.2 and 5.3 are examples of PERT/Time (events) networks.

In the third element of LOB, the Progress section, are found three interesting variations as reflected in figures 5.1, 5.2, and 5.3. In the production application, figure 5.1, progress was measured by reflecting each of the individual activities of the Production Plan, in a barometer type display, compared to the 80 units in the vertical scale.

Figure 5.2   LOB on One-Time Project

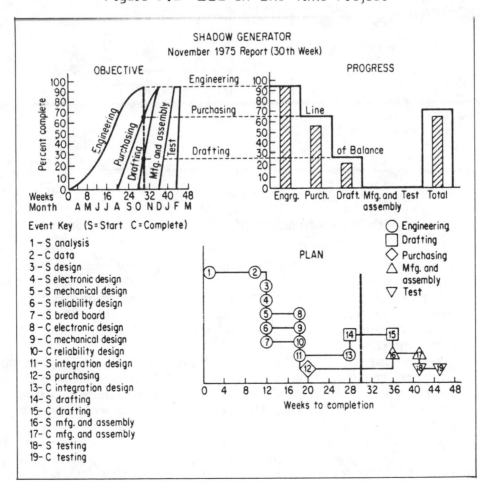

36

Figure 5.3   LOB on Another One-Time Project

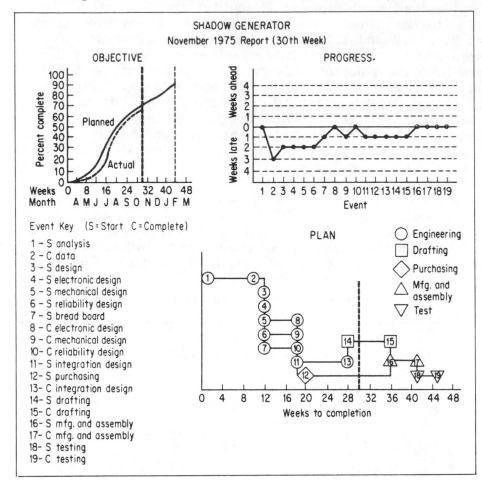

In the developmental project, figure 5.2, progress is measured
against the "percent complete" of the functions listed in the Objective
element, again using barometer type charts.   In the other developmental display, figure 5.3, progress is measured by events of the Plan,
reflecting an ahead or behind schedule status, using the time needed
dates of the Plan.

The last element of LOB is the striking of the Line of Balance,
and again there are some interesting contrasts between production and
developmental uses.   In a production mode, using the set-back need
dates from the Production Plan, the Line is struck to reflect status as
of 1 May in figure 5.1

In figure 5.2, the need dates as shown in the Plan determine what
"percent complete" need be achieved by various functions on the
Objective part, in order to strike the Line.   In figure 5.3 no Line is

actually used, since status as of a given date is reflected in the ahead/behind schedule condition of the progress display.

What these three displays of LOB reflect is that the technique may be used for both production and developmental type jobs. In the production mode, the rules are precise and each element is well defined. On developmental projects, LOB displays may be tailored to the specific tasks to be done.

***

Since this is a book on the subject of an earned value management control system, as typified by C/SCS, and the basics of budgeting and scheduling were covered to provide a proper understanding of management methods, it is appropriate to point out an example of the differences between earned value management control and what might be called conventional management control. It is a small, but critical point to keep in mind in understanding the distinction between the two approaches.

Back in figure 5.3, in the display of the Objective, were shown two cumulative curves over time, reflecting the Planned and the Actual work to be done. This approach illustrates what should be referred to as the conventional management approach. The Planned work to be done reflects what management hopes to accomplish, phased by time over the term of a project.

The Actuals curve reflects the actual costs of work done to date. It is assumed (note this distinction) that actual costs spent represents actual work accomplished, or what is called earned value. Fifteen years of experience with the application of C/SCS on hundreds of separate contracts across this nation have proved that this basic assumption is wrong. Actual Costs do not necessarily reflect Work Performed. This being the case then, management needs additional visibility in order to assess the true status of jobs it intends to monitor.

The addition is, of course, earned value, or what was actually accomplished from the work planned to be done. This third point of reference provides management with the detail it properly needs to get a true status of the project, and of greater consequence, it gives them a better estimate of what the final bill is likely to run.

SUMMARY ON LINE OF BALANCE

Line of Balance -- LOB as a technique is best suited for large quantity production type jobs, to show the status of the effort as of a point in time. It is well suited for use as a reporting requirement, even on firm-fixed price type contracts, when the procuring customer needs assurances that the articles it is buying will be available when needed. LOB displays the status of hardware, on an exception basis, as of a point in time.

38

LOB also has some applications on one-time only developmental tasks, somewhat as PERT/Time is used, but usually on less complex efforts. This application allows for the user to display whatever he/she feels is appropriate for the task being performed. This expanded role for LOB is not completely accepted in the engineering community, where it could have its greatest utility. EZPERT (covered in the last chapter) is more frequently used in these developmental type situations.

Lastly, as added proof of the value of LOB, there are commercial jetliners flying today which were developed by private industry funds, where the private contractors used the LOB technique to monitor the status of their inhouse developments. This is the ultimate compliment to a governmental reporting requirement.

ENDNOTES

1. Robert W. Miller, Schedule, Cost and Profit Control with PERT (New York: McGraw-Hill Book Co., Inc., 1963), Page 17.
2. Anthony L. Iannone, Management Program Planning and Control with PERT, MOST AND LOB (Englewood Cliffs, N.J.: Prentice-Hall Inc., 1967), page 129.
3. Victor G. Hajek, Management of Engineering Projects (New York: McGraw-Hill Book Co., 1977), page 139.
4. Commander Gerald J. Chasko, from a Defense Systems Management College paper, September 1, 1978 "Line of Balance" appearing in J.S. Baumgartner, Systems Management (Washington, D.C.: The Bureau of National Affairs, Inc., 1979), page 238.
5. Victor G. Hajek, Management of Engineering Projects (New York: McGraw-Hill Book Co., 1977).

PART III
THE COST/SCHEDULE
CONTROL SYSTEM
CRITERIA CONCEPT

Figure 6.1 First Half Status (conventional method)

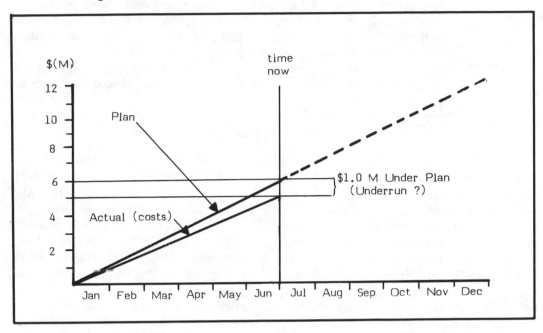

To pause for just a moment and reflect on what this book is attempting to do, its purpose is to describe the generic concept of performance measurement/earned value as a management control concept. While there are numerous such systems now in place at firms across the nation, each firm uses its own variation, its own flavor, its own definitions. To eliminate any possible confusion that could result from different interpretations of the same titles, the definitions used by the Department of Defense's C/SCS Criteria will be used throughout. Not only will that approach allow for preciseness, but perhaps of greater consequence, the DOD's 15 years of experience with these terms should provide for greater confidence in the material being covered.

However -- and this is the bad part -- in order to build on the DOD's C/SCSC experience, certain of their definitions must be used in order to properly cover the subject. The first five such C/SCSC definitions to be used are as follows:

1. The Plan or Budgeted Cost for Work Scheduled (BCWS) is the numerical representation (dollars/hours/or other measurable units) of the budgeted value of all work scheduled to be accomplished in a given period of time. This may be called Work Scheduled, which is synonymous with Budget or Plan.

2. Earned Value or Budgeted Costs for Work Performed (BCWP) is the numerical representation of the budgeted value of all work actually accomplished in a given period of time. This may be referred to as Work Performed, which is synonymous with the term Earned Value.

3.   <u>Actuals or Actual Costs of Work Performed (ACWP)</u> are the costs actually incurred and recorded for performance measurement purposes, in accomplishing the work performed within a given time period. This is called simply Cost Actuals, or Actuals.

4.   <u>Schedule Variance (SV)</u> is the numerical difference between Work Performed (BCWP) less Work Scheduled (BCWS).

5.   <u>Cost Variance (CV)</u> is the numerical difference between Work Performed (BCWP) less Actual Costs (ACWP).

Now to apply these new definitions to the illustration above. Keeping the case in very simple terms, but extending it to incorporate C/SCS methodology, assume the firm's contract called for the construction of 12 buildings, at the rate of one complete unit per month (start to finish). But instead of constructing one per month, all 12 were started in the beginning. At the end of six months they have 12 buildings, each 25 percent completed. What they really have then are 12 buildings times 25 percent complete, or the equivalent of three fully completed units. Their plan called for six completed buildings at the end of six months. Since they spent $5.0 million in Actual Costs, their first half performance now takes on a different perspective, as is shown in figure 6.2, using the C/SCS method.

There are three variances shown on the right of figure 6.2. First is PSV, which will be called Plan-Spending Variance. This was all that was available to review under the conventional approach, shown earlier in figure 6.1. All that PSV shows is that they had planned to spend $6.0 million in the first six months, and $5.0 million was actually spent. Not only does the plan-spending variance have little real meaning, it would actually distort the facts by permitting one to believe that they had an underrun of costs in the first half. Plan-Spending Variance is not used in C/SCS and it shall not be referred to further.

Of importance, however, are the variances shown as SV and CV in figure 6.2. These variances are available in C/SCS because the criteria require: (1) a detailed, bottom-up, measurable plan against which results can be measured (BCWS); and (2) a detailed, bottom-up, measurable assessment of performance against the plan (BCWP), called Earned Value, on a monthly basis.

Thus, by establishing the Earned Value of three equivalent buildings (12 x .25 = 3), or the BCWP at $3.0 million, it is possible to relate that value against the original work scheduled or Plan at the first half point, and to determine the Schedule Variance is $3.0 million behind (BCWP $3.0 million, less BCWS $6.0 million equals minus $3.0 million), and to reflect graphically 3 months behind schedule.

Also, it is possible to relate the Earned Value of $3.0 million against the Cost Actuals of $5.0 million and to shatter any thoughts of an underrun. What they have at the six month point is a negative

Figure 6.2 First Half Status (C/SCS method)

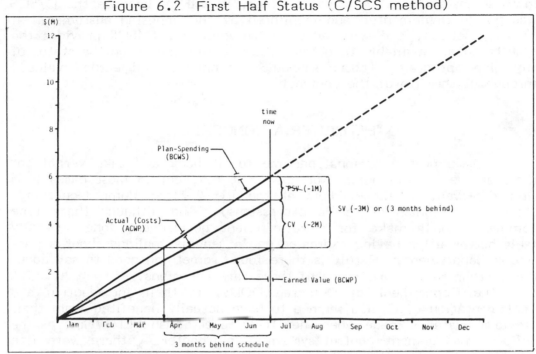

($2.0 million) Cost Variance, and a negative ($3.0 million) Schedule Variance. Not a good picture at the half way point.

Thus by using the C/SCS method in this very simple illustration, it can be seen that the technique shows a very different picture from the conventional management approach of merely equating Planned costs vs. Actual costs.

***

From the individual contractor's standpoint, C/SCS or performance measurement may not absolutely be required to provide good program management. Although there are many who believe that performance measurement/earned value has important features that should always be present in every firm's management control system, realistically, the technique is not critical to the survival of private industry. Some private firms have found C/SCS to be useful, however, and have adopted it as their sole management control system. There are sound reasons for this which will be discussed throughout this book.

But from the United States Government's perspective, which must allocate resources between competing products, the performance measurement concept has provided a good (but less than perfect) method to obtain an accurate assessment of the cost and schedule status of their procurements, on a monthly basis, and it has improved their ability to ascertain the true final costs.

Certainly individual contractors will still attempt to hide a schedule slip, or disguise a cost overrun, even with C/SCS imposed. But in these instances, if allowed to occur, it will be because the C/SCS was poorly implemented and monitored by the imposing customer. If properly set up, and with adequate surveillance, C/SCS provides the best technique available to obtain accurate information on the status of any given program, (cost, schedule, technical, and earned value), throughout the life of the contract.

THE CRITERIA CONCEPT

It is almost a national pastime to sit back and take verbal pot shots at the government. Not only is it fun, but in most cases it is well deserved. "Those idiots at the IRS," "that dumb Congress," etc., are common household expressions. And although these type comments don't make for more efficient government, one generally feels better after having expressed one's genuine feelings about a particular department. Rarely is there found something good to say about the government. This is one of those rare occasions.

The Department of Defense (DOD), in their introduction and implementation of C/SCS seemed to have actually benefited from their previous mistakes made when they tried to establish PERT/Cost as the uniform management control system. In Chapter 4, there were five reasons listed for the demise of PERT/Cost. Excluding reason 5, which was that the DOD had a better idea, namely C/SCS, objections 1 through 4 seemed to have been overcome with the implementation of the new system utilizing a nonoffensive approach called: the "Criteria Concept."

Like them or not, some of the smartest people in this nation are the senior military officers and civilians of the defense community. Generally, they have risen to their positions because they have demonstrated efficiency and leadership. They have their counterparts on the corporate scene, usually called vice presidents and program managers, who likewise have risen in most cases because of demonstrated leadership. It was quite natural, therefore, that these leaders would feel just a bit insulted by the arrogant manner in which PERT/Cost was forced on their establishments. The fact that they were told to use the new technique by extra bright academicians, with little or no practical management experience, merely added to the insult. Even a good idea would have had little chance with that load to carry.

Under the criteria approach, the DOD took the nonoffensive position that they simply needed certain information on all major procurements where the government had more to lose from poor cost/schedule performance than the contractor, namely, on all cost reimbursement type buys. Under these contractual arrangements, a 100 percent overrun in costs, a year's slip in schedule, impacts the government in a major way, with little lasting impact on the individual contractors, since overruns are not that uncommon. The DOD deserved information that presented the true status of all their programs. Rather than telling the private contractors that they had to use a specific management control system on their procurements, as they had with PERT/Cost, the DOD merely laid down criteria which had to be met on all major acquisitions. In their Joint Implementation Guide they stated:

> It is recognized that no single set of management control systems will meet every DOD and contractor management data need for performance measurement. Due to variations in organizations, products, and working relationships, it is not feasible to prescribe a universal system for cost and schedule controls. DOD has adopted an approach which simply defines the criteria that contractor's management control systems must meet. The criteria provide the basis for determining whether contractor management control systems are acceptable.[1]

And still later:

> By applying criteria, rather than specific DOD proscribed management control systems, contractors have the latitude and flexibility for meeting their unique management needs. This approach allows contractors to use existing management control systems or other systems of their choice, provided they meet the criteria.[2]

Make no mistake, the criteria laid down by the DOD were not easy to meet. Contractors across the country put forth much individual effort demonstrating that their systems (often requiring some modification) met these criteria. However, there was no ground swell of individual and corporate resistance to C/SCS, as there had been to PERT/Cost, although the DOD accomplished essentially the same result.

The introduction and imposition of C/SCS on both industry and the military departments was accomplished in a brief 11 page document on December 22, 1967 entitled: DOD Instruction 7000.2, Performance Measurement for Selected Acquisitions. This concise document and the subsequent 80 page Joint Implementation Guide (called the JIG) are copied in their entirety in Appendix B and E of this book. These documents will be referred to often in the next few chapters as the basic workings of performance measurement/earned value are reviewed.

The C/SCS Criteria will be covered in full detail in a later chapter. The criteria are divided into five groups covering: Organization; Planning and Budgeting; Accounting; Analysis; and Revisions and Access to Data. But before getting too deep into a discussion on the criteria, however, there is still another basic building block to cover: the concept of the Work Breakdown Structure, most commonly referred to as the WBS. The WBS concept is so basic to the DOD C/SCSC that an incomplete understanding of the WBS would result in a similar incomplete grasp of C/SCSC.

48

ENDNOTES

1. Departments of the Air Force (AFSCP/AFLCP 173-5), the Army (DARCOM-P 715-5), the Navy (NAVMAT P5240), and the Defense Supply Agency (DSAH 8315-2), <u>Cost Schedule Control Systems Criteria -- Joint Implementation Guide</u>, 1980, Page 5.

2. Ibid, Page 6.

WORK BREAKDOWN STRUCTURES— WBS: SATISFYING TWO WORLDS WITH ONE TECHNIQUE

Once upon a time there was a young man who was given his first cost/schedule control assignment, although at the time he thought he was an administrative assistant (an administrative assistant to a program manager has its inherent dangers). His company had just won a $3 million contract from the Air Force, and in those days (1958) that was still a lot of money.

The program manager handed this young man a copy of the contract with instructions to go out and set up budgets for the effort. He had had no special training for such an exercise, so he started with the newly issued organizational charts for the program. He contacted the manager of design, the manager of systems engineering, the manager of testing, the manager of manufacturing, etc., and carefully made his way through the organization, reaching agreements with each of them on their budget needs. When he finished, he had budgeted the entire contract, with a little left over for a management reserve. He was really proud of himself, and so was the program manager.

About a month later the Air Force came in for their periodic review of the program, and the young man was asked to present the budgets to them. In his presentation he traced through the budgeting approach, relating cost actuals to the plan. To his surprise and disappointment, instead of the accolades he was expecting, the Air Force was quite upset with what they saw. "Why are you budgeting the program to your internal organizational structure," and "don't you know you have a contract with us with a definite statement of work" were some of the kinder remarks being sent in his direction that morning.

On that day this young man made an important discovery, one which he has never since forgotten. The social scientists have a word for what happened that morning: EGOCENTRISM. It simply means viewing the world in relation to oneself. The Air Force had awarded his firm a contract with a statement of work. They felt -- rightfully

-- that everything that was done should be in relation to that statement of work. By contrast, the project also had an organization, and each of the department managers felt -- also rightfully -- that what they did should be in relationship to their organization. What could be done to satisfy both his primary goal of controlling contract costs as well as satisfying a customer demand, both of which seemed to be in conflict?

The young man continued to internally control the program with budgets structured around the organization, to satisfy the needs of the department managers. However, just prior to each customer review, he would stay up late into the night and recut the budget and actuals to present the very same data the way the Air Force wanted it: structured by the contract tasks.

No one should misunderstand the point being made here: both the customer and the department managers had valid reasons to look at the same effort (the work to be accomplished) from their own, but differing perspectives. Nowadays the young man's dilemma is satisfied routinely. It is done with two important tools not available to him back in those early days: (1) improved computers, and (2) a management technique called the Work Breakdown Structure.

ENTER THE WBS CONCEPT

By the mid-1960s, there was no such thing as a WBS concept, rather there were multiple WBS concepts in existence. A given statement of work could be and was often being displayed: by the contractor's functional organization; by contract phase; by contract tasks; by a PERT/Cost network; by financial reporting requirements; by demands from configuration management; etc., depending on the particular preferences of individual buyers or contractor management. In order to establish some semblance of consistency between various major systems acquisitions, and to create a historical data base to improve their future procurements, the defense establishment had to take steps to standardize the collection of costs according to some common language. Thus, in August 1965, the Department of Defense initiated a special study "to develop guidelines for the preparation and application of a WBS for a single project that would satisfy multiple user needs in DOD and industry ... "and to develop a practical minimum of uniform WBSs that could be applied to the widest possible variety of both large and small system/projects."[1]

The result of this special study was the issuance of Department of Defense Directive 5010.20 on July 31, 1968, and later of Military Standard 881 on November 1, 1968, both bearing the same title: "Work Breakdown Structures for Defense Materiel Items." The DOD Directive set forth the policy, and the Military Standard was the detailed implementing document, the latter containing specific instructions as to the preparation of all future WBSs. Both documents included the very same definition of a WBS, which was:

A work breakdown structure is a product-oriented family tree composed of hardware, services and data which result from project engineering efforts during the development and production of a defense materiel item, and which completely defines the project/program. A WBS displays and defines the product(s) to be developed or produced and relates the elements of work to be accomplished to each other and to the end product.[2]

With the creation of a standard WBS format, the DOD was able thereafter to be in a position to compare the cost proposals of all new procurements, or subtasks therein, to those of previous similar buys, to test for reasonableness, and to test the final estimates for existing programs against their historical data base, again, to test the reasonableness of such estimates. Henceforth, with the implementation of a common WBS format, the DOD was able to independently assess the validity of the costs for future and existing buys. Thereafter, it became more difficult -- but still not impossible -- for contractors to "buy into" individual procurements, and to keep their cost overruns hidden until it was too late to do anything about them.

JUST WHAT IS A WBS

When one sees a WBS on a wall it looks like an organization chart, but it is definitely not an organization chart although some have attempted to use it as such. But there are similarities between the methodology of both organization chart displays and WBS displays.

Whereas an organization chart will graphically portray a given company's executive reporting structure, a WBS will likewise graphically display a given contract's statement of work, specifically calling out the hardware, software, and services to be performed, and their relationship to each other.

The single most important document to assist in the preparation of the WBS is Military Standard 881 for the DOD (or other related documents depending on the buying customer). And although all new program managers feel that their activity is unique and different from anything that has come along before, all new DOD contracts can be, should be, and must be portrayed in a WBS according to Military Standard 881. Certainly, a given new system may have unique features, such as the swing wing aspect of the F-111 Fighter, but the basic system and its unique features will fit within a standard WBS in conformance with the requirement. They all have, they all will.

A WBS will start out with a single box at the top, into which everything below will flow. This single box represents the total system and is referred to as WBS level 1. Lower levels are appropriately numbered levels 2, 3, 4, etc. In figure 7.1 is shown a WBS down to level 3, for a complete aircraft system. A level 3 display is significant in that most contracts will call for cost/schedule status reports in detail down to level 3, although actual cost collection on larger programs may go to lower WBS levels, perhaps down to levels 5, 6, or 7. Typically, hardware legs go lower, versus non-hardware items, e.g., training, data, program management, etc., which are usually limited to levels 3 or 4. A display of a WBS down to level 5 is shown in figure 7.2 for a full missile system. A WBS may be used also to reflect a subsystem only, i.e., a navigation unit, or wing structure. Or, it may reflect something completely unrelated to military hardware, example: a hotel, commercial center, factory, a new city, a harbor, utility plant, a training program, and so forth, to mention just a few.

The lowest levels of a WBS have importance because each box or element as they are called represents a discrete segment of work identifying hardware, data, or the services to be performed. It is into these lowest WBS elements where a performing contractor must provide for a given department's budget and create a detailed standard against which future performance may be measured. These detailed, low level efforts are referred to in C/SCS as cost accounts, and are defined as:

Cost Account. A management control point at which actual costs can be accumulated and compared to budgeted costs for work performed. A cost account is a natural control point for cost/schedule planning and control, since it represents the work assigned to one responsible organizational element on one contract work breakdown structure (CWBS) element.[3]

By providing for budgets, work definition, schedules, cost accumulation, and work measurement in detail at the lowest level of the WBS, a contractor, with the aid of the computer processing equipment now available, may sort the same data in two ways: vertically to reflect WBS displays and satisfy the customer, or horizontally to reflect organizational breakouts and thereby satisfy the interests of individual department managers. This approach is reflected in figure 7.3.

WBS Terminology

The collection of costs by the WBS breakout is primarily of interest to the buying customer, and the contractor is normally only interested in looking at costs by its functional organizational display, but there are exceptions. One such exception could exist where there are known subsystem risks on a program, and management, therefore, wants to focus closely on how well those risk areas are being worked and eliminated.

For example, perhaps the development of the guidance and control unit is felt to be a high risk area of a given missile weapon system design. Management will want to follow the monthly performance of the guidance unit. By an organizational display, the guidance unit cannot be tracked exclusively because several different departments in

Figure 7.1 Work Breakdown Structure -- Aircraft System

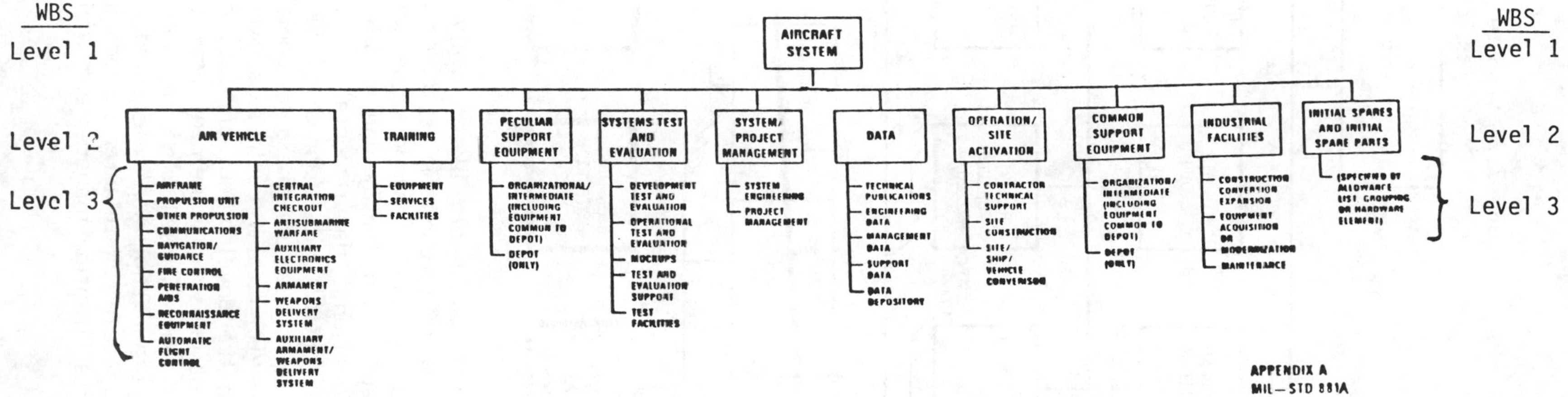

APPENDIX A
MIL—STD 881A

54

Figure 7.2   WBS to Level 5

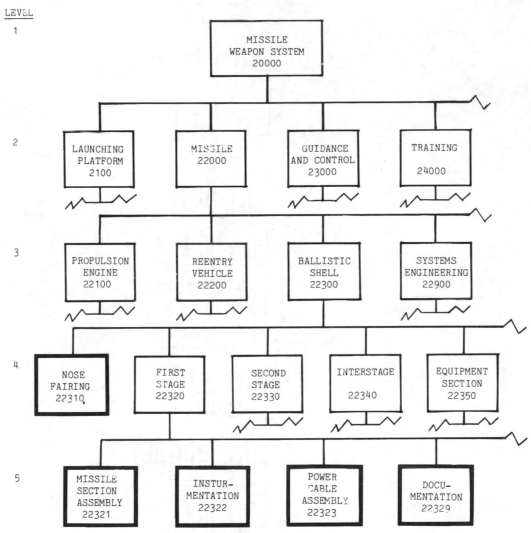

the contractor's plant are likely involved in the development of the unit.   Under these circumstances, contractor management may want to review the performance (earned value against plan and actual costs) of the WBS element on the guidance unit, in addition to their normal review of functional departmental costs.   Back in figure 7.2, the guidance and control unit is shown as WBS element 23000, on level 2.

Another example of where a contractor might have a definite interest in a WBS display could exist where there were severe funding constraints in the development of, say, a new aircraft system.   Under these circumstances, management may feel it desirable to accelerate the design of the aircraft structure, but since the radar, navigation system, and other equipment are standard units in existence, work on them could be deferred to later periods in order to preserve near-term funds.   In this situation management would want to focus its attention

Figure 7.3 Satisfying Two Worlds with a single WBS

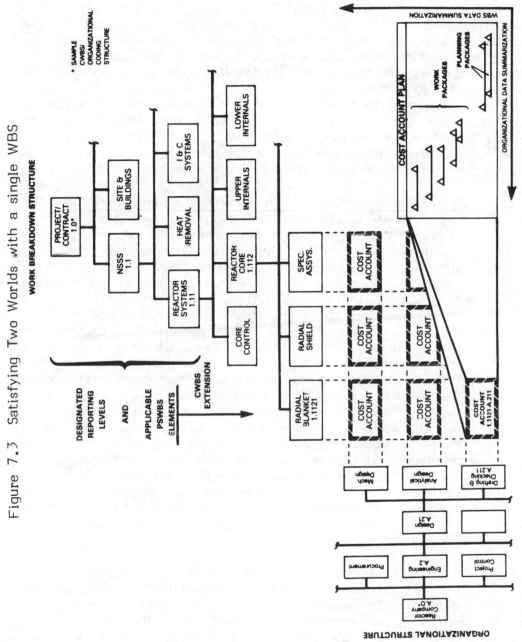

Source: Department of Energy, DCE/CR-0015, Cost and Schedule Control Systems Criteria for Contract Performance: Implementation Guide, May, 1980, Page 15.

of performance by WBS at level 3, in addition to its normal review of functional cost categories.

In the next chapter, the C/SCS Criteria will be discussed in detail one by one. Of the 35 such criteria which a contractor must meet in order to comply with the C/SCS requirement, criterion number one requires that there be only one WBS on any given program. This means that a contractor may not use one WBS to report to the customer, and another WBS for its internal management or for any other purpose. Only one WBS is allowed, and if multiple charts are found to exist by the customer, the violation is serious enough to withhold validation of the contractor's C/SCS compliance.

Now, having said that only one WBS is allowed on any program, shown below are four definitions of WBSs which may exist on a given program, as defined in Military Standard 881. Confusing? Not really. As one reviews these four definitions it becomes apparent that each is but a special purpose derivative from a single WBS concept.

1. Summary Work Breakdown Structure (Summary WBS) The upper three levels of a full WBS represent the Summary WBS. Figure 7.1 was a Summary WBS. It has primary significance in that the first three levels usually represent the formal cost/schedule reporting levels for any given contract. In order to allow for comparison of one program to another, uniform definitions and terminology must be strictly adhered to as defined in Military Standard 881.

2. Project Summary WBS is a special purpose WBS prepared by the customer, for its exclusive use. A Project Summary WBS is used when the customer desires to define a conceptual design of a total system that may have unique configuration elements or unique features.

3. Contract WBS is normally prepared by a contractor in accordance with Military Standard 881 to reflect the statement of work in a specific contract and/or a request for proposal. A Contract WBS describes the total product and work to be done to satisfy a specific contract.

4. Project WBS is used by the customer to define a total program and is made up by merging all the Contract WBSs with all other in-house WBSs to form one consolidated Project WBS.

From an individual contractor's standpoint, the Contract WBS above is of primary concern, for here the particular contractor extends the WBS down to the appropriate levels for cost budgeting and tracking. However, everyone should be aware that the customer may be looking at derivations and extensions of several WBSs on any particular program.

Before leaving the subject of WBS, the following three additional definitions are needed in order to fully appreciate the daily workings of the WBS concept.

WBS Index.   An indentured listing of WBS elements.   Taking figure 7.2, the Index would look something like this:

WBS Level	WBS Element
1 2 3 4 5	
2 0 0 0 0	Missile Weapon System
2 1 0 0 0	Launching Platform
2 2 0 0 0	Missile
2 2 2 0 0	Reentry Vehicle
2 2 3 0 0	Ballistic Shell
2 2 3 1 0	Nose Fairing
2 2 3 2 0	First Stage
2 2 3 2 1	Missile Section Assembly
2 2 3 2 2	Instrumentation

WBS Dictionary.   A book which takes each WBS element and describes the statement of work associated with the element, together with the functional organizations responsible for performance of the element.

Cost Account Matrix.   A summary one page chart or conversion table which relates the functional organizations to the WBS elements. If one would take figure 7.3, and list the WBS Elements horizontally across the top, list the functional departments vertically in the left column, then place an "x" in the middle where each organization has work to do in the WBS element, one would have a Cost Account Matrix. The Cost Account Matrix sometimes gets quite large on certain programs, but provides a useful summary of the work contained in the WBS dictionary.

SUMMARY

The WBS technique is important to the buying customer because it aids in the definition of work to be done in total, and it allows the supplier to break the total effort down into manageable pieces for purposes of defining specific procurement packages. Once under contract, a standardized WBS reporting format allows the customer to compare proposals for new efforts and estimates to complete existing jobs, with its historical data bank, to independently assess the reasonableness of such forecasts.

A WBS is important to individual contractors because it allows them to plan a new project and to fully demonstrate to the buying customer that it is completely knowledgeable about the proposed job.

Lastly, the WBS concept allows contractors to take the same data and sort it vertically by WBS to satisfy the buying customer or horizontally to satisfy the needs for internal management controls. Back in 1958 if the WBS technique had been in place, that young man would have spent less late nights in his office grinding out numbers on his bread-basket size Friden calculator.

ENDNOTES

1. E.J. Nucci and A.L. Jackson, Jr., "Work Breakdown Structures for Defense Materiel Items", in Defense Industry Bulletin, February, 1969, as reprinted in J. Stanley Baumgartner, Systems Management (Washington, D.C.: The Bureau of National Affairs, 1979) page 198.

2. Department of Defense Military Standard 881A, Work Breakdown Structures for Defense Materiel Items, 1975, page 2.

3. Department of Defense Instruction 7000.2, Performance Measurement for Selected Acquisitions, 1977, page 2.

THE CRITERIA IN DETAIL

All wish to possess knowledge, but few, comparatively speaking, are willing to pay the price.

Juvenal

The Roman poet Decimus Junius Juvenal, writing almost two thousand years ago somehow described today's business attitude toward the government's Cost/Schedule Control System. Many in the industry would like to be knowledgeable about C/SCS and possibly use it in their particular application. But few, very very few, have been willing to pay the price of sitting down and doing the necessary homework to allow for even a basic grasp of the technique. But one cannot learn accounting by simply discussing accounting theory -- at some point, one must sit down and work out accounting problems. One cannot learn about life by simply reading Harold Robbin's novels -- at some point one must go out and "find a friend." Likewise, in order to learn about C/SCS and performance measurement/earned value, one has no choice but to review and to reflect on and to absorb the criteria -- one by one.

There are some 35 C/SCS Criteria, with which any contractor dealing with the Department of Defense must be in compliance in order to be considered as having a valid C/SCS management control system. Any contractor's system will do, as long as it can be demonstrated that it meets these 35 criteria. The burden of proof rests with the contractor to demonstrate that its system does, in fact, comply with the criteria. It is not an easy task.

For the convenience of those attempting to understand the criteria, the creators divided them into five logical categories: I -- Organization; II -- Planning and Budgeting; III --Accounting; IV -- Analysis; and V -- Revisions and Access to Data. As mentioned earlier, the criteria were first issued in 1967 in the brief DOD Instruction 7000.2 Performance Measurement for Selected Acquisitions, and they were later updated in 1972 and 1977. This concise document contained little more than a statement of objectives, a listing of the criteria, and related definitions. A more comprehensive treatment of the criteria was later contained in the multi-service procedure: Cost/Schedule Control Systems Criteria-Joint Implementation Guide. This 71-page document is the workhorse of C/SCS and will be referred to often as these criteria are discussed. The JIG (Joint Implementation Guide) is copied in total in Appendix E to this book.

But before each of the criteria are reviewed in detail, including the impact each will have on a particular contractor's management control system in order to be in compliance with the intent of the requirement, it may be useful to examine an overview of the criteria. The criteria were placed into five logical groupings, and each group has a special thrust. Shown in figure 8.1 is a summary of the five criteria groups, with a brief statement of what each group requires from a contractor.

And now each of the 35 criteria will be examined, one by one, within each of the five groupings. At the end of each discussion will be a reference to specific pages in the Joint Implementation Guide (JIG), should the reader care to obtain additional information on a given subject.

I -- ORGANIZATION

These initial five criteria are aimed at demonstrating that the contractor fully understands the contractual statement of work by requiring a definition of same by use of a Work Breakdown Structure (WBS) and also that all work has been assigned to a specific organization for performance.

---

1. **Define all the authorized work and related resources to meet the requirements of the contract, using the framework of the CWBS.**

The first criterion requires the use of a single WBS to define all contractual effort. By definition, a WBS specifically tailored to a given contract becomes a Contract Work Breakdown Structure -- CWBS. All WBSs must be prepared strictly in compliance with Military Standard 881 on DOD contracts (utility companies, etc., may reference other documents).

Probably the very quickest way to fail or be in conflict with this criterion is to have in use more than one WBS on a given contract. Only one WBS is allowed for any given effort, and within it must be shown all contract line items, deliverable end-items, and elements needed for customer reporting. The elements that will contain cost accounts must be identified, which are usually the lowest elements displayed on the CWBS. (JIG 9,36).

Figure 8.1 C/SCS Criteria Summary

GENERAL

Company Policy for Cost and Schedule Control
Administration of Policy
Systems Summary

I ORGANIZATION

CWBS Development and Control
Organizational Structure & Responsibility
Integration of CWBS with Organizational Structure
Systems Integration
Subcontract Management

II PLANNING & BUDGETING

Work Authorization
Schedule Development & Control
Cost Account/Work Package Development & Planning
Establishment of Performance Measurement Baseline
Overhead Planning & Budgeting
Management Reserve Budget Control
Undistributed Budget Control

III ACCOUNTING

Procedures
Elements of Cost
Materials Cost Control
Purchase Order System
Recurring/Nonrecurring Costs
Overhead Procedures and Control
Data Base Description
Data Reconciliation

IV ANALYSIS

Earned Value Methods Determination & Use
Comparison of Actual versus Planned Performance
Variance Analysis
Estimate at Completion Derivation

V REVISIONS & ACCESS TO DATA

Baseline Maintenance
Change Incorporation
Internal Replanning
Formal Reprogramming
Internal & External Reporting Procedures
Systems Surveillance
Access to Data

Source: Department of Energy, DOE/CR-0015, Cost & Schedule Control Systems Criteria For Contract Performance: Implementation Guide, May 1980, Page 66.

---

2. Identify the internal organizational elements and the major subcontractors responsible for accomplishing the authorized work.

Here the contractor must take each of the identified tasks in the WBS and assign performance responsibility to a specific organization. On those items in which a make-or-buy decision has been made and it has been decided to subcontract the effort, the subcontractor should be identified if one has been selected. As make-or-buy and organizational changes occur, such changes should be referenced in an updated Cost Account Matrix. (JIG 9,36).

---

3. Provide for the integration of the contractor's planning, scheduling, budgeting, work authorization, and cost accumulation systems with each other, the CWBS, and the organizational structure.

This is perhaps one of the most important and difficult of the criteria to meet for here the contractor must demonstrate that its management control system integrates its overall program planning with all aspects of master and detail scheduling, with its budgeting formats, with work authorizations (if separate from budgets), with its cost actual system, and each of these within the framework of the CWBS and contractor's organization.

The heart of the integration of these facets of management is the cost account, which by definition must combine one CWBS element with one responsible organizational unit. Cost accounts define three types of effort, the most important of which is the discrete or work package, and the other two listed below must be kept to a minimum:

1. Discrete or Work Packages are short timespan, measurable jobs, which have a definite start and stop point, and which can be used to measure work performance or earned value.
2. Level of Effort (LOE) are general or supportive activities, which have no definite or deliverable products, which are more time related, and sometimes continue for the life of a program (example the program manager).
3. Apportioned Effort is related to some other discrete or measurable effort, usually as a constant percentage of that other effort, but by themselves are not measurable as work packages (example quality control).

The fact that in order to meet the C/SCS standards a management control system must integrate the multiple management functions of planning, scheduling, budgeting, cost accumulation, etc., with the work to be done is likely one of the primary differences between C/SCS and most other type management systems. (JIG 9,14,36,50).

---

4. Identify the managerial positions responsible for controlling overhead (indirect costs).

Nothing in the criteria requires that a contractor's indirect or overhead burdens be applied at the cost account level, i.e., these types of burden costs may be added at a higher summation point than the cost account level. However, the criteria do require that indirect costs be clearly defined, uniformly and fairly applied to all direct costs and all contracts in accordance with documented procedures, and that responsible managers be identified and delegated with authority to control these nondirect burden costs (JIG 10,36).

---

5. Provide for integration of the CWBS with the contractor's functional organizational structure in a manner that permits cost and schedule performance measurement for CWBS and organizational elements. (Provide matrix showing integration.)

One of the requirements of C/SCS is to be able to take the same data, building from the cost accounts, and to measure performance, both by CWBS and by contractor organization. To demonstrate that the system has this capability, the contractor must first prepare a matrix that lists CWBS numbers on one scale, the departmental organizations on the other scale, and that indicates which organizations have effort in which CWBS elements. This summary is called a Cost Account Matrix and was covered earlier in Chapter 7 on Work Breakdown Structures. A closely related activity is the preparation of the WBS Dictionary, which provides a summary statement of work for each WBS element, and, most important, it provides a listing of all organizations that have effort in each WBS element. Obviously, all of the activities (CWBS, WBS Dictionary, Cost Account Matrix, and cost accounts) are so interrelated that preparation of one logically leads to the preparation of the next.

In each cost account established, the contractor must be able to formulate and determine status on a monthly basis, three activities which allow for earned value/performance measurement, as well as allow for an estimate at completion, also monthly.

1. Budgeted Costs for Work Scheduled -- BCWS, i.e., the plan.

2. Actual Costs for Work Performed -- ACWP, i.e., actual costs.

3. Budgeted Costs for Work Performed -- BCWP, i.e., earned value. (JIG 10,11,37).

II -- PLANNING AND BUDGETING

In group two there are 11 criteria to satisfy, and here it must be demonstrated that the contractor has in place an integrated management control system which can implement the organizational theory discussed in group I above. The total contract funds must be provided for using a performance measurement baseline, and any management reserve must be allotted and controlled outside of such performance baseline. All growth or changes to the contract must be tightly controlled, and implemented in an expedient manner, normally on a monthly basis.

> 1. Schedule the authorized work in a manner which describes the sequence of work and identifies the significant task interdependencies required to meet the development, production, and delivery requirements of the contract.

This criterion requires the use of some type of a master program schedule, out of which will come major program milestones. Such milestones set the wide parameters which are usually then supported by intermediate level schedules, and further supported by functional departmental schedules down to the work package level. Shown in figure 8.2 is a Department of Energy chart which illustrates the scheduling flow from a Project Master Schedule at the top, down to the Cost Account and even Work Package Schedules at the bottom. Out of the scheduling activity must come the sequence of work to be accomplished, within the framework of the contract period. Each cost account must provide a specific start and stop date, from which a forecast of program completion can be made by summation of all the cost accounts.

Nowhere in the criteria do they specify that any particular scheduling technique must be used. However, here they do require that schedule interdependencies and constraints be shown. As was discussed earlier in the scheduling chapters, only a network type schedule will truly show dependencies and constraints. Therefore, almost by elimination, a strict interpretation of the criteria would suggest that this criterion insists that some type of PERT or CPM type network schedule be used. However, a contractor may employ any scheduling technique as long as the full intent of the criterion is satisfied. (JIG 14,15,37).

> 2. Identify physical products, milestones, technical performance goals, or other indicators that will be used to measure output.

Here, the contractor must demonstrate in detail, precisely how it will measure earned value, what milestone/technical goals it will establish, and the techniques to be used to reflect accomplishments against its plan. There will be a full discussion in Chapter 11 on the subject of how various contractors provide earned value to meet this criterion. (JIG 16,37,38).

> 3. Establish and maintain a time-phase budget baseline at the cost account level against which contract performance can be measured. Initial budgets established for this purpose will be based on the negotiated target cost. Any other amount used for performance measurement purposes must be formally recognized by both the contractor and the government.

First, the term Performance Measurement Baseline must be defined and fully understood. From the JIG (page 6) a PMB is defined as:

> The time-phased budget plan against which contract performance is measured. It is formed by the budgets assigned to scheduled cost accounts and the applicable indirect budgets. For future effort, not planned to the cost account level, the performance measurement baseline also includes budgets assigned to higher level CWBS elements, and undistributed budgets. It equals the total allocated budget less management reserve.

65

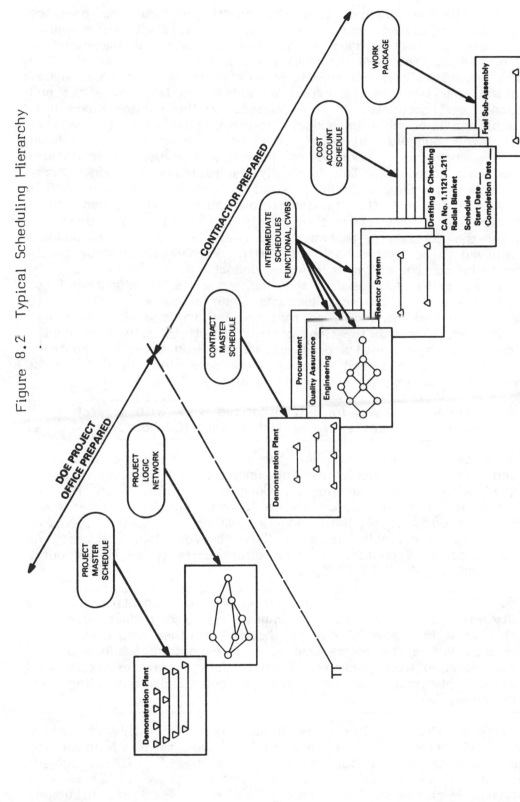

Figure 8.2 Typical Scheduling Hierarchy.

Source: Department of Energy, DOE/CR-0015, Cost & Schedule Control Systems Criteria For Contract Performance: Implementation Guide, May 1980, Page 26.

This criterion requires that the contractor take the contract budget base (negotiated + authorized contract costs), subtract a management reserve, and produce a top level Performance Measurement Baseline - PMB, then take the PMB and produce a bottom-up, detailed budget plan. The PMB will consist of short-span discrete work packages in the near-term to the extent possible, plus level of effort and apportioned cost accounts, all time-phased. In those cases where it is inadvisable or impossible to budget far-term effort down to the cost account level, budgets will be allocated and kept at the higher level CWBS elements and controlled to prevent their use in near-term budgeted cost accounts. This is simply the rolling-wave budget technique which was discussed earlier. What is very important in C/SCS is the tight control of the far-term/gross budgets to prevent their reallocation into the near-term fully budgeted cost accounts. Obviously the concern is that overruns could be disguised if budgets were allowed to be shifted back and forth. Procedures must be specific about the control of far-term/gross budgets.

This criterion also requires that indirect costs be allocated if not included as a part of the cost accounts (indirect costs do not have to be included in cost accounts) so that the full value of the PMB may be established. Through the tight control of bottom-up cost accounts, each one time-phased with a precise start and stop date, the contractor will produce a Budgeted Cost for Work Scheduled (BCWS) against which performance may be measured. (JIG 16,17,38,51,59).

> **4. Establish budgets for all authorized work with separate identification of cost elements (labor, material, etc.).**

This criterion requires that the total contract be budgeted, including that effort which may be unpriced but authorized to be proceeded with by the customer. Budgets and work authorizations must be issued in a formal, documented, and controlled manner down to the cost account level. All budgets must be expressed in terms of cost elements, example labor dollars and/or labor hours; or material/subcontract dollars; or other direct costs (example computer costs). (JIG 16,38,39,51,52,53).

> **5. To the extent the authorized work can be identified in discrete, short-span work packages, establish budgets for this work in terms of dollars, hours, or other measurable units. Where the entire cost account cannot be subdivided into detailed work packages, identify the far-term effort in larger planning packages for budget and scheduling purposes.**

Many of the 35 criteria are interrelated, as is this one which addresses discrete work packages in the near-term, followed by planning packages in the far-term, all time-phased. If the subject sounds familiar, it should, for it was covered above in #3 when a time-phased Performance Measurement Baseline -- PMB was discussed.

Here the contractor must show that he/she establishes discrete budgets to the greatest extent possible, in a way which represents the manner in which the job is being planned. In the later or far-term, the effort may be shown in time-phased planning packages, which will subsequently become work package(s) as their term approaches. Discrete work packages must be relatively short and contain measurable activity to allow for the calculation of work measurement or earned value. The contractor must be able to differentiate between work packages and planning packages, so that work cannot be shifted either way. Likewise long-term discrete packages must be measurable and controlled to also prevent a shift of budget.

All budgets must be expressed in measurable units, i.e., dollars or hours or other types of direct costs. Work packages must be assigned to a specific department for performance. (JIG 16,17,39,40,55,56,57).

> 6. Provide that the sum of all work package budgets plus planning packages within a cost account equals the cost account budget.

This criterion requires a reconciliation to show that the sum of all work packages and planning packages within a cost account equals the budget for the cost account, no more no less. (JIG 15,40,51).

> 7. Identify relationships of budgets or standards in underlying work authorization systems to budgets for work packages.

Some firms that have been in business for a number of years, that have a fairly consistent product and consistent way of producing it, and that have kept good records of such activities are able to establish work standards for their performance. If conditions do not change from one contract to the next, such standards provide an excellent basis for budgeting selected activities. Examples of such standards are the number of hours to produce a typical drawing; the number of hours to check/release a typical drawing; the number of hours to produce a typical tool; to manufacture a typical part, and so forth.

This criterion requires some type of formal relationship between the work performance standard used and the work package budget. Normally a published work standard book, directive, procedure, or memorandum will satisfy this requirement. (JIG 15,40).

> 8. Identify and control level of effort activity by time-phased budgets established for this purpose. Only that effort which cannot be identified as discrete, short-span work packages or as apportioned effort will be classed as LOE.

Of the three types of cost accounts allowed (Discrete, Level of Effort, and Apportioned), the level of effort type is the least desirable one to be used. LOE cost accounts must be kept to a minimum.

However, as this criterion states, LOE must be time-phased with a budget and controlled as with any other cost account. Neither budget nor earned value may be shifted in either direction, for such would distort the true status. Examples of LOE functions would be a program manager, a field support engineer, sometimes a guard, or scheduler, etc., all of whom perform activities which are more time related than output related. Thus they are justified as LOE activity. (JIG 13,14,18,40,55).

---

9. Establish overhead budgets for the total costs of each significant organizational component whose expenses will become indirect costs. Reflect in the contract budgets at the appropriate level, the amounts in overhead pools that will be allocated to the contract as indirect costs. (Reference DCAA Audit Manual and DAR 15-203.)

The customer needs assurances that there is an orderly way to forecast, budget, control, and allocate indirect burdens over all direct costs. What makes up the burdens, do they represent the full plant or only part of it, and on what cycle are such budgets created, must be shown to satisfy this criterion. Each organization that can incur such costs should be making commitments from its own budget (not someone else's), and all elements of such expenses should be included in the budgets.

Each company, and frequently each major division or operating unit within a company, must submit a financial disclosure statement outlining the way in which they plan to operate their business in a financial sense. All contractors must subsequently be able to prove that their operations are consistent with what they said in their disclosure statement. Of particular interest is the makeup of burden costs, including what types and amounts of Independent Research and Development (IR&D) costs will be allotted to their indirect pools. Also of interest is the makeup of the direct base, the types of firm, non-firm, and potential business included in their base. The relationship between the projected direct base and overhead pools must be shown, including what types of costs are included in the burdens.

Most larger firms have more than one type of indirect pool. Typical of the types of such pools are engineering burden, manufacturing burden, material burden, general and administrative, and sometimes a study or partial burden. The contractor must specify exactly the number of indirect pools it has, and the types of costs which go into each of these separate pools. Costs must be tightly controlled to each of the pools, to preclude the manipulation of costs by the contractor. How far into the future the burdens and burden bases are projected, and the makeup and methodology behind them, must be shown to satisfy this requirement. When changes in either the burden base or projected pools occur, how the contractor adjusts its forecast to accommodate these changes must be described.

Lastly, in the event that burdens are not applied to individual cost accounts (and the criteria do not require application of burdens to cost accounts), the contractor must indicate at what point in the CWBS and organizational summaries burden costs will be added. (JIG 18,40,41,58).

---
10.   Identify management reserves and undistributed budget.

Before beginning this discussion, the JIG (page 6) will be referred to for two additional definitions:

Management Reserve (synonymous with Management Reserve Budget).
> An amount of the total allocated budget withheld for management control purposes rather than designated for the accomplishment of a specific task or set of tasks. It is not a part of the Performance Measurement Baseline.

Undistributed Budget.
> Budget applicable to contract effort which has not yet been identified to CWBS elements at or below the lowest level of reporting to the Government.

Undistributed Budget, therefore, is a part of the PMB, whereas Management Reserve is outside the PMB until a management decision is made to transfer some or all into the PMB.

Management Reserve goes under other titles such as contingency reserve, etc. However, until the contract is ended, Management Reserve (MR) must be tightly controlled and every transaction which either takes from or adds to the MR must be documented and done so with the approval of the program manager. Since MR is by definition outside the PMB, effort must be made to make sure that no management or contingency reserve is allowed to stay in the PMB, e.g., at cost account levels or organizational budgets.

Undistributed Budget, by contrast, is expected to be used in the performance of the contract and is, therefore, a part of the PMB. In all cases, undistributed budget must be allotted to a specific statement of work, time-phased, and tightly controlled so as to not be used for other work. There are two situations in which undistributed budget may be used:

1. For contract changes, authorized but not definitized, where the interim budgets are kept at a higher CWBS level until negotiations are concluded;
2. For far-term effort where it might prove fruitless to define the planning and budgeting down to the detailed cost account level (rolling-wave budgeting).

However, there is not universal agreement as to the use of undistributed budget in the second situation, as the following somewhat unique application would imply:

> In the 1970-1975 time frame contractors were allowed to use undistributed budgets to hold future budgets until the cost account manager approached the proper time period when the work was going to be accomplished. In recent years most government review teams held with the concept that undistributed budget was only for use at the very early stages of a new contract, or when work had been authorized but the contract had not been definitized.[1]

The author has never experienced or heard of a government review team being unreasonable in the interpretation of the criteria as they apply to a particular situation. In those developmental programs which are relatively short in duration, perhaps three to five years in length, the use of undistributed budget would likely be limited to only the first application, as the white paper would imply. However, in those developmental contracts that extend eight to ten years or more in duration, the contractor could likely receive approval for the use of undistributed budgets in both situations. The contractor would likely be allowed to define only the near-term effort (three to five years) down to the cost account level, and leave the far-term effort in time-phased, tightly controlled, but higher CWBS level undistributed budgets. (JIG 15,21,41).

---

11. Provide that the contract target cost plus the estimated cost of authorized but unpriced work is reconciled with the sum of all internal contract budgets and management reserves.

All contractors' management control systems, which are in compliance with the C/SCS Criteria, must be defined in what is termed a system description and further supported by detailed working procedures, most frequently outside of the system description to allow for flexibility. This criterion requires simply that somewhere in the written definition of a contractor's C/SCS, that the following be specified and followed, representing the Contract Budget Base - CBB:

Contract Target Costs Plus Authorized but Unpriced Work at the Cost Level	EQUALS	PMB (sum of all internal contract budgets and undistributed budgets) Plus Management Reserve

(JIG 15,41,42,52-54).

III -- ACCOUNTING

In this the third grouping of criteria, the purpose is as the name implies, to define and reach agreement on the accounting rules governing the C/SCS activity. All firms doing a public business must have some type of accounting system which incorporates acceptable standards of accounting, and which has records available for audit if necessary. Firms doing business with the government must also satisfy the additional requirements of the audit branch of the DOD, the Defense Contract Audit Agency -- DCAA.

With all these rules and standards governing accounting activity, why is it necessary to define additional rules just for C/SCS? The answer is simple. C/SCS requires an additional dimension beyond that which is required in the public sector. C/SCS requires a performance measurement plan (BCWS) against which actual performance will be measured (BCWP). Such activity does not exist in other public management control or accounting systems, where they focus only on a plan and actuals, but do not concern themselves with performance measurement/earned value.

In order to accept existing financial systems from public firms, and to add the performance measurement dimension, the criteria must define certain additional rules which govern accounting systems. Hence, the requirement for a group of seven criteria that focus on accounting and require agreement on the accounting methodology.

> 1. Record direct costs on an applied or other acceptable basis consistent with the budgets in a formal system that is controlled by the general books of account.

Here the criteria insist on an agreement as to the acceptable method of accounting. They will allow any conventional method of accounting, but seem to encourage the applied method. Since this term is not universally known in the accounting world, the JIG (page 5) will be used to provide a definition: "Applied Direct Costs. The amounts recognized in the time period associated with the consumption of labor, material, and other direct resources, without regard to the date of commitment or date of payment." In simple terms this means to account for items when they are consumed, not when ordered or when bills are paid.

This criterion requires that direct costs be budgeted and costs accumulated in a consistent manner, down to the cost account level. It also requires that all C/SCS accounting be done within the framework of the firm's general books of account, i.e., their official accounting system. (JIG 17,18,42).

> 2. Summarize direct costs from the cost accounts into the WBS without allocation of a single cost account to two or more WBS elements.

72

> 3. Summarize direct costs from the cost accounts into the contractor's functional organizational elements without allocation of a single cost account to two or more organizational elements.

Criteria 2 and 3 are related, the only difference between them is the direction of the summation. The first requires the ability to sum cost accounts upward in the WBS, to a reporting level, 2 or 3. The latter criterion requires the summation of cost accounts by functional organization, to some higher organizational grouping, i.e., engineering, manufacturing, etc. Both criteria prohibit the allocation of a single cost account to either two or more WBS elements, or two or more organizational units. Such prohibition is consistent with the definition of a cost account, which is that point at which one WBS element intersects with one organizational unit. Hence, it would not be proper to allocate costs from one cost account to more than one WBS element or organizational unit. (JIG 17,18,42,52,53).

> 4. Record all indirect costs which will be allocated to the contract.

Once again, a criterion addresses the issue of indirect costs. Here the requirement is that the contractor be able to sum indirect costs from the point where allocation is made, upward to a contract total, and that actual costs be compared with the budget plan. There must be a relationship between those persons who have responsibility for indirect budgets, to those who can incur costs against these budgets.

The government is always concerned that the allocation of indirect costs from point of accumulation to final source be equitably applied over both government and commercial work. Here the contractor must show that there is no distortion in the allocation of such costs, and that both the commercial work and government contracts are treated fairly in the allotment of burden costs.

Lastly, the contractor must show the methods it uses to allocate indirect costs to the final source. Whether the method calls for a monthly adjustment of indirect actuals against a yearly plan, or a constant rate adjusted at year-end for such actuals, the procedure must be formally documented and be auditable by the DCAA. (JIG 17,18,42,43).

> 5. Identify the bases for allocating the cost of apportioned effort.

Under C/SCS, there are three types of cost accounts allowed: Discrete/Work Package, Level of Effort, and Apportioned. Apportioned cost accounts are those which have some historical direct relationship to a discrete work package; therefore, the earned value of the discrete work package will also be the earned value of its apportioned cost accounts. Example, the function of quality inspection often has a direct relationship with the function of manufacturing assembly, depending upon the business, of course. Each firm will have its unique situations. The point is that apportioned cost accounts (quality inspection in this case) need not be measured for its own performance. All that is needed is that the primary cost account (manufacturing assembly) be measured and the progress of one represents the progress of the other.

This criterion requires that the bases (cost accounts that have a direct relationship to apportioned functions) against which apportioned cost accounts will be measured be specified and defined in a specific way. (JIG 18,43).

---

6. Identify unit costs, equivalent unit costs, or lot costs as applicable.

Any new product at the start must go through a development phase, which goes by several titles: research and development; development; full scale development; nonrecurring effort; and so forth. Included in these categories will be the costs to engineer, produce one or more units for test, and to test these articles until management is satisfied with the end product. Then the product is ready for the production phase, which also goes under several titles: production; manufacturing; recurring effort; etc. One important distinction between these two phases is the need to establish the costs per unit of the article produced. In the nonrecurring developmental phase, tasks generally happen once and do not occur again. By contrast, in the recurring production phase, the same tasks happen again and again. Therefore, one will want to know if improvements in performance are made when producing each subsequent unit. To do this, one must have the ability to know the costs of unit 1, versus unit 10, versus unit 100, versus unit 1,000, and so on. This allows progress to be displayed on a learning or experience curve.

Under this criterion, the contractor must be able to distinguish between nonrecurring developmental effort, and the recurring production effort and have such documented in procedures. It also requires the contractor to be able to establish unit or equivalent unit or lot costs for articles produced in the recurring phase. Unit costs may be developed by hours, labor dollars, material dollars, or total unit price.

Unit costs may be established by isolating the individual costs of one unit, or by equivalents of units, or with probably the most common production method: lot costs. Under lot costs, a block of selected units are started all at once. The contractor merely has to be able to fix the actual average cost of one unit in a given block to satisfy this criterion. The average cost of units in, say, block 1 are then equated to the average costs of units in subsequent blocks -- 10, 100, 1,000, -- to determine if unit costs are being reduced, as the units produced goes up. (JIG 17,18,43).

> 7. The contractor's material accounting system will provide for: accurate cost accumulation and assignment of costs to cost accounts in a manner consistent with the budgets using recognized, acceptable costing techniques; determination of price variances by comparing planned versus actual commitments; cost performance measurement at the point in time most suitable for the category of material involved, but no earlier than the time of actual receipt of material; determination of cost variances attributable to the excess usage of material; determination of unit or lot costs when applicable; and full accountability for all material purchased for the contract including the residual inventory.

Material is a big and difficult subject to discuss with respect to budgeting, and here only those aspects related to meeting the criterion will be covered.

Material costs may be tracked at several points in time:

- when the order is placed, i.e., commitments made (not usually allowed under C/SCS);
- when the articles are received;
- when the units received have passed inspection;
- when paid for, i.e., expenditures recorded;
- when withdrawn from the stockroom (if previously put into stock);
- when incorporated into an assembly or final product.

This criterion requires that whatever point is tracked, the budget plan (BCWS) and the actual costs (ACWP) and the earned value /performance measurement (BCWP) use the same point in time, or adjust to the differences. If budgets are set on one basis, say when materials are received, and actual costs are related to expenditures, a distortion in the true status may occur. The contractor must either use the same basis to report BCWS, BCWP, and ACWP, or make an adjustment in one or two so that the status will relate equal points in time.

The contractor's system must be able to identify variances in both material quantities used, as well as differences in material prices. Merely because there is no variance at the top does not mean that a variance hasn't taken place at lower levels, as for example:

BCWS 15 units at $10.00 = $150

ACWP 10 units at $15.00 = $150

The contractor's material system must be able to reflect any differences in either quantities used or in unit prices.

Lastly, the material system must have a documented way to set unit or lot prices, including how it will account for any residual material inventory, if appropriate. (JIG 17,18,43).

IV -- ANALYSIS

This fourth grouping of the criteria assumes that the foundation has been laid against which work measurement may be performed during the period of a contract. If during the life of the contract everything went exactly as planned, then this fourth group would not be needed, for its main purpose is the analysis of the results versus the plan. If there were no variances then, obviously, no analysis would be needed, and this fourth group could be eliminated.

It is doubtful that in the history of the world that a project of any substance has ever been undertaken and completed exactly as originally planned. Therefore, it is wise to allow for some provision, in a formal way, for the analysis of what is presently happening, and to forecast what the final results might be, if one desires to follow the status of a contract during the term of its performance.

To provide the necessary measurement tools, the criterion requires that the following five types of data be made available from the contractor's management control system:

1. BCWS -- Budgeted Cost of Work Scheduled, i.e., the budget,
2. ACWP -- Actual Cost of Work Performed, i.e., cost actuals,
3. BCWP -- Budgeted Cost of Work Performed, i.e., work accomplished,
4. BAC -- Budget At Completion, i.e., the sum of all cost accounts budgeted for the contract,
5. EAC -- Estimate At Completion, i.e., the estimated cost required to actually complete the total contract.

With these five data elements clearly established and tightly controlled, the contractor has the basis to determine and to report status during the term of the contract.

The Analysis group insists that a contractor define Variance Thresholds against which plan versus actuals may be compared, and when these thresholds are penetrated, that some type of formal analysis take place, and a corrective plan be implemented. And now for a review of the six criteria in this group.

> 1. Identify at the cost account level on a monthly basis using data from, or reconcilable with, the accounting system; BCWS and BCWP; BCWP and Applied (actual where appropriate) Direct Costs for the same work; variances resulting from the above comparisons classified in terms of labor, material, or other appropriate elements, together with the reasons for significant variances.

Here the requirement is for a monthly comparison, down to the cost account level, of the results of the BCWS (plan) less BCWP (work accomplished), and BCWP less ACWP (cost actuals). The results of such comparisons will provide a Schedule Variance (BCWP less BCWS) as well as a Cost Variance (BCWP less ACWP). When either the SV or CV exceeds a previously established parameter, called in C/SCSC a variance threshold, the contractor must perform a variance analysis to determine precisely why the threshold was broken. The analysis must specify the types of costs involved, e.g., labor, material, other direct costs, and provide a plan for recovery.

When the contractor has a major part of the effort performed by another company, a subcontractor, and when the value of the subcontract exceeds a specific dollar value, the prime contractor must impose C/SCSC on the subcontracted effort and have the same capability to measure and report progress as is contained in the prime contract effort. Chapter 13 is devoted to the flow down of C/SCSC to subcontractors. (JIG 18,19,44).

---

2. Identify on a monthly basis, in the detail needed by management for effective control, budgeted indirect costs, actual indirect costs, and variances, along with the reasons.

The contractor must have the ability, and actually perform, an analysis of the variances of indirect expenses, if any. The analysis must cover the type of cost, and the indirect pool or pools involved, as appropriate. Indirect expenses can increase for two principal reasons:

- because indirect expenses exceed the original budgeted amounts, or
- because the direct base over which the indirect costs are allocated has shrunk, and the indirect costs have not been cut back in a corresponding manner, resulting in an increase of allocated costs to a given contract.

The contractor's analysis must be specific as to exactly what is causing the variances, and what steps are being taken to correct the condition. (JIG 18,19,44,45,58).

---

3. Summarize the data elements and associated variances listed in items 1 and 2 above through the contractor organization and WBS to the reporting level specified in the contract.

Although contractors are required to analyze all significant variances at the cost account level, normally they are not required to report all such variances to the customer. Rather, formal customer reporting usually takes place up the WBS to higher levels, usually 3 and sometimes at level 2. This higher level formal reporting allows the contractor some flexibility in managing the contract, for many variances are never actually reported to the customer, simply because there are offsetting variances at lower levels of the WBS which cancel out at the reporting levels of 3 or 2. Through internal corrective actions contractors are able to bring most variances back on track without involvement by the customer. There is nothing wrong with this concept, which gives contractors the opportunity to manage their programs without customer involvement.

This criterion requires that a contractor have the ability to summarize variances upward through the WBS, as well as horizontally by organizational unit. (JIG 19,45,51-54,61,62).

> **4. Identify on a monthly basis significant differences between planned and actual schedule accomplishment together with the reasons.**

While it is the purpose of this book to describe the merits of C/SCS, and they are considerable, it would be naive and misleading to present the system as being totally foolproof. The technique provides an excellent means of systematically ascertaining both cost and schedule status of an activity throughout its life. But there are shortcomings, and one is in the ability of C/SCS to precisely reflect the true schedule position of a program.

Schedule Variances (SV) reflect the differences between the work performed (BCWP) less work originally scheduled (BCWS). What this really reflects is the <u>dollar value</u> of work accomplished less work scheduled, which may or may not necessarily reflect the true critical schedule position. Some work may be accomplished ahead of schedule, or out of sequence, representing considerable dollar amounts, but leaving critical milestones unfinished, thereby adversely affecting the overall schedule position of the effort. Therefore, Schedule Variances (SV) must be viewed as a general indicator of the overall schedule position of a program, but SV should <u>not</u> be used as a substitute for intelligent program management, either with the contractor or with the customer.

This criterion, if properly imposed, requires the contractor to integrate into its C/SCS a scheduling system which focuses on tangible milestones, (such as Preliminary Design Reviews - PDR; Critical Design Reviews - CDR; test completions) and not simply on the summation of BCWP results of all cost accounts, which could be misleading. The contractor with its PERT networks and master schedules must be alert to meeting all key milestones when scheduled, and to integrate these into its C/SCS. (JIG 20,45).

> **5. Identify managerial actions taken as a result of criteria items 1 through 4 above.**

This criterion deals with the issue of whether or not performance information is disseminated down to the lowest level cost account managers, what if anything is done with the information by them, and if there is a system in effect which requires that certain corrective actions be taken when established cost/schedule performance parameters (variance thresholds) have been penetrated.

Each contractor may establish its own variance thresholds, which when approved by the procuring customer, serve to trigger certain internal actions when exceeded. There are three primary points at which thresholds may be established, and most contractors use a combination of two or all three for following performance. Variances in either direction, over or under a standard, can reflect a problem of sorts, although positive parameters are sometimes allowed to exist at a greater percentage level than negative ones before corrective action is required. For example, if a negative (overrun) parameter is say $100,000, a positive (underrun) parameter might be $200,000. The thinking here is that a negative variance reflects a potentially more serious problem, although there is no universal agreement on this concept.

The most common variance parameters will focus on:

1. the cumulative to date position;
2. the current month/period;
3. the estimate at completion.

Variances in excess of a percentage of a base, and/or in excess of an absolute value, call for management action.

The most common type of management action is the requirement to prepare a variance analysis report, which exists by several titles in the industry (e.g., Problem Analysis Report -- PAR). Such reports must reflect the cost account manager's statement of the problem causing the variance and what actions will be taken to remedy the problem. At a minimum, the next level of management must sign the report to indicate a concurrence with the actions proposed. Sometimes, the program manager must also concur on the PAR report. Such reports are reviewed internally, and top level WBS summaries are submitted to the customer monthly as one part of the Cost Performance Report -- CPR.

When such actions are required of all organizations through formalized procedures, this criterion is normally met. (JIG 19,20,45,46).

> 6. Based on performance to date and on estimates of future conditions, develop revised estimates of cost at completion for WBS elements identified in the contract and compare these with the contract budget base and the latest statement of funds requirements report to the government.

In the last criterion of the Analysis group, the focus is on the contractor's projection of the final costs to complete the total job, i.e., the Estimate At Completion -- EAC. While misleading information may be contained in several sources of programmatic data, the EAC is where the contractor could (if it so desired) mislead a customer into an unrealistic expectation of the final bill, or costs of the total job. Call it being overly-optimistic, call it being unrealistic, call it deliberately lying, whatever, some firms have established for themselves a reputation of making poor projections of the total bill on cost reimbursable contracts. Therefore, an essential part of any management control system must be the ability to make a reasonably accurate forecast of final costs, the EAC.

This criterion insists that an EAC be based on an assessment of the work remaining to complete all contract tasks unfinished, taking off from the work performed to date -- BCWP. These estimates must be compared with original estimates for each WBS element, the Contract Budget Base, and functional estimates. In effect, the government insists on what was referred to earlier as a bottom-up (comprehensive) estimate of the remaining costs, as contrasted with the gross top-down projections.

Again, overhead or indirect costs are emphasized as being an essential part of each individual contract's costs, even though these costs are shared with all contracts in an organization. Historical performance of the indirect pools should be examined to see if there is some obvious pattern which must be considered when making the EAC. For example, changes in indirect pools rarely take place in absolute concert with changes in the direct bases over which these costs must be allocated. Certain of the overhead costs are essentially fixed (e.g., an engineering building) and are not easily changed as the direct base goes up or down.

Normally, direct bases go up, or go down, and there is usually some time delay before the burdens adjust proportionately. Thus, if a firm's direct base is going down, one must be alert to a possible increase in burden rates, no matter what the experts forecast. Why -- because history has shown that cuts in indirect costs seldom take place with the same speed as a reduced direct base. Most people are optimistic by nature, and they refuse to believe company projections of a downturn in business. Therefore, managers are slow to take the necessary actions to cut out indirect costs with the same speed as the direct base goes down, hence, the indirect rate goes up.

The opposite condition can also take place, i.e., the direct base can increase faster than indirect expenses and result in decreasing burden rates. This condition must also be considered when making the EAC. However, because of the very nature of most people, their optimistic attitudes of not wanting to believe downward business projections, and because of their reluctance to implement cuts in indirect costs (sometimes affecting discretionary but important projects), the danger of burden rates going up is far greater than that of burden rates coming down.

There are a series of issues with respect to the EAC preparation, which can be best handled through internal procedures. An example is the frequency with which EACs must be prepared from the bottom-up, comparing cost account estimates with functional estimates and WBS elements, including inputs from major subcontractors. Whether or not the latest EAC is coordinated with plantwide management to make certain that all critical resources are available when needed is also an important factor. Procedures specifying a broad management approval of an EAC is one way to require such plantwide coordination.

Lastly, a contract calling for full C/SCS implementation will usually require at least three types of reports as follows (which will be discussed in more detail in Chapter 12):

- CPR -- Cost Performance Report -- normally due monthly, reporting cost and schedule progress and reporting earned value
- CCDR -- Contractor Cost Data Reports -- due quarterly, or semiannually, or annually, for the purpose of establishing a historical cost data base
- CFSR -- Contract Funds Status Report -- normally due quarterly, specifying a forecast of funds required to complete the program, but displayed at the price level (cost + fee)

This criterion insists that the contractor's EAC be consistent with the CPR, the CCDR, and the CFSR, certainly not an unreasonable requirement. (JIG 20,46,47,63,64,65).

V -- REVISIONS AND ACCESS TO DATA

This last of the five groupings of criteria deals with revisions to the program plan that result from contractual changes either from external redirection or internally generated redirection, while attempting to satisfy the contract statement of work. No program of any significance ever runs the full course without some changes, and it is incumbent upon a contractor, in order to meet the criteria, that it accommodate such changes in an orderly and controlled manner, in accordance with its written procedures.

Lastly, the requirement is imposed on a contractor to open its books to the contracting officer or other customer representatives, as requested, in order to support C/SCS data.

> 1. Incorporate contractual changes in a timely manner, recording the effects of such changes in budgets and schedules, in the directed effort before negotiation of a change, base such revisions on the amount estimated and budgeted to the functional organizations.

Since all programs encounter changes, both external and internal, in order to maintain some relationship between the work authorized and the physical work going on, a contractor must by necessity, incorporate changes in budgets and schedules in a timely manner. Just what constitutes timely is a question of fact. In some cases timely could represent minutes or hours, as when stopping work at the direction or redirection of the customer; in other situations timely might allow for days or weeks before reprogramming. The outer limit of timely would likely be dictated by the monthly reporting cycle of the Cost Performance Report -- CPR. There must be consistency on what is being reported to the customer.

Changes to the working budgets and schedules must be accommodated in an expeditious manner and reflected in the Performance Measurement Baseline -- PMB. Work which has been authorized, but not negotiated with the customer, must be folded into the PMB, based on the estimated value of the new work, and once negotiated, adjusted to reflect the final settlement with the customer. Obviously, all changes must be tightly controlled to allow for a complete understanding of what is in and what is outside of the Performance Measurement Baseline -- PMB. (JIG 20,21,47).

---

2. Reconcile original budgets for those elements of the WBS identified as price line items in the contract, and for those elements at the lowest level of the DOD project summary WBS, with current performance measurement budgets in terms of changes to the authorized work and internal replanning in the detail needed by management for effective control.

Many government contracts contain selected articles in the statement of work which must be priced as line items, and in which the customer has a special interest in knowing what their actual costs will be. As changes occur in the total effort the contractor must provide sufficient traceability of such changes to tell if the price of these contract line items has changed.

Closely related to this requirement is the customer interest in knowing the costs of selected hardware it is buying, as reflected in the lowest WBS elements of its Project Summary Work Breakdown Structure -- PSWBS. For example, if the Air Force is buying several aircraft, it may want to know the costs of the navigation systems on each airplane, as a way of determining whether or not it is procuring these units at a fair price. To accomplish this a PSWBS is established for all aircraft, with a standardized breakout of the WBS elements isolating specific hardware, such as the navigation system. Through the Contractor Cost Data Reporting -- CCDR, it requires cost actuals in a prescribed format, to allow for the establishment of a historical cost data bank. With the data bank, costs of similar hardware may be related, system by system. This criterion requires traceability of changes, down to the lowest level PSWBS, to reflect the final costs of each PSWBS elements. (JIG 20,21,47,59,60).

---

3. Prohibit retroactive changes to records pertaining to work performed that will change previously reported amounts for direct costs, indirect costs, or budgets, except for correction of errors and routine accounting adjustments.

Perhaps the single most unique feature of C/SCS is the performance measurement aspect (Budgeted Costs for Work Performed --BCWP), i.e., what work was actually accomplished. When BCWP is compared to actual costs -- ACWP, the Cost Variance is known; when BCWP is related to work scheduled (BCWS), the Schedule Variance is shown. With the significance of earned value to the technique, it should be no wonder that the rules prohibit after-the-fact changes in the measurement by contractors. Two exceptions to this rule are allowed: correction of errors in calculation, and legitimate accounting adjustments. (JIG 21,47,48).

---

4. Prevent revisions to the contract budget base except for government directed changes to contractual effort.

With a new term, a new definition is probably in order, (from page 6 of the JIG): "Contract Budget Base. The negotiated contract cost plus the estimated cost of authorized unpriced work." The Contract Budget Base (CBB) is nothing more than the Performance Measurement Baseline (PMB), plus Management Reserve, if any. If there is no management reserve, the PMB equals the CBB. Since it is rare, and foolhardy, not to have a Management Reserve, the PMB is more significant in daily activity of C/SCS than is the CBB.

Sometimes a program will experience difficulties in staying within the total limits of its Contract Budget Base (CBB), and after careful analysis of the work remaining, it would make no sense to continue to measure progress against unrealistic and unattainable goals. When such conditions occur, this criterion permits a formal reprogramming of the work remaining, but the contractor should have procedures which prevent proceeding with the remaining effort until approval is received from the customer. Such remaining activity should have at least six months to run after the reprogramming effort, and generally it is not to occur more than once during the life of a contract, but there are exceptions. Often, the Limitation of Government Funds clause in contracts provides strong inducements to not proceed with effort beyond the CBB and without customer approval. (JIG 21,48).

---

5. Document, internally, changes to the performance measurement baseline and, on a timely basis, notify the procuring activity through prescribed procedures.

Maintenance of the Performance Measurement Baseline (PMB) is fundamental to C/SCS, and Chapter 10 will be devoted to the subject later. This criterion requires that the contractor have in place the necessary procedures to preclude unauthorized changes to the PMB, that all such changes be traceable, and that the status of the baseline be specified each month as one part of the Cost Performance Report - CPR. (JIG 21,48).

---

6. Provide the contracting officer and duly authorized representatives access to all of the foregoing information and supporting documents.

Undoubtedly, sometime in the past a contractor must have refused to provide supporting data to the customer, not a wise move. Hence, this criterion insists on such data being made available to the contracting officer and other customer representatives. Any wise contractor would normally do so, even without this criterion.

However, in the early years of C/SCS, there was some confusion as to whether or not C/SCS applied to firm fixed price contractual arrangements. It does not, and the previous ambiguity has been eliminated with specific language incorporated in the JIG (page 5): "Firm-fixed price or firm-fixed price-with-economic price-adjustment contracts or subcontracts will not be selected for application of C/SCS." Earlier C/SCS documents did not specifically exclude fixed price contracts and, thus, caused some problems. When certain contractors (the author's for example), extended their C/SCS from cost reimbursable to firm-fixed-price contracts, and then rightfully refused to either submit Cost Performance Reports or allow customer examination of C/SCS documents, there were some hurt feelings. However, the issue is now settled, and neither this last criterion, nor C/SCS applies to firm-fixed-price efforts, under which the contractor assumes all financial risks of the program. (JIG 29,48).

There could be exceptions, however, and all parties should be aware of them. If a particular system being bought was of a critical nature to the military operations, or if the size of the buy was large compared to the contractor performing it (where a failure to perform could bankrupt the company), the buying command might be justified in requiring a Cost Performance Report -- even on a firm-fixed-price contract.

***

The 35 C/SCS Criteria have been scrutinized, and although it has been a long and tedious exercise, it was absolutely necessary. The criteria form the foundation for a C/SCS management control system, and it would not be possible to fully understand the concept without having first visited these criteria.

Other aspects of C/SCS will now be covered, building upon the understanding of these criteria.

ENDNOTE

1. Air Force Institute of Technology -- AFIT white paper dated June 23, 1981.

9

THE SACRED RITUAL
OF VALIDATION

There is an expression in legal parlance which seems to fit nicely with the next subject. The expression is "condition precedent." In very simple terms, a condition precedent is something that must happen before a second something can take place. Up to this point the discussion has focused on a C/SCS management control system. However, before the C/SCS can be fully operational, there is something which must happen beforehand. That something is validation. The management control system must be validated by the customer before earned value measurement and Cost Performance Reporting can have any meaning. Hence, the process of validation should be viewed as a condition precedent to having an operational C/SCS management control system.

The process of validating C/SCSC compliance goes by two frequently used terms. The initial validation activity is called a Demonstration Review (Demonstration), which is an examination by the customer of a contractor's management control system to verify that it meets the 35 criteria previously discussed. The second term that is used is called a SAR, or Subsequent Application Review.* In a SAR, the reviewing team understands that the contractor has a validated C/SCS management control system, but it wants verification that the system which was previously approved is in fact being used, either on a newly awarded contract or on the same contract after a lapse of time. A different application, (such as production after development) would require another full Demonstration Review.

When a contractor forms a new organizational unit -- new division or subsidiary -- or moves to a new location in which new personnel or

---

* Do not confuse the C/SCS SAR above with the DOD's Selected Acquisition Report, also SAR, which is a separate unrelated task, but unfortunately is imposed in a closely numbered document DODI 7000.3.

new procedures are put in place, the customer will usually insist on at least a SAR, and sometimes a full Demonstration depending upon the circumstances. The concern is that the changed environment will have an adverse effect on the previously approved control techniques and procedures.

If a contractor expects to both develop and produce a given new product, it is wise to request a simultaneous review of its systems and procedures as they apply to both developmental and to production activities. To do otherwise, the contractor must later pass a second demonstration review for the recurring or production effort. However, the production activity must exist in the plant in order to be examined, i.e., it cannot simply be a plan. When a contractor has or anticipates multi-service contracts (Army, Navy, Air Force), it should also request a multi-service review team so it will have what is called tri-service validation. In the validation and revalidation process "the burden of proof necessarily rests with the contractor."[1] It is up to the contractor to demonstrate that its management control system, the supporting procedures, and its staff have implemented their system in full compliance with the criteria.

The principal difference between the full demonstration review and the SAR is one of degree. In simple pragmatic terms, the team arriving at a contractor's facility to conduct a demonstration review is likely to be made up of anywhere from 15 to 30 people, and they are likely to stay two to four weeks reviewing every policy and procedure, and interviewing most cost account managers. The Joint Implementation Guide describes the process well:

> The C/SCSC review team will examine the contractor's working papers and documents to ascertain compliance and document their findings. For this purpose, the contractor will be required to make available to the team the documents used in the contractor's management control systems; for example, budgeting, work authorization, accounting, and other functional documents which apply to the specific contracts being reviewed. The documentation must be current and accurate.... Detailed operating procedures should delineate the following:
>
> a) Responsibilities of operating personnel.
> b) Limitations on action.
> c) Internal authorization required.[2]

The goal of the demonstration review is to prove that the contractor's management control system meets the criteria and is being used.

In the case of the SAR (Subsequent Application Review), the goal is simply to show that the previously validated system is still being used. Back to pragmatic terms, the reviewing team is usually much smaller, 5 to 15 people, and their stay is normally shorter, running 3 to 10 work days. The SAR is less formal, and the team merely makes spot checks on the system. They are not trying to prove that a system exists, for that is a basic assumption, rather they are verifying that the approved system is still in use:

> The objective of a subsequent application review is to insure that, on a new contract, the contractor is properly and effectively using the accepted system, revised in accordance with approved changes. It is not the purpose of the review to reassess the contractor's previously accepted system.[3]

The "approved changes" referred to above are those evolutionary modifications which take place from time to time in any management system. The author's company received a tri-service validation for both development and production contracts in 1971. Over the years there have been numerous minor changes made to the original system. In every case, the proposed C/SCS modification resulted in a documented procedural change which was coordinated with and approved by the local government representative (called the AFPRO-Air Force Plant Representative Office*) prior to implementation. In this case, the AFPRO was delegated authority to monitor and approve on-site changes to the C/SCS management control system.

In the above descriptions, the demonstration review has been referred to as a larger task than that of the SAR. This is the norm, but there are exceptions. One example is the contractor which failed to pass its SAR after two attempts, going for some 18 months without receiving approval of its management control system. The team which arrived for the third SAR attempt, interviewed all cost account managers, and traced through their entire management system in a totally comprehensive way. In this case there was no fundamental difference between the typical demonstration and their third attempted SAR. The customer was justifiably concerned that the system under review had experienced fundamental changes in its operation. Instead of simply working off the discrepancy list from the previously failed SAR, the customer's team performed a comprehensive review of their total C/SCS compliance, much in the spirit of a full demonstration review.

PREPARATION FOR THE DEMONSTRATION REVIEW OR SAR

According to the standard clause inserted in the language of a contract, one must be prepared to demonstrate one's C/SCS compliance within 90 days after award, or as otherwise agreed to by the parties.[4] The 90-day period has only happened a very few times, and the norm for both the demonstration and the SAR is more like 9 to 11 months after contract award. Sometimes SARs for follow-on options to the same contract will happen in the 90-day period. The customer

---

*   Sometimes called the Contract Administration Office -- CAO, NAVPRO, DCASO, ETC.

also has a vested interest in passing the first review and will not be unreasonable in reaching an agreement as to the exact timing of their arrival. Before they arrive to examine the system, certain activities must have been accomplished. The best tangible proof of one's preparation, and a general rule of thumb, is the Cost Performance Report -- CPR. After a firm has submitted two successive CPRs that measure earned value, and they look acceptable, and all procedures, bulletins, manuals, etc., have been issued defining the system, a firm is normally considered ready for the team to arrive to trace through the C/SCS management control system.

Prior to the demonstration or SAR, two events will generally take place preparatory to the actual review. The first is the implementation visit by the customer team that will monitor C/SCS compliance and performance. In this initial visit, the customer will impress on the contractor the importance of C/SCS reporting, if this is an unsettled issue. Usually the contractor will provide a presentation of its C/SCS management control system, if it is being used on other contracts. The specific C/SCS reports which are due, their frequency, and variance thresholds are normally discussed. Typically, prior to leaving, the customer will provide a list of documents it will want to review on their next visit, illustrated by the following:

1. Organization charts
2. Listing of burden pools, and their content
3. List of major vendors, and their dollar value
4. Work Breakdown Structure/Index/Dictionary
5. Work authorization methods, for each functional area, i.e., engineering, manufacturing, etc., including the review of actual documents and their flow
6. Budget methods, as per 5
7. Cost accumulation methods, as per 5
8. Variance analysis procedures
9. Baseline Management; change control; undistributed budget procedures; and associated logs
10. Cost Account Matrix, listing the WBS across the top, the organization along the side, and reflecting which intersect with which, and the dollar values of each
11. Master Schedule
12. Intermediate Schedules associated with the work authorization, as per 5
13. Detailed Schedules associated with work authorization, as per 5
14. Most recent Cost Performance Report -- CPR
15. Specific examples of engineering and manufacturing cost accounts reflecting discretely measured effort, apportioned effort, and Level of Effort-LOE
16. Management Reserve Log
17. List of cost account managers, by function
18. Statistical summaries of measured cost account/work package time-spans[5]

The next visit by the customer C/SCS team will usually take place about four weeks prior to the actual demonstration or SAR date; the visit is called a readiness review or assessment. Such visits usually take three to five days, and the purpose is to decide whether or not the contractor will be in a position to have a demonstration or SAR. This is a serious effort, and the documents listed above will be examined in considerable detail. Selected interviews will also be conducted with a few cost account managers to determine the preparedness of the contractor, and to give it a flavor of what to expect in the forthcoming review. Prior to leaving, the customer team will debrief the contractor on its findings and will list all obvious deficiencies. If the contractor is significantly unprepared for the readiness review, or the list of deficiencies is extensive, by mutual agreement the demonstration or SAR date is usually delayed, and another readiness review is normally scheduled in its place. This is not a good omen for a contractor.

In preparation for the actual demonstration or SAR, two essential ingredients are needed; there should be a broad company team formed to support the activity; and there must be genuine support from all levels of management, especially top management. The review cannot be done by a handful of people, working outside of the mainstream of program activity. If the program manager and other functional management do not view the validation effort in a serious way and are not fully committed to giving C/SCS their complete support, then the best advice for anyone is to seek another assignment -- early. Failure to pass the review has an adverse effect on a program, as will be discussed later. If the management is only partially committed to C/SCS and intends to give only lip-service to the system and to the review, a graceful exit for participants is suggested. If one's contract calls for full C/SCS in accordance with DODI 7000.2, management has no alternative but to fully support the effort. Unfortunately, such realization is sometimes delayed until the first or second demonstration or SAR failure has had its impact on a firm's management.

The demonstration review and/or SAR is a major exercise, not too dissimilar from a major proposal. An initial step is, therefore, the preparation of an outline and plan of action. The Joint Implementation Guide -- JIG (Appendix E) is an excellent starting point, and it contains much information on the review process. Of particular significance is the fact that the reviewing team will use the JIG as their outline for the review. Four of the appendices in the JIG pertain directly to the review process. (Note, these four appendices are a part of the JIG, which is copied in Appendix E to this book.)

- Appendix C -- C/SCSC review report format provides a suggested format for the report to be submitted by the team conducting the review. The outline provides a glimpse of what the team must cover.
- Appendix E -- Evaluation/Demonstration Review Checklist for C/SCSC is the listing of the 35 criteria and supporting questions. This checklist provides blank spaces to the right

of each question, which should be used to make reference to one's specific procedures, schedules, budgets, documents, etc., which will be cited as being in compliance with the requirement of the criteria. Prior to the team arrival this checklist is frequently displayed across a blank wall, with referenced documents, and is discussed by the internal team which will ask the question: Does this satisfy the requirement of the criterion? Much discussion will be focused on Appendix E.

- Appendix F -- C/SCSC review worksheets and exhibits contains 14 separate formats for reviewing the C/SCS in very specific detail. Example: Format 3 aids the team with the reconciliation of the total budget, to allow traceability up the WBS. Considerable time should be spent with Appendix F prior to the arrival of the reviewing team.

- Appendix G -- C/SCSC Subsequent Application Reviews Policy and Guidance contains the ground rules for the SAR, which the reviewing team will follow. For example, Appendix G states that the checklist in Appendix E above is not appropriate for the SAR, except on an abbreviated and exception basis. If a firm is preparing for its first SAR, it will want to read Appendix G closely, for these are the guidelines that the review team will be following. The last page of G contains an outline for the SAR report, similar to what Appendix C does for the demonstration review.

Just as with a major proposal, the team preparing for the demonstration or SAR will find a large conference room dedicated to its exclusive use to be most helpful. On the blank walls can be displayed the appendices discussed above. In addition, one wall should display a flow diagram of all company documents which form an integral part of the C/SCS compliance, including delegations of authority, procedures, organization charts, and other related documents. Such displays are useful both to the team preparing for the review, as well as a quick overview for the customer team itself, which hopefully will understand C/SCS, but likely not be familiar with a given firm's systems or particular approach. Space permitting, the WBS, organization charts, and a Cost Account Matrix of WBS elements versus the organization should be displayed.

Training is an essential part of the C/SCS validation process. One's organization, particularly the cost account managers and management at all levels, must be familiar with the system being demonstrated. In addition to knowing how to use the system, as a practical matter, all personnel must be able to recite C/SCS buzzwords and must know how to respond to questions they will be asked from the reviewing team. Many firms find it useful to prepare a list of most likely questions their managers are probably going to be asked during the process. Many a SAR deficiency has been listed because someone failed to use the proper term to describe the workings of C/SCS, and conversely, many a snow job has been performed by those who don't actually know or use the system, but do know the critical C/SCS jargon. Whether one intends to genuinely implement C/SCS in the firm, and hopefully that is the case, or merely put on a show for the reviewing team, a listing of most likely questions will be beneficial. The following are some 20 questions found to be frequently used by reviewing teams when interviewing members of the contractor's organization. Obviously, no single list will be absolutely complete or foolproof.

Most Likely Review Questions

1. What is your job and where do you fit in the organization?
2. Do you use C/SCS in your job?
3. What is your role?
4. Do you understand the need for C/SCS?
5. Are you a cost account manager, and if so, how many cost accounts do you manage?
6. From whom do you receive your budget, and in what form?
7. Do you presently have a copy of your budget?
8. How do you plan your work?
9. How is work performance measured (earned value), and who does it?
10. How is your plan revised?
11. What schedules do you use in your job, and where do they come from?
12. What is a work package, and do you use them?
13. Do you provide inputs to the CPR, and do you ever see a full CPR document?
14. How is your performance to your BCWS?
15. Do you have variance thresholds; what are they?
16. What happens when you exceed a variance threshold, describe the process?
17. Do you prepare PARs, who must see them, what happens to them?
18. Do you do an ETC and EAC, or is it done for you? By Whom? How often?
19. What procedures do you use, do you have a copy?
20. Do you like C/SCS?

It is always important to know the make-up of the team about to descend on a firm and to prepare to answer likely questions from them, based on their backgrounds. While no two teams are exactly alike, there is a pattern which is generally followed:

● Team Director from headquarters command of AFSC, DARCOM, NAVMAT, is the expert on C/SCS. This person may head up more than one team at the same time and will provide policy guidelines and the interpretation of criteria to members of the team.

- **Team Chief** may come from the lead command headquarters or a subordinate command. This person is responsible for the organization of the team, for the conduct of the review, for preparing the written report, and for reporting the findings to the team director, who may or may not take an active part in the review itself. Most team chiefs have been through several reviews prior to being designated chief.

- **Team Members** generally represent a balanced mix of backgrounds including engineering, testing, manufacturing, accounting (DCAA), program control, cost/price analysis, contract administration, and customer plant representatives (AFPRO).

Once assembled, the reviewing teams generally take one of two approaches in the conduct of the review, and sometimes a third composite approach. Depending upon the backgrounds of the team members, they normally structure the review process either along the lines of the criteria or on the functions to be reviewed. Probably the most effective approach is the criteria, but the approach requires highly experienced C/SCS team members who are not always available. This approach simply focuses on the five criteria groupings covered in Chapter 8 -- organization, planning and budgeting, accounting, analysis, and revisions. These teams are usually smaller in size, and their findings are well integrated.

When experienced team members are not available, the approach is usually along functional lines, out of necessity. The team has to be larger than the criteria approach, simply because each person brought in covers a particular specialty only. Integration of their findings is more difficult because of the size of the team. The third approach, the mix, is a composite of the two, depending upon the availability of experienced C/SCS members. Most C/SCS review teams use the mix approach.

Prior to the arrival of the reviewing team, certain homework will have to be done. One will want to analyze the initial budget baseline, examining in detail the distribution of all cost accounts issued. All should want to have some just-in-case statistics, or one may want to actually put such data in presentation form. Of particular interest will be:

- the number of cost accounts used;
- the average length, maximum and minimum lengths;
- the average dollar size, maximum and minimum size;
- the percentage of discrete/work package, apportioned, and Level of Effort - LOE cost accounts.

In figure 9.1, A Summary of Cost Accounts, is shown a typical display of these types of data.

93

Figure 9.1   A Summary of Cost Accounts (594 total)

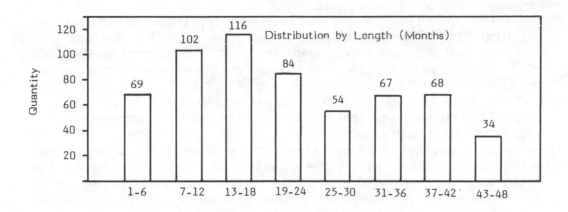

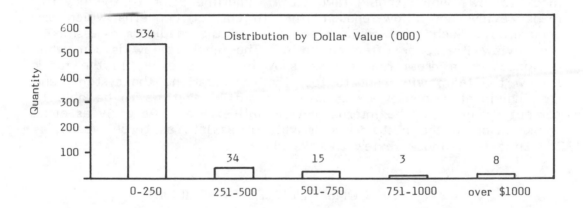

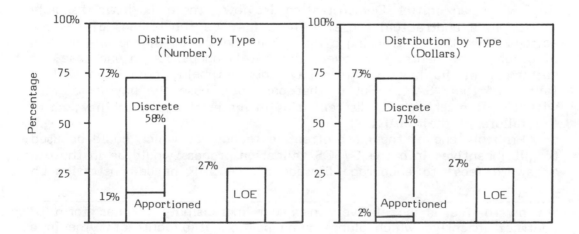

94

A decade or so ago when most defense contractors were preparing for their initial C/SCS reviews, there was little outside help available. Today, all is different, and there is considerable advisory talent available. In most larger firms, sister divisions frequently have experienced personnel who have worked with C/SCS and have been through the validation process. Unfortunately, these experts in any given firm also have their own jobs and responsibilities and are thus not always available when one needs them, or for as long as they are needed. While as a general rule the author has never been an advocate of outside consultants, there are exceptions. One of these exceptions is in the use of outside consultants to come in and critique a C/SCS management control system and to assist in preparations for the demonstration process. Not only is one able to get them when they are needed, but they can stay for the duration of one's needs. The outside consultant can be the expert on the validation process and is often used to convince the internal management to act or not act in a certain way. They can also be used to structure a training course unique to a company's particular needs.

Perhaps the most critical use of the outside consultant is in the mock review, which should take place sometime prior to the government review and allow enough time to correct concerns which are uncovered. Such mock reviews are done on the readiness assessment, the review itself, or often on both. The mock review is somewhat analogous to a dress rehearsal in show-biz. However, in the mock review the team will want to test the organization, the system, and the individual responses to questions in sufficient time to be able to correct deficiencies the internal review will expose. As early as eight weeks prior to the customer's arrival, or as late as three weeks, is the time for a mock review to take place.

THE CONSEQUENCES OF FAILURE

When a contractor fails to pass either a Subsequent Application Review or an initial Demonstration Review, there is little tangible impact in a contractual sense. There may be suggestions of adverse actions from the contracting officer, say the threat of the withholding of progress payments. However, that rarely happens. In one case, an eastern firm did have progress payments withheld, coinciding with a failure of their SAR. But in that particular case the payments were withheld as much due to discrepancies in material accountability, as to the failure of their SAR.

Probably one of the most effective techniques which could be used to put incentives into the C/SCS validation process would be in the use of award fees* to encourage passage of the SAR or demonstration on

*An award fee is a relatively new but increasingly popular form of contract incentive which places some portion of a contract's fee in a pool, and makes the earning of these fees dependent on the occurrence of certain program events, as determined solely by the customer.

the first try. Perhaps the future will see more of this concept used to put muscle into the C/SCS enforcement.

Repeated failures of a SAR, suggesting fundamental adverse changes in a contractor's management control system, could result in a total rescission of a previous C/SCS validation, and thus put the contractor back to square one. But so what? Without a contract clause stipulating a penalty for failure, why should a contractor even be concerned?

Well, the first thing that happens after a SAR failure is the immediate drain on the effective use of all personnel, i.e., engineering, manufacturing, and other human resources needed to perform the contract's statement of work. Suddenly, everyone is working on that "damned C/SCS ----," and how to work off the discrepancy list left by the customer's reviewing team. Management at all levels suddenly becomes interested in the subject. And additionally, the customer comes around more often.

But the most profound and devastating effect of a failed SAR or demonstration is in the political realm. Government programs must be approved by, and funded by, the United States Congress, and the Congress is a political body. No program can ever expect to have total Congressional support if for no other reason than the fact that firms are located in specific states and particularly in specific Congressional districts. It would not be possible to precisely quantify the political impact that resulted when the builder of a new aircraft system failed to pass a C/SCS demonstration review for its newly formed division. However, it may safely be assumed that the failed C/SCS review did give opponents of the new aircraft the means to impugn the overall program, and thereby contributed in some way to its cancellation in the late 1970s. No company or management needs a reputation of failure with respect to its internal management systems.

The reasons for failure are numerous. Quite often failure occurs because management simply does not believe in the C/SCS concept or feels they can have both their preferred approach and C/SCS. In these cases all the planning, work measurement, estimates to complete, etc., are done, not by the cost account managers as it should be, but rather by personnel brought in to perform these tasks, with instructions: "Do not bother my engineers." The customer reviewing teams are not stupid, and they quickly see through such a facade when interviewing cost account managers and other company personnel. In such cases, failure of the demonstration or SAR is preordained.

THE FRUITS OF PASSAGE

Passage of a Demonstration Review or Subsequent Applications Review creates an immediate organizational high, probably not too dissimilar from the feeling one gets from walking out of a dentist's office after a series of "close encounters." The most tangible result of passage will be the signing of a Memorandum of Understanding (MOU) by the contractor and the government. The Joint Implementation Guide (page 28) defines the MOU as:

> The memorandum of understanding is not a contract clause, but it may be incorporated in any contract by appropriate reference when the contract includes a requirement for compliance with the criteria. This document serves to clarify intent of the contractor and DOD components relative to implementation of the criteria. It contains reference to a description of accepted systems and subsystems and provides for Government access to pertinent contractor records and data for surveillance purposes. Provision is also made to permit accepted changes to accepted systems.

A sample MOU is contained in Appendix D to the JIG (the JIG may be found in Appendix E of this text).

Also resulting from the successful passage of the validation process will be the approval of the contractor's C/SCS System Description, mentioned in the above quote. The system description provides a defined baseline against which all future C/SCS compliance may be measured, and it gives the customer a reference point for continued contract surveillance. As of this writing the author's company is still using the same C/SCSC Systems Description originally approved on May 10, 1971.

ENDNOTES

1. Joint Implementation Guide, JIG, page 27.
2. Ibid, page 27.
3. Ibid, page 66.
4. Ibid, DAR 7-104.87, page 32.
5. List provided by Don Schild (modified) of USAF WPAFB.

10

BASELINE MANAGEMENT

Now that the validation process has been covered, the criteria have been reviewed in detail, and all parties understand the importance of the Work Breakdown Structure, it is time to take the next logical step of discussing the subject of Baseline Management. In a C/SCS management control system, the baseline has particular importance because of what the technique attempts to do. C/SCS is nothing more than conventional budgeting and cost/schedule reporting, but with one important addition: earned value measurement. Thus, if one is attempting to measure work progress, on a monthly basis, one must know in precise terms what one is attempting to measure. Almost as important as knowing what one is measuring, is to know what one is not measuring, i.e., what is outside of the baseline. Hence, in C/SCS, it is of paramount importance to know how to establish a baseline, how to maintain the baseline, and how to monitor departures from it, which in C/SCS is referred to as the Performance Measurement Baseline (PMB).

This chapter will cover three large but related subjects:

- The Baseline -- what it is, how it is established, why it is needed, and how it is maintained
- Variances from the Baseline -- when they occur, how to recognize, how to analyze, what corrective actions are required
- Estimate at Completion -- the C/SCS bottom line, i.e., what the project is likely to cost when it's over

THE BASELINE

The next few sections will cover material in very specific detail, using terms which have definite meanings in C/SCSC. Thus, there is

97

no choice but to present six definitions, certain of which may be new to the reader, and some that have been discussed earlier.

1. PMB -- Performance Measurement Baseline is the time-phased budget plan against which work performance (earned value) is measured and is formed by the assignment of detailed budgets to scheduled tasks, with the addition of appropriate indirect costs. On future effort which is not planned down to the cost account level, the PMB includes budgets assigned to higher CWBS elements and the undistributed budget. Management Reserve is outside of the PMB.

2. CBB -- Contract Budget Base is the value of all negotiated contract costs, plus the estimated cost of authorized unpriced work.

3. Authorized Unpriced Work refers to those additions or deletions to the contract statement of work, which have been authorized by the customer, and which are being worked on by an organization prior to their being negotiated. These are costs over the negotiated contract cost value (which are referred to as Contract Target Costs -- CTC).

4. CTC -- Contract Target Costs represent the total value of all the negotiated costs in a contract, excluding fee and excluding authorized unpriced work (CTC + Fee = Contract Price).

5. Management Reserve sometimes called management reserve budget, contingency reserve, etc., is that portion of the CBB which management sets aside outside of the PMB to be used to cover unplanned contract activity as determined by management, such as test failures, redesign, etc. During the life of a contract, it is expected that the management reserve will be totally consumed.

6. Undistributed Budget refers to those budgets that are a part of the PMB, but have not yet been defined down to the cost account level. They are budgets which are to the right of the near-term cost account budgets of the rolling-wave concept, and are in the "to be defined" category.

These six definitions are shown graphically in figure 10.1, the Performance Measurement Baseline (PMB), with each of the definitions listed above referenced by number.

Back when the criteria were discussed, the second of the five criteria groupings was entitled Planning and Budgeting. This is simply another way of describing the process of establishing a Performance Measurement Baseline -- PMB against which all actual work accomplishment will be measured. The process can be thought of as a three step, iterative one as shown in figure 10.2.

Step 1 reflects the definition of the contract work, with use of the Work Breakdown Structure. Step 2 takes the lowest level CWBS elements and schedules them down to cost accounts, within the framework of the overall master program schedules and intermediate schedules. Step 3 is the allocation of budget to the cost account and work package levels, as specified in the cost account tasks. Once completed, the time-phased PMB is created, as reflected in figure 10.2.

The process looks simple enough and in theory it is. However, just as the validation of a C/SCS management control system rarely

Figure 10.1 The Performance Measurement Baseline -- PMB

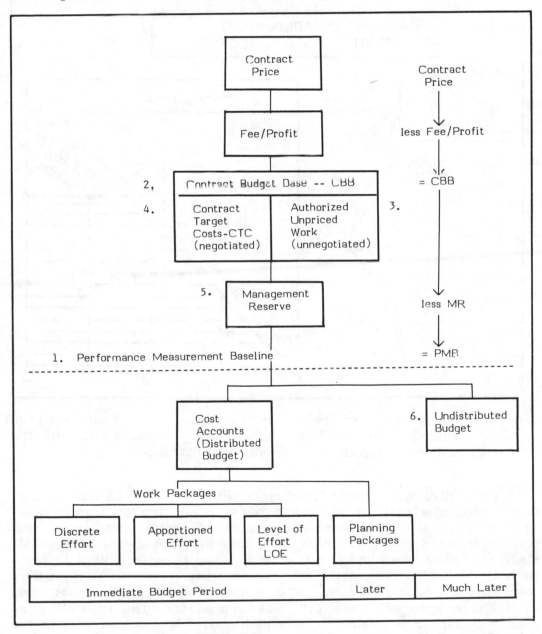

Source: Chart courtesy of Humphreys & Associates, Newport Beach, California, modified slightly.

takes place within "90 days after contract award," also the establishment of the performance baseline takes time.   As one who was on the customer side of the house for many years described it: "It normally takes anywhere between 9 to 12 months after a contract go-ahead to get a good budget baseline established on a major effort."[1]

Figure 10.2 Establishing the PMB

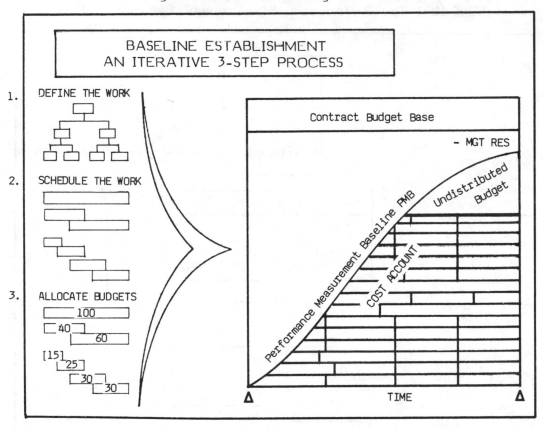

Source: Charts courtesy Humphreys & Associates, from material originally presented by Robert R. Kemps, Office of the Assistant Secretary of Defense (Comptroller).

Certainly, some might take issue with the 9 to 12 month forecast, particularly those who have never been through the process. That does seem like an excessive amount of time.   But anyone who has experienced the excitement of a new program award, and particularly a major one, knows well that it takes time for things to come to order.   Engineers want to start engineering -- immediately; buyers want to start buying -- now.   What a good program manager has to do in this case is to say "hold it," and keep all activities to a minimum until a definitive program plan is established.   An essential part of the program plan is the PMB, which defines down to the very lowest levels the tasks, schedules, and budgets to be performed.

However, no matter how adamant the program manager may be about slowing down the initial activity until a plan is established, certain activities will start. Therefore, an initial budget is normally issued to authorize work which will start anyway. The initial budget is usually for three to six months. Shown in figure 10.3 are six steps which typically take place in some form on most programs after award. Program planning becomes progressively more specific until all areas understand what they are to do and are all marching in step with the program plan (and PMB).

Figure 10.3 Steps from Program Award to PMB

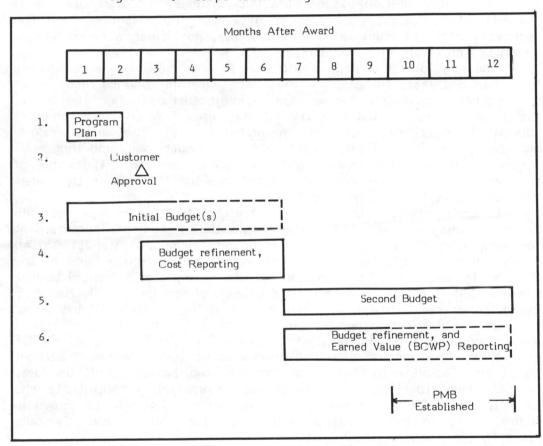

Thus, it takes until step 6 (figure 10.3) to produce a "good" PMB on major programs. No matter how detailed the original proposal may have seemed, no matter how long one's firm may have had a cadre of people working on pre-contract activity, "day one" happens when the contract is awarded, not before. And after award (day one), there is a definite sequence of activities and events which must happen before the program is fully underway. Therefore, the above expert's statement of taking 9 to 12 months to reach a good PMB is quite accurate, and representative, even though the length of time suggested might seem on the surface to be unduly long.

Once the budget and schedule baseline (PMB or BCWS) is established, to a degree which allows for earned value measurement and customer reporting to take place, an equally difficult task, and one which will last for the duration of a program, will be that of maintaining the baseline. Programs in their developmental or nonrecurring phase are dynamic in nature. Changes are the rule, not the exception. That is precisely what makes the establishment of the PMB so very difficult and yet so very essential: to define a budget baseline for the original work, before the changes hit. There have been cases where contracts were awarded on day one and contract change notices received the very next day. There have been construction contracts which have had well in excess of 1,000 changes over the duration of the effort! Without the creation of an original baseline, and the positive control of changes to that baseline, performance measurement becomes impossible and meaningless.

Changes to the contract, and thus to the PMB, come essentially from two sources: internal and external. Internal changes result from the engineers finding a better way, manufacturing finding the initial design impossible to build, test failures, etc. When these changes happen, it is critical that they be managed, i.e., that such work is not started until specifically authorized by the customer, and then subsequently authorized internally by the program manager. The value of such work must be estimated and folded into the PMB under the category of "authorized unpriced work."

External changes are normally straightforward, from a program control standpoint, and they result from the customer's requirement for something different from what is presently under contract. In all cases, however, it is mandatory that work coming from outside of the PMB be logged and tightly monitored. An example of a typical budget baseline log is shown in figure 10.4 below. Each individual change is listed and tracked until it becomes a part of the approved PMB.

During the life of a program, changes to the baseline (PMB) will take place almost continually, and it is vital to the integrity of C/SCS monitoring that such changes be traceable to their source. Without the tight discipline of managing changes, the baseline will be lost. Special thanks to Humphreys & Associates, management consultants who specialize in C/SCS, for allowing the use of the four charts shown in figure 10.5, to illustrate the various changes which commonly take place to the PMB.

Often, an initial program plan will call for certain tasks to be worked according to a given schedule, and a baseline is thus established. Later, as the program progresses, it may be found necessary or desirable to replan certain of the tasks into a later time frame. A contractor may on its own, replan the program, as long as it stays within the total Contract Target Costs and completes the activity within the contract schedule. No retroactive changes for completed work may be made, however. This situation is shown in figure 10.5A. All that is required of the contractor is to have a traceable record of the reprogrammed effort, and to report same in the monthly reports to the customer, called a CPR (Cost Performance

Figure 10.4   Typical Budget Baseline Log

BUDGET BASELINE LOG

DATE	CHANGE TITLE	TARGET COST	AUTH UN-PRICED	CBB	MGMT RE-SERVE	PMB	UNDIST BUDGET	DIRECT BUDGET	O/H BUDGET	G&A BUDGET
1/14	ABC CONTRACT	120	—	120	10	110	10	40	40	20
1/31	JANUARY 79 SUMMARY	120	—	120	10	110	10	40	40	20
2/5	CONTRACT CHANGE NO. 001	—	45	45	5	40	—	16	16	8
2/15	P.O. LTR—ADDITIONAL MGMT RPTS	—	30	30	—	30	—	12	12	6
2/23	P.O. LTR—MOTOR REDESIGN	—	30	30	—	30	—	12	12	6
2/28	FEBRUARY 79 SUMMARY	120	105	225	15	210	10	80	80	40
3/11	P.O. LTR—6 MO. SCHEDULE EXTEN	—	40	40	10	30	—	12	12	6
3/20	ECP 10-3 ENGR STUDIES	—	10	10	—	10	—	4	4	2
3/26	CONTRACT CHANGE NO. 001	42	(45)	(3)	(3)	—	—	—	—	—
3/31	MARCH 79 SUMMARY	162	110	272	22	250	10	96	96	48
4/3	P.O. LTR—DELETION GFP	—	20	20	2	18	—	12	—	6
4/10	CONTRACT CHANGE NO. 002	—	90	90	10	80	—	32	32	16
4/19	SUBCONTRACT ENVIRONMENTAL TESTING	—	—	—	—	—	(10)	7	—	3
4/30	APRIL 79 SUMMARY	162	220	382	34	348	—	147	128	73
5/7	CCN NO. 3 — REDUCED SUPPORT	—	(50)	(50)	(4)	(46)	—	(19)	(19)	(8)
5/31	MAY 79 SUMMARY	162	170	332	30	302	—	128	109	65
6/4	ECP 14 — ALTERNATE MATERIAL	—	10	10	—	10	—	7	—	3

Source: Chart courtesy Humphreys & Associates, Newport Beach, California.

Report).   Here, it is assumed that the replan is the result of prudent management choice and does not reflect fundamental problems, such as cost overruns or possible delays in schedule.

All programs are planned with success in mind, and that is quite reasonable.   However, it is always prudent to set aside some "just in case" budget in the form of a Management Reserve, in the (likely) event that everything doesn't go exactly as planned.   Thus, if a program is planned with the assumption that all testing will be a success, and test failures occur, there obviously will be some additional budget required.   These values come from the shifting of Management Reserve, which by definition is outside of the PMB, into the baseline. Customer approval is not required in these cases, but traceability and reporting of the changes to the Management Reserve is and must be described in the monthly CPR.   This condition is illustrated in figure 10.5B.   Note once again, that no changes are made to either the Contract Target Costs or program duration.   Only Management Reserve is shifted, and is to be used for statement of work changes, not to hide bad performance.

In figure 10.5C is shown the effects of official contract changes to a baseline.   In effect, each contract change, adding or removing work, calls for a revised PMB, or budget baseline.   Frequently, the addition of contract changes also moves the program completion date to the right.

Finally, it is necessary to face that abhorrent word which management and contracting officers only speak of in whispers --"overrun." Realistically, overruns do happen, even in the best of families. But it is a difficult subject to rationally discuss, because an overrun connotes a previous flaw in the plan, or the approach taken, or in a management judgment. Even the Joint Implementation Guide (page 16), which has been quoted so often in this work, seems to avoid the direct use of the word overrun:

> Any increase which results in a total allocated budget in excess of the contract budget base constitutes formal reprogramming and must be formally submitted by the contractor and formally recognized by the procuring activity.

In this case, and in the chart shown in figure 10.5D, the term "formal reprogramming" is just another way of describing the condition of overrun. In such cases, specific customer approval is required for a number of reasons, particularly since some additional contract funding may be needed. Note: this discussion only applies to cost reimbursable contracts, any cost growth under firm-fixed priced arrangements is on the contractor anyway. Also formal reprogramming does not always imply an overrun -- just most of the time.

If there was any doubt that the term formal reprogramming in the previous quote was referring to an overrun condition, the next page of the JIG quickly clarifies the issue:

> When a contractor formally notifies the procuring agency of a total allocated budget in excess of the contract budget base and the revised plan is accepted for reporting performance to the Government, then it should also be recognized that this condition may be an indicator to the Administrative Contracting Officer (ACO) that progress payments, liquidation rates, or cost reimbursement fee vouchers may require review for appropriate adjustment.

In very dignified terms, the JIG has alluded to a contractor overrun, which means that the approved PMB will be exceeded. Additional funds may be required in order to complete the job, and the "appropriate adjustment" referred to in the above quote could affect the contractor's fee on a cost share incentive contract to pay for a portion of the overrun, i.e., formal reprogramming.

Lastly, there are some replanning rules which must be followed and these were discussed in Chapter 8 on the criteria, under Revisions. A contractor may on its own, use management reserve to change cost account budgets and may reprogram unopened cost accounts. Transfers of effort may take place between cost accounts, as long as budget is transferred along with the work. Transfers of work alone, or budgets alone, between cost accounts is prohibited. Retroactive changes to completed cost accounts is also not allowed, except to correct errors and routine accounting adjustments. Closed cost accounts may not be reopened.

If this last set of rules seems unduly confining, it must be remembered that C/SCS allows for almost any type of reprogramming to take place, as long as it is done in concert with, and with the approval of, the customer.

Figure 10.5 Changes to the PMB Baseline

EFFECTS OF INTERNAL REPLANNING

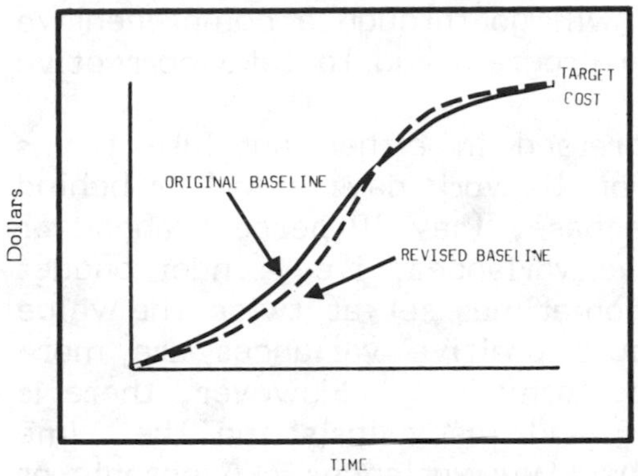

Figure 10.5A   Replanning

USE OF MANAGEMENT RESERVE

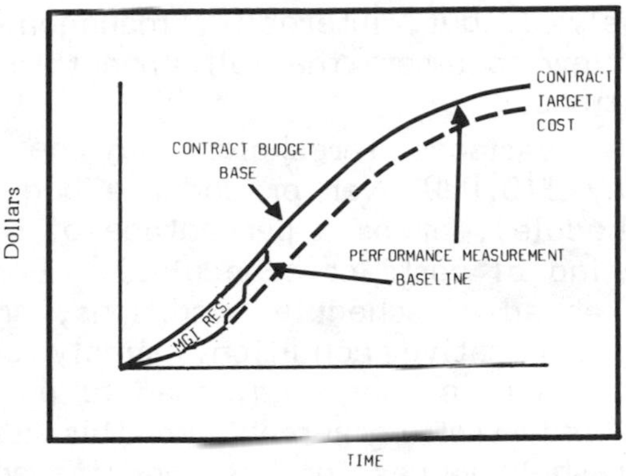

Figure 10.5B   Use of Management Reserve

EFFECTS OF CONTRACT CHANGES

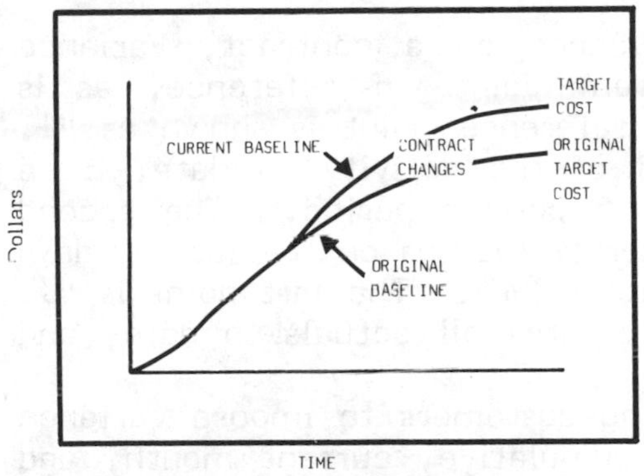

Figure 10.5C   Contract Changes

REVISIONS
FORMAL REPROGRAMMING

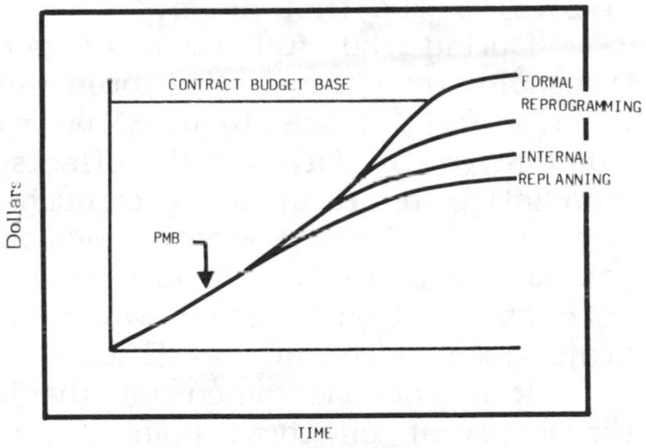

Figure 10.5D   Formal Reprogramming

Source: Chart supplied by Humphreys & Associates, from material originally presented by Robert R. Kemps, Office of the Assistant Secretary of Defense (Comptroller).

VARIANCES FROM THE BASELINE

Once the budget baseline (PMB or BCWS) is established, the next required step is to monitor and report progress against the plan. While it may seem appropriate to do a comprehensive review of all approved budgets and schedules each month, a more efficient way to monitor performance is on an exception basis. Particular attention should be focused on those areas that have exceeded reasonable, and previously set limits. These reasonable limits are called Variance Thresholds and are nothing more than outside cost/schedule parameters. Once such parameters or thresholds are exceeded, C/SCS procedures call for a special type of analysis to take place and for the formal reporting of the results. These special studies are typically called variance analysis reports, or sometimes problem analysis reports. Thus in a C/SCS management control system, when a performance threshold has been exceeded by a previously agreed to value, a sort of "buzzer" goes off, and certain actions must take place in order to comply with the rules of C/SCS. The customer normally sees only a portion of such variance analysis, but, internally, management will go through a comprehensive review to assess the full impact to the program and to take corrective actions.

Variance thresholds may be expressed in either absolute terms (say $10,000 over or under a budget or 10 work days ahead or behind schedule), or as a percentage of some base, (say 10 percent ahead or behind of costs or schedules). Positive variances, i.e., under budget or ahead of schedule conditions, are sometimes set at twice the value of a negative condition, simply because positive variances are more related to a poor plan, than to poor performance. However, there is no universal agreement on this issue, and many insist on the same threshold values for both positive and negative variances. A chronic or continuing positive performance of large proportions could reflect significant problems, as for example, ones method of planning the work (BCWS) in the first place.

During the full term of performance on a contract, variance thresholds can focus on three different points of reference, as is illustrated in figure 10.6. The first reference point is shown as "1. Cumulative to date." It reflects all of the activity to date, on a cumulative or total basis through the reporting period. The second point is "2. Current Month," which merely focuses on the last 30 days and is a part of the cumulative to date values. The last point is "3. Estimate at Completion," which incorporates all actuals to date, and projections to the end -- EAC.

It is not uncommon for the buying customers to impose variance thresholds at all three points, e.g., cumulative, current month, and EAC, although there are some who would consider that to be excessive reporting requirements. This latter group feels that the cumulative position is all that is needed for good performance monitoring. They claim that the current month is too prone to accounting fluctuations to measure progress and will only result in excessive paperwork (PAR reports). They also feel that the EAC thresholds are often subjectively influenced by people unwilling to admit the real estimate to complete and are, therefore, unreliable as a monitoring point.

To pause on this point for a minute, the C/SCS concept can be an excellent management tool, but it is not intended to be a substitute for good management. It merely complements and assists good management. If a customer or contractor program manager fails to spot a potential problem from data reflecting variances to the baseline at the cumulative position, chances are likely they will also miss the added data from the current period and EAC points also. But by way of

Figure 10.6 Three Variance Threshold Points

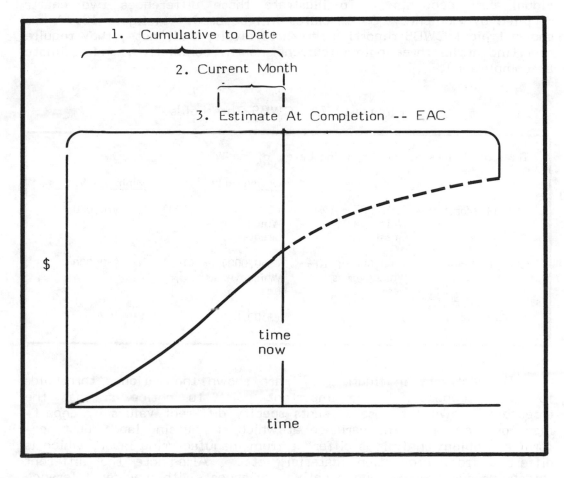

work on the contractor and added costs to the program, however, the current month and EAC reports place much burden on the cost account managers, who must prepare such variance reports. And when PARs become excessive, they are rarely read anyway.   When private contractors self-impose C/SCS internally on their commercial or firm-fixed price work (which require no external customer reporting), variance thresholds for the current month and EAC are one of the first things to go because of their high cost to prepare and questionable value in monitoring status. A busy program manager will often ask to see the five most critical variances each month . . . period.

Whether a contract requires reporting at all three reference points, or relaxes the requirement to focus on a few critical variances, it is important to understand just where such analysis takes place. Variance analysis takes place at the individual cost account level, which by definition is where a single functional department intersects at the lowest element of the CWBS. However, the customer will only see a summary report at a higher CWBS level, typically level 3. When there are offsetting variances within the same CWBS summary level, the customer may never see a reported variance. But internally, the contractor will require a review of variances down to individual cost accounts. To illustrate these differences two charts supplied by Humphreys & Associates will be used. In figure 10.7A are shown typical CWBS reporting threshold levels, and, note, they require reporting at all three points (current month, cumulative, and estimate at completion).

Figure 10.7A   CWBS Thresholds

Threshold Values at the Reporting Levels of the WBS			
	Favorable	Unfavorable	Minimum Values
Current Month	$20,000 or 15% Whichever is Greater	($10,000) or (15%) Whichever is Greater	$10,000
CUM to Date	$100,000 or 10% Whichever is Less	($50,000) or (10%) Whichever is Less	$50,000
At Completion	$200,000	($100,000)	

By contrast, in figure 10.7B are shown the variance thresholds for cost accounts. One important point to notice is that the thresholds shown for cost accounts specify different values by department or function. The variance at which engineering labor must perform a problem analysis is different from manufacturing labor, which is different from production material, etc. Also note the different thresholds for positive and negative variances, with a wider tolerance allowed for positive variances.

At present, there is no such thing as a standard variance threshold at the customer (CWBS) reporting level. Each customer sets the values at which it will require formal variance reporting from a contractor and, then, imposes these in the contract. If a customer insists on reports in excess of a contractor's normal reporting level, as reflected in its validated C/SCS systems description and procedures, then the customer will likely have to pay additional costs for these added C/SCS reports.

For a comparison with figure 10.7A, which outlined typical CWBS reporting thresholds, shown in figure 10.8 are thresholds specified in an actual (unnamed) contract. Note, in figure 10.8, that the cumulative thresholds decrease from 10 percent initially down to 2 percent as the program moves toward completion. Also note, that the EAC threshold stays constant at 2 percent throughout the term of the contract. To keep such thresholds from inundating the program with variance analysis reports, often a percentage is combined with an absolute value, say $100,000, so that the threshold is 10 percent and $100,000, which seems to reduce the monitoring to meaningful levels only.

Figure 10.7B   Thresholds for Cost Accounts

Threshold Values at the Cost Account Level:

	Minimum Value	Cost -%	Cost +%	Schedule -%	Schedule +%
Current Month					
Engineering Labor	100 Hrs	15	20	15	20
Manufacturing Labor	250 Hrs	15	20	15	20
Production Material	$2,500	15	20	15	20
Tooling Material	$1,200	15	20	15	20
Subcontractors	TO BE DETERMINED ***				
CUM to Date					
Engineering Labor	250 Hrs	10	15	10	15
Manufacturing Labor	500 Hrs	10	15	10	15
Production Material	$5,000	10	15	10	15
Tooling Material	$2,500	10	15	10	15
Subcontractors	TO BE DETERMINED ***				
At Completion					
Engineering Labor	250 Hrs	10	10	10	10
Manufacturing Labor	500 Hrs	10	10	10	10
Production Material	$5,000	10	10	10	10
Tooling Material	$2,500	10	10	10	10
Subcontractors	TO BE DETERMINED ***				

$$-\% = \frac{BCWP - ACWP}{BCWP} \qquad +\% = \frac{BCWP - BCWS}{BCWS}$$

*** Based on Subcontractor Dollars and Criticality

The formula used to set the values in figure 10.8 are listed as follows and are slightly different from those shown in the Humphreys table in figure 10.7B:

1. Program Completed % = $\dfrac{\text{Budgeted Cost Work Performed}}{\text{Budget at Completion}}$ = _____ %

2. Cost Variance % = $\dfrac{\text{Cum BCWP less Cum ACWP}}{\text{Budgeted Costs Work Performed}}$ = _____ %

3. Schedule Variance % = $\dfrac{\text{Cum BCWP less Cum BCWS}}{\text{Budgeted Costs Work Scheduled}}$ = _____ %

4. Estimate at Completion Variance % = $\dfrac{\text{BAC less EAC}}{\text{BAC}}$ = _____ %

110

Figure 10.8   Cost/Schedule Variance Thresholds

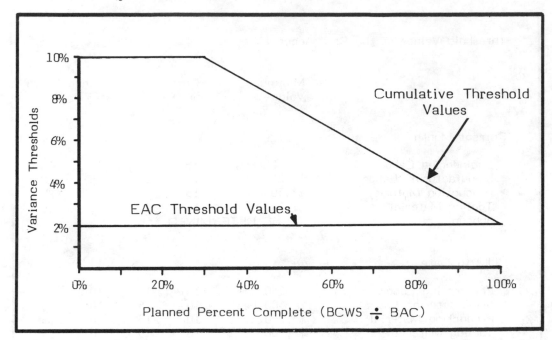

In addition to there being no set standard customer variance thresholds, also, there are no standard cost account thresholds for the industry.   Each contractor may set its own threshold levels by function, which must be defined in its procedures, and approved by the validation team in its demonstration review.   It is up to the contractor to propose threshold levels, by function, which in turn must be approved by the customer.   Hopefully (but not always) such thresholds will strike a balance between providing adequate visibility, but doing so at a reasonable cost to the program.

Once a variance threshold has been penetrated, certain formal actions must take place in order to meet the spirit of the six C/SCS Criteria contained, in group IV: Analysis.   These formal actions are the preparation and review (summary) and submittal of variance analysis reports, most frequently called Problem Analysis Reports (PARs).   The PAR is a brief one-page summary of the analysis of the variance to the budget/schedule plan, reporting formats will vary by contractor.   However, all effective PARs must address four issues:

1.   They must be prepared by the lowest responsible cost account manager, the one closest to the variant condition, and not by an outside planner/scheduler/or budgeter.

2.   The PAR must explain separately each cost and schedule variance and its present and potential impact on the program.

3. Actions taken/or to be taken to resolve the variance must be detailed.
4. The PAR must be reviewed with, and signed by, the next higher level of management (sometimes two levels of management).

What the formalizing of the variance analysis does in effect is require that a contractor go through a series of steps any time its performance is outside of the plan by a previously set tolerance. It also requires that such analysis be documented, so that a contractor's program manager and, if need be, the customer may trace through each problem area at a subsequent date.

The PAR is an essential part of the monthly Cost Performance Report (CPR) and is specifically called out as Format 5 of DOD Instruction 7000.10, which sets forth the requirements for the CPR (Appendix C to this book). A typical PAR report is shown in figure 10.9.

ESTIMATE AT COMPLETION (EAC)

Some might quarrel with the placement of the subject of Estimate At Completion - EAC at this point in a book on a C/SCS management control system. One could argue that the EAC represents a projection of the final costs of a program; therefore, the subject rightfully belongs in the final chapter. But the EAC has been intentionally combined with the subject of baseline management to emphasize the point that in C/SCS the estimated costs at the completion of the program is but a logical extention of work accomplished along the Performance Measurement Baseline - PMB. How well one has been performing (BCWP) along the PMB (BCWS), and its relationship to how much money has been spent (ACWP), will determine the final costs (EAC) on a program.

In an ideal world, or before a program gets underway, several of the terms used during this discussion are synonymous. For example, prior to the start of a program:

*   BCWS (Budgeted Costs for Work Scheduled)
                    equals
*   PMB (Performance Measurement Baseline)
                    equals
*   BAC (Budget At Completion)
                    equals
*   EAC (Estimate At Completion)

Unfortunately, this is hardly a perfect world, and a program only experiences the above condition for a brief moment before starting performance against the plan. This ideal condition is illustrated in figure 10.10.

However, as performance begins against the plan, what was a common projection now separates into distinct curves as deviations take place

112

Figure 10.9 Problem Analysis Report -- PAR

PMB PROBLEM ANALYSIS REPORT

PROGRAM _____
COST ACCOUNT _____
SALES ORDER _____
WBS _____

DATE _____
AS OF _____

IMPACT: SCHED.   COST

RECOVERABLE   ☐   ☐

IRRECOVERABLE ☐   ☐

A. PROBLEM

B. CORRECTIVE ACTION

VARIANCES	SCHEDULE		COST	
	$	HOURS	$	HOURS
CURRENT				
CUM TO DATE				
AT COMPLETION				

	CUM TO DATE	MONTHLY											CUM AT COMPLETION
BCWS													
BCWP													
ACWP													
RECOVERY PLAN													

RESPONSIBLE ANALYST _____

COST ACCOUNT MANAGER _____

Figure   10.10   Conditions before a Program Starts

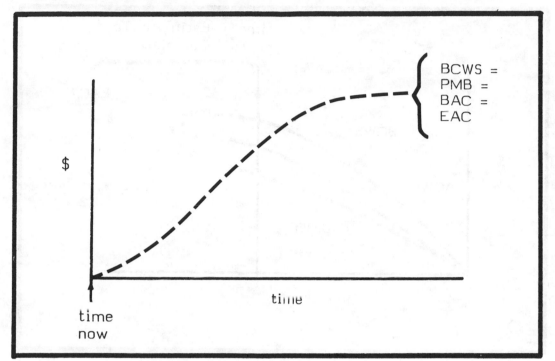

from the plan. Thus, the same program which was displayed in figure 10.10, would now start to resemble the one shown in figure 10.11.

What figure 10.11 displays is a program behind schedule (BCWP less BCWS) and a program overrunning its costs (BCWP less ACWP). In order to forecast the EAC (Estimate At Completion) costs, one must quantify the costs of the ETC (Estimate To Complete). Question: When doing an ETC cost projection, which of the three performance curves shown in figure 10.11 should be used: BCWS, BCWP, or ACWP? Answer: All three.

The BCWS curve to the end represented the PMB, or all the work required to complete the job. When one subtracts the BCWP, or work accomplished, from the BCWS, the result is the balance of the work necessary to finish the job. When one adds a cost estimate to the work remaining to finish the job, one has forecasted the ETC. When one adds the ETC to the ACWP, or cost actuals, one has established the EAC (Estimate At Completion). Thus all three performance curves shown above must be considered when estimating the final costs of a program.

The author's company has perfected an effective method to forecast the Estimate At Completion - EAC on their programs, and it might be worthwhile to review their technique at this time. In brief, their procedure requires two factors to be present in all such EAC forecasts:

1. Balanced organizational inputs to the estimate (EAC), repre-

114

Figure 10.11 Status after a Program Starts

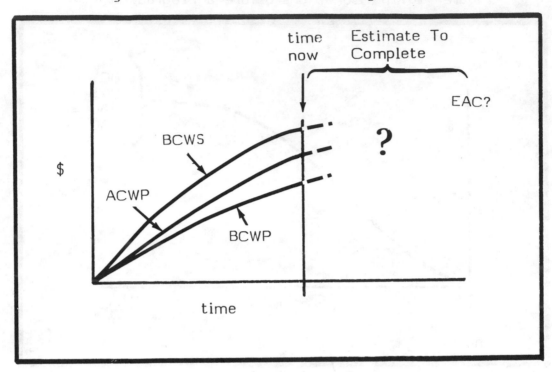

senting all organizations which have a vested interest in the
forecast and will be performing to them.
2. Periodically, two independent forecasts are required to project the Estimate At Completion: a Mathematical EAC and
an Analytical EAC Override.

Organizationally, the preparation and submittal of all C/SCS
reports are the responsibility of the division controller, who is a part
of the finance department. Within the controller's organization are
two separate controller activities: (1) program controllers, who are
assigned to specific program managers to represent their interests, and
who consolidate all C/SCS data related to a particular contract for
reporting to the customer; and (2) the functional controllers, who are
assigned to specific functional departments, who typically support
multiple contracts for that function. A classic matrix relationship.
As a routine practice, estimates to complete are assembled from
cost account managers by functional controllers only, for submittal to
and consolidation by a given program controller. Program controllers
manage the baseline and management reserve and assemble the data in
report form for transmittal to a customer. However, when there is
any indication that a given function is either overestimating a job, or
underestimating it for some reason, the program controller has
authority to make an independent forecast of the effort and to use it
in the C/SCS report. The program controller has final say on the
estimate used unless the functional controller insists on elevating the

issue to the division controller for a final resolution. The process works well and recognizes the diverse interests and pressures which exist on program managers versus functional performing managers, each of whom are represented by specific controllers assigned to support them.

With respect to the Estimate At Completion - EAC, two distinct methods are used:

- Mathematical EAC is derived by subtracting the work accomplished (BCWP) from the total work scheduled (BAC), both of which have costs allocated by detailed subtask, and by adding the difference to the actual costs to date (ACWP). This approach assumes that the original detailed estimates are still valid.
- Analytical EAC Override is derived by review of detailed performance and trend analysis of work completed and in process, and preparing a detailed estimate to complete for all remaining work.

The Mathematical EAC is probably typical of most estimating approaches used in the industry. There is nothing inherently wrong with the method, as long as the original planning estimates were valid and nothing has happened since the program began to alter these original planning asssumptions. Two big Ifs. Unfortunately, few programs (perhaps none) ever finish exactly as first planned. Tests fail, requirements change, better ideas are conceived, and soon the current modified plan hardly resembles the original plan. Also, hopefully, people do get smarter as they work on a program. Thus, the Analytical EAC Override method takes on real significance as experience and knowledge is gained through trial and error.

The Mathematical EAC is mechanical in form and, thus, lends itself nicely to computer applications. By contrast, the Analytical EAC Override does not, and the approach takes more seasoned controller personnel working closely with a program manager to give the method any meaning. The use of both these EAC techniques, in conjunction with balanced organizational estimates and frequent and very critical internal management reviews, does add confidence in the forecasted final estimates (EAC) with at least one company in the industry.

***

And now for a return to yesteryear for one more "war story." It was during that time when a million dollars was still a lot of money, and if the values listed seem too insignificant, one can simply add two or three digits. It will not alter the principle involved.

Many years ago a young man worked for a firm which was relatively new in the industry and which had set highly ambitious growth goals for itself. In those days (prior to C/SCSC) the single best way for a firm to achieve rapid growth was to obtain a cost reimbursable contract, and then to use it to build a technical base, while hopefully performing on the contracted effort. Finally, this firm got its chance.

A request for proposal was received calling for activity for which they had some experience. They immediately decided to submit a proposal (which was a common happening in those days) and quickly formed a proposal team. The pricing people requested organizational estimates and reviewed their cost projections with management. The price they were proposing was slightly over $5.0 million.

Management reviewed the values and reacted decisively: "Too high, cut the price." Another review was held with the price set at $3.5 million, and the reaction was the same: "Cut." Still another review was held with a $2.5 million price, and although it took slightly longer for the decision, the result was the same: "Too high -- cut." When the proposal was finally submitted, the proposed costs were $1.7 million, with a one dollar fee for their services! To no one's real surprise, this company won the competition.

Unfortunately, the unnamed young man was given the honor of being the cost controller on that high priority effort, and he spent the next 24 months attempting to issue budgets. He had an impossible task, and fortunately for him at the time, he was not aware of the events that had taken place in setting the price for his program. As for controls, he was only able to monitor costs from the top down; he could never issue detailed bottom-up budgets. Why? Because he found the individual engineering and manufacturing managers had too much personal integrity to sign up for budgets at roughly one-half of the values they knew they needed to do the job. They would have accepted ambitious targets; they flatly refused unattainable budgets.

When the dust finally settled some three years later, those individuals who had worked on the program had done an outstanding job under a very difficult set of conditions. However, not everyone saw it that way. The very same management which during the proposal had said, "Too high -- cut," now criticized the program manager for his "inability to keep costs under control." The original contract of $1.7 million with a one-dollar fee was negotiated up to a $4.5 million contract value incorporating all changes, and the added contract value received a full fee. However, they ended the program having spent some $9.2 million --a 100 percent pure overrun, or + 500 percent over the original negotiated price!

Now just what does this story have to do with C/SCSC? Well, as was indicated earlier, this program was awarded prior to the development of C/SCSC. One of the absolute requirements of the criteria is the creation of a Performance Measurement Baseline -PMB, which is made up of detailed individual cost account budgets. The cost accounts must be verifiable by a customer team performing either a Demonstration Review or Subsequent Application Review -SAR.

In the first two years of the effort this young man was never able to issue individual budgets, today called cost accounts. Hence, he would have never been able to establish a Performance Measurement Baseline - PMB. And without a PMB, this contractor could not have passed a validation test. Thus, by imposing a C/SCSC requirement on all major contracts, the buying customer is able to verify the likelihood of a contract staying within the target costs in the early months of a program. If a contractor has "bought into" an effort, and the procuring activity allowed it to happen, the C/SCSC requirement, if properly implemented and enforced, will expose such a condition early in the program start-up phase. An overrun or schedule slip will be obvious.

Updating the values of yesteryear to today's prices, if a contractor today were to win a $1.7 billion contract, and then in the first few months of the effort not be able to establish a PMB (and thus not comply with C/SCSC), the customer would have just cause to probe deeply into the validity of their cost proposal and Estimate At Completion - EAC values. If a realistic assessment of the EAC were to show a value of, say, $9.2 billion, or $7.5 billion over their original estimates, the customer would have a right to know it -- early. In such a case, the customer may want to take their $9.2 billion and buy something else with it. The customer has a right to know the full truth.

C/SCSC is not a perfect management control aid. But if implemented and properly used by management, it will cure many of the ailments that were common in industry only a few years back.

ENDNOTES

1. Interview with Lloyd L. Carter, USAF retired, recently a director with Humphreys & Associates, March 19, 1981.

11

HOW EARNED VALUE
IS DETERMINED

Half the work that is done in the world is to make things appear what they are not.[1]

E. R. Beadle

About a century ago Mr. Beadle made this amusing remark, which in one brief statement represents both the basis for, and the antithesis of, C/SCSC.

It represents the basis for C/SCSC because, somehow, the procuring customers had to get at the truth. Contractors were winning $1.7 million contracts and spending $9.2 million, and at no time until the programs were over, would anyone admit to the total costs. This could not continue. The government needed some device to ascertain the true status of all contracts at any point in time and to obtain reliable Estimates At Completion, so they could project their total funding requirements in a reasonably accurate way. Hence, the need for C/SCSC.

But the quote also represents the very opposite of what the criteria attempt to do. The principal difference between the C/SCSC and other management approaches is that of measuring the earned value. "What you got for what you spent," is the often used battle cry of the proponents of the system.

Thus, if one were to take the opposite of Mr. Beadle's statement and apply it to this subject, it might come out as: all the work that is done in C/SCSC is to make things appear as they really are.

"The what you got," which C/SCSC attempts to quantify in a systematic way, is referred to by the technique as the BCWP, or Budgeted Cost for Work Performed. Over the years, if the procuring customers had known what they got for what they spent, or more cynically, how little they were getting for what they were spending, the requirements for C/SCSC and a monthly BCWP would likely have originated decades earlier. This chapter will discuss how the BCWP is measured, that is, how earned value is actually established by contractors attempting to comply with the C/SCS Criteria.

Throughout this chapter, five terms will be used which are synonymous with each other: BCWP = Earned Value = Work Performed = "What you got for what you spent" = Performance Measurement.

There are numerous government publications on C/SCSC. However, nowhere, in any of these works, do they give one any clue as to "how" one is to measure performance. They merely set forth the requirements for work measurement in the criteria. The "how to" is strictly up to the contractor to propose in its management control system; and the government to approve or reject the approach being offered while validating their cost/schedule system.

Fundamental to making an assessment of the BCWP (or earned value) is that previously a BCWS (or work scheduled, or plan) had been established, against which performance could be measured. Without a baseline plan (BCWS or PMB) there can be no basis for determining earned value.

In C/SCS the PMB -- Performance Measurement Baseline -- is made up of the sum of cost accounts, and cost accounts come in three distinct types: Discrete or Work Package; LOE -- Level of Effort; and Apportioned. While the main thrust of C/SCS and work measurement is focused on discrete/work package cost accounts, there are instances where the other two are appropriately used, and their performances must also be quantified.

LEVEL OF EFFORT -- LOE -- COST ACCOUNTS

LOE cost accounts are those which are necessary to a program, but which are more time oriented than task related. Examples of these activities are program management, scheduling, field engineering support, etc. When these functions are charged directly to a contract, they continue for the full term of a program, but they have no measurable outputs. In these cases work performance (BCWP) is always assumed to equal the plan or work scheduled (BCWS), no more, no less. Therefore, LOE cost accounts by definition can have no Schedule Variance (BCWP less BCWS). But they can have cost variances (BCWP less ACWP).

On LOE cost accounts, the BCWP, monthly and cumulative, always matches the BCWS, up to 100 percent of the budget, or BCWS. BCWP can never exceed 100 percent of BCWS. With respect to cost actuals (ACWP), any differences between BCWP and ACWP will cause a positive or negative Cost Variance.

APPORTIONED COST ACCOUNTS

Apportioned cost accounts are those which have been shown to have a direct performance relationship to some other discrete activity, called their reference base. A good example is that of assembly inspection, which normally has a direct relationship to assembly hours, but, of course, at a fraction (say 10 percent of the related base, i.e., assembly hours). When the apportioned cost account for assembly inspection is issued, it must state in writing that the BCWP for inspection will be the same as that for assembly hours, its related base.

When determining the monthly or cumulative BCWP for the inspection (apportioned) cost account, the value will always equal the percentage BCWP for the base assembly hours (discrete) cost account. If the assembly hours cost account is experiencing a negative schedule variance (BCWP less BCWS), likewise, the inspection cost account must reflect the same negative schedule variance.

The cost status for this same apportioned cost account, however, will reflect the Actual Costs of Work Performed (ACWP) of the inspection cost account, and not of the base cost account for assembly hours. The Cost Variance position of the apportioned inspection cost account will be the difference between the ACWP for its own activity versus the derived BCWP of its base, i.e., assembly hours. Thus, if the manager of inspection were to double the inspectors from the 10 percent normal rate that was budgeted to, say, 20 percent, the inspection cost account would reflect a negative Cost Variance, even if its base cost account for assembly hours showed no such Cost Variance.

With respect to Schedule Variances, apportioned cost accounts reflect the position of their related base cost accounts. With respect to Cost Variances, however, they reflect their own costs as related to the derived BCWP (as a percentage) of their related bases.

DISCRETE/WORK PACKAGE COST ACCOUNTS ON LABOR FUNCTIONS

The methodology for measuring performance (BCWP) of both LOE and apportioned cost accounts is consistent throughout the industry. However, these two types of cost accounts by the very rules of C/SCS are to represent only a small portion of all active cost accounts in use. The majority of cost accounts are required to be of the discrete/work package type, and the methodology for measuring performance of the discrete/work package cost accounts is, by no means, uniform throughout the industry.

While attempting to establish the earned value position each month, discrete/work packages can be placed into three categories: (1) those completed, (2) those not yet started, and (3) those in process. The cost accounts which are completed and those not yet started are both easy to assess; they earn 100 percent and zero percent respectively. But those work packages which are in process as of the reporting period are not easy to quantify in any meaningful way, particularly those which are delinquent or late in being completed. The Joint Implementation Guide states:

The major difficulty encountered in the determination of BCWP is the evaluation of in-process work (work packages which have been started but have not been completed at the time of cutoff for the report).[2]

Therefore, most of the attention of those attempting to determine the earned value will be focused on the active, in process discrete cost accounts.

While the techniques used to measure performance do vary in the industry, and various contractors may use some unique terms to describe their particular approach, there are essentially six distinct methods used to measure "what you got for what you spent" (BCWP):

1.   The 50/50 Technique -- This approach was popular in the early days of C/SCS, but its use has diminished somewhat of late. The 50/50 technique is used for work packages with a duration of not more than three accounting periods, preferably two maximum. Fifty percent of the Plan value is earned when the activity starts, and the balance is earned when the effort is completed. Some contractors use a modified approach which allows the cost account manager to set the percentage values to other than 50/50, say 25/75, or 40/60, etc.

2.   The 0/100 Technique -- This approach is applied to work packages which start and hopefully complete within one accounting month. Nothing is earned when the activity starts, but 100 percent is earned when completed.

3.   Milestone Method -- This approach works well when work packages exceed three or more months in duration. Objective milestones are established, preferably one or more each month, and the assigned budget for the work package is divided up based on a weighted value assigned to each milestone. In those instances where there are no milestones in a given month, an estimate of work completed may allow for additional earned value of the work package during the month.

4.   Percent Complete -- This approach allows for an estimate of percent complete, usually cumulative, to be made each month by the manager of the work package.

Over the years, the latter two methods, milestone and percent complete, or a combination of both, have received increasingly wide industry use. There is nothing inherently wrong with this direction as long as the work packages stay short in duration, and internal company management goes through a periodic review process where each work package manager must justify the completion value assigned to their activity. The author has witnessed many a heated and strained discussion for work package managers when their next level supervision and/or their colleagues felt they were claiming too much or too little completion value for their activities in a status review meeting. If a company management (and lower level managers in particular) truly utilize the C/SCS approach in the management of a program, the professional integrity of employees and supervision provides a sort of unwritten check and balance on the accuracy of the monthly earned value estimate. Conversely, if a firm gives lip service only to C/SCS and really uses some other control technique, the monthly BCWP can have wide distortions using the percent complete method to measure performance, since this approach is, in effect, a subjective assessment of status.

One approach used to minimize the subjectivity factor in the percent completion/milestone methods to set earned value is to limit the maximum amount allowed to be earned in any work package until it is completed. While the percentages allowed do vary from company to company, 80 percent to 90 percent maximum is typical of most firms. Thus, a given work package may earn only up to say 80 percent until the task is 100 percent complete, and then it earns the balance.

The four methods listed above to measure performance, apply well to engineering type activity. There are two additional techniques that apply best to manufacturing efforts:

5. Equivalent Units -- This method places a given value on each unit completed, say $25, or 25 hours per unit, as the basis for setting both the budget and earned value.

6. Standards -- This approach to budgeting and measuring performance is the most sophisticated and requires the most discipline on the part of the contractor. It requires the establishment of standards for the performance of the tasks to be worked. Historical cost data, time and motion studies, etc., are all essential to the process of setting work standards. This approach may well be the one increasingly used in the future, based on the requirements of Military Standard 1567, to be discussed later in this chapter.

There is no single method which works best in all types of activity. Probably the best approach for a firm to take is to allow several different methods to be used, based on the collective judgments of the cost account managers, working closely with their C/SCS specialists and the customer.

To assess the methods actually being used in the defense industry, a survey of five major contractors was made, and the results are summarized in figure 11.1. Contractor A has four major divisions; note that each division is allowed to select its own techniques to measure earned value, which emphasizes the uniqueness of C/SCSC applications. The actual identity of each firm is disguised to respect the proprietary nature of this information. Each of the five firms is a major defense contractor, and all have their own validated C/SCS management control systems (Contractor A has four separate validations).

Note that no two of these five contractors uses exactly the same combination of techniques, each has some unique feature. Since all have approved C/SCS systems, a safe conclusion is that the govern-

124

Figure 11.1 Survey of Earned Value Techniques

Earned Value Technique	Contractor A-1	A-2	A-3	A-4	B	C	D	E
1. 50/50	No	No	Yes	Yes	Yes	Yes	Yes	No
2. 0/100	No	No	Yes	Yes	Yes	No	Yes	No
3. Milestone	Yes	Yes	Yes	Yes	Yes	Yes	Yes	Yes
4. Percent Complete	Yes	Yes	Yes	Yes	Yes	Yes	Yes	Yes
Maximum EV allowed until 100% Complete	85%	80%	80%	80%	100%	85% (95% LOE)	100%	90%
5. Equivalent Units	Yes	Yes	No	Yes	Yes	No	No	No
6. Standards	Yes	Yes	Yes	Yes	No	Yes	No	No

Source: Author survey.

ment, when validating a given contractor's C/SCSC approach, will allow the contractor its own choice of methods, as long as they meet the intent of the criteria. The one consistent pattern, however, is the frequent use of the milestone and percent complete methods. All contractors listed use these methods.

To illustrate how the earned value (BCWP) is determined using four of the six techniques listed earlier, Humphreys & Associates provided the display for figure 11.2, which shows the methods used to set the earned value using the 50/50, Equivalent Unit, Percent Complete, and Milestone techniques.

Work Package 1 uses the 50/50 technique. In month 1 the WP was started, so 50 percent of the plan (BCWP) was earned, i.e., the BCWP was 100 in month 1. In month 2, the scheduled completion date was slipped to month 4. Therefore, the BCWP status at the end of the month 3, time now, is still only 100 since the balance of the BCWP, the other 50 percent, cannot be earned until the WP is completed.

Likewise, in WP 2, the planned (BCWS) values are shown on the above portion of each month, and the earned (BCWP) values are shown below. In month 2, the BCWS was 6 units, or $150, compared with the performance (BCWP) of 2, or $50. In the 3rd month, BCWP was increased to 6 units, or $150, a nice recovery.

One can trace through WPs 3 and 4 and compare planned (BCWS) versus earned value (BCWP) for each approach.

Figure 11.2 Earned Value Techniques

SAMPLE COST ACCOUNT
EARNED VALUE CONCEPT
BUDGETED COST FOR WORK PERFORMED (BCWP)

MONTH		1	2	3	4	5	6
WP1	50/50	▲100 / 100	100△ / 0	- - - -	△		
WP2	EQ/UNITS $25/UNIT	▲	- -△150 / 2 UNITS 50	75 / 6 UNITS 150	100	250 △	
WP3	% COMP	▲50 / 16.7%	100 / 33%	150 / 33%	- - - -	△	△
	CUMULATIVE	50	50	0			
WP4	MILESTONE				△150	△200	50 △
	BCWS/-CUM	150	500	725	975	1425	1475
	BCWP-INCRE.	150	100	150			
	BCWP-CUM	150	250	400			

↑
TIME NOW

Source: Chart courtesy of Humphreys & Associates.

SETTING THE EARNED VALUE ON MATERIALS AND OTHER DIRECT COSTS

It is doubtful if there is any single issue which has given people implementing C/SCSC more headaches or difficulty than that of materials. Many a contractor has failed to pass its initial validation review because it could not demonstrate an ability to measure the earned value of materials in the same time period as when actual costs were recorded on their books. At least one contractor lost its existing validation because of materials. With anything as straight forward as the buying of a few parts, why should it be so tough to account for materials under C/SCSC? In order to answer this question, one must step back and compare the requirements of C/SCSC with the normal flow of material purchases, and perhaps the answer will be obvious.

Under typical cost control systems, materials are normally tracked at two reference points only:

1. The Plan which usually represents the point at which engineering or manufacturing or others initiate the order for the parts, regardless of when such parts are actually ordered or received.

2. The Actuals which is ordinarily the point at which the costs of the parts are recorded on the firm's accounting books, i.e., when the bill is paid.

Those firms that have a material commitment system are able to record the liability for purchased goods at the point at which engineering or manufacturing initiates the order, later updated when ordered by purchasing, later updated when parts are received, and finally updated when the bill is paid and the costs are recorded on the accounting books. While a material commitment system does allow for the synchronization of the plan with actuals at the point at which orders for parts are initiated, such an approach does not meet the specific language of Criterion III, 7, on material accounting to be discussed later.

Under C/SCS requirements, a third reference point must be added to the above two reference points:

1.   The Plan -- now called BCWS -- Budgeted Cost for Work Scheduled

2.   The Actuals -- now called ACWP -- Actual Costs of Work Performed

3.   The Performance -- called earned value or BCWP --Budgeted Costs for Work Performed

With the third added dimension, BCWP, the problems of those attempting to synchronize the three reference points have increased greatly.

And now for the clincher, i.e., the requirements of C/SCS Criterion III, 7, which states:

> The contractor's material accounting system will provide for: accurate cost accumulation and assignment of costs to cost accounts in a manner consistent with the budgets using recognized, acceptable costing techniques; determination of price variances by comparing planned versus actual commitments; cost performance measurement at the point in time most suitable for the category of material involved, but no earlier than the time of actual receipt of material; determination of cost variances attributable to the excess usage of material; determination of unit or lot cost when applicable; and full accountability for all material purchased for the contract including the residual inventory.[3]

This criterion tells a contractor what it must do, and also what it must not do. For example, while a contractor must measure performance of its materials, it cannot measure them until the materials are actually received. Thus, the point of commitment of the material liability is eliminated as an option to measure BCWP, since that is prior to receipt of materials.

The criterion also requires that budgets (BCWS) and cost accumulation (ACWP) be consistent, which is easy, by and of itself. It also requires that price variations be isolated between BCWS and ACWP, adding a further complexity. But the real difficulty comes with the full accountability requirement, the setting of both unit and lot costs, and the isolation of any residual inventory purchased under the contract. These are no small tasks, for now such factors as handling attrition, machine scrappage, and surplus inventory must be considered in accounting for all purchased parts.

If one traces through the detailed flow of parts acquisition, one finds that materials have some ten points at which visibility is possible. Admittedly, the distinction between some may seem quite fine:

One -- When the parts request is initiated by the using groups. This usually consists of preparing a document called a purchase requisition by engineering or manufacturing, or others.

Two -- When the purchase requisition is approved by management, and perhaps the value committed on a material commitment report.

Three -- When the order for the parts is officially placed by the buyer, usually issuing a purchase order, somtimes resulting in a commitment.

Four -- When the parts have arrived at the receiving dock, but prior to acceptance.

Five -- When the parts have been inspected and accepted, usually by someone from quality control.

Six -- When the parts are placed into a storage room.

Seven -- When the parts are taken from the storage room, for use on the contract.

Eight -- When the parts are incorporated into the end-item hardware.

Nine -- When an invoice is received, approved for payment, and perhaps committed in an accounts payable report.

Ten -- When the invoice is paid, the cost expenditures are recorded on the company books.

While these ten reference points might seem trivial to those attempting to establish a system which sets the BCWS, ACWP, and BCWP at exactly the same point of reference in order to comply with the C/SCS Criteria, they all have particular meaning. The illustration of a typical procurement system given above would set the BCWS using One or Two or Three, while the ACWP would use Ten and, thus, not comply with the material criterion. In order for firms to measure the acquisition of parts, and to place their plan, their cost actuals, and their work performance in a consistent manner, they had to create a new or substantially modified procurement control system. Not all firms understood that fact initially, and it took the harsh lessons of a failed demonstration review to cause some to modify their control systems.

Returning again to the survey of five companies summarized earlier in figure 11.1, there is a fairly consistent pattern. Contractor A-3 sets the BCWS, ACWP, and BCWP at point Five, when parts are accepted by quality control, and Contractor E at point Six, when the parts are placed into the storage room, ready for use. However, the other six contractors and divisions all use point Seven, when the parts are taken out of storage for use on a particular contract. This point, when materials are actually disbursed for use on a specific contract, recognizes the fact that many parts and materials may be used on any one of several contracts, and it is only when they are taken from storage and actually assigned to a specific contract that the BCWP can really be set with certainty.

With respect to Other Direct Costs (ODC), which covers such things as travel, computer usage, and a host of other activity chargeable directly to a contract, the BCWP is usually set either when costs are incurred or when costs are recorded. if the cost incurred method is used, the ACWP must be shifted to the earlier time frame, which is sometimes accomplished by use of a commitment report. If the cost recorded method is used, the BCWS must be shifted to a later time frame, to compensate for the time delay, normally about two months, between when costs are incurred until payment is made. Since Other Direct Costs are normally relatively small compared to labor and materials with their burdens, they do not usually present a major problem.

PERFORMANCE MEASUREMENT OF INDIRECT COSTS

There is another group of costs that are not exclusive to any single contract or program, but which apply to all contracts within a given company. These costs represent the single largest category of costs on all contracts, and are referred to as indirect costs, sometimes called overheads or burdens. They are collected in accounting pools for distribution over all direct costs by some approved method. The treatment of these costs must be consistent, fair, and apply to all programs in an equitable way. Costs which are charged into indirect pools (or burden centers), as with direct costs, must be defined, approved by the government, and applied thereafter in accordance with the financial disclosure statement for the company. Smaller firms may have only one such indirect pool. Larger companies often have six or seven or more such indirect pools, and charges going into each pool must be approved by category, and consistently applied to a pool in a manner similar to the distinction between direct and indirect costs. To allow uncontrolled shifting of costs between indirect pools, or between direct and indirect, would allow contractors to manipulate costs between different types of contracts (firm and cost), obviously a practice which is prohibited.

Indirect costs are those which, by definition, are impossible or at least difficult to identify to any one contract, and are of a benefit to all programs. A firm with only one contract might be able to charge everything directly to their one contract. However, the minute they get a second contract, or start to pursue additional business, it would no longer be appropriate to charge everything to the one contract only.

Hence, at the point at which two or more programs/activities exist in a given firm, there is a need for some type of indirect accounting approach, to equitably allocate the nondirect activity over the multiple contract direct base.

The allocation of the costs of indirect activity is generally provided for as a percentage rate of total direct activity. For example, for every dollar of direct costs the plan may call for, indirect costs would be allocated at say 110 percent based on the following:

$$\frac{\text{Total Indirect Pool} \quad \$110,000}{\text{Total Direct Base (all contracts)} \quad \$100,000} = \text{Indirect Rate of } 110\%$$

The difficulty of forecasting these burdens is that indirect costs must relate to direct costs, but indirect pools are made up of two types of costs:

1. Fixed Costs (e.g., facility rental/depreciation; company president; etc.) which do not vary with changes in the direct base.
2. Variable Costs (e.g., fringe benefits; telephones; accounting personnel; supplies; etc.) which will vary with changes in the direct base.

A given program has virtually no control over fixed indirect costs (one rarely fires a company president to save money) and only limited influence over variable indirect costs. While fringe benefit costs may go down roughly proportionate to the number of people on the indirect payroll, it is not an absolute relationship. In a declining business environment, it is a simple truth that the first people to be cut are those who are lowest paid and with no seniority. Thus, if the indirect work force is cut from 1,000 to 500, to adjust to a 50 percent loss of direct base, the indirect cost savings will never reach the same proportion as the reduction in people. The high priced company officers are still left, as are the people with the extra weeks vacation because of long-term service with the company.

Still another difficulty of forecasting indirect burden rates is that of forecasting the direct base, over which indirect costs will be allocated. A direct base forecast will be made up of two categories of business: (1) Firm Business (contracts in hand); and (2) New or Follow-On Business (with a high likelihood of capture).

The new or follow-on business doesn't always materialize, in which case the indirect rates go up on existing contracts because indirect costs are never adjusted with the same speed or in the same proportions as the declining direct base. Admittedly, "never" is a strong word to use. But if there has ever been a situation in which indirect costs were cut in the same proportions as the direct bases, the author has never been there to witness it. Thus, changes in the direct base will have the following impact on a given contract:

1. When the total direct base goes down -- the burden rates increase (always).
2. When the total direct base goes up -- the burden rates come down (sometimes, but slowly).

When a given contract establishes a PMB, Performance Measurement Baseline, which calls for indirect costs at the 110 percent planned rate, and indirect actuals reflect a higher percentage, say 200 percent of direct costs, the contractor must be in a position to isolate what took place. Assuming that cost actuals reflected the cost plan, i.e., that there was no shifting of costs between direct and indirect, and between indirect pools, a change in burden percentage rates must be the result of two factors, or a combination of the two:

- A change in the direct base (higher or lower)
- A change in the indirect pool costs (higher or lower)
- A combination of the two

A contractor must be in a position to trace the reasons why indirect burdens deviated from the plan and adversely impacted all contracts in the company. Was there a change in the direct base over which indirect costs were allocated; or was there a change in the amount of indirect costs charged to the burden pools; or was it a combination of both, which is usually the case.

So much for indirect accounting basics; back to C/SCS performance measurement. To assess such performance, one must understand that indirect rates fall into four categories:

1. Negotiated Bidding Rates (long-term forecast) often referred to as Forward Pricing Rates, are those burdens agreed to with the government, based on a reasonable projection of direct base as related to a projection of indirect costs, usually reaching three years into the future.
2. Applied Rates (current year) are those used by internal management for budgeting and reporting for the current period. These rates do not have to match the negotiated bidding rates, and conservative management will often set them slightly above the bidding rates.
3. Actual Incurred Rates (current year) are those which reflect actual expenditures as they appear on the company books. Each firm is likely to be different because of its accounting system. For example, some firms use a monthly cumulative adjustment, while others make their adjustments only periodically, but always at year end. Whatever method is used, it is important that actual overhead rates approximate the approved negotiated bidding rates.
4. Negotiated Final Rates (subsequent periods) are the actual rates agreed to between the company and the government after

the fact, sometimes long after the fact. Actual costs are adjusted to exclude those items which the government refuses to allow, such as entertainment costs. Adverse disallowances to the indirect pools impact company profits, but not individual contracts.

In order to measure C/SCS performance on a given contract it is necessary that in all cases BCWS (work scheduled) use the same category of indirect burdens as that of BCWP (work performed), and that no retroactive revisions be allowed to either the BCWS or BCWP. The category to use for the plan and earned value is the Applied Rate, #2 above, less the estimated value of disallowed costs in overheads.

With respect to ACWP (actual costs) it is appropriate to also use applied rates even though the actual incurred rates may be running above or below them, as long as one has confidence that the applied rates can be achieved. In such cases, any adjustments to the actual incurred rates are allowed for customer reports with a careful explanation in the Cost Performance Report. If, however, one has reason to suspect that indirect rates will go up or down for reasons discussed earlier, the ACWP must reflect the latest updated forecasts and let the cost variance (BCWP less ACWP) show.

Earned value in C/SCS refers to the performance measurement of a single contract. The performance of a firm's indirect activity affects all contracts in the company and is normally beyond the ability of a single program to control or influence. Nevertheless, as deviations to plan occur, a firm must have the ability to analyze and explain just what happened to their indirect costs.

HOW EARNED VALUE IS ESTABLISHED ON A CONTRACT

The earned value position (BCWP) for a given contract is simply the summation of all its cost accounts, those either completed or in process, expressed in either hours or dollars including burdens. It is a derived estimate. Each cost account must be assessed individually, and the summation of all cost accounts represents the contract's earned value or BCWP position.

***

No discussion of performance measurement under C/SCSC would be complete without some mention of Military Standard 1567, issued exclusively by the Air Force on 30 June 1975. A military standard (sometimes called a DOD Standard) should apply to all departments of the defense establishment, not just one. Whether the Air Force will be able to convince the other services to join them in a joint service endorsement of 1567, and just what impact the standard will have on the C/SCSC and their present Joint Implementation approach is an open issue. In the meantime, it is important that everyone understand what at least one service is planning to require from the private sector should they desire to receive Air Force contracts in the future.

Military Standard 1567 is intended to apply to all Air Force contracts of: (1) $100 million or more for full scale developments; (2) production or major system modifications which exceed $30 million annually or $100 million in total; and (3) subcontracts which exceed $5 million annually or $25 million cumulative. Excluded will be contracts for facilities, construction, shelf-items, time and material, research, study, and fixed-price efforts. The Standard will require a documented Work Measurement Plan from contractors which will outline:

- the organizational responsibilities to implement Military Standard 1567;
- the company procedures required to be added or modified, in order to comply;
- an agreement to establish and maintain engineered labor standards of known accuracy for all the "touch labor" functions of machining, welding, fabricating, cleaning, painting, assembling, and production functional testing;
- an agreement to continue to improve work methods associated with the established labor standards;
- an agreement to use the approved labor standards in their budgeting, estimating, production planning, and "touch labor" performance evaluations;
- an agreement to conduct internal audits of the implementation of Military Standard 1567, and to make the results of such audits available to the customer;
- an agreement to allow government surveillance of the implemention of the plan.

If the government surveillance personnel determines that the contractor's system does not meet the 1567 requirements, they can mandate an immediate corrective action plan subject to their approval. Should the contractor then fail to meet the corrective action plan, their approved manufacturing work measurement system can be invalidated by the government. Sounds much like C/SCSC doesn't it?

The implementation of Military Standard 1567 on contracts will have a very profound impact on C/SCSC, although interestingly, nowhere in the 1567 document does it even make reference to C/SCSC. It will also have a very profound impact on private contractors and the way they do business in the future.

There is an important distinction between the implementation approach used by Military Standard 1567 and that taken by the C/SCS Criteria. Under the criteria approach, the government merely indicated that they needed certain data, and the contractors could choose any method to provide the data to meet the criteria, as long as the information was available. Hence, different firms have used different methods to meet the requirements of C/SCSC. Nowhere in any government C/SCSC document does it tell industry "how" to provide such data.

Military Standard 1567, on the other hand, not only specifies the requirement for certain data, but it also essentially provides the "how" to do it. It assumes that its way is the best way and allows little flexibility to the private firm. In this regard, their implementation approach is not too dissimilar from the one used two decades earlier to impose PERT/Cost on industry.

What the final impact Military Standard 1567 will have on the defense procurement business is anybody's guess. If the 1567 approach turns out to be a viable, efficient way for all contractors to conduct their business, then it will survive the test of time. However, the joint service implementation approach taken on the C/SCSC will have to be modified to incorporate the requirements of 1567. Although not presently cross-referenced in any government document, Military Standard 1567 and the C/SCSC are on a collision course.

ENDNOTES

1. Herbert V. Prochnow and Herbert V. Prochnow, Jr., The Public Speaker's Treasure Chest (New York: Harper & Row, 1964), page 376.
2. JIG page 18, Appendix E of this text.
3. Joint Implementation Guide, page 43.

12

C/SCSC REPORTS

No management control system would be complete without some provision for the formal reporting of contract status to the customer. C/SCSC is no exception. There are four distinct reports which, while technically not a part of the criteria, are nevertheless an important adjunct to it. Based on the size of a program, however, not more than three are ever required on any single contract.

These four reports were designed to satisfy the diverse needs for information by the customer, recognizing that when the customer is the defense arm of the United States government, that multiple uses will be made from the same data. For example, the actual procurements are made by the separate military departments, as with the Department of the Air Force. This group will need current information on the cost schedule status of the contract in order to perform their role as program manager. Their next higher level leaders at Air Force headquarters will want the same information as assurance that the program is going well, and they will also need an accurate projection of the funding requirements on the program in order to submit their funding needs to the Department of Defense. At the DOD, they will also need status and funding information on all contracts, and, additionally, they will want historical cost data to compare the costs of one program against others. At the DOD, further cost analysis by program will take place as an added check that funding projections are adequate to complete all aspects of their programs.

All data submitted in conjunction with C/SCSC must be in a sufficiently standardized format to allow for the comparison of one program with another, and with programs of the various procuring services. The costs of a Navy fighter aircraft must be comparable with the costs of an Air Force fighter. The Work Breakdown Structure (WBS) as specified in Military Standard 881 is the vehicle used to standardize the cost reporting format.

The four reports due in concert with the C/SCSC are listed in figure 12.1, and each will be discussed individually in this chapter. Also shown are the approximate frequencies of reporting dates, the purpose of the reports, the applicable DOD Instruction, and the related DOD Joint Implementation Guide.

Figure 12.1 C/SCSC Reports

REPORT	FREQUENCY	PURPOSE	DOD INSTRUCTION	DOD JOINT GUIDELINE	DOLLAR THRESHOLD*
CFSR-Contract Funds Status Report	Quarterly	Forecast Funding Requirements, with Fee and Termination Liability	DODI 7000.10 (see Appendix C)	AFSCP 173-5 AFLCP 173-5 DARCOM P715 -5; NAVMAT P5240; DLAH 8315.2 (Appendix E)	$500,000
CPR-Cost Performance Report	Monthly	Summary of Cost/ Schedule Position	same	same	$40 million on FSD $160 million on Production
C/SSR-Cost/ Schedule Status Report	Monthly	Cost/Schedule Information on smaller contracts (mini-CPR)	same	AFSCP 173-3 AFLCP 173-2 DARCOM P715 -13;NAVMAT P5244; DLAH8315.3	$2 million
CCDR-Contractor Cost Data Reporting	Quarterly, or Semi-Annual or Annually	Four separate reports providing a Historical Data Base	DODI 7000.11 (see Appendix D)	AFSCP 800-15 AFLCP 800-15 AMCP 715-8 NAVMAT P5241	all critical hardware; $75 million on FSD; $300 million on Production

* Dollar thresholds vary with procuring command and over time. Each procuring command will set their own threshold values.

CFSR -- CONTRACT FUNDS STATUS REPORT

On all cost reimbursable type contracts, at the time of award, a funding profile is normally established. However, the very conditions which make a cost type contract appropriate (i.e., the likelihood of changes and redirection) will also most probably cause the funding profile to change. Therefore, on all DOD cost type contracts of six months duration or more, and over $500,000 in value, a CFSR is required quarterly to forecast the necessary program funding. Firm-fixed price contracts do not call for a CFSR because their funding is usually provided for in a separate delivery or billing schedule.

In these days of high interest rates, it is particularly important that a contractor give adequate attention to the projections in the CFSR. The funding projection must be properly balanced to keep a firm's cash flow adequate on a contract, but it must do so without requesting funds surplus to its needs. In figure 12.2, this process is illustrated.

Figure 12.2 Customer Funding

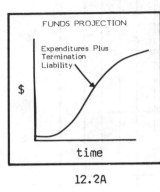 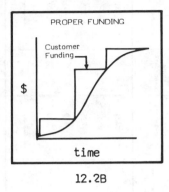 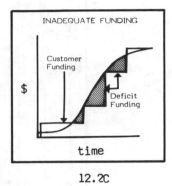

Figure 12.2A reflects the projection of expenditures on a hypothetical program, plus the estimated value of termination liability at any point in time. The next box, figure 12.2B, illustrates a program with adequate customer funding, i.e., at no time does the contractor have to wait for reimbursement for costs incurred, because funds have been sufficiently allocated to cover all expenditures.

The last figure, 12.2C, reflects an undesirable condition for several reasons. In the first place, the contractor has assumed the role of financier of the contract. Since the government cannot recognize interest as an element of reimbursable cost, all costs of the deficit funding, i.e., expenditures ahead of reimbursements, come out of the contractor's profits. With the high cost of money, deficit funding costs could well exceed profits on a given contract.

But perhaps of greater importance is the fact that when a contractor exceeds the funding of a program, it does so at its own risk. Should the contract be terminated for any reason while the contractor has exceeded the funding, the government is under no legal obligation to cover the exposure. One of the most common causes of deficit funding, however, is that unspoken problem referred to as overrun. In such cases, the contractor must assume at least part of the blame.

The precise format for the CFSR is specified in DOD Instruction 7000.10 (Appendix C to this book), and in more exact detail by DID (Data Item Description) DI-F-6004-B, a part of 7000.10. For those interested in the report, they can read the instructions contained in that Appendix. All categories of costs are tightly structured in Form DD 1586, illustrated in figure 12.3.

CPR -- COST PERFORMANCE REPORT

Probably one of the most important and frequently used acronyms in C/SCSC is that of CPR, which stands for the Cost Performance Report. It should not be confused with the medical term CPR, which stands for Cardio Pulmonary Resuscitation, a technique used on

138

Figure 12.3 Contract Funds Status Report -- CFSR

(CLASSIFICATION)

CONTRACT FUNDS STATUS REPORT (Dollars in ____000'S____)

Form Approved
Budget Bureau No.: 22-R0180

1. CONTRACT NUMBER		7. CONTRACTOR (NAME, ADDRESS & ZIP CODE)	9. INITIAL CONTRACT PRICE:
3. CONTRACT FUNDING FOR FY FY 1980	5. PREVIOUS REPORT DATE 27 March 1981		TARGET (1) CEILING (1)
2. CONTRACT TYPE FPI	4. APPROPRIATION	6. CURRENT REPORT DATE 26 June 1981	8. PROGRAM	10. ADJUSTED CONTRACT PRICE: TARGET (1) CEILING (1)

11.

		FUNDING INFORMATION										
			CONTRACT WORK AUTHORIZED				FORECAST					
LINE ITEM/WBS ELEMENT	APPROPRIATION IDENTIFICATION	FUNDING AUTHORIZED TO DATE	ACCRUED EXPENDITURES PLUS UNLIQUIDATED COMMITMENTS TOTAL	DEFINITIZED	EST. OVER/UNDER TARGET COST	NOT DEFINITIZED	SUBTOTAL	NOT YET AUTHORIZED	ALL OTHER WORK	SUBTOTAL	TOTAL REQUIREMENTS	FUNDS CARRYOVER	NET FUNDS REQUIRED
A	B	C	D	E	F	G	H	I	J	K	L	M	N
1000			$101,296	$86,647	$12,126	$2,958	$101,731				$101,731		$101,731
2000				Ø	Ø	Ø	Ø						Ø
3000			5,993	5,558	237	Ø	5,795				5,795		5,795
4000			461	447	(139)	181	489				489		489
5000			7,260	2,290	771	5,959	9,020				9,020		9,020
6000			230	58	190	8	256				256		256
TOTAL		(1)	$115,240	$95,000	$13,185	$9,106	$117,291				$117,291		$117,291

CONTRACT WORK AUTHORIZED (WITH FEE/PROFIT) - ACTUAL OR PROJECTED

12.

	ACTUAL TO DATE	3rd Q '81										AT COMPLETION
A. UNLIQUIDATED COMMITMENTS	458	Ø										Ø
B. ACCRUED EXPENDITURES	114,782	117,291										117,291
C. TOTAL (12A + 12B)	115,240	117,291										117,291
13. FORECAST OF BILLINGS TO THE GOVERNMENT	114,782	2,509										117,291

REMARKS:

DD FORM NO. 1586
1 JAN 72

(CLASSIFICATION)

Page ____ of ____ Pages

patients who denote "the absense of any clinical signs of consciousness and pulse, and who if not treated immediately, will experience permanent neurological damage." Well perhaps -- just perhaps -- the creators of the Cost Performance Report knew exactly what they were doing when they coined the term: CPR.

The CPR is a monthly report which is used by the customer and company management to monitor and assess status of a given program. It includes the typical subjects contained in such reports, i.e., the plan (BCWS) and actual costs (ACWP). But in addition, the CPR includes an estimate of the work performed (BCWP), and a forecast of the ultimate impact on costs at completion (EAC).

The format for the CPR is also shown in DODI 700.10 (Appendix C), and the precise requirements are specified in DID DI-F-6000B, contained therein. Five formats are called out:

    Format 1 -- Work Breakdown Structure
    Format 2 -- Functional Categories
    Format 3 -- Baseline
    Format 4 -- Manpower Loading
    Format 5 -- Problem Analysis Report

Each section has its own particular reason for being, therefore, each will be reviewed separately.

CPR Format 1 -- Work Breakdown Structure

Early in a new program, usually 30 days after contract award, a WBS (Work Breakdown Structure) will be required. Typically, this WBS will merely be an update of the WBS submitted with the proposal, and if all things are perfect, the contractual Statement of Work (SOW) will be an exact reflection of the WBS, item by item. Once approved by the customer, the WBS will serve to define the categories of costs required under Format 1.

Although a WBS will likely go down to levels 5, 6, or 7, reporting under Format 1 is usually held to level 3 only, (level 4 on primary hardware, e.g., air vehicle), as instructed in DODI 7000.10. However, there have been instances where the customer has required Format 1 reporting down to the very lowest level of the WBS. Not only does this type of requirement provide more data than is humanly possible to assimilate, but it is costly, and certainly not required for proper management. Since the contractor must be collecting costs at the lowest level of the WBS anyway, summary reporting at WBS level 3 or even 2 is adequate, because anytime a variance threshold is penetrated, the contractor must describe what is happening as required under Format 5 (Problem Analysis Reporting).

WBS reports are a customer requirement, used almost exclusively by the customer. Contractors normally manage a contract by functional organization only, and not by WBS. Therefore, if contractors were given a free choice, the WBS reports required by Format 1 would likely be the first to go. But there are exceptions.

140

In defense of the WBS report, however, is what can and should be done with it. Every new program, particularly those pushing the state of the art in technology, faces certain risks. Management, both with the customer and contractor, can have these program risks isolated, and the best place to monitor the progress toward elimination of such risks is with the WBS report. For example, a new radar development may be the major risk on a new aircraft program. Functional organizational displays will only partially isolate and focus on the radar. But the combination of functional sorting and a WBS breakout should provide adequate monitoring of program risk areas, whatever they are judged to be.

But to stay with the radar as an example, under a typical WBS the radar would likely fall on levels 4 or 5. If management determines that the radar is a high program risk area, there is nothing wrong with having the monthly WBS format contain routine summaries at level 2 or 3, but in addition, it can require the radar WBS element as a special item. Such an approach would reflect the intelligent use of CPR requirements, and this seems to be the direction of both industry and government. Rather than monitor every nut and bolt in a system, the trend is toward higher level summaries, but with special focus on potential program risks, i.e., the radar as an example.

Contained in figure 12.4 is Format 1, covering the WBS. There are special government forms which may be used by the contractor. However, a contractor may substitute a photo/copy of a computer report printout, in lieu of these special forms, as long as all of the same data are included.

The next four figures will cover CPR Formats 1 through 4, and will use as examples charts provided by the Department of Energy (DOE). This is done to emphasize the point that the earned value approach has broader applications than simply the procurement of DOD hardware.

CPR Format 2 -- Functional Categories

The data contained in Format 1 -- WBS, and Format 2 --Functional Categories, must contain the same bottom line, i.e., they must both add up to the same totals. Prior to the introduction of computers, this requirement kept certain young men at work all night long preparing for a customer review, since the customer always wanted to see the data by hardware/statement of work, and the normal practice in industry was, and is, to manage a contract by functional organization. All this was covered earlier in Chapter 7 on the "Work Breakdown Structure."

Format 2 reports reflect the contractor's normal organizational departments or functional categories, usually those that were reviewed at the time of validation. However, if a given program manager prefers a different organizational breakout, the government would likely accede to the request because, typically, Format 2 reports are used by the contractor for their internal management of a contract. These reports are at the top contract level (WBS Level 1), and figure 12.5

Figure 12.4 CPR Format 1 -- Work Breakdown Structures

FORM ERDA-144 (3-76)

U.S. ENERGY RESEARCH AND DEVELOPMENT ADMINISTRATION

COST PERFORMANCE REPORT—WORK BREAKDOWN STRUCTURE (Format 1)   Page ____ of ____

| CONTRACTOR: A.U.S., Inc. | CONTRACT TYPE/NO. CPFF(10-10-10-2) (2222) | PROJECT NAME/NUMBER Energistic | REPORT PERIOD 12-1-75 to 12-31-75 | SIGNATURE J. S. Browning |
| LOCATION: Germantown, Maryland | | | | TITLE Project Director   DATE 1-8-76 |

| QUANTITY 1 | NEGOTIATED COST $292,420 | EST. COST OF AUTH. UNPRICED WORK -0- | TARGET PROFIT/FEE % $8773/3% | TARGET PRICE $301,193 | ESTIMATED PRICE $290,4?9 | SHARE RATIO N/A |

| ITEM (1) WORK BREAKDOWN STRUCTURE | CURRENT PERIOD | | | | | CUMULATIVE TO DATE | | | | | AT COMPLETION | | |
| | BUDGETED COST | | ACTUAL COST WORK PERFORMED (4) | VARIANCE | | BUDGETED COST | | ACTUAL COST WORK PERFORMED (9) | VARIANCE | | BUDGETED (12) | LATEST REVISED ESTIMATE (13) | VARIANCE (14) |
	WORK SCHEDULED (2)	WORK PERFORMED (3)		SCHEDULE (5)	COST (6)	WORK SCHEDULED (7)	WORK PERFORMED (8)		SCHEDULE (10)	COST (11)			
NSSS	4140	3901	4134	(239)	(233)	29775	25348	32235	(4427)	(6887)	76234	76584	(350)
SITE AND BLDGS.	5076	5064	5147	(12)	(83)	24772	23506	26008	(1266)	(2502)	82494	83255	(761)
BALANCE OF PLANT	1080	1076	1055	(4)	21	6399	6185	6496	(214)	(311)	23026	23239	(213)
TRAINING	72	75	80	3	(5)	274	271	285	(3)	(14)	1930	1930	0
SUPPORT EQUIP.	24	23	23	(1)	0	119	115	114	(4)	1	2386	2386	0
SYS. TEST & EVAL.	760	685	788	(75)	(103)	6487	5655	6975	(832)	(1320)	26681	26995	(314)
PROJECT MGT.	630	642	624	12	18	7570	7380	7470	(190)	(90)	18836	18836	0
DATA	136	147	140	11	7	886	911	911	25	0	8362	8062	300
FUEL	0	0	0	0	0	0	0	0	0	0	6699	6699	0
GENERAL AND ADMINISTRATIVE	1632	1591	1643	(41)	(52)	10451	9504	11028	(947)	(1524)	35234	33974	1260
UNDISTRIBUTED BUDGET											-	-	
SUBTOTAL (Less G&A)	11918	11613	11991	(305)	(378)	76282	69371	80494	(5911)	(11123)	246648	247986	9200
MANAGEMENT RESERVE											10538		10538
TOTAL	13550	13204	13634	(346)	(430)	86733	78875	91522	(7858)	(12647)	292420	281960	10460

(All Entries in Thousands of Dollars)

RECONCILIATION TO CONTRACT BUDGET BASELINE

| VARIANCE ADJUSTMENT | | |
| TOTAL CONTRACT VARIANCE | | |

Source: U.S. Department of Energy, Performance Management System-Data Analysis Guide (Washington, D.C., 1976), page 4.

reflects the Format 2 report. Once again, a photocopy of a computer printout may be substituted.

CPR Format 3 -- Baseline

A couple of chapters ago there was a discussion on baseline management, which in C/SCSC is called the Performance Measurement Baseline or PMB. As a way of review, included in the PMB are all the issued budgets, plus the assigned but undistributed budget. Outside of the PMB is the management reserve. The purpose of this report is to tell the government precisely what is included in the current CPR and, by elimination, what is not in the CPR.

Format 3, as shown in figure 12.6, starts with the original target costs and traces all changes made thereto. Particular detail is provided by item, for all changes which occurred to the PMB during the month.

CPR Format 4 -- Manpower Loading

This report uses the same functional or organizational categories as those used in Format 2. But while Format 2 expressed costs in dollars, this report reflects equivalent manpower. For those who might have forgotten what constitutes an equivalent man month, such represents a value equal to one month's work, regardless of how many persons it took to achieve it. For example, two people working half-time equals 1.0 man month. Two people working 50 percent overtime, or 60 hours per week, would equal 3.0 man months. The format requires the rounding off of values, for example 11.6 MM would be rounded to 12.

Figure 12.7 illustrates a specific format for Format 4. This type of report also lends itself nicely to a computer printout, which may be substituted for the form. The report calls for a display of actual man months for the current period, total man months to date, a six-month projection, and the total man months at completion -- EAC. If there are significant differences between a previous and the current EAC, the differences must be explained in a Problem Analysis Report.

CPR Format 5 -- Problem Analysis Report
(or Variance Analysis Report)

This report is a narrative summary of what went wrong in CPR Formats 1 through 4. The subject was covered earlier under Baseline Management, and the only point worth repeating is that while the specific format is essentially left up to the contractor, each PAR must cover the following matters:

1. Prepared by the lowest responsible manager of the work package, and not by an outsider

Figure 12.5 CPR Format 2 -- Functional Categories

FORM E₁ A
(1-76)

U.S. ENERGY RESEARCH AND ...PMENT ADMINISTRATION
COST PERFORMANCE REPORT–FUNCTIONAL CATEGORIES Format 2

CONTRACTOR: A.U.S. Inc.

LOCATION: Germantown, Maryland

CONTRACT TYPE/NUMBER: CPFF/(10-10-10-2) (2222)

PROJECT NAME/NUMBER: Energistic

Page 2 of ____

REPORT PERIOD 12-1-75 to 12-31-75

ORGANIZATIONAL OR FUNCTIONAL CATEGORY	CURRENT PERIOD					CUMULATIVE TO DATE					AT COMPLETION		
	BUDGETED COST WORK SCHED-ULED	BUDGETED COST WORK PER-FORMED	ACTUAL COST WORK PER-FORMED	VARIANCE SCHEDULE	VARIANCE COST	BUDGETED COST WORK SCHED-ULED	BUDGETED COST WORK PER-FORMED	ACTUAL COST WORK PER-FORMED	VARIANCE SCHEDULE	VARIANCE COST	BUDGETED	LATEST REVISED ESTIMATE	VARI-ANCE
(1)	(2)	(3)	(4)	(5)	(6)	(7)	(8)	(9)	(10)	(11)	(12)	(13)	(14)
Engineering	6351	6173	6664	(178)	(491)	37249	33493	40455	(3756)	(6962)	108798	109536	(738)
Tooling	12	11	13	(1)	(2)	88	76	83	(12)	(7)	4257	4257	0
Quality Control	15	15	16	0	(1)	162	162	170	0	(8)	876	876	0
Construction	526	524	532	(2)	(8)	3005	2997	3119	(8)	(122)	27463	27463	0
Procurement	231	230	232	(1)	(2)	1874	1870	1901	(4)	(31)	13729	13729	0
Material Overhead	12	12	12	0	0	94	94	95	0	(1)	686	686	0
Subcontract	3933	3784	3678	(149)	106	25080	22117	26005	(2963)	(3888)	63418	64018	(600)
Other:													
Training	72	75	80	3	(5)	274	271	285	(3)	(14)	2386	2386	0
Proj. Management	630	642	624	12	18	7570	7380	7470	(190)	(90)	18336	18336	0
Data	136	147	140	11	7	886	911	911	25	0	6699	6699	0
Mgment Reserve											10538		10538
GENERAL AND ADMINISTRATIVE	1632	1591	1643	(305)	(378)	10451	9504	11028	(947)	(1524)	35234	33974	1260
UNDISTRIBUTED BUDGET											-	-	
TOTAL	13550	13204	13634	(346)	(430)	86733	78875	91522	(7858)	(12647)	292420	281960	10460

Source: U.S. Department of Energy, Performance Management System-Data Analysis Guide (Washington, D.C., 1976), page 5.

Figure 12.6 CPR Format 3 -- Baseline

FORM ERDA-144B (3-76)

U.S. ENERGY RESEARCH AND DEVELOPMENT ADMINISTRATION
COST PERFORMANCE REPORT—BASELINE (Format 3)

Page 3 of 7

CONTRACTOR: A.U.S., Inc.
LOCATION: Germantown, Md.
CONTRACT TYPE/NUMBER: CPFF/(10-10-10-2) (2222)
PROJECT NAME/NUMBER: Energistic
REPORT PERIOD: 12-1-75 to 12-31-75

(1) ORIGINAL CONTRACT TARGET COST	(2) NEGOTIATED CONTRACT CHANGES	(3) CURRENT TARGET COST (1)+(2)	(4) ESTIMATED COST OF AUTHORIZED, UNPRICED WORK	(5) CONTRACT BUDGET BASELINE (3)+(4)	(6) TOTAL ALLOCATED BUDGET	(7) DIFFERENCE (5)-(6) (See Form ERDA-144D)
$228900	$63520	$292420	-0-	$292420	$292420	-0-

BUDGETED COST FOR WORK SCHEDULED (NON-CUMULATIVE)

ITEM	BCWS CUMULATIVE TO DATE (2)	SIX MONTH FORECAST +1 (3)	+2 (4)	+3 (5)	+4 (6)	+5 (7)	+6 (8)	ENTER SPECIFIED PERIOD 3 Q (9)	4 Q (10)	2 Y (11)	3 Y (12)	(13)	TOTAL BUDGET (14)
PM BASELINE (BEGINNING OF PERIOD)	76282	11095	11461	11461	11461	11461	11461	17192	17192	45027	12555		236648
(LIST BASELINE CHANGES AUTHORIZED DURING REPORT PERIOD)													
None													- 0 -
Management Reserve Applied													10000
GENERAL AND ADMINISTRATIVE	10451	1534	1707	1844	1844	1844	1844	2479	2355	6169	1720		35234
UNDISTRIBUTED BUDGET													-
PM BASELINE (END OF PERIOD)	76282	11195	12461	13461	13461	13461	13461	1C092	17192	45027	12555		246648
MANAGEMENT RESERVE													10538
TOTAL	86733	12729	14168	15305	15305	15305	15305	20571	19547	51196	14275		292420

Source: U.S. Department of Energy, Performance Management System-Data Analysis Guide (Washington, D.C., 1976), page 6.

Figure 12.7 CPR Format 4 -- Manpower Loading

FORM ...44C (3-76)

U.S. ENERGY RESEARCH AND ...VELOPMENT ADMINISTRATION
COST PERFORMANCE REPORT—MANPOWER LOADING (Format 4)

CONTRACTOR: A.U.S. Inc.
LOCATION: Germantown, Maryland

CONTRACT TYPE/NUMBER: CPFF/ (10-10-10-2) (2222)
PROJECT NAME/NUMBER: Energistic
Page 4 of 7
REPORT PERIOD: 12-1-75 to 12-31-75

ORGANIZATIONAL OR FUNCTIONAL CATEGORY	CURRENT MONTH		CURRENT FY 76		CUM. ACTUAL TO DATE	FORECAST FY 1976						BALANCE FY 77	NEXT FY 78	BALANCE TO COMPLETE	ESTIMATE AT COMPLETION
	Planned	Actual	Planned	Actual		Jan	Feb	Mar	Apr	May	June				
	(1)	(2)	(3)	(4)	(5)	(6)	(7)	(8)	(9)	(10)	(11)	(12)	(13)	(14)	(15)
Direct															
Engineering	2658	2680	9908	10100	15086	2734	2812	2972	2972	2972	2972	8018	7236	78	47852
Tooling	12	12	36	30	42	15	15	15	315	315	315	997	123	0	2152
Quality Ctl.	15	15	84	83	96	17	17	17	17	17	17	108	177	9	492
Construction	440	426	2120	2204	2754	608	608	608	608	508	608	3648	6936	315	17301
Other															
Training	25	20	50	50	96	25	60	60	60	50	50	300	43	0	744
Proj. Mgt.	128	130	1600	1630	1821	158	158	158	158	158	158	948	1500	263	5480
Data	90	90	110	116	320	107	107	107	107	107	107	1324	2735	289	5310
Total Direct	3368	3373	13908	14213	20215	3664	3777	3937	4237	4227	4227	15343	18750	954	79331
Total Indirect	672	680	2810	3012	4043	733	755	787	847	845	845	3068	3750	191	15864
TOTAL	4040	4053	16718	17225	24258	4397	4532	4724	5084	5072	5072	18411	22500	1145	95195

(Figures Are Equivalent Man-Months)

Source: U.S. Department of Energy, Performance Management System-Data Analysis Guide (Washington, D.C., 1976), page 7.

2. Each cost and/or schedule variance must be explained with a separate PAR, and its full impact outlined.
3. A recovery plan must be specified
4. The next higher supervision must review and sign the PAR

Figure 12.8 illustrates a PAR, here termed a Variance Analysis Report. Although the format is different, all the essential points are covered.

The CPR is the heart of C/SCSC and provides demonstrative proof to a customer that the intent of DODI 7000.2, which imposes the criteria on a contract, has been properly implemented. It provides the customer with a status position which can be verified on site at the contractor's plant.

The CPR is used by the customer to:

- monitor and evaluate contract performance;
- to isolate the early identification of problems, and their size;
- to provide status information.

The inability of a contractor to submit a CPR for whatever reason, and to consistently track performance to it, sends out a clear signal to the customer that something is wrong. In such cases a detailed management probe might be in order. Thus, the CPR is an extremely important document for management, both contractor and customer.

C/SSR -- THE POOR MAN'S CPR

There is another report that is used on contracts which are not of sufficient size to warrant a CPR. This report is called a C/SSR, Cost/Schedule Status Report.

The present threshold at which a C/SSR is generally required is $2 million and a contract period in excess of 12 months. With continuing inflation, a more reasonable dollar value may well be $5 or $10 million in the future. However, programs of a critical nature in the defense establishment may well require a full CPR no matter what their size. It is inappropriate to require either a CPR or C/SSR under a firm-fixed price contractual arrangement, in most situations. While the total dollar value of contracts requiring a CPR is greater, the C/SSR has had a broader impact on the industry. As one Air Force official states: "Here at ASD for every CPR we impose, we receive over seven C/SSRs from contractors."[1]

Under the rules which govern the C/SSR, a contractor must be in a position to describe how the work was measured (BCWP), and most of the same definitions which govern C/SCSC activity, as specified in DODI 7000.2, apply to the C/SSR. Reporting of costs is typically at WBS level 3, but a contractor must be in a position to trace deeper if

Figure 12.8 CPR Format 5 -- Problem Analysis Report

VARIANCE ANALYSIS REPORT

CONTRACT NAME	DATE

TO:	CC:

SUMMARY LEVEL DESCRIPTION	SUMMARY LEVEL NO.

TYPE OF PROBLEM	VARIANCE		TREND ANALYSIS	CUM TO DATE VARIANCE			
	$	%		SCHEDULE		COST	
				$	%	$	%
☐ CUM. TO DATE SCHEDULE (BCWP-BSWS)			CURRENT MONTH				
☐ CUM. TO DATE COST (BCWP-ACTUALS)			LAST MONTH				
☐ COST AT COMPL. (BAC-EAC)							
☐ TECHNICAL PERFORMANCE			MONTH BEFORE LAST				

PROBLEM DESCRIPTION/CAUSE

IMPACT (NOTE: EFFECT ON TECH. PERF., COST AND/OR SCHEDULE)

ACTION REQUIRED/TAKEN	RESP. ORG/ INDIVIDUAL	SCH. DATE	COMP DATE

PREPARED BY	APPROVED BY	
		PAGE _____ OF _____

Source: Form courtesy of Aeronutronic, Newport Beach, California.

148

variance parameters are exceeded. Therefore, cost segregation must be at the lowest WBS Levels, as with the CPR. No Validation or Subsequent Application Review is required of the contractor under the C/SSR approach. While the rules on the CPR are firm, on the C/SSR they are negotiable between the customer and contractor or sub-contractor.

The C/SSR has three sections:

1. The C/SSR summary form (see figure 12.9)
2. A brief narrative on status
3. Problem Analysis Reports -- PARs (if thresholds are exceeded)

Note that the C/SSR summary, as shown in figure 12.9, reflects only the cumulative to date position and the Estimate At Completion (EAC). It does not require the current period (monthly) status. Considerable contractor preparation costs are saved by dropping the monthly status period. All work authorized, both priced and unpriced, must be included in the C/SSR, as with the CPR.

The C/SSR was devised by the DOD in an attempt to improve the management of small contracts, but without imposing excessive reporting requirements (i.e., CPRs). By standardizing the format, the proliferation of unique reports is somewhat avoided. But the very nature of the C/SSR allows for flexibility, as the joint service guide which covers the report states:

> For CPR reporting, BCWS and BCWP must be the result of the direct summation of work package budgets. The C/SSR permits the determination of these values through any reasonably accurate, mutually acceptable means.... Thus, the C/SSR allows the contractor greater flexibility in the selection of internal performance measurement techniques than does the CPR.[2]

In addition to the C/SSR, the smaller contracts may well require the submission of the Contractor Funds Status Report -- CFSR, mentioned earlier, as well as the CCDR, to be covered next.

CCDR -- CONTRACTOR COST DATA REPORTING

The fourth and last report specifically required in conjunction with C/SCSC goes by the title of Contractor Cost Data Reporting -- CCDR, a generic name actually covering four distinct cost reports. The purpose of the CCDR is to provide the procuring military command and, likely more importantly, the Department of Defense with the means to prepare an independent cost estimate of all their major acquisitions, and the means to compare one system (e.g., aircraft)

Figure 12.9 The Cost/Schedule Status Report

COST/SCHEDULE STATUS REPORT

CONTRACTOR		CONTRACT TYPE/NO. F33615-80-C-	PROGRAM NAME/NUMBER ASSEMBLY REQUIREMENTS AND DESIGN	REPORT PERIOD 9-25-81	SIGNATURE TITLE & DATE	FORM APPROVED OMB NUMBER
LOCATION						
RDT&E ☑ PRODUCTION ☐						

CONTRACT DATA

(1) ORIGINAL CONTRACT TARGET COST	(2) NEGOTIATED CONTRACT CHANGES	(3) CURRENT TARGET COST (1) + (2)	(4) ESTIMATED COST OF AUTHORIZED, UNPRICED WORK	(5) CONTRACT BUDGET BASELINE (1) + (4)
$1,138,090	-	$1,138,090		$1,138,090

PERFORMANCE DATA

WORK BREAKDOWN STRUCTURE	BUDGETED COST WORK SCHEDULED	BUDGETED COST WORK PERFORMED	ACTUAL COST WORK PERFORMED	VARIANCE SCHEDULE	VARIANCE COST	AT COMPLETION BUDGETED	AT COMPLETION LATEST REVISED ESTIMATE	AT COMPLETION VARIANCE
PHASE I								
4.1 TASK I–ESTABLISH PROJECT MASTER PLAN & SCHEDULE	$ 31,361	$ 31,361	$ 31,420	$ -0-	(59)	$ 31,361	$ 30,625	$ 736
4.2 TASK II–UNDERSTAND THE ASSEMBLY PROBLEM	261,553	211,961	*206,348	(49,592)	5,613	1,013,061	1,060,235	(47,174)
5.0/6.0 DOCUMENTATION	20,161	20,161	8,006	-0-	12,155	87,283	84,720	2,563
SUBTOTAL	$313,075	$263,483	$245,774	(49,592)	$ 17,709	$1,131,705	$1,175,580	(43,875)
COST OF MONEY	1,617	1,617	3,927	-0-	(2,310)	6,385	17,536	(11,151)
MANAGEMENT RESERVE						-0-		
TOTAL	$314,692	$265,100	$249,701	(49,592)	$ 15,339	$1,138,090	$1,193,116	(55,026)

*NOTE: Actuals include $113,893 subcontractor costs invoiced but not booked, $1,598 travel costs not booked.

with all other related systems. The CCDR provides the defense establishment with its historical cost data bank.

The CCDR is a requirement defined in DODI 7000.11, (Appendix D to this book) and is implemented under a joint service approach with a guide entitled appropriately: Contractor Cost Data Reporting (CCDR), (NAVMAT P-5241; AMCP 715-8; AFLC P800-15; AFSCP 800-15) dated 5 November 1973. The CCDR superceded two earlier reports entitled the CIR -- Cost Information Reports and the PIR -- Procurement Information Reports.

Contracts with a value of less than $2 million are not generally required to prepare a CCDR, but all programs which exceed that value are placed into two categories for purposes of defining reporting requirements:

- Category I are acquisitions estimated to require in excess of $75 million for research, development, test, and evaluation; or production in excess of $300 million. All four reports are required.

- Category II are selected contracts, or specific line items from Category I above. Only two of the four reports are required (1921-1 and 1921-2) in this category, generally at contract completion.

And contrary to the normal rule with respect to fixed-price contracts, Category I procurements sometimes require the submittal of a CCDR when the effort is deemed to be of particular importance to the DOD. The CCDR applies to both prime and subcontracted efforts.

Since the primary purpose of the CCDR is to provide the defense establishment with the ability to make independent cost estimates, and to compare the costs of one system against all other similar systems, the data must obviously be reported in a standardized format to be useful. The WBS concept as specified under Military Standard 881 provides the definition of reporting format for the CCDR.

While the responsibility for implementing the CCDR on contracts rests with the major command buying the system (e.g., Air Force Systems Command), they must do so in accordance with a CCDR Plan, submitted to the Department of Defense, more specifically to the Cost Analysis Improvement Group (CAIG) of the Office of the Secretary of Defense (OSD), for approval. One of the principal reasons for the CAIG review and approval is to assess the compatibility of reporting format being proposed in the plan with other elements of its historical data base, using the proposed WBS as the standardized format. Figure 12.10 illustrates the CCDR Plan, as specified in the CCDR joint implementation guide.

And now for a brief description of each of the four parts of the CCDR, which are:

1. Cost Data Summary Report -- DD Form 1921
2. Functional Cost-Hour Report -- DD Form 1921-1
3. Progress Curve Report -- DD Form 1921-2
4. Plant-Wide Data Report -- DD Form 1921-3

Figure 12.10 Contractor Cost Data Reporting Plan

CONTRACTOR COST DATA REPORTING PLAN	1. PROGRAM	2. ☐ CAT I ☐ CAT II	3. ☐ INITIAL SUBMISSION ☐ CHANGE ☐ RFP ☐ CONTRACT	4. ☐ PBS ☐ CONTRACT WBS

5. DATA AS OF	6. REVIEW & REFERENCE NO.	7. REPORT DATE	8. PREPARED BY	9. LOCATION	10. DATA STORAGE LOCATION

11. LINE NO.	12. WBS LEVEL	13. REPORTING ELEMENTS	14. PROGRAM CODE	15. CONTRACTOR	16. TYPE CONTRACT	17. PROGRAM TOTALS				18. REPORT FREQUENCY									
						RDT&E		PROCUREMENT		CCDR FORM NOS									
						UNITS	COST (Million)	UNITS	COST (Million)	DD FORM 1921		DD FORM 1921-1		DD FORM 1921-2	DD FORM 1921-3				
										C	P	C	P						

The Cost Data Summary Report (1921)

This report provides cost data by WBS element, separating the nonrecurring from recurring costs, displaying total costs to date, and the EAC. Costs by WBS element normally go to level 3, but they may by agreement go to lower WBS levels on selected elements of particular interest, e.g., program risk areas. Costs for each WBS element represent total burdened costs, but without G & A and profit. On the last page of the report, the subtotal of WBS element costs are shown, then management reserve, G & A, and profits are added to reach a total price for the contract. Form 1921 is shown in figure 12.11.

A report with perhaps 75 WBS reporting elements will run about three pages in length. This report is due not less than annually, and frequently quarterly or semiannually depending upon the critical nature of the program.

The Functional Cost-Hour Report (1921-1)

In this report, each of the WBS elements shown as a one-line entry in the Cost Data Summary Report above are broken down into a one-page summary by detail cost element, and then further subdivided into a separate page on nonrecurring and another page for recurring costs. Therefore, a program reporting 75 WBS elements will run 225 pages in length.

All of the CCDRs may be reported using a photocopy of a contractor's computer report as long as the same data and format are used. Because of the size of this report, the use of computer reporting is almost a necessity. The Functional Cost-Hour report format is shown in figure 12.12, using a computer printout to satisfy this report.

The Progress Curve Report (1921-2)

This report is prepared to reflect the hours and costs required to manufacture the production units/lots on a contract. It measures progress toward the reduction in hours/costs to build each article. The data from this report are displayed on learning curves to highlight how well, or poorly, a contractor is doing to reduce the hours required per unit. It is an important report used by the DOD to prepare parametric cost estimates by program, costs per pound, etc., and to compare one system against other systems.

These reports are due at the completion of each production lot, but not less frequently than annually. Actual costs for units completed are shown, plus a projection of estimated future performance. Figure 12.13 reflects the report format.

The Plant-Wide Data Report (1921-3)

This is a report that reflects the indirect costs for all activity in a contractor's plant, with particular emphasis on any differences bet-

Figure 12.11 CCDR Cost Data Summary Report (1921)

CLASSIFICATION

COST DATA SUMMARY REPORT (Dollars in Thousands)

Form Approved OMB No. 22R0222

1. PROGRAM	2.		5. REPORT AS OF
XYZ	[X] CONTRACT [ ] RFP [ ] PROGRAM ESTIMATE	[X] RDT&E [ ] PROCUREMENT	26 June 1981
			6. FY FUNDED: 1981

7. CONTRACT TYPE	8. CONTRACT PRICE	9. CONTRACT CEILING	10. [ ] PRIME/ASSOCIATE [X] SUBCONTRACTOR (Name and Address, include ZIP Code)	MULTIPLE YEAR CONTRACT [X] YES [ ] NO	11. NAME OF CUSTOMER (Subcontractor use only)
CPIF/AF	N/A	N/A	Ajax Aircraft		USAF

CONTRACT LINE ITEM	REPORTING ELEMENTS	ELEMENT CODE	TO DATE – COSTS INCURRED			AT COMPLETION			
			NON-RECURRING	RECURRING	TOTAL	UNITS	NON-RECURRING	RECURRING	TOTAL
314	AIR VEHICLE/SUBSYSTEM GROUND TESTS	2114	18003	–	18003		18556	–	18556
355	ARMAMENT/WEAPON DELIVERY INTEG. TESTS	2117	10	–	10		10	–	10
358	FLIGHT SIMULATION PROGRAM	2118	–	–	–		–	–	–
361	CONTRACTOR FLIGHT TESTS	2119	8452	–	8452		8712	–	8712
376	MISCELLANEOUS TEST PROGRAM	2190	4181	–	4181		4310	–	4310
390	DROP AND ACCELERATED LOADS TEST PROGRAM	2191	4337	–	4337		4470	–	4470
395	TECHNICAL EVALUATION	2200	–	–	–		–	–	–
396	FLIGHT TEST SUPPORT SYSTEM	2220	–	–	–		–	–	–
402	MOCKUPS	2400	4621	–	4621		4625	–	4625
406	TEST AND EVALUATION	2500	3243	–	3243		3270	–	3270
423	SYSTEM ENGR./PROJECT MGMT. (Other than ILS)	3XXX	27223	–	27228		27231	–	27231
424	SYSTEM ENGINEERING (Other than ILS)	3100	11503	–	11508		11508	–	11508
440	PROJECT MANAGEMENT (Other than ILS)	3200	6465	–	6466		6469	–	6469
457	SYSTEM ENGINEERING (ILS)	5100	7154	–	7154		7154	–	7154
458	LOGISTIC SUPPORT ANALYSIS PROCESS	5110	6594	–	6594		6594	–	6594
467	ILS FOR ENGINEERING CHANGE PROPOSALS	5120	–	–	–		–	–	–
468	DEPOT AND INTERMEDIATE REWORK ANALYSIS	5130	–	–	–		–	–	–
472	FACILITIES REQUIREMENTS ANALYSIS	5140	–	–	–		–	–	–
473	GROUND SUPPORT EQUIP. REQMTS. PROGRAM	5150	55	–	55		55	–	55
474	SPARE AND REPAIR PARTS PROGRAM	5150	310	–	310		310	–	310
475	TRAINING SYSTEM DEVELOPMENT	5170	195	–	195		195	–	195
476	PKG. HANDLING STORAGE & TRANSP. (PHS & T)	5180	–	–	–		–	–	–
477	PROJECT MANAGEMENT (ILS)	5200	2100	–	2100		2100	–	2100
478	ILS PLANNING	5210	1396	–	1396		1396	–	1396
480	ILS, DEMO & EVALUATION PROGRAM	5220	9	–	9		9	–	9
485	SITE/UNIT ACTIVATION PROGRAM	5230	–	–	–		–	–	–
486	PREOPERATIONAL (INTERIM) SUPPORT	5240	695	–	695		695	–	695
446	DATA (Other than ILS)	4XXX	2401	–	2401		2428	–	2428
447	ENGINEERING (Other than ILS)	4100	938	–	938		937	–	937
451	MANAGEMENT DATA (Other than ILS)	4200	1121	–	1121		1149	–	1149

REMARKS

NAME OF PERSON TO BE CONTACTED	SIGNATURE	DATE
		23 July 1981

DD FORM 1921, 1 AUG 73

CLASSIFICATION

Figure 12.12 CCDR Functional Cost-Hour Report (1921-1)

FUNCTIONAL COST-HOUR REPORT   PROGRAM: **XYZ**   REPORT AS OF: 26 JUNE 1981
DOLLARS IN: THOUSANDS   HOURS IN: THOUSANDS   X CONTRACT PROGRAM ESTIMATE   RFP

RDT&E   X   PROCUREMENT   OTHER   MULTIPLE YEAR CONTRACT: YES   X   NO   FY FUNDED: 1979

X   SUBCONTRACTOR: **Ajax Aircraft**

NAME OF CUSTOMER: **USAF**
REPORTING ELEMENT: TOTAL WBS 1100 AIRFRAME RECURRING

FUNCTIONAL CATEGORIES	ADJUSTMENTS TO PREVIOUS REPORTS	CONTRACTOR		SUBCONTRACT OR OUTSIDE PROD AND SERV		TOTAL	
		TO DATE	AT COMPL.	TO DATE	AT COMPL.	TO DATE	AT COMPL.
DIRECT LABOR HOURS	0	369	370	11	11	380	381
DIRECT LABOR DOLLARS	0	4480	4486	135	135	4615	4622
OVERHEAD	0	7392	7401	203	204	7595	7605
MATERIAL	0	72	72	10	10	82	82
OTHER DIRECT CHARGES	0	2284	2278	35	35	2319	2313
TOTAL ENGINEERING DOLLARS	0	14228	14237	384	385	14612	14622
DIRECT LABOR HOURS	0	238	238	9	9	247	247
DIRECT LABOR DOLLARS	0	2405	2406	81	81	2485	2487
OVERHEAD	0	4109	4111	115	115	4224	4226
MATERIALS AND PURCHASED TOOLS	0	1483	1489	28	28	1511	1517
OTHER DIRECT CHARGES	0	191	190	6	5	197	196
TOTAL TOOLING DOLLARS	0	8188	8196	230	230	8418	8425
DIRECT LABOR HOURS	0	222	223	23	23	245	245
DIRECT LABOR DOLLARS	0	2140	2141	214	214	2354	2355
OVERHEAD	0	3667	3665	299	299	3966	3964
OTHER DIRECT CHARGES	0	222	228	16	15	238	244
TOTAL QUALITY CONTOL DOLLARS	0	6029	6034	529	529	6558	6563
DIRECT LABOR HOURS	0	1412	1412	162	162	1574	1574
DIRECT LABOR DOLLARS	0	13280	13276	1393	1394	14673	14670
OVERHEAD	0	22830	22816	1949	1950	24779	24766
MATERIALS AND PURCHASED PARTS	0	7076	7241	503	505	7579	7745
OTHER DIRECT CHARGES	0	1387	1393	100	104	1487	1497
TOTAL MANUFACTURING DOLLARS	0	44573	44726	3945	3953	48518	48679
PURCHASED EQUIPMENT	0	4894	4933	0	0	4894	4933
MATERIAL OVERHEAD	0	1961	1979	57	58	2018	2037
OTHER COSTS NOT SHOWN ELSEWHERE	0					0	
TOTAL COST LESS G&A	0	79873	80105	5145	5155	85018	85260
G&A	0	0	0	411	413	411	413
TOTAL PLUS G&A	0	79873	80105	5556	5568	85429	85673
FEE OR PROFIT	0	0	0	499	501	499	501
TOTAL OF LINES 29 AND 30	0	79873	80105	6055	6069	85928	86174

DD 1921-1

Figure 12.13 CCDR Progress Curve Report (1921-2)

SECURITY CLASSIFICATION

PROGRESS CURVE REPORT (Recurring Cost Only)		1. PROGRAM		Form Approved OMB No. 22R0322	
2. DOLLARS IN	3. HOURS IN	5. CONTRACT		6. REPORT FOR _____ MONTHS	
4. TOTAL UNITS ACCEPTED PRIOR TO THIS REPORT				ENDING: _____	
7. MULTIPLE YEAR CONTRACT [ ] YES [ ] NO 8. FY FUNDED:	9. [ ] PRIME/ASSOCIATE [ ] SUBCONTRACTOR (Name and address; Include ZIP Code)			10. NAME OF CUSTOMER (Subcontractor use only)	

SECTION A

11. REPORTING ELEMENT(S)

ITEM	UNITS/LOTS ACCEPTED					ESTIMATE OF NEXT UNIT/LOT TO BE ACCEPTED	TO COMPLETE CONTRACT
	a	b	c	d	e	f	g
1. MODEL AND SERIES							
2. FIRST UNIT OF LOT							
3. LAST UNIT OF LOT							
4. CONCURRENT UNITS							
CHARACTERISTICS 5. 6. 7.							
CONTRACTOR DATA (PER UNIT/LOT)							
8. DIRECT QUALITY CONTROL MAN-HOURS							
9. DIRECT MANUFACTURING MAN-HOURS							
10. QUALITY CONTROL DIRECT LABOR DOLLARS	$	$	$	$	$	$	$
11. MANUFACTURING DIRECT LABOR DOLLARS	$	$	$	$	$	$	$
12. RAW MATERIAL & PURCHASED PARTS DOLLARS	$	$	$	$	$	$	$
13. PURCHASED EQUIPMENT DOLLARS	$	$	$	$	$	$	$
14. TOTAL DOLLARS	$	$	$	$	$	$	$
SUBCONTRACT/OUTSIDE PROD. & SERV.							
15. DIRECT QUALITY CONTROL MAN-HOURS							
16. DIRECT MANUFACTURING MAN-HOURS							
17. TOTAL MAN-HOURS							
18. QUALITY CONTROL DIRECT LABOR DOLLARS	$	$	$	$	$	$	$
19. MANUFACTURING DIRECT LABOR DOLLARS	$	$	$	$	$	$	$
20. RAW MATERIAL & PURCHASED PARTS DOLLARS	$	$	$	$	$	$	$
21. PURCHASED EQUIPMENT DOLLARS	$	$	$	$	$	$	$
22. TOTAL DOLLARS	$	$	$	$	$	$	$
UNIT TOTAL [ ] AVERAGE [ ]							
23. DIRECT QUALITY CONTROL MAN-HOURS							
24. DIRECT MANUFACTURING MAN-HOURS							
25. TOTAL MAN-HOURS							
26. QUALITY CONTROL DIRECT LABOR DOLLARS	$	$	$	$	$	$	$
27. MANUFACTURING DIRECT LABOR DOLLARS	$	$	$	$	$	$	$
28. RAW MATERIAL & PURCHASED PARTS DOLLARS	$	$	$	$	$	$	$
29. PURCHASED EQUIPMENT DOLLARS	$	$	$	$	$	$	$
30. TOTAL DOLLARS	$	$	$	$	$	$	$
31. % SUBCONTRACT OR OUTSIDE PROD. & SERV.							
MFG FLOW TIME							
MOS OR QTRS 32. START							
33. FINISH							
34.							
35.							
36.							
37.							
38.							
39.							

SECTION B

DD FORM 1 AUG 73 1921-2

156

ween commercial and government programs. While the other three CCDRs are program specific, this one deals with all contracts and business in a given firm.

The reports are due annually, and if submitted on one contract, a photocopy will suffice for all other requests. The report covers the current period, and projects two years into the future. Figure 12.14 illustrates the format for this report.

Because the Plant-Wide Data Report contains a company's proprietary or business sensitive data, these reports are normally sent directly to the government, i.e., the prime contractor (if a private firm) is bypassed with this submittal.

CONSISTENCY AND RECONCILIATION
BETWEEN C/SCS REPORTS

Without belaboring the subject of reporting, it must be mentioned that when multiple reports are due on a given contract, they must be consistent with each other, or at least be reconcilable to each other. This is particularly true when they are reporting data as of the same time period, e.g., December 31 of a given year.

While any given contract is likely to have three reports due (a CFSR, CPR or C/SSR, and CCDR), the primary difficulty seems to be between the quarterly CFSR and the monthly CPR or C/SSR. Two issues seem to cause the problem: Profit/Fee and Termination Liability. If one understands that the primary purpose of the CFSR is to forecast the government's liability at any point in time, including the contractor's profit and estimated termination liabilities, and that the CPR is a monthly status report which focuses on the Performance Measurement Baseline -- PMB -- which excludes both profit and termination liability, much of the confusion vanishes.

Perhaps a specific illustration, using charts from the CFSR and CPR will eliminate the difficulty. Shown in figure 12.15 are the forms used in the CFSR and Format 1 from the CPR covering the WBS. The five letters shown in figure 12.15 relate specific sections to each other and are summarized as follows:

Letter	Subject	CFSR	CPR
Ⓐ	Reporting Date/Period	same	same
Ⓑ	Definitized Work/ Target Price	same	same
Ⓒ	Non Definitized Work	price with fee	costs without fee
Ⓓ	Actual Costs to Date	includes both fee and estimated value of termination liability	costs only, no fee and no termination liability
Ⓔ	Estimate at Completion	price with fee	costs only

Figure 12.14 CCDR Plant-Wide Data Report (1921-3)

PLANT-WIDE DATA REPORT

1. CONTRACTOR
2. PLANT LOCATION
3. REPORT PERIOD ENDING
4. DATE SUBMITTED

OVERHEAD ACCUMULATION, DISTRIBUTION AND APPLICATION

☐ ACTUAL ☐ ESTIMATE

SECTION A

TIME PERIOD			① FROM / TO — DIRECT COST				② FROM / TO — DIRECT COST				③ FROM / TO — DIRECT COST			
QTY.	BUYER		ENG.	MFG.	MAT'L	OTHER	ENG.	MFG.	MAT'L	OTHER	ENG.	MFG.	MAT'L	OTHER

PROGRAM PROJECT a b c

1.
2.
3.
4.
5.
6.
7.
8.
9.
10.
11.
12. OTHER GOVT. EFFORT
13. COMMERCIAL EFFORT
14. TOTAL DIRECT COST BASE

SECTION B

INDIRECT COST CATEGORY	INDIRECT COST					INDIRECT COST					
	ENG.	MFG.	MAT'L	OTHER	G&A	ENG.	MFG.	MAT'L	OTHER	G&A	

15. INDIRECT LABOR
16. EMPLOYEE BENEFITS
17. PAYROLL TAXES
18. EMPLOYMENT
19. COMMUNICATION TRAVEL
20. PRODUCTION RELATED
21. FACILITIES-BUILDING LAND
22. FACILITIES-FURNITURE EQUIPMENT
23. ADMINISTRATION
24. FUTURE BUSINESS
25. OTHER MISCELLANEOUS
26. CREDITS
27. TOTAL OVERHEAD COST
28. TOTAL G&A COST
29. OVERHEAD / G&A RATE

EMPLOYMENT - INDIRECT

B. WORKERS

DD FORM 1921-3

158

Figure 12.15 Reconciliation of C/SCSC Reports

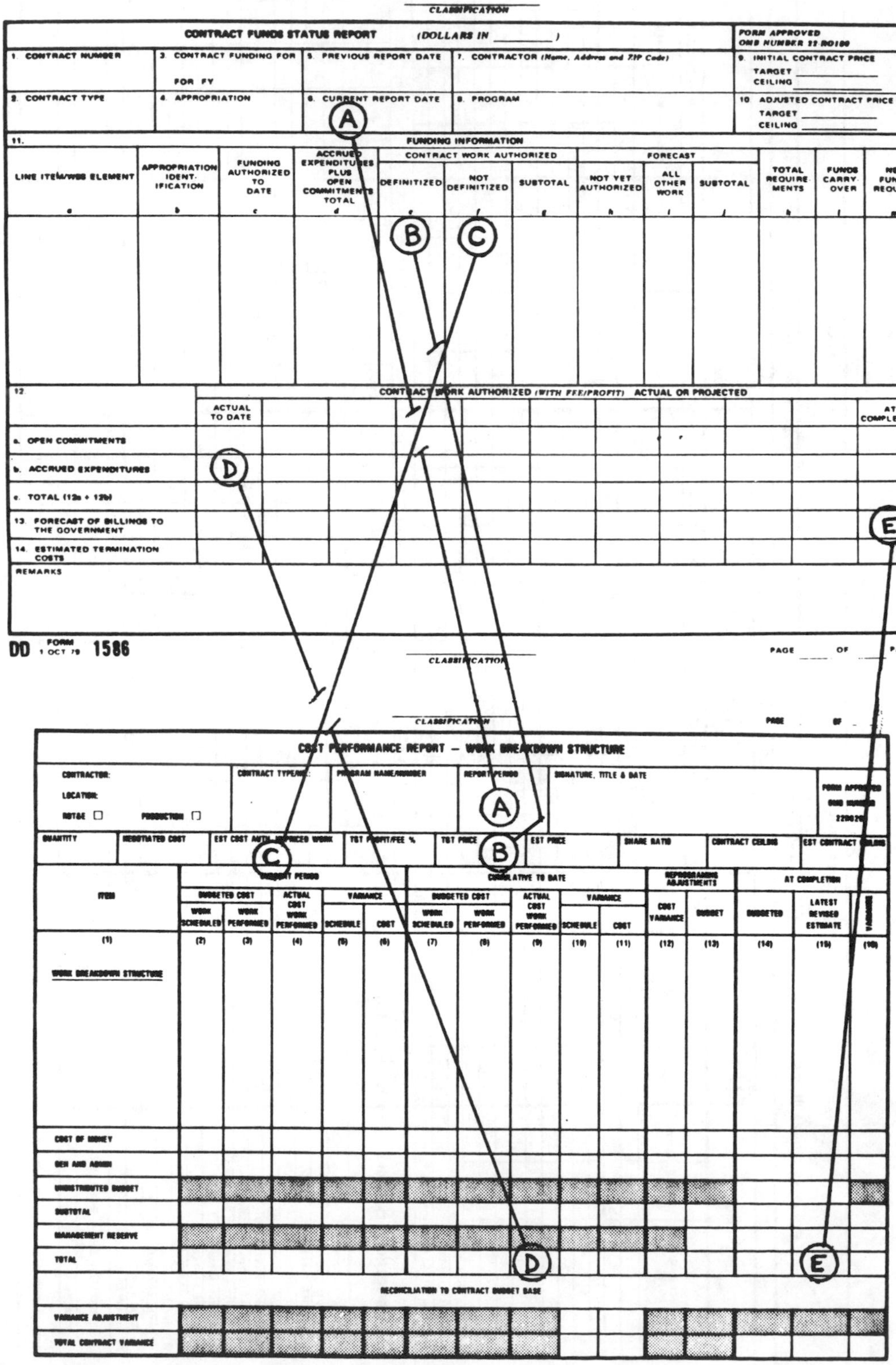

Source: Chart courtesy Humphreys & Associates

So much for C/SCSC reporting. Should anyone need additional information on the subject, the specific report requirements may be reviewed in the DOD documents contained in Appendices C and D to this book.

ENDNOTES

1. Interview with Dan Schild, Chief of the Cost Management Systems Division, Aeronautical Systems Division, Wright Patterson Air Force Base, Ohio, July 7, 1982.
2. Departments of the Air Force (AFSCP 173-3 & AFLCP 173-2), the Army (DARCOM-P 715-13), the Navy (NAVMAT P 5244), and the Defense Logistics Command (DLAH 8315.3), Cost/Schedule Management of Non-Major Contracts (C/SSR Guide), 1978, page 1-5.

13

IMPOSING C/SCSC ON SUBCONTRACTORS

The typical buyer is a man past middle life, spare, wrinkled, intelligent, cold, passive, noncommittal, with eyes like a codfish, polite in contact, but, at the same time, unresponsive, cool, calm, and damnably composed as a concrete post or a plaster of Paris cat; a human petrification with a heart of feldspar and without charm, or the friendly germ, minus bowels, passions, or a sense of humor. Happily they never reproduce, and all of them finally go to Hell.[1]

It ain't easy finding great buyers these days. Because of their complete dedication to the job and through a general lack of use, they have lost their capacity to reproduce and are now on the endangered species list. Such being the case, what is management to do when a particular job calls for the work of a really great buyer? Simple. Management merely takes an average buyer and gives him an exciting tool called C/SCSC. That seems to make the difference.

Up to this point the discussion has centered on having the criteria imposed downward from a customer. Now the recipient is the customer, and he has assumed his rightful role as that of the "imposer." Out there somewhere are thousands of "imposees" just waiting for his instructions. Exciting isn't it!

But prior to covering the subject of flowing the criteria downward to the subcontractors, perhaps it would be wise to stand back and examine the function of subcontract management. What is subcontract management, how significant is it to the total prime contract effort, and is there a proper role for C/SCSC in this process?

THE ROLE OF SUBCONTRACT MANAGEMENT

Starting sometime in the 1960s, there began a subtle, almost unnoticed shifting in the amount of effort prime government contractors were keeping for themselves. More and more they were asking other firms (once prime contractors themselves) to perform significant portions of their prime contracts.

There were numerous reasons for this change. The "pay dirt" in prime contracting activity isn't the research and development efforts, they are merely a necessary means to the end. The real objective and value of prime contracting is in the long-term production run. And the competition for the very few production runs was becoming progressively more severe. Not only were there fewer production runs started, but the cost of competing for them, i.e., the costs of specialized assets, professional staff, long-time commitments of facilities, was making it a high risk business. Private industry doesn't enjoy high risks unless there are correspondingly high profit potentials to be gained. Subcontracting part of the action was a way of spreading the costs to compete and the associated business risks among several firms.

In addition to the benefits of diluting the business risks of the stretched-out competitions, prime contractors found they could enhance the chances of success by forming strong prime/subcontractor teams which complemented obvious weaknesses in an individual firm's technical capability.

While it is unlikely that one could ever determine exactly how much of the prime contracts' efforts are being sent outside for performance, there is general agreement that it is well in excess of half of the prime effort:

> Few people realize that since 1970, 50 percent or more of every defense dollar eventually ends up going to a subcontractor. All evidence indicates that this trend will not only continue but probably increase. Thus, through subcontracting, a prime contractor is becoming a manager of resources rather than a producer of goods.[2]

Still others place the value of subcontracting even higher:

> On almost every defense system acquisition program, subcontracts account for more than half of the prime contractor's costs. One prime contractor, for example, subcontracts 66 percent of a missile program while two others have subcontracted 60 to 70 percent of aircraft and destroyer programs, respectfully.[3]

The increased amount of work going to other firms for performance brought with it certain challenges to management. Instead of work being accomplished in-house, where one could, if one wanted to, keep close surveillance on the activity and exert considerable pressure on fellow employees, now jobs had to be precisely defined in advance, and all monitoring was restricted to areas specifically authorized in the subcontract document. Managers who once prided themselves on their effectiveness in getting work done in their own company, suddenly got all entangled in terms and conditions, statements of work, authorities and responsibilities, when trying to get the same job done through a subcontract with another company. Just who in the prime company was responsible for what, opened a whole new set of jurisdictional disputes, as this illustration shows:

> Sometimes the fault for loss of subcontractor's control of costs is traceable to the prime contractor and, more specifically, to the matter of who in the prime's organization has responsibility for what. On a large aerospace program a few years ago a company's program engineer for propulsion assumed that he had full responsibility for both in-house and subcontract propulsion work because a documented company policy assigned this responsibility to the program engineer. At the same time a subcontract administrator in the prime contractor organization assumed he had full responsibility for propulsion subcontracts on the program because another numbered company policy assigned responsibility for subcontracts to the procurement organization. Company management was (and may still be) unaware of these conflicting directives. The net result was that, although it was clear to the individuals involved who was responsible for strictly technical and subcontract administration aspects, neither was directly responsible for cost or schedule management and neither took effective steps to control the two propulsion subcontractors. The company's program manager, more interested in technical aspects than in cost and controls, assumed no direct responsibility for subcontract management. Costs galloped out of control while progress inched along on subcontractor's work.[4]

In addition to the organizational issue of who does what with respect to subcontract management is a related issue of which is the best vehicle to define the prime/subcontractor relationship. While there are multiple types of contractual arrangements available, most are derivatives of two diverse types: the cost reimbursable and the fixed price.

Under the various fixed price type contracts available, the most stringent is the Firm Fixed Price, commonly referred to as FFP. This type of contract is the most desirable to use, as long as one knows exactly what one wants from the subcontractor. If the definition of work is apt to change for whatever reason, a fixed price contract is not good to use. Under FFP contracts, the subcontractor agrees to perform services and/or to deliver hardware according to an agreed to price that is not subject to change. All the risks are on the subcontractor for performance, as long as the agreed to statement of work and/or schedules do not change. However, in the defense industry, many a low-bidding subcontractor got well through negotiated changes in the statement of work and delays in the "official" schedule. Under FFP subcontracts one has to know exactly what one wants, and be able to define it in a legal document.

The opposite of the FFP subcontract is the cost reimbursable type, of various varieties, the most common of which is the Cost-Plus-Fixed-Fee (CPFF) type. Here, the subcontractor agrees on a cost which can vary, but a fee which is set, unless the statement of work changes. Such an arrangement allows for the easy incorporation of changes and redirection, without causing a major disruption of the effort. The CPFF subcontract is appropriate when the activity cannot be properly defined, and when there is little or no performance history to establish a fair price. However, the CPFF subcontract places the risks of performance, not on the subcontractor, but on the prime contractor.

What all of this basic contract information means, while attempting to understand the mission of subcontract management, is that studies have shown that although fixed price subcontracts represent the largest number of activities in the industry, they represent a lesser percentage of subcontracted dollars. Conversely, although cost reimbursable type subcontracts are used less frequently than fixed price types, they do represent the largest dollar volume.[5] Hence, in terms of prime contractor exposure, the risks of performance remain with the prime contractor and are represented by just a few cost type subcontracts. Thus, if the prime contractors are able to find a way to manage well their few cost type subcontracts, they will reduce their own risks on any given program.

But what has history shown about the ability of a prime contractor to control its subcontractors and, thus, to minimize program risks? As two gentlemen with over 50 years of collective subcontract management experience point out:

> ...statistically, subcontracts invariably will overrun more, in percent, than the prime contract. Analysis of a selective sample of major defense contracts shows that work done in-house is more likely to be accomplished at the cost predicted than work done through subcontracts.[6]

In its broadest sense, the role of subcontract management includes the administration of all activity which goes outside of a firm for performance. Realistically, however, the activity should be focused on where the risks to the program lie.

> Subcontract management is primarily the management of cost-plus contracts. The principal characteristic of a cost-plus contract is that it provides for work that carries a substantial degree of risk. The risk results from an inability to define the requirement or from an effort involving very advanced technology. Were these risks not present, a no risk, firm, fixed-price contract could and should have been used.[7]

Going one step beyond the cost type subcontracts, which would appear to represent the primary business risks connected with the non-in-house activity, these two authors have further emphasized where they feel the heart of most subcontract problems are.

> Although cost, schedule, and technical achievement are involved in subcontract management, the principal problem is one of cost. This is not to minimize either delivery to schedule or achievement of the technical goals, but when one raises the subject of subcontract problems, he is usually talking about a cost overrun.[8]

If one were to take what these two seasoned experts in the field of subcontract management say literally, and there is no reason to refute their position, and now understanding the full utility of a management concept using earned value measurement, can there be any doubt but that one of the most valuable tools available to any prime contractor's procurement department is in the selected use of C/SCSC on just a few critical subcontract buys, and thus improve the cost/schedule performance of the prime contract.

THE REQUIREMENT TO USE C/SCSC ON SUBCONTRACTS

The requirement to use C/SCSC on procurements of a selected size is imposed in the Department of Defense with DODI 7000.2, Appendix B to this book. The instruction further requires that prime contractors use C/SCSC on their critical subcontractors, as agreed to between the government and prime, on all but firm fixed price subcontracts. On the smaller subcontracts, which do not warrant the use of a full CPR, the requirement is to impose C/SSR type reporting.[9]

Within the defense establishment, there are two organizations whose role it is to watch closely the procurement activities of the various military departments: the Defense Contract Audit Agency -- commonly referred to as DCAA and the Contract Administration Offices -- CAO, represented by the AFPRO, NAVPRO, etc. These groups have their own C/SCSC manual entitled: <u>C/SCSC Joint Surveillance Guide</u>. In it, the requirement to use the criteria on selected buys is also specified:

> Subcontracts, excluding those that are firm-fixed-price, may be selected for C/SCSC application by mutual agreement between the prime contractor and the procuring activity based upon dollar value and/or criticality of the subcontract to which C/SCSC will be extended. Subcontracts selected should be identified in the prime contract.[10]

In an earlier chapter the necessity for contractors to define all of their contractual effort using a method called the WBS (Work Breakdown Structure) was covered. This is an absolute requirement, whether the work is performed in-house by its own departments, or purchased outside from a subcontractor. All effort must be called out in the prime contractor's WBS, subcontractors included.

Returning once again to the Military Standard 881 which specifies the requirement, there is the following statement:

> The prime contractor shall be responsible for traceable summarization of subcontractor data supporting his prime contract WBS elements. The prime contractor may negotiate any WBS with a subcontractor that permits the prime contractor to fulfill his contract WBS requirements and which provides adequate control of the subcontractor.[11]

Thus, when the very first of the 35 criteria states that "all" of the work must be defined within the framework of the WBS, it means all of the work, including that which goes outside of the prime contractor's plant for performance.

In Chapter 9, the subject of validation was discussed. If a major subcontractor is performing under a requirement for C/SCSC, it too must go through a validation, either an initial demonstration review, or more likely a SAR to verify that it is properly using its earned value system on the new subcontract. The Joint Implementation Guide specifies who may perform the actual SAR.

> The prime contractor will contractually require the selected subcontractors to comply with the criteria. However, demonstrations and reviews of these selected subcontractor's management systems may be performed by the procuring authority when requested by either the prime or subcontactor.[12]

Thus, it is apparent from this language that a subcontractor's SAR may be performed by any one of four teams:

1. Military team exclusively
2. Military team, assisted by the prime contractor
3. Prime contractor exclusively
4. Prime contractor, assisted by military personnel

Under no circumstances should the prime contractor ever allow the number one option above to be used to do its work for them. There is too much at stake, too much vital subcontractor information to be gained in the review process. While a subcontractor may rightfully take the position that certain information is proprietary to it, particularly overhead rates if the prime and subcontractor are competitors on other programs, that type of data may rightfully be withheld from prime contractor personnel and only be reviewed with the military team members. However, most of the SAR activity will focus on the planning and performance of direct costs only (with overheads applied as a rate) and that data cannot be considered proprietary to the prime contractor. There is a great deal of critical information to be gained from a SAR, and, therefore, the prime contractor must insist on its personnel being a part of the reviewing team. The most appropriate reviewing teams are likely the joint military/prime contractor teams, number 2 above. And from the subcontractor's point of view, a review team headed by the military, but with prime contractor's personnel participating (#2 above) may be useful in future DOD work.

THE REQUIREMENT FOR SUBCONTRACTOR C/SCSC REPORTS

The proper implementation of C/SCSC with a subcontractor must include the formal submittal of certain standardized reports, as a necessary complement to the process. These reports were covered in full in Chapter 12, and the discussion here will emphasize how these same structured reports, plus certain others, may assist the prime contractor in the management of selected subcontracts in which some type of C/SCSC implementation is deemed appropriate because of the size or the critical nature of the procurement. The implementation of C/SCSC reporting with selected subcontractors will allow the prime contractor to: (1) receive a monthly assessment of the cost/schedule status position; (2) observe any adverse trends in performance; and (3) be in a position to make an independent (from the subcontractor) estimate of what the final cost and schedule position is likely to be.

Before discussing what type of data might be obtained from the subcontractor, it is probably important to stress the point that such data does not come free. There is a cost to prepare and submit reports and these costs -- directly or indirectly -- will be included in the price of the subcontract. Therefore, it is imperative that the "I'll take one of each" approach to data selection be avoided. Only those reports that are needed for sound management reasons should be requested. The risk of doing without the data should be weighed against the costs and benefits of having the visibility, and, hopefully, a proper balance will be struck. The dollar value of certain procurements (exceeding the C/SCSC thresholds) or the critical nature of certain buys will sometimes automatically dictate the reporting requirements for the prime contractor.

Shown in figure 12.1 in Chapter 12 was a table of four cost reports, any three of which are required from a contractor when the C/SCSC provision is in their contract. To quickly recap these reports, they are:

1. CFSR-Contract Funds Status Report -- due quarterly on cost reimbursable contracts to forecast the funding requirements, typically, only those activities over $500,000 in value.
2. CPR-Cost Performance Report or the C/SSR-Cost/Schedule Status Report -- for any cost reimbursable contract in excess of $2 million the C/SSR should be imposed, and cost contracts reaching the value of $40 million or more should require a full CPR. Critical buys may lower these thresholds.
3. CCDR-Contractor Cost Data Reporting -- provides historical cost data and is useful when attempting to project future costs, e.g., costs of a planned production run. The CCDR is

also useful to help maintain a competition between multiple subcontractors by providing comparative data. It normally applies to cost reimbursable contracts, but it may also apply to fixed price efforts if the equipment is deemed critical to the prime effort.

In addition to these cost/schedule reports, there are two scheduling-only reports which should be considered on certain procurements.

4. <u>PERT/Time</u> or <u>EZPERT</u> is useful when a cost reimbursable development subcontract calls for a series of complex tasks, and the final product is required by the prime contractor on a specific need date.

5. <u>Line of Balance-LOB</u> provides good visibility on equipment buys where large quantities are involved, on both cost and fixed price subcontracts.

One of the most overlooked and underused reports which provides excellent cost/schedule status in a structured format, and with a minimal impact on the supplier, is that of the mini-CPR, or the C/SSR-Cost/Schedule Status Report. As was mentioned earlier about this report, one major procurement command uses the C/SSR seven times as often as the CPR, i.e., they receive over 200 C/SSRs each month from their suppliers. By contrast, few private firms receive even one C/SSR, even though they often have cost type procurements representing millions of dollars. Why is this the case?

The full CPR came into being along with the introduction of the criteria in the late 1960s. Many procurement departments at private firms reviewed the criteria and CPR and decided, rightfully, that the imposition of these requirements on their small suppliers, even on cost type buys, would place an undue hardship on them. Some seven years later, in 1974, when the C/SSR was introduced, it was largely unnoticed by most buyers with private firms. The joint military guide which covers this report described its purpose:

. The Cost/Schedule Status Report (C/SSR) was established in 1974 to meet the needs of all managers within the Military Departments for cost and schedule information on non-major contracts in which the Government shares or assumes all of the cost risk.[13]

If one would substitute "prime contractor" for "Military Departments," the C/SSR might be considered useful to a private contractor when it "assumes all of the cost risk," i.e., anytime a cost reimbursable type contract is used.

The guide goes on to state:

. . . The C/SSR requirement does not establish any minimum requirements (standards) with respect to the contractor's management systems, nor does it involve the evaluation, acceptance, or rejection of the contractors' internal management procedures, except where compliance with contractual provisions relative to the report is in question.[14]

Thus the C/SSR, which is used extensively by the military buyers, but rarely in private industry, may well be an excellent device to increase visibility on selected minor procurements in which the prime contractor assumes the costs risks on the activity, i.e., any cost type contract. The DOD imposes the C/SSR on all cost type contracts in excess of $2 million, which would likely be appropriate for private firms as well.

Specific instructions for the preparation of the C/SSR are contained in DODI 7000.10 (Appendix C to this book). In addition, included in Appendix F are two clauses which would be required by any private firm when defining a contractual relationship with a subcontractor: (1) sample solicitation clause, and (2) a sample contract clause.

In many cases, procurement personnel in private firms will be unfamiliar with the Criteria, the CPR, CFSR, CCDR, and the C/SSR in particular. In such cases, it might be advisable for the private firm to consider some type of special training class, similar to those used when the firm prepared for their validation review. Often there are experienced C/SCSC people within a company who could prepare a special training seminar, and/or sometimes it might be advisable to go outside to one of the management consultant firms which specialize in such training.

CONCLUSION

In the opening of this chapter certain frivolous remarks were made about buyers, their physical presence, and the demise of certain of their vital parts. Also, the statement was made that one could simply take an average buyer, give him C/SCSC, and make him into a superstar. Such statements should have been taken in the spirit in which they were given -- complete BLANK BLANK. But there was one important message that was intended in all this triviality.

Coming to grips with the proper control of subcontractors, which now represents 50 percent or more of most prime contracts, and perhaps an even higher percentage of the prime contractor's risks, is an important part of the process of management. The successful control of the subcontractor's performance is the collective result of several people in the prime contractor's organization, but two people in particular are vital to the process: the program manager and the buyer.

The program manager must set forth the policy, the direction, and the performance targets for all aspects of a given program, including that which goes to some other firm for execution. The buyer must take this direction, define it in a way to be understood by mortals, and monitor compliance as some other firm performs to the contractual document.

The theme of this chapter has been that these two essential players, plus the introduction of C/SCSC to its fullest and proper level, will provide an awesome triad in the control of the largest segment of prime contracts today.

ENDNOTES

1. Elbert Hubbard in <u>Plant Production Control</u> by Charles A. Koepke (New York, John Wiley & Sons Inc., 1941), page 104.

2. Reprinted by permission of the publisher, from George Sammet, Jr., and Clifton G. Kelly, <u>Subcontract Management Handbook</u> (New York: AMACOM, a division of American Management Associations, 1981), page 2.

3. J. S. Baumgartner, "The program manager and subcontractor: hands on or hands off?" in <u>Systems Management</u>, edited by J. S. Baumgartner (Washington, D.C.: The Bureau of National Affairs, Inc., 1979), page 160.

4. Ibid., page 162-163.

5. Sammet and Kelly, <u>Subcontract Management Handbook</u>, New York: AMACOM, 1981, page 11.

6. Ibid., page 3.

7. Ibid., page 1.

8. Ibid., page 10.

9. DODI 7000.2, Paragraph D.3, page 2.

10. AMCP 715-10; NAVMAT P5243; AFLCP/AFSCP 173-6; DSAH 8315.1; DCAAP 7641.46, 1974, page 2-5.

11. Military Standard 881, 1975, Paragraph 5.5.6, page 15.

12. <u>Cost-Schedule Control Systems Criteria Joint Implementation Guide</u>, 1980, item (e), page 31.

13. <u>Cost/Schedule Management of Non-Major Contracts-C/SSR Joint Guide</u>, DARCOM 715-13; NAVMAT P5244; AFLCP 173-2; AFSCP 173-3; DLAH 8315.3, 1978, page 3.

14. Ibid., page 3.

14

ANALYSIS OF C/SCSC DATA

A few years ago a young man got involved in a project for his city to help define the "official list of trees." The goal was to obtain a consensus from experts in the field, and then to publish a list of 15 approved trees which could be used in a city ordinance requiring parkway planting. After weeks and months of discussions with landscape architects, nursery owners, gardeners, etc., they could not agree on a single list. Finally, the exasperated young man asked a landscape architect for his opinion as to why they couldn't reach an agreement on such a simple task. After a pause the architect replied, "It's because you are asking for the impossible -- it's like asking an astronomer to specify his five favorite stars -- too many beautiful stars -- too many beautiful trees."

That night the young man sat down and made a list of his 15 favorite trees, which he presented to the city council the following night as the "consensus of experts." No one objected to the list. The city council then passed their ordinance.

There is a parallel between the above story and defining the proper data to be analyzed in an C/SCSC management control system. Obtaining a consensus from experts would be a difficult, perhaps impossible task. Too many beautiful data points -- too many beautiful analyses which could be performed. Therefore, what is to follow in this last chapter on the Criteria, is the single best approach to C/SCSC data analysis, representing a "consensus of one."

Before starting a discussion on the various methods used to analyze and display C/SCSC data, it would likely be beneficial to revisit five specific terms, for in the illustrations which will follow, they will be used often. These terms are:

1. BCWS-Budgeted Costs for Work Scheduled is the plan against which performance will be measured.
2. BCWP-Budgeted Costs for Work Performed is the earned value or dollar value of the work accomplished against the plan.

3. ACWP-Actual Costs of Work Performed are the cost actuals.
4. BAC-Budget at Completion is the projected value of the plan (BCWS) at the end of the effort.
5. EAC-Estimate at Completion is the projected value of what the effort will actually cost (ACWP) at the end.

In the following discussion the data could be viewed from at least three vantage points:

1. From government buyers examining prime contractor data,
2. From prime contractors examining their in-house performance,
3. From prime contractors examining their subcontractor's data.

The last perspective will be assumed, i.e., prime to subcontractor. The prime contractor will be attempting to do the following two things with the data it is receiving from its subcontractor:

• Determine current status and performance trends
• Make an independent (from the subcontractor) estimate of what the final position will likely be

DETERMINING CURRENT STATUS AND PERFORMANCE TRENDS

Seven types of analyses will be examined.

Cumulative Status Display

The most common display in C/SCSC is simply the cumulative curve, showing dollars over time. A cumulative curve is best represented by one-half of a Bell-shaped curve, which visually displays a slow build-up, fastest acceleration in the middle, and a slow ending. Any cumulative program curve which doesn't approximate roughly one-half a Bell-shaped curve, is highly suspected of displaying a faulty plan.

To display a typical C/SCSC cumulative curve, figure 14.1 reflects a fictitious program called XYZ (to be used several times) which will run for three years, and which has a cost value for performance purposes of $100 million. The most significant differences between C/SCSC and the conventional cost control methods are reflected in figure 14.1.

Under the conventional approach, one focuses on two aspects only: (1) the plan (BCWS) and (2) actuals (ACWP), and the differences between the two. By contrast, C/SCSC focuses on these two, plus what was actually accomplished or earned value (BCWP). Variances are related to the earned value (BCWP) only.

A close look at the XYZ program after only one year reflects a program off to a bad start. The plan (BCWS) called for performance of $25 million after year one, whereas performance or earned value

(BCWP) only hit $15 million. To make matters worse, actual costs (ACWP) came in at $30 million. Thus, the program has a Schedule Variance (SV) of minus $10 million (which equates to roughly 4 months behind schedule) and a Cost Variance (CV) of minus $15 million.

Figure 14.1 Cumulative Status Display

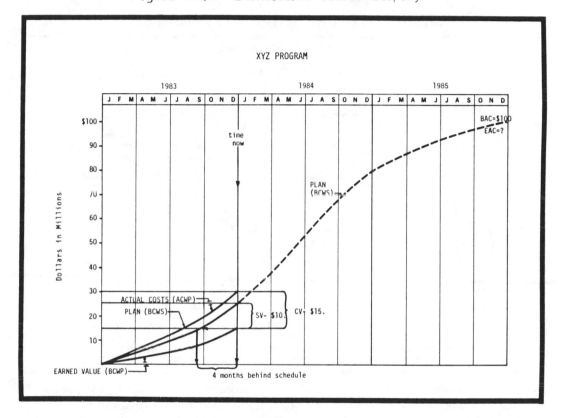

Tracking Variances from a Standard (BCWP)

In C/SCS the standard is earned value, or the budgeted value of work performed (BCWP). Therefore, the tracking of costs and schedule performance against the standard, i.e., earned value, gives one a clue as to how well or poorly the program is doing. In the XYZ program these variances are as follows:

- Cost variance: CV = BCWP less ACWP, or $15 million less $30 million = ($15 million)
- Schedule Variance: SV = BCWP less BCWS, or $15 million less $25 million or ($10 million).

When the SV and CV are displayed graphically, they resemble the chart shown in figure 14.2, as used by the U.S. Army. In this chart the CV and SV are plotted monthly, and the trend can immediately be seen. To be over the line is good, and represents an underrun or

174

ahead of schedule condition. Under the line represents an overrun or behind schedule condition.

This chart represents variances in absolute terms, i.e., total dollar variances. Such displays may represent the total program at WBS level 1, or they may go down to a lower WBS level to reflect an area of interest or special concern, for example, program risk areas.

Figure 14.2 Cost and Schedule Variances

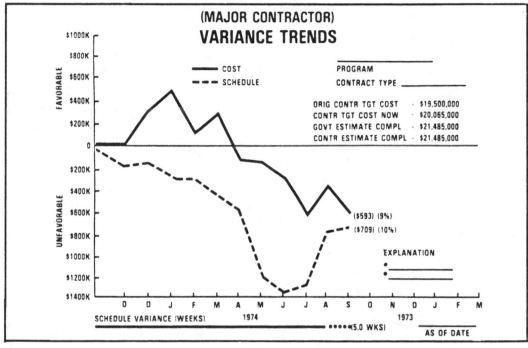

Source: "Army Research and Development News Magazine," November-December 1974, page 13-15, from an article by Major General George Sammet Jr., appearing in J.S. Baumgartner, Systems Management (Washington, D.C.: The Bureau of National Affairs, Inc. 1979), page 282.

Determining the Efficiency Factor for Work Performed

In addition to absolute variances, one would likely want to know how efficient the performance has been. Two indices are available to provide performance as a percentage of the standard, BCWP.

Returning once again to the XYZ program as an example, two performance indices may be used to determine the efficiency factors.

- CPI (Cost Performance Index) $= \dfrac{BCWP}{ACWP} = \dfrac{\$15.M}{\$30.M} = 50\%$

- SPI (Schedule Performance Index) $= \dfrac{BCWP}{BCWS} = \dfrac{\$15.M}{\$25.M} = 60\%$

175

Graphically, the CPI and SPI may be plotted using a display similar to that used above to show the absolute variances. In figure 14.3 is shown a plotting of the CPI and SPI, not at WBS level 1 which is possible, but at WBS level 4, to reflect the development of, say, the radar unit, which might be of special interest to management because of a previous risk analysis. These types of charts may be plotted to reflect either the monthly position or, of more significance, the cumulative position.

Figure 14.3   Plotting of CPI and SPI

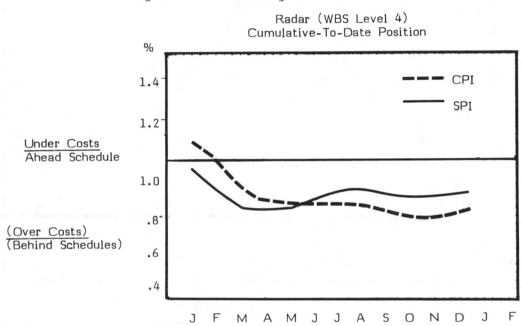

Source: United States Air Force Systems Command, Guide to Analysis of Contractor Cost Data, 1 June 1977, revised 1 August 1979, page 4-26, (as modified by author).

These two indices, CPI and SPI, will be used later to prepare an independent (from what the subcontractor may be saying) estimate of what the program will likely cost (EAC), and how long it will probably take to complete.

Tracking Manpower

One of the most important indicators to watch on all programs is that of labor, usually expressed as manpower loading. Format 4 of the monthly CPR reflects manloads by function, actuals to date, a projection, and the latest estimate at completion. Shown in figure 14.4 is a typical display, with a supporting table reflected at the bottom.

Figure 14.4   Manpower Loading Display

AS OF DATE 7-25-78
ISSUE DATE 8-18-78

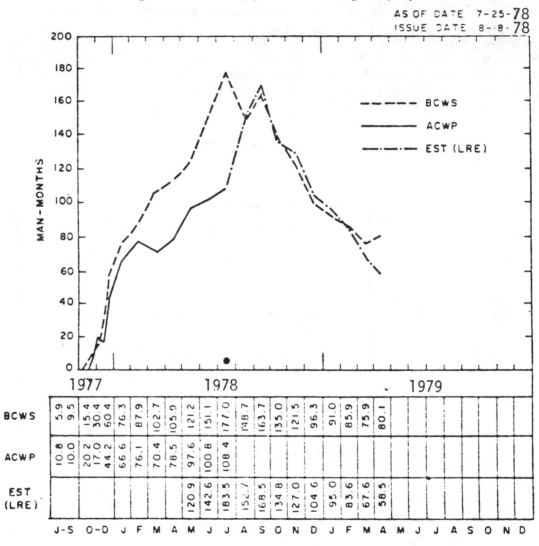

	J-S	O-D	J	F	M	A	M	J	J	A	S	O	N	D	J	F	M	A	M	J	J	A	S	O	N	D
BCWS	5.9 / 9.5	15.4 / 30.4 / 60.4	76.3	87.9	102.7	105.9	121.2	151.1	177.0	148.7	163.7	135.0	121.5	96.3	91.0	85.9	75.9	80.1								
ACWP	10.8 / 10.0	20.2 / 17.0 / 44.2	66.6	76.1	70.4	78.5	97.6	100.8	108.4																	
EST (LRE)					120.9	142.6	183.5	152.7	168.5	134.8	127.0	104.6	95.0	83.6	67.6	58.5										

Source: USAFSC Guide to Analysis of Contractor Cost Data,
          page 4-21.

In addition to tracking total program manpower, as reflected by the figure, depending upon the phase of a given program, selected specific functions should also be monitored. Early in all programs, engineering is a logical candidate to be watched, as shown in figure 14.5.

Looking ahead once again to having an ability to do an independent EAC, the manload data by specific function may be used to make such a projection.

Tracking the Use of Management Reserve

One of the most important indicators of program condition and, therefore, something which should be watched closely is that of the

Figure 14.5 Engineering Manpower Loading

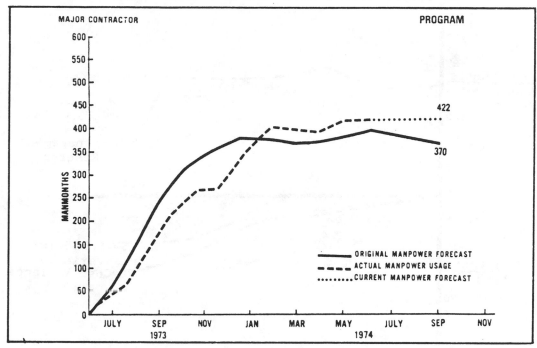

Source: "Army Research and Development News Magazine," November-December 1974, page 13-15, from an article by Major General George Sammet Jr., appearing in J.S. Baumgartner, Systems Management (Washington, D.C.: The Bureau of National Affairs, Inc. 1979), page 286.

use of management reserve over the life of a contract. Management Reserve is budget which is set aside in the beginning of a program to cover contingencies, i.e., in-scope problems as they occur. Management Reserve is expected to be utilized before the end of a contract; however, if it is utilized too early in a program, it could reflect some type of difficulty which should be probed by the prime contractor.

One of the most useful displays of Management Reserve (MR) is to compare on one chart both the CV and SV and their relationship in dollars to the MR. Figure 14.6 is such a display. This display reflects a substantial depletion of MR in December, which should be explained in either the CPR, or in person at the subcontractor's plant.

Another technique used to monitor MR is to relate its use in a straight-line application over the life of a contract. The straight line merely provides a point of reference, as is shown in figure 14.7.

Tracking Technical Performance

Monitoring the cost and schedule status of a program, even if one could determine the true position with absolute certainty, tells only

178

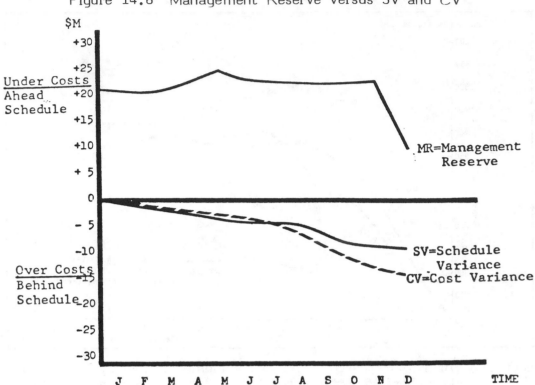

Figure 14.6   Management Reserve versus SV and CV

Source: USAFSC Guide to Analysis of Contractor Cost Data, page 4-10.

part of the story.   There are technical performance targets for every developmental program which are of equal, and likely of greater importance than either the cost or schedule status.   For example, it would be of small comfort to have a program end exactly within its costs, and on schedule, only to have it perform at one-half the required operating levels.   A fighter aircraft that must have a flight range of 1,000 miles would be of little value if it came in within the cost and schedule targets, but with a range of only 500 miles. Technical performance targets must be met.

The technical performance goals of all programs are unique and must be specifically tailored by the prime customer.   Shown in figures 14.8A and B are illustrative examples of some technical indicators used to monitor a U.S. Army developmental program.   When these technical indicators are used in conjunction with cost and schedule indicators provided from C/SCSC reporting data, the prime contractor has good visibility on the full status of its subcontractor.

Analysis of What the Subcontractor is Saying

Format 5 of the monthly CPR is a section entitled Problem Analysis Report (PAR).   A PAR is required any time either cost or

Figure 14.7   Management Reserve versus Linear Time

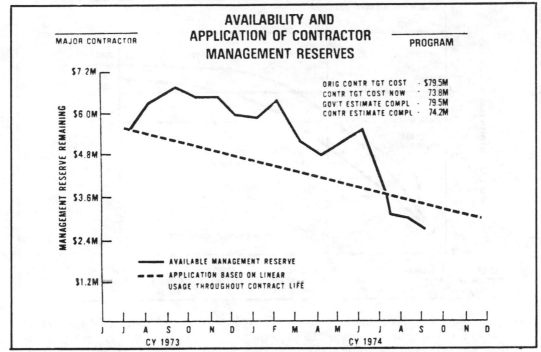

Source: "Army   Research   and   Development   News   Magazine,"
November-December 1974, page 13-15, from an article by
Major   General   George   Sammet Jr.,   appearing   in   J.S.
Baumgartner, Systems Management (Washington, D.C.:   The
Bureau of National Affairs, Inc. 1979), page 283.

Figure 14.8A   Technical Performance Indicators

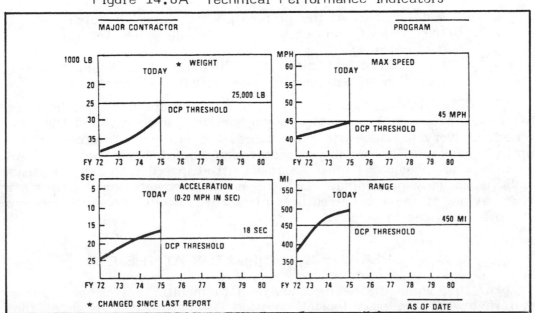

180

Figure 14.8B Reliability Performance Indicators

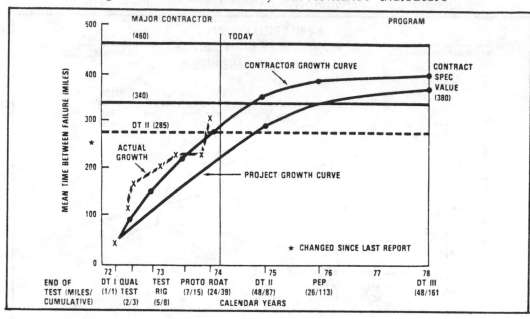

Source: "Army Research and Development News Magazine,"
November-December 1974, page 13-15, from an article by
Major General George Sammet Jr., appearing in J.S.
Baumgartner, Systems Management (Washington, D.C.: The
Bureau of National Affairs, Inc. 1979), pages 284 and 285.

schedule variances exceed a previously set threshold level. Thus, if
the radar development WBS element experiences a negative cost
variance of say 12 percent, the subcontractor is required to submit a
PAR each month which sets forth:

● a description of the problem, what caused it, etc;
● the impact on cost and schedule and technical
performance;
● the corrective plan to eliminate the variance,
including an estimate of when it will be corrected.

PARs are intended to enlighten and if there are questions lingering
after a review of the reasons given for the variances, and the proposed recovery plan doesn't make sense, the prime contractor has two
options available. The subcontractor can be informed that the PAR
write-ups are weak and must be resubmitted in order to fully describe
what is actually happening. Or, the prime contractor may call for a
cost review at the subcontractor's plant to carefully probe the reasons
for the variances in person.

FORECASTING THE POSITON AT THE END

Now that some of the methods used to monitor performance have
been reviewed, the next logical question is what will it mean at the

end? In C/SCSC the forecasted costs to complete the program are termed the Estimate At Completion (EAC). What impact will the performance to date have on the EAC? Three forecasting techniques will be discussed·to answer this question.

EAC Projection Based on CPI

Earlier, the Cost Performance Index (CPI), which is an indicator of cost efficiency of work accomplished to date, was discussed. The CPI on the XYZ program (shown in figure 14.1) after the first year was:

$$CPI = \frac{BCWP}{ACWP} = \frac{\$15.M}{\$30.M} = 50\%$$

The most frequently used method to forecast the EAC by the Air Force Systems Command is to assume that the same efficiency which is reflected in the actuals to date, i.e., the CPI, will continue to the end of the program. Thus, it uses the following formula:

$$Estimate\ At\ Completion = \frac{Budget\ At\ Completion\ less\ Mgmt\ Reserve}{CPI\ Cumulative}$$

On the XYZ Program the EAC would be:

$$EAC = \frac{\$100.M}{50\%} = \$200.M$$

This method merely extrapolates the actual performance to date to the end. It makes no attempt to consider the possibility that the subcontractor's performance may improve or be improving with time.

EAC by Function

Probably, a more accurate and sophisticated method to forecast the ending cost result would be to take the same technique discussed above and apply it individually to each of the subcontractor's organizational functions. In the monthly CPR formats 2 and 4 report performance by function, and a CPI may be determined for each function.

In all developmental programs certain functions will be performed prior to other functions. The most pronounced example of this phasing by function is that of the relationship between engineering and manufacturing. Obviously, the engineers must set the design before the factory can build it. An example of the historical phasing of the various functions is shown in figure 14.9. Each firm with its unique product lines will have a slightly different phasing of each function, which its historical records will show.

182

Figure 14.9   Time Phases by Function

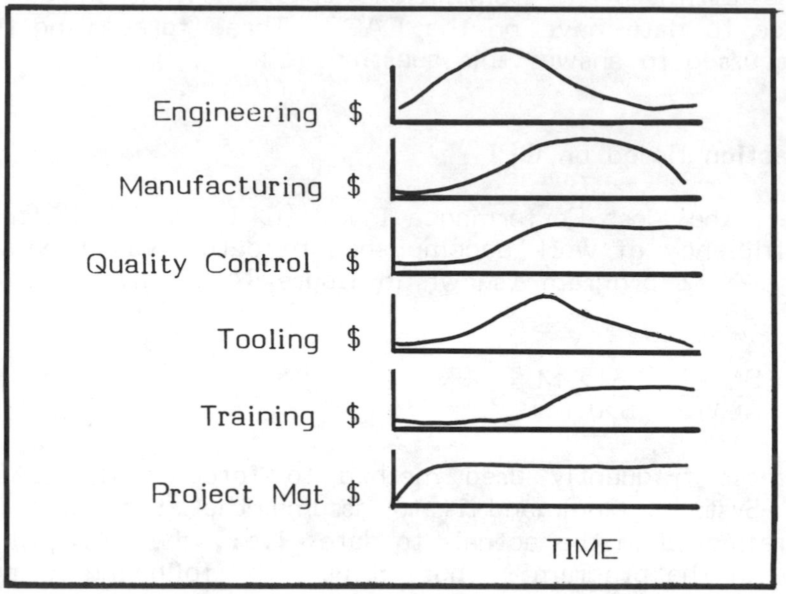

Engineering $

Manufacturing $

Quality Control $

Tooling $

Training $

Project Mgt $

TIME

Source: USAFSC Guide to Analysis of Contractor Cost Data, page 4-27.

Figure 14.10   EAC Forecast by Function

FUNCTION	ACWP	BCWP	CPI	BAC	EAC
Engineering	40455	33493	.828	108798	131399
Manufacturing	3119	2997	.961	27463	28578
Quality Control	170	162	.953	876	919
Tooling	83	76	.916	4257	4647
Training	285	271	.951	2386	2509
Project Mgt	7470	7380	.988	18336	18559
Subcontract	26005	22117	.850	63418	74609
Other	2907	2875	---	21114	21114
Mgt Reserve	---	---	---	10538	---
G & A	11028	9504	---	35234	38680
TOTAL	91522	78875	---	292420	321014

Source: USAFSC Guide to Analysis of Contractor Cost Data, page 4-27.

Cost Performance Index -- To Go

The last method to be discusssed takes the cost efficiency experience to date, as reflected in the CPI, and determines what level of cost efficiency will be required for the remainder of the program in order to stay within the present budget at completion. Throughout history, contractors and subcontractors have often taken the position that in spite of the results thus far, "we expect to stay within the present budgeted costs." This technique attempts to quantify exactly what it will take to achieve that noble result.

Going again back to the XYZ program for an example, the CPI for the first year of the program was 50 percent, not very impressive. If the subcontractor took the position that it will stay within the budgeted costs, it would have to perform as follows:

$$CPItg = \frac{BAC \ less \ BCWP}{BAC \ less \ ACWP} = \frac{\$100.M \ less \ \$15.M}{\$100.M \ less \ \$30.M} = \frac{\$85.M}{\$70.M} = 1.21\%$$

Thus, the subcontractor for the last two years will have to achieve a cost efficiency of 1.21 percent, highly, highly, unlikely based on performance to date. A cost overrun is the more probable forecast for the XYZ program.

The same techniques discussed above to estimate the final cost position may also be used to forecast the likely schedule position at the end. However, one important point should be stressed with regard to schedule forecasting with C/SCSC.

C/SCSC is a technique which can show the cost and schedule position of a given contract, but in gross terms only. True, by tracing down the WBS the problem or problems can be isolated, but as a forecasting tool, the 10 percent overrun of costs has more significance than is reflected in a 10 percent behind schedule condition. The reason is that a schedule is likely to have certain critical events which may not be reflectd in the gross look provided by the earned value technique. Whereas dollar costs are interchangeable and may be expressed in gross terms, schedule events are not so interchangeable. A given progam could be showing a favorable schedule variance using earned value, but in fact, be behind schedule because certain critical events are not being reflected in the summaries. The gross look, as provided by C/SCSC, does not always work with respect to schedule status. Therefore, the earned value technique works best when used in conjunction with other scheduling techniques, e.g., PERT-Time, master and detail schedules, in order to properly reflect the true schedule condition of a given program.

In the foregoing pages only a small sampling of the many techniques available to analyze and assess data made available from the monthly CPR has been covered. Additional analysis may be made from the Contract Funds Status Report and the four separate reports from the Contractor Cost Data Reporting, particularly the performance learning curves which may be prepared from the 1921-1 forms. But no matter how much data is available from any management control system, the limiting factors usually turn out to be the analysis of the data, the displays of the data, and the management review. In short, the C/SCSC management control system will provide the monitoring structure and information, but only intelligent management can put it to effective use.

PART IV
FURTHER APPLICATIONS
AND
EXECUTIVE SUMMARY

15

FURTHER APPLICATIONS OF
A C/SCSC MANAGEMENT
CONTROL SYSTEM

A few years back there was a restructuring of charters within the author's company and suddenly they, who were the builders of aircraft, assumed responsibility for the completion of a major construction program in the Middle East. There were logical reasons for the realignment which need not be covered here. The decision impacted on the author quickly, for with their newly acquired responsibility, the California management wanted their own people on the local job immediately to assume management of the construction activity. Fortunately -- or unfortunately -- the author was selected to represent the financial organization until a permanent candidate could be located and sent over.

The construction job represented several hundred million dollars, and, even considering inflation, that still constituted a lot of money. While the overall job was being monitored at a centralized headquarters in-country, actual construction was taking place at three separate locations, each several hundred miles apart. For ease of discussion, reference to the three sites will be simply A, B, and C. Each site had some 25 or more buildings to construct, some quite large and very complex. It was what is called a "turn-key" project, i.e., they were responsible for the total job from the initial design through to the point where the buildings were ready for user occupancy.

Although the construction company which now reported to them had been in existence for more years than they had been building aircraft, to their amazement the construction group had no standardized management control system that could be used to uniformly monitor progress at each of the three sites. They simply left it to each superintendent at the sites to implement his own monitoring methods and to report status to headquarters each month based on his own assessment of how they were performing. With a high turnover of construction site personnel, and lacking a uniform monitoring approach, it was no wonder that on arrival there was little confidence in the progress being reported from the three sites. Each location was missing their early completion goals, and they knew they had a problem. But they had no way to quantify the total problem, or to relate status from one site to another.

The obvious message here, in a book on earned value, is that this construction job would have been an ideal place to impose the C/SCS Criteria, and to implement a "uniform" management control system with uniform status reporting. In retrospect the progress reporting from site A was quite good, based on the competence of individuals and the techniques they used at that location. It is likely that site A could have met the 35 Criteria had they been imposed, for the methods they were using were quite similar to those required by the Criteria. At sites B and C they had little visibility and the progress being reported turned out to be overoptimistic (to be kind). Their "seat-of-the pants" assessment of accomplishments turned out to be totally misleading.

By the time the author's firm took over the project it was too late to then impose their earned value technique. At 35 percent complete, running behind schedule, and lacking the detailed initial planning so vital to implementing a C/SCSC management control system, all they could do was to quick-fix the condition with more management personnel than they would normally use on any project. They did make a recovery and completed the total contract (which was more than just construction) in a respectable fashion. The author left the country after seven months with a feeling of satisfaction and two distinct impressions on the use of an earned value management control approach:

1. The management of a large, complex, multi-location program cannot be accomplished by relying on individual managers to select, monitor, and report on those activities which they feel are important; rather, a systematic approach is needed to implement a uniform management control method with uniform progress reporting. A management control system which would satisfy the C/SCS Criteria would fill this requirement completely.

2. The applications of an earned value management control system are not limited to military procurement alone; they fit nicely on other selected applications, e.g., housing projects, nuclear power plants, dam construction, shopping centers, highway projects, to name only a few.

***

It has never been the purpose of this book to in any way suggest that the performance measurement/earned value approach be incorporated in all management systems everywhere and used in every situation where tight control is desired. That would be foolhardy, and costly, and much in the same way the fine technique of PERT was misdirected in the beginning. There are appropriate applications for C/SCSC, and there are inappropriate applications for the concept. In the final analysis, individual managements must decide what is right for them.

But it is the intended purpose of this book to make management everywhere aware of the performance measurement/earned value concept, and to point out that there may be ideal applications in one's own business where the concept could improve organizational performance. Perhaps some specific illustrations will emphasize this point.

For the past 15 years, or since they implemented the concept, the Department of Defense has used earned value/performance measurement on all non-fixed-price new developmental programs reaching a certain value. And while cost overruns and schedule delays have not been eliminated, it can safely be said that the DOD buyers, program managers, their respective commanders, headquarters, and the Congress (which has its own role in monitoring contracts for which they must approve such funds) all have had better visibility into individual programs with C/SCSC imposed than they would have had without it. C/SCSC is best at identifying problems, not at eliminating them completely.

Across town in the nation's capital, the Department of Energy had substantial funding in the late 1970s (and will likely again as world energy continues to run short) and transplanted the C/SCSC concept in total to monitor their developmental/construction projects. They issued a series of new books on the subject specific to their needs. But the 35 DOD criteria were adopted verbatim, without a change.

Over at the Federal Aviation Agency (FAA), they have imposed the criteria concept on the suppliers of equipment in their multibillion dollar upgrade of computer controls at locations throughout the country.

These are illustrations of where C/SCSC has been effectively implemented on large government programs. But the real potential for the performance measurement/earned value concept may well be in the private/nongovernment sector, where there are literally thousands of businesses and industries that may not be aware of the concept. Some of these possibilities should be mentioned.

Banks, insurance firms, savings and loan associations, money lenders, etc., all have something in common: they all finance the construction of new projects. A construction job is a nonrecurring, complex series of tasks, and, as was discussed earlier, it lends itself nicely to the C/SCSC. With the high cost of borrowing money these days, the old rule of thumb method used in housing and light construction of advancing 1/3 of the funds when ground is broken, 1/3 when the roof is on, and the last 1/3 when completed is no longer appropriate. A more precise way to estimate and monitor the proper level of funding is needed by both lender and borrower. This is particularly true on large construction jobs that span many months/years before completion. In these situations, the C/SCSC concept could provide a standard language system and monitoring approach for all parties to the agreement.

Architectural and engineering (A & E) firms are constantly involved in the planning of long-range projects. They plan and design and (sometimes) implement huge projects, many lasting several years. Examples are shopping centers, large hotel complexes, planned living communities, downtown/center-city rejuvenation, to mention only a few. Often A & E and construction firms do well in preparing such plans and forecasts and completing the jobs. Other times they don't do quite so well, as many a lender has learned the hard way. The interesting fact is that there is no common or one standard method used by such A & E and construction firms to prepare and implement these plans. Each uses its own method to plan, quantify, and implement future projects. Some are quite good, some not so good, but nothing is uniform.

There are at least six reasons why the A & E firms, builders, the money lenders, and others might want to consider the adoption of the DOD's C/SCSC approach sometime in the future. The earned value system resulting from the criteria approach would provide them with:

1. a standard or common language management control system which all parties would understand;
2. standardized reporting of progress;
3. a standardized historical cost data base by WBS, which would prove invaluable forecasting future jobs;
4. ease of definition in legally enforceable terms, in contracts between the parties;
5. ease of surveillance at headquarters and on location, with the ability to verify that the technique is actually being used;
6. a technique with 15 years of proven success, with the confidence that such would bring, plus thousands of trained personnel fully experienced with the concept.

There is nothing inherent in the C/SCS Criteria which makes them useful only in the United States. On the contrary, if the approach is valuable here, likewise, the concept could be adopted for use overseas, both with various government ministries and with their businesses, private and government sponsored. Picture a hypothetical situation in which a nation in the underdeveloped world category might set for itself the goal of becoming capable of defending itself from external threats. Such an objective would be an ambitious national undertaking and would take both a considerable amount of resources as well as time (in years) to achieve. Once started, this hypothetical nation would want to monitor progress (monthly) as they make their way toward the goal. The C/SCSC concept could be adopted by such a nation to help plan, implement, and monitor progress in the acquisition of the necessary equipment, the construction of the needed facilities, and the difficult job of training their own people to reach the point of self-sufficiency at a point in time. Unfortunately for these smaller

16

EXECUTIVE SUMMARY

A management or executive summary at the ond of a work has essentially three reasons for its existence:

- To provide those executives who have very limited discretionary time to themselves (and that includes most) with the means to have an overview on a subject prior to deciding on whether or not to undertake the entire reading
- To recapitulate the major points in the book for those readers who have trekked their way through the full subject
- To provide a "sneaky" introduction to a subject for those who are about to start the reading of a book

The author hopes this executive summary will accomplish all three purposes.

There are 15 points which should be understood when completing a study on the Cost/Schedule Control System Criteria (C/SCSC).

1. The 35 C/SCS Criteria were introduced by the Department of Defense in 1967 to specify the minimum management information requirements needed from all contractors wishing to do business with the DOD. Once a contractor has complied with these 35 Criteria they have what may be termed an "earned value" management control system.

2. The C/SCSC concept rejects the notion that there is some absolute or even coincidental relationship between actual costs and actual work accomplished (also called earned value, work performed, and "what you got for

what you spent"). Thus, the traditional/conventional review method of comparing the plan/budget to actual costs is rejected by C/SCSC.

3. The C/SCSC requires the preparation of a detailed plan (called a Performance Measurement Baseline -- PMB) against which cost and schedule performance may be ascertained (called earned value), and focuses management's attention on earned value as a way of determining status at any point in time.

4. Schedule Variances (SV) are defined as any differences between the earned value less the plan.

5. Cost Variances (CV) are defined as any differences between the earned value less cost actuals.

6. C/SCSC requires that all program effort be defined using one (and only one) Work Breakdown Structure (WBS); that all tasks be budgeted at the lowest elements of the WBS where a single organization is responsible for a single WBS element (called a cost account) so that work may be summarized in either of two directions: by WBS item or by contractor functional organization.

7. C/SCSC requires that a given contractor use one (only) management control system and that their system incorporate all planning, work definition, work authorization, budgeting, and scheduling into this single system.

8. Contractors in compliance with the 35 Criteria must prove it in what is called a validation of two types: an initial Demonstration Review or a Subsequent Applications Review (SAR).

9. As an adjunct to the C/SCSC, three formal reports are normally required:

   a. CFSR -- Contract Funds Status Report
   b. CPR -- Cost Performance Report or a C/SSR -- Cost/Schedule Status Report.
   c. CCDR -- Contractor Cost Data Reporting

10. The methods to determine earned value are up to a contractor to propose; however, there are essentially only six methods used by most contractors, and the most frequently used one is the milestone method, which assigns specific values to milestones in a short-span measurable cost account.

11. C/SCSC provides a fairly accurate assessment of cost status, but only a gross assessment of schedule status. This is because cost resources are interchangeable, but schedule resources are not necessarily so. However, of greater importance is the fact that C/SCSC may not expose the true status of Critical Milestones, which may pace the completion of the effort.

12.   Therefore, C/SCSC works best to provide schedule status when used in conjunction with a complementary scheduling approach, e.g., PERT/Time Networks.

13.   C/SCSC must be passed on to certain subcontractors who are under a cost reimbursable type contract and reach a specific threshold value.

14.   The earned value concept not only provides an excellent means to determine current status, but of equal importance, the performance to date (Cost Variances and Schedule Variances) allows one to make an independent forecast of the final program costs and ending schedule position.

15.   The C/SCSC earned value concept has been successfully used by the United States government since 1967, but it has not -- at present -- had much impact on private industry, which may well hold the greatest potential for the technique.

In the foregoing pages a very simple management concept has been discussed at considerable length. This concept, the C/SCSC, has impacted well in excess of 100 American firms and their operating divisions across the nation. Tens of thousands of people have been specifically trained in the subject preparatory to doing business with the United States government. It is hoped that this book will in some way facilitate/reinforce that learning process.

A WORD ABOUT THE AUTHOR

Quentin W. Fleming is a manager in the Northrop Corporation's newly formed Advanced Systems Division, in the greater Los Angeles area. In 1971, on a leave of absence from Northrop, he received an appointment with the United States government. He and his family moved initially to Washington, D.C., and later to Tehran, Iran, where he became the seventh and last Peace Corps Director in that country (program terminated in 1976). Concurrently, he managed the Peace Corps program on the small island nation of Bahrain, on the south side of the Arabian/Persian Gulf. He rejoined Northrop in 1976.

Mr. Fleming is the author of <u>Doing Business on the Arabian Peninsula</u>, published by AMACOM Division of the American Management Associations, New York, 1981. He holds the degrees of BS and MA in Management and an LLB. He and his family make their home in Southern California.

APPENDICES

APPENDIX A
SUMMARY OF GOVERNMENT
C/SCSC DOCUMENTS

DEPARTMENT OF DEFENSE

TITLE	DATE	REFERENCE NUMBER	PURPOSE
Resource Management Systems of the DOD	Aug. 22, 1966	DODD 7000.1	Sets objective and policies for the improvement of DOD resource management systems.
Performance Measurement for Selected Acquisitions	June 10, 1977	DODI 7000.2	C/SCSC objectives and criteria for uniform DOD requirements on selected acquisitions.
Selected Acquisition Reports (SARs)	Apr. 4, 1979	DODI 7000.3	Standardized format for reporting technical, schedule, quantity, and cost information on major defense systems to the Secretary of Defense.
Contract Cost Performance, Funds Status and Cost/Schedule Status Reports	Dec. 3, 1979	DODI 7000.10	C/SCSC related reporting requirements.
Contractor Cost Data Reporting (CCDR)	Sept. 5, 1973	DODI 7000.11	C/SCSC related historical cost requirements.
Economic Analysis and Program Evaluation for Resource Management	Oct. 18, 1972	DODI 7041.3	Outlines policy on economic analysis of proposed programs, and program evaluation of on-going activities.
The Planning, Programming, and Budgeting System	Oct. 29, 1969	DODI 7045.7	Contains instructions for the DOD Five Year Defense Program (FYDP).
Guide to Analysis of Contractor Cost Data--Air Force Systems Command	Aug. 1, 1979	---	Provides a source of selected techniques for the analysis of contractor cost data.
Cost/Schedule Control System Criteria--Joint Implementation Guide	Oct. 1, 1980	AFSCP 173-5 AFLCP 173-5 DARCOM-P 715-5 NAVMAT P5240 DLAH 8315.2	The "JIG", the working procedures for C/SCSC used by all services.
C/SCSC Joint Surveillance Guide	July 1, 1974	AFLCP/AFSCP 173-6 AMCP 715-10 NAVMAT P5243 DSAH 8315.1 DCAAP 7641.46	Guidance procedures for contract administration services, and DCAA.
Cost/Schedule Management of Non-Major Contracts (C/SSR Guide)	Nov. 1, 1978	AFSCP 173-3 AFLCP 173-2 DARCOM P 715-13 NAVMAT P5244 DLAH 8315.3	The joint service procedure on the C/SSR.
Contractor Cost Data Reporting (CCDR) System	Nov. 5, 1973	AFSCP 800-15 AFLCP 800-15 AMCP 715-8 NAVMAP P5241	The joint service definition for the CCDR.

DEPARTMENT OF DEFENSE (continued):

TITLE	DATE	REFERENCE NUMBER	PURPOSE
Major System Acquisitions	March 29, 1982	DODD 5000.1	States the DOD Policy for major systems or major modifications to existing systems.
Major System Acquisition Procedures	March 19, 1980	DODI 5000.2	The procedure for DODD 5000.1
OSD Cost Analysis Improvement Group	June 13, 1973	DODD 5000.4	Provides a permanent charter for the CAIG within the Office of the Secretary of Defense-works with CCDR historical cost data.
Policies for the Management and Control of Information Requirements	March 12, 1976	DODD 5000.19	Uniform policy on information requirements, including acquisition management.
Design to Cost	May 23, 1975	DODD 5000.28	Establishes policy on design to cost requirements.
DOD Acquisition Management Systems and Data Requirements Control Program	March 10, 1977	DODI 5000.32	Implements DODD 5000.19
Work Breakdown Structures For Defense Materiel Items	July 31, 1968	DODD 5010.20	Sets forth policy on use of the WBS.
Work Breakdown Structures for Defense Materiel Items	Apr. 25, 1975	Military Standard 881A	Implements the DOD policy on the use of the WBS.
Military Standard Work Measurement	June 30, 1975 (USAF only)	Military Standard 1567	Defines requirements for work measurement on touch labor for Air Force contracts.

DEPARTMENT OF ENERGY

TITLE	DATE	REFERENCE NUMBER	PURPOSE
C/SCS Criteria for Contract Contract Performance Measurement	Sept. 25, 1979	DOE Order 2250.1	Establishes the policy for using C/SCS Criteria on major acquisition projects.
C/SCSC Summary Description	Aug., 1979	DOE/CR-0014	Provides an overview of the DOE C/SCSC.
C/SCSC Implementation Guide	May, 1980	DOE/CR-0015	Uniform guidance for implementation of C/SCSC. (DOE version of the DOD JIG).
C/SCSC Work Breakdown Structure Guide	Oct., 1981	DOE/MA-0040	Provides the DOE guidance on the use of the WBS for work definition. (DOE version of Military Standard 881).
C/SCSC Contractor Reporting/ Data Analysis Guide	Nov., 1980	DOE/CR-0017	Aides both DOE and industry in the effective use and analysis of performance measurement data.
C/SCSC Systems Review/ Surveillance Guide	Nov., 1981	DOE/MA-0047	Guidance to DOE personnel in the validation process: demonstration review and subsequent applications review.
C/SCSC Checklist Handbook	Sept., 1981	DOE/MA-0017	Provides a "pocket sized" book for use of a validation team.

APPENDIX B
DODI 7000.2
PERFORMANCE MEASUREMENT
FOR SELECTED APPLICATIONS

NUMBER 7000.2
DATE June 10, 1977

Department of Defense Instruction
ASD(C)

SUBJECT   Performance Measurement for Selected Acquisitions

References: (a) DoD Directive 7000.1, "Resource Management Systems
                   of the Department of Defense," August 22, 1966
               (b) DoD Directive 5000.1, "Major System Acquisitions,"
                   January 18, 1977
               (c) DoD Directive 5000.2, "Major System Acquisition
                   Process," January 18, 1977
               (d) through (i), see enclosure 2.

A. REISSUANCE AND PURPOSE

This Instruction reissues reference (f) and sets forth objectives and
criteria for the application of uniform DoD requirements to selected defense contracts. The provisions of this Instruction specifically require
the use of Cost/Schedule Control Systems Criteria (C/SCSC) in selected
acquisitions. Reference (f) is hereby superseded and cancelled.

B. APPLICABILITY AND SCOPE

1. The provisions of this Instruction apply to all Military Departments and Defense Agencies (hereafter referred to as "DoD Components") which
are responsible for acquisitions during systems development and production.

2. The acquisitions governed by this Instruction are in selected contracts and subcontracts within programs designated as major system acquisition programs in accordance with reference (b). Firm-fixed-price and firm-
fixed-price-with-economic-price-adjustment contracts are excluded. Application of the C/SCSC to major construction projects is also encouraged where
appropriate.

C. OBJECTIVES

1. To provide an adequate basis for responsible decision-making by
both contractor management and DoD Components, contractors' internal management control systems must provide data which (a) indicate work progress,
(b) properly relate cost, schedule and technical accomplishment, (c) are
valid, timely and auditable, and (d) supply DoD managers with information
at a practicable level of summarization.

2. To bring to the attention of, and encourage, DoD contractors to
accept and install management control systems and procedures which are
most effective in meeting their requirements and controlling contract performance. DoD contractors also should be continuously alert to advances
in management control systems which will improve their internal operations.

D. POLICY

1. It shall be the general policy to (a) require applications of the C/SCSC as stated in enclosure 1 to programs that are within the scope of section B., above, (b) require no changes in contractors' existing cost/schedule control systems except those necessary to meet the C/SCSC, and (c) require the contractor to provide to the Government performance data directly from the same system used for internal management.

2. The policies and criteria contained herein will not be construed as requiring the use of specific systems or changes in accounting systems which will adversely affect (a) the equitable distribution of costs to all contracts, or (b) compliance with the standards, rules, and regulations promulgated by the Cost Accounting Standards Board.

3. Subcontracts within applicable programs, excluding those that are firm-fixed-price, may be selected for application of these criteria by mutual agreement between prime contractors and the contracting DoD Component, according to the criticality of the subcontract to the program. Coverage of certain critical subcontracts may be directed by the Department of Defense, subject to the changes article of the contracts. In those cases where a subcontractor is not required to comply with the criteria, the Cost/Schedule Status Report (C/SSR) approach to performance measurement set forth in DoD Instruction 7000.10 (reference (g)) will normally be used. The limitations in reference (g) apply.

4. The applicability of C/SCSC and provisions concerning the acceptability and use of contractor's cost/schedule control systems shall be (a) included in the Decision Coordinating Papers (DCP) leading to the decisions for full-scale development and production, (b) addressed in procurement plans, (c) set forth in Requests for Proposal (RFP), and (d) made a contractual requirement in appropriate procurements.

a. Reviews of Systems. To ensure compliance with the Cost/Schedule Control Systems Criteria, contractors' systems will be reviewed during various phases of the contracting process.

(1) Where the C/SCSC are included as a requirement in the RFP, an Evaluation Review will be performed as an integral part of the source selection process.

(2) After contract award, an in-plant Demonstration Review will be made to verify that the contractor is operating systems which meet the criteria.

(3) Upon successful completion of the Demonstration Review, contractors will not be subjected to another Demonstration Review unless there are positive indications that the contractor's systems no longer operate so as to meet the criteria.

(4) Subsequent contracts may require a review of shorter duration and less depth to ensure the appropriate and effective application of the accepted systems to the new contract.

(5) Detailed procedures relating to contractual application, interpretative guidance, interservice relationships, and conduct of systems reviews are contained in the Cost/Schedule Control Systems Criteria Joint Implementation Guide (reference (h)).

b. Memorandum of Understanding. After determination that a management system meets C/SCSC, a Memorandum of Understanding may be established between the Department of Defense and the contractor to apply to future contracts.

(1) The use of a Memorandum of Understanding contemplates the execution of a written instrument which references the C/SCSC and negotiated provisions which (a) reflect an understanding between the contractor and the DoD of the requirements of the DoD criteria, and (b) identify the specific system(s) which the contractor intends to use on applicable contracts with DoD Components.

(2) The Memorandum of Understanding will include or make reference to a written description of the system(s) accepted in a Demonstration Review. The system description should be of sufficient detail to permit adequate surveillance by responsible parties. The use of a Memorandum of Understanding is preferred where a number of separate contracts between one or more DoD Component(s) and the contractor may be entered into during the term of the Memorandum of Understanding. It contemplates the delegation of authority to the DoD Component negotiating the Memorandum of Understanding with the contractor to make the agreement on behalf of all prospective DoD contracting components.

(3) Action to develop a Memorandum of Understanding may be initiated by either the contractor or the DoD Component, but will usually be in connection with a contractual requirement. In a proposal, reference to a Memorandum of Understanding satisfies the C/SCSC requirement in RFP's and normally obviates the need for further Evaluation Review during source selection. Procedures for executing Memorandums of Understanding are included in the Cost/Schedule Control Systems Criteria Joint Implementation Guide (reference (h)).

c. Surveillance. Recurring evaluations of the effectiveness of the contractor's policies and procedures will be performed to ensure that the contractor's system continues to meet the C/SCSC and provides valid data consistent with the intent of this Instruction. Surveillance reviews will be based on selective tests of reported data and periodic evaluations of internal practices during the life of the contract. Guidance for surveillance is set forth in the C/SCSC Joint Surveillance Guide (reference (i)).

E. RESPONSIBILITIES

Pursuant to authority contained in DoD Directive 7000.1 (reference (a)):

1. The Assistant Secretary of Defense (Comptroller) will establish policy guidance pertaining to the Cost/Schedule Control Systems Criteria and will monitor their implementation to ensure consistent application throughout the Department of Defense.

2. The Secretaries of the Military Departments will issue appropriate instructions which promulgate the policies contained herein and which assign responsibilities for accomplishing the actions required to validate contractors' compliance with the C/SCSC.

3. The Joint Logistics Commanders will develop and issue joint implementing instructions which outline the procedures to be used in applying, testing and monitoring the C/SCSC on applicable contracts and will ensure that adequate reviews of contractors' systems are performed. The joint implementing procedures and their revisions will be coordinated among all affected DoD Components and submitted to the Assistant Secretary of Defense (Comptroller) for review prior to publication.

4. The Defense Contract Audit Agency and the appropriate Contract Administration Service office will participate in reviews of contractors' systems under their cognizance and will perform required surveillance, collaborating with each other and with the procuring DoD Component in reviewing areas of joint interest.

F. EFFECTIVE DATE AND IMPLEMENTATION

This Instruction is effective immediately. Forward two copies of the implementing documents to the Assistant Secretary of Defense (Comptroller) within 60 days.

Fred P. Wacker

Assistant Secretary of Defense
(Comptroller)

Enclosures - 2
1. Cost/Schedule Control Systems Criteria
2. List of additional references

COST/SCHEDULE CONTROL SYSTEMS CRITERIA

1. GENERAL

a. Any system used by the contractor in planning and controlling the performance of the contract shall meet the criteria set forth in paragraph 3., below. Nothing in these criteria is intended to affect the basis on which costs are reimbursed and progress payments are made, and nothing herein will be construed as requiring the use of any single system, or specific method of management control or evaluation of performance. The contractor's internal systems need not be changed, provided they satisfy these criteria.

b. An element in the evaluation of proposals will be the proposer's system for planning and controlling contract performance. The proposer will fully describe the system to be used. The prospective contractor's cost/schedule control system proposal will be evaluated to determine if it meets these criteria. The prospective contractor will agree to operate a compliant system throughout the period of contract performance if awarded the contract. The DoD will agree to rely on the contractor's compliant system and therefore will not impose a separate planning and control system.

2. DEFINITIONS

a. ACTUAL COST OF WORK PERFORMED (ACWP). The costs actually incurred and recorded in accomplishing the work performed within a given time period.

b. ACTUAL DIRECT COSTS. Those costs identified specifically with a contract, based upon the contractor's cost identification and accumulation system as accepted by the cognizant DCAA representatives. (See Direct Costs.)

c. ALLOCATED BUDGET. (See Total Allocated Budget.)

d. APPLIED DIRECT COSTS. The amounts recognized in the time period associated with the consumption of labor, material, and other direct resources, without regard to the date of commitment or the date of payment. These amounts are to be charged to work-in-process in the time period that any one of the following takes place:

(1) When labor, material and other direct resources are actually consumed, or

(2) When material resources are withdrawn from inventory for use, or

(3) When material resources are received that are uniquely identified to the contract and scheduled for use within 60 days, or

(4) When major components or assemblies are received on a line flow basis that are specifically and uniquely identified to a single serially numbered end item.

e. APPORTIONED EFFORT. Effort that by itself is not readily divisible into short-span work packages but which is related in direct proportion to measured effort.

f. AUTHORIZED WORK. That effort which has been definitized and is on contract, plus that for which definitized contract costs have not been agreed to but for which written authorization has been received.

g. BASELINE. (See Performance Measurement Baseline.)

h. BUDGETED COST FOR WORK PERFORMED (BCWP). The sum of the budgets for completed work packages and completed portions of open work packages, plus the appropriate portion of the budgets for level of effort and apportioned effort.

i. BUDGETED COST FOR WORK SCHEDULED (BCWS). The sum of budgets for all work packages, planning packages, etc., scheduled to be accomplished (including in-process work packages), plus the amount of level of effort and apportioned effort scheduled to be accomplished within a given time period.

j. BUDGETS FOR WORK PACKAGES. (See Work Package Budgets.)

k. CONTRACT BUDGET BASE. The negotiated contract cost plus the estimated cost of authorized unpriced work.

l. CONTRACTOR. An entity in private industry which enters into contracts with the Government. In this Instruction, the word may also apply to Government-owned, Government-operated activities which perform work on major defense programs.

m. COST ACCOUNT. A management control point at which actual costs can be accumulated and compared to budgeted costs for work performed. A cost account is a natural control point for cost/schedule planning and control, since it represents the work assigned to one responsible organizational element on one contract work breakdown structure (CWBS) element.

n. DIRECT COSTS. Any costs which can be identified specifically with a particular final cost objective. This term is explained in ASPR 15-202.

o. ESTIMATED COST AT COMPLETION OR ESTIMATE AT COMPLETION (EAC). Actual direct costs, plus indirect costs allocable to the contract, plus the estimate of costs (direct and indirect) for authorized work remaining.

p. INDIRECT COSTS. Costs, which because of their incurrence for common or joint objectives, are not readily subject to treatment as direct costs. This term is further defined in ASPR 3-701.3 and ASPR 15-203.

213

q. INITIAL BUDGET. (See Original Budget.)

r. INTERNAL REPLANNING. Replanning actions performed by the contractor for remaining effort within the recognized total allocated budget.

s. LEVEL OF EFFORT (LOE). Effort of a general or supportive nature which does not produce definite end products or results.

t. MANAGEMENT RESERVE. (Synonymous with Management Reserve Budget). An amount of the total allocated budget withheld for management control purposes rather than designated for the accomplishment of a specific task or set of tasks. It is not a part of the Performance Measurement Baseline.

u. NEGOTIATED CONTRACT COST. The estimated cost negotiated in a cost-plus-fixed-fee contract, or the negotiated contract target cost in either a fixed-price-incentive contract or a cost-plus-incentive-fee contract.

v. ORIGINAL BUDGET. The budget established at, or near, the time the contract was signed, based on the negotiated contract cost.

w. OVERHEAD. (See Indirect Costs.)

x. PERFORMANCE MEASUREMENT BASELINE. The time-phased budget plan against which contract performance is measured. It is formed by the budgets assigned to scheduled cost accounts and the applicable indirect budgets. For future effort, not planned to the cost account level, the performance measurement baseline also includes budgets assigned to higher level CWBS elements, and undistributed budgets. It equals the total allocated budget less management reserve.

y. PERFORMING ORGANIZATION. A defined unit within the contractor's organization structure, which applies the resources to perform the work.

z. PLANNING PACKAGE. A logical aggregation of work within a cost account, normally the far term effort, that can be identified and budgeted in early baseline planning, but is not yet defined into work packages.

aa. PROCURING ACTIVITY. The subordinate command in which the Procuring Contracting Office (PCO) is located. It may include the program office, related functional support offices, and procurement offices. Examples of procuring activities are AFSC/ESD, AFLC/OC-ALC, DARCOM/MIRADCOM, and NMC/NAVAIRSYSCOM.

bb. REPLANNING. (See Internal Replanning.)

cc. REPROGRAMMING. Replanning of the effort remaining in the contract, resulting in a new budget allocation which exceeds the contract budget base.

dd. RESPONSIBLE ORGANIZATION. A defined unit within the contractor's organization structure which is assigned responsibility for accomplishing specific tasks.

ee. SIGNIFICANT VARIANCES. Those differences between planned and actual performance which require further review, analysis, or action. Appropriate thresholds should be established as to the magnitude of variances which will require variance analysis.

ff. TOTAL ALLOCATED BUDGET. The sum of all budgets allocated to the contract. Total allocated budget consists of the performance measurement baseline and all management reserve. The total allocated budget will reconcile directly to the contract budget base. Any differences will be documented as to quantity and cause.

gg. UNDISTRIBUTED BUDGET. Budget applicable to contract effort which has not yet been identified to CWBS elements at or below the lowest level of reporting to the Government.

hh. VARIANCES. (See Significant Variances.)

ii. WORK BREAKDOWN STRUCTURE. A product-oriented family tree division of hardware, software, services, and other work tasks which organizes, defines, and graphically displays the product to be produced, as well as the work to be accomplished to achieve the specified product.

    (1) Project Summary Work Breakdown Structure. A summary WBS tailored to a specific defense materiel item by selecting applicable elements from one or more summary WBS's or by adding equivalent elements unique to the project (MIL-STD-881A).

    (2) Contract Work Breakdown Structure (CWBS). The complete WBS for a contract, developed and used by a contractor within the guidelines of MIL-STD-881A, and according to the contract work statement.

jj. WORK PACKAGE BUDGETS. Resources which are formally assigned by the contractor to accomplish a work package, expressed in dollars, hours, standards, or other definitive units.

kk. WORK PACKAGES. Detailed short-span jobs, or material items, identified by the contractor for accomplishing work required to complete the contract. A work package has the following characteristics:

    (1) It represents units of work at levels where work is performed.

    (2) It is clearly distinguishable from all other work packages.

    (3) It is assignable to a single organizational element.

    (4) It has scheduled start and completion dates and, as applicable, interim milestones, all of which are representative of physical accomplishment.

(5) It has a budget or assigned value expressed in terms of dollars, man-hours, or other measurable units.

(6) Its duration is limited to a relatively short span of time or it is subdivided by discrete value-milestones to facilitate the objective measurement of work performed.

(7) It is integrated with detailed engineering, manufacturing, or other schedules.

3. CRITERIA

The contractors' management control systems will include policies, procedures, and methods which are designed to ensure that they will accomplish the following:

a. Organization

(1) Define all authorized work and related resources to meet the requirements of the contract, using the framework of the CWBS.

(2) Identify the internal organizational elements and the major subcontractors responsible for accomplishing the authorized work.

(3) Provide for the integration of the contractor's planning, scheduling, budgeting, work authorization and cost accumulation systems with each other, the CWBS, and the organizational structure.

(4) Identify the managerial positions responsible for controlling overhead (indirect costs).

(5) Provide for integration of the CWBS with the contractor's functional organizational structure in a manner that permits cost and schedule performance measurement for CWBS and organizational elements.

b. Planning and Budgeting

(1) Schedule the authorized work in a manner which describes the sequence of work and identifies the significant task interdependencies required to meet the development, production and delivery requirements of the contract.

(2) Identify physical products, milestones, technical performance goals, or other indicators that will be used to measure output.

(3) Establish and maintain a time-phased budget baseline at the cost account level against which contract performance can be measured. Initial budgets established for this purpose will be based on the negotiated target cost. Any other amount used for performance measurement purposes must be formally recognized by both the contractor and the Government.

(4) Establish budgets for all authorized work with separate identification of cost elements (labor, material, etc.).

(5) To the extent the authorized work can be identified in discrete, short-span work packages, establish budgets for this work in terms of dollars, hours, or other measurable units. Where the entire cost account cannot be subdivided into detailed work packages, identify the far term effort in larger planning packages for budget and scheduling purposes.

(6) Provide that the sum of all work package budgets, plus planning package budgets within a cost account equals the cost account budget.

(7) Identify relationships of budgets or standards in underlying work authorization systems to budgets for work packages.

(8) Identify and control level of effort activity by time-phased budgets established for this purpose. Only that effort which cannot be identifed as discrete, short-span work packages or as apportioned effort will be classed as level of effort.

(9) Establish overhead budgets for the total costs of each significant organizational component whose expenses will become indirect costs. Reflect in the contract budgets at the appropriate level the amounts in overhead pools that will be allocated to the contract as indirect costs.

(10) Identify management reserves and undistributed budget.

(11) Provide that the contract target cost plus the estimated cost of authorized but unpriced work is reconciled with the sum of all internal contract budgets and management reserves.

c. Accounting

(1) Record direct costs on an applied or other acceptable basis in a formal system that is controlled by the general books of account.

(2) Summarize direct costs from cost accounts into the WBS without allocation of a single cost account to two or more WBS elements.

(3) Summarize direct costs from the cost accounts into the contractor's functional organizational elements without allocation of a single cost account to two or more organizational elements.

(4) Record all indirect costs which will be allocated to the contract.

(5) Identify the bases for allocating the cost of apportioned effort.

(6) Identify unit costs, equivalent unit costs, or lot costs as applicable.

(7) The contractor's material accounting system will provide for:

(a) Accurate cost accumulation and assignment of costs to cost accounts in a manner consistent with the budgets using recognized, acceptable costing techniques.

(b) Determination of price variances by comparing planned versus actual commitments.

(c) Cost performance measurement at the point in time most suitable for the category of material involved, but no earlier than the time of actual receipt of material.

(d) Determination of cost variances attributable to the excess usage of material.

(e) Determination of unit or lot costs when applicable.

(f) Full accountability for all material purchased for the contract, including the residual inventory.

d. Analysis

(1) Identify at the cost account level on a monthly basis using data from, or reconcilable with, the accounting system:

(a) Budgeted cost for work scheduled and budgeted cost for work performed.

(b) Budgeted cost for work performed and applied (actual where appropriate) direct costs for the same work.

(c) Variances resulting from the above comparisons classified in terms of labor, material, or other appropriate elements together with the reasons for significant variances.

(2) Identify on a monthly basis, in the detail needed by management for effective control, budgeted indirect costs, actual indirect costs, and variances along with the reasons.

(3) Summarize the data elements and associated variances listed in (1) and (2) above through the contractor organization and WBS to the reporting level specified in the contract.

(4) Identify significant differences on a monthly basis between planned and actual schedule accomplishment and the reasons.

(5) Identify managerial actions taken as a result of criteria items (1) through (4) above.

(6) Based on performance to date and on estimates of future conditions, develop revised estimates of cost at completion for WBS elements identified in the contract and compare these with the contract budget base and the latest statement of funds requirements reported to the Government.

e. Revisions and Access to Data

(1) Incorporate contractual changes in a timely manner recording the effects of such changes in budgets and schedules. In the directed effort prior to negotiation of a change, base such revisions on the amount estimated and budgeted to the functional organizations.

(2) Reconcile original budgets for those elements of the work breakdown structure identified as priced line items in the contract, and for those elements at the lowest level of the DoD Project Summary WBS, with current performance measurement budgets in terms of (a) changes to the authorized work and (b) internal replanning in the detail needed by management for effective control.

(3) Prohibit retroactive changes to records pertaining to work performed that will change previously reported amounts for direct costs, indirect costs, or budgets, except for correction of errors and routine accounting adjustments.

(4) Prevent revisions to the contract budget base (paragraph 2.k.) except for Government directed changes to contractual effort.

(5) Document, internally, changes to the performance measurement baseline (paragraph 2.x.) and, on a timely basis, notify the procuring activity through prescribed procedures.

(6) Provide the contracting officer and his duly authorized representatives access to all of the foregoing information and supporting documents.

REFERENCES

(d) Armed Services Procurement Regulation (1976 Edition)
(e) MIL-STD-881A, "Work Breakdown Structures for Defense Material
    Items," April 25, 1975
(f) DoD Instruction 7000.2, "Performance Measurement for Selected
    Acquisitions," April 25, 1972 (hereby cancelled)
(g) DoD Instruction 7000.10, "Contract Cost Performance, Funds
    Status and Cost/Schedule Status Reports," August 6, 1974
(h) AFSCP/AFLCP 173-5, DARCOM-P 715-5, NAVMAT P5240, DSAH 8315.2
    "Cost/Schedule Control Systems Criteria Joint Implementation
    Guide," October 1, 1976
(i) DARCOM-P 715-10, NAVMAT P5243, AFLCP/AFSCP 173-6, DSAH 8315.1,
    DCAAP 7641.46, "C/SCSC Joint Surveillance Guide," July 1, 1974
    and Change 1, October 1, 1976

APPENDIX C
DODI 7000.10
C/SCSC REPORTS:
CPR; CFSF; C/SSR

December 3, 1979
NUMBER 7000.10

Department of Defense Instruction^{ASD(C)}

SUBJECT   Contract Cost Performance, Funds Status and Cost/Schedule Status Reports

References: (a) DoD Instruction 7000.10, "Contract Cost Performance, Funds Status and Cost/Schedule Status Reports," August 6, 1974 (hereby canceled)
               (b) DoD Directive 7000.1, "Resource Management Systems of the Department of Defense," August 22, 1966
               (c) DoD Directive 5000.1, "Major System Acquisitions," January 18, 1977
               (d) through (j), see enclosure 1

A. REISSUANCE AND PURPOSE

This Instruction:

1. Reissues reference (a) to revise the Cost Performance Report (CPR), the Contract Funds Status Report (CFSR), and the Cost/Schedule Status Report (C/SSR);

2. Assigns responsibilities and provides uniform guidance for implementation of the CPR, the CFSR, and the C/SSR; and

3. Provides procedures for collecting summary level cost, and schedule performance and funding data from contractors for program management purposes, pursuant to references (b), (c), and DoD Directive 5000.2 (reference (d)), and for responding to requests for program status information on major system acquisitions, primarily by means of DoD Instruction 7000.3 (reference (e)).

B. APPLICABILITY AND SCOPE

The provisions of this Instruction apply to the Office of the Secretary of Defense, the Military Departments, the Defense Agencies, and the Unified and Specified Commands (hereafter referred to as "DoD Components") responsible for (1) managing acquisition contracts falling within the scope of section C., and (2) determining fund requirements for contracts and managing the flow of such funds. Application of the provisions of this Instruction to construction contracts is encouraged where appropriate.

C. POLICIES

1. In concert with the policies established in DoD Directive 5000.2 (reference (d)), utilization of the CPR, CFSR, and C/SSR shall

be limited by system managers to that necessary to achieve essential management control.

    a. Contractors are encouraged to substitute internal reports for CPR, CFSR, and C/SSR provided that (1) data elements and definitions used in the reports are comparable to CPR, CFSR and C/SSR requirements, and (2) the reports are in forms suitable for management use.

    b. As applicable, provisions of DoD Directive 5000.19 (reference (f)) concerning the tailoring of management systems may be employed by system managers in the implementation of CPR, CFSR, and C/SSR.

  2. Instructions regarding levels of detail and frequencies of reporting are contained in the Data Item Descriptions (DD Forms 1664) in enclosures 2, 3, and 4 of this Instruction. Local reproduction of formats contained in these enclosures is authorized.

  3. The Cost Performance Report (CPR):

    a. Provides (1) contract cost/schedule status information for use in making and validating management decisions, (2) early indicators of contract cost/schedule problems, and (3) effects of management actions taken to resolve problems affecting cost/schedule performance.

    b. Applies to selected contracts within those programs designated as major system acquisitions in accordance with the criteria of DoD Directive 5000.1 (reference (c)). CPRs will be applied to all contracts which require compliance with the Cost/Schedule Control Systems Criteria (C/SCSC) of DoD Instruction 7000.2 (reference (g)).

    c. Will not be required on firm fixed-price contracts (as defined in Section 3-404.2 of the Defense Acquisition Regulation (reference (h)), unless those contracts represent the development or production of a major defense system or a major component thereof and circumstances require cost/schedule visibility.

    d. Applies to ongoing contracts only in those cases where the procuring agencies consider it necessary to support program management needs and DoD requirements for information. Some of the factors which may affect applications to ongoing contracts are anticipated time to contract completion, anticipated program deferrals, and the relative importance of subcontracts.

    e. Is assigned OMB Approval No. 22-R0280.

4. The Contract Funds Status Report (CFSR):

     a. Supplies funding data that, with other related inputs, provides DoD management with information to assist in (1) updating and forecasting contract fund requirements, (2) planning and decision-making on funding changes, (3) developing fund requirements and budget estimates in support of approved programs, and (4) determining funds in excess of contract needs and available for deobligation.

     b. Applies to all contracts greater than $500,000.

     c. Will not apply to firm fixed-price contracts unless the contract represents the development or production of a major defense system or a major component thereof and specific funding visibility is required. CFSR may be applied to unpriced portions of firm fixed-price contracts that individually or collectively are estimated by the Government to be in excess of 20 percent of the initial contract value. In such cases, the contract will delineate the specific CFSR requirements, if any, to be imposed on the contractor to fit the circumstances of each particular case.

     d. May be implemented at a reduced level of reporting for (1) those contracts with a dollar value between $100,000 and $500,000; (2) time and material contracts; and (3) contractual effort for which the entire CFSR report is not required by the procuring activity, but limited funding requirements information is needed.

     e. Will not be required on:

        (1) Contracts with a total value of less than $100,000, or

        (2) Contracts expected to be completed within 6 months.

     f. Is assigned OMB Approval No. 22-R0180.

5. The Cost/Schedule Status Report (C/SSR):

     a. Provides summarized cost and schedule performance status information on contracts where application of the CPR is not appropriate.

     b. Applies to contracts of $2,000,000 or over and 12 months' duration or more which do not use the CPR. (DoD Instruction 7000.11 (reference (i)) provides for application of Contractor Cost Data Reporting (CCDR) to Category II contracts. To avoid the possibility of duplicative reporting, those elements of cost which are provided by the C/SSR will not be required by CCDR.)

c. Will not be required on firm fixed-price contracts unless those contracts represent the development or production of a critical component of a major defense system, and circumstances require cost/ schedule visibility.

d. Is assigned OMB Approval No. 22-R0327.

D. RESPONSIBILITIES

1. The Heads of DoD Components will assure that:

a. Contractor reports are timely and submitted in accordance with the instructions contained in enclosures 2, 3, and 4.

b. Submitted data are checked for discrepancies and necessary corrections are furnished by contractors.

c. Application of the CPR, CFSR, and C/SSR to ongoing programs or firm fixed-price contracts is held to the minimum essential to support program management needs and DoD requirements for information.

d. Appropriate members of the Performance Measurement Joint Executive Group (reference (j)) provide a forum to arbitrate misapplications of CPR or C/SSR requirements that cannot be resolved amicably through focal points established in the headquarters of the procuring commands.

2. The Director of the cognizant Defense Contract Audit Agency (DCAA) office shall:

a. At the request of a DoD Component, provide advice at the time of preaward evaluations as to whether the contractor's accounting and control systems are adequate and reliable for CPR, CFSR, and C/SSR reporting purposes.

b. Review selected CPR, CFSR, and C/SSR reports when it is considered necessary to assure the continuing adequacy and reliability of procedures and the validity of reported data.

c. Review selected individual CPR, CFSR, and C/SSR reports when requested by the Procuring Contracting Officer (PCO) or Administrative Contracting Officer (ACO) and submit a report thereon.

Dec 3, 79
7000.10

E. EFFECTIVE DATE AND IMPLEMENTATION

This Instruction is effective immediately. Forward two copies of implementing documents to the Assistant Secretary of Defense (Comptroller) within 120 days.

Fred P. Wacker
Assistant Secretary of Defense
(Comptroller)

Enclosures - 4
   1. References
   2. DD Form 1664, DI Number DI-F-6000B,
        Cost Performance Report (CPR)
   3. DD Form 1664, DI Number DI-F-6004B,
        Contract Funds Status Report (CFSR)
   4. DD Form 1664, DI Number DI-F-6010A,
        Cost/Schedule Status Report (C/SSR)

References, continued

(d) DoD Directive 5000.2, "Major System Acquisition Process,"
January 18, 1977

(e) DoD Instruction 7000.3, "Selected Acquisition Reports (SARs),"
April 4, 1979

(f) DoD Directive 5000.19, "Policies for the Management and Control
of Information Requirements," March 12, 1976

(g) DoD Instruction 7000.2, "Performance Measurement for Selected
Acquisitions," June 10, 1977

(h) Defense Acquisition Regulation (1976), Section 3-404.2

(i) DoD Instruction 7000.11, "Contractor Cost Data Reporting (CCDR),"
September 5, 1973

(j) AFSCP/AFLCP 173-5, DARCOM-P 715-5, NAVMAT P5240, DSAH 8315.2,
"Cost/Schedule Control Systems Criteria Joint Implementation Guide,"
October 1, 1976

Dec 3, 79
7000.10 (Encl 2)

DATA ITEM DESCRIPTION	2. IDENTIFICATION NO(S).	
	AGENCY	NUMBER

1. TITLE		
COST PERFORMANCE REPORT (CPR)	DOD	DI-F-6000B

3. DESCRIPTION/PURPOSE

3.1 This report is prepared by contractors and consists of five formats containing cost and related data for measuring contractors' cost and schedule performance. Format 1 provides data to measure cost and schedule performance by summary level work breakdown structure elements. Format 2 provides a similar measurement by organizational or functional cost categories. Format 3 provides the budget baseline plan against which performance is measured. Format 4 provides manpower loading forecasts for   (Continued on page 2)

4. APPROVAL DATE

1 February 1979

5. OFFICE OF PRIMARY RESPONSIBILITY

OASD(C)MS

6. DDC REQUIRED

8. APPROVAL LIMITATION

7. APPLICATION/INTERRELATIONSHIP

7.1 The CPR normally will be required for selected contracts within those programs designated as major programs in accordance with DoD Directive 5000.1, "Major System Acquisitions." It will be established as a contractual requirement as set forth in the DD Form 1423 Contract Data Requirements List (CDRL), and DD Form 1660, Management System Summary List.

7.2 If the CPR supports a contractual requirement for contractor compliance with the Cost/Schedule Control Systems Criteria (C/SCSC), the CPR data elements will reflect the contractor's implementation in accordance with DoD Instruction 7000.2, "Performance Measurement for Selected Acquisitions." If compliance with the C/SCSC is not contractually required,

(Continued on pages 2 and 3)

9. REFERENCES (Mandatory as cited in block 10)

DoD 4120.3M, Aug 78
DoDD 5000.1, 18 Jan 77
DoDD 5000.19, 12 Mar 76
DoDD 5000.32, 10 Mar 77
DoDI 7000.2, 10 Jun 77
DoDI 7000.10, 6 Aug 74
Cost Accounting
    Standard 414, 1 Sep 76

MCSL NUMBER(S)

00934

10. PREPARATION INSTRUCTIONS

10.1 Unless otherwise stated in the solicitation, the effective issue of the document(s) cited in the referenced document(s) in this block shall be that listed in the issue of the DoD Index of Specifications and Standards (reference DoD 4120.3M) and the supplements thereto specified in the solicitation and will form a part of this data item description to the extent defined within.

10.2 Hard copy printouts from contractors' internal mechanized reporting systems may be substituted for CPR formats provided the printouts contain all the required data elements at the specified reporting levels in a form suitable for DoD management use. Where data are furnished which require mechanized processing, narrative remarks should accompany tapes or cards and identify pertinent items to which they apply, and a listing of the tape or card data should be included to expedite processing. CPR formats will be completed in accordance with the following instructions:

10.2.1 Heading Information - Formats 1 through 5

10.2.1.1 CONTRACTOR NAME AND LOCATION : Enter the name, division, if applicable, plant location and mailing address of the reporting contractor.

10.2.1.2 RDT&E ☐ PRODUCTION ☐: Check appropriate box. Separate reports are required for each type of contract.

10.2.1.3 CONTRACT TYPE/NUMBER: Enter the contract type, contract number and the number of the latest contract change or supplemental agreement applicable to the contract.

(Continued on pages 3 through 13)

DD FORM 1664

DI-F-6000B (Continued)
3.   DESCRIPTION/PURPOSE (Continued)

correlation with the budget plan and cost estimate predictions.
Format 5 is a narrative report used to explain significant cost and
schedule variances and other identified contract problems.

3.2 CPR data will be used by DoD system managers to: (a) evaluate
contract performance, (b) identify the magnitude and impact of actual
and potential problem areas causing significant cost and schedule
variances, and (c) provide valid, timely program status information
to higher headquarters.

---

7.   APPLICATION/INTERRELATIONSHIP (Continued)

the data elements to be reported on the CPR will be as specified in
the solicitation document or as subsequently negotiated.

7.3 Unless otherwise provided for in the contract, the CPR normally
will be required on a monthly basis and submitted to the procuring
activity no later than 25 calendar days following the reporting
cutoff date. Reports may reflect data either as of the end of the
calendar month or as of the contractor's accounting period cutoff
date.

7.4 Data reported in the CPR will pertain to all authorized contract
work, including both priced and unpriced effort. The level of detail
to be reported normally will be limited to level three of the Contract
Work Breakdown Structure (WBS) or higher. If a problem area is
indicated at a lower level of the WBS, more detailed data will be
provided until the problem is resolved. Functional data normally
will be reported at the total contract level rather than by individual
WBS elements. Certain aspects of the report are subject to negotiation between the Government and the contractor, such as:

7.4.1 The specific variance thresholds which, if exceeded, require
problem analysis and narrative explanations.

7.4.2 The specific organizational or functional categories to be
reported on Formats 2 and 4.

7.4.3 The specific time increments to be used for the baseline and
manpower loading projections required by Formats 3 and 4.

7.4.4 The reporting provisions which apply to the COST OF MONEY line
on Formats 1 and 2.

7.4.5 The reporting provisions which apply if compliance with C/SCSC
is not contractually required.

DI-F-6000B (Continued)
7. APPLICATION/INTERRELATIONSHIP (Continued)

7.5 In all cases, the CPR is subject to "tailoring" to require less
data in accordance with the provisions of DoD Directive 5000.19,
"Policies for the Management and Control of Information Requirements,"
and DoD Instruction 5000.32, "DoD Acquisition Management Systems and
Data Requirements Control Program." All negotiated reporting provisions
will be specified in the contract, including the reporting frequency,
specific variance thresholds, and the WBS elements to be reported.

7.6 The prescribing document which generates this reporting requirement is DoD Instruction 7000.10, "Contract Cost Performance, Funds
Status and Cost/Schedule Status Reports."

7.7 This Data Item Description supersedes DI-F-6000A.

---

10. PREPARATION INSTRUCTIONS (Continued)

10.2.1.4 PROGRAM NAME/NUMBER: Enter the program name, number,
acronym and/or the type, model and series or other designation of the
prime items purchased under the contract.

10.2.1.5 REPORT PERIOD: Enter the beginning and ending dates of the
period covered by the report.

10.2.1.6 SECURITY CLASSIFICATION: Enter the appropriate security
classification.

10.2.2 FORMAT 1 - WORK BREAKDOWN STRUCTURE:

10.2.2.1 SIGNATURE, TITLE AND DATE: The contractor's authorized
representative will sign the report and enter his title and the date
of signature.

10.2.2.2 QUANTITY: Enter the number of prime items to be procured on
this contract.

10.2.2.3 NEGOTIATED COST: Enter the dollar value (excluding fee or
profit) on which contractual agreement has been reached as of the
cutoff date of the report. For an incentive contract, enter the
definitized contract target cost. Amounts for changes will not be
included in this item until they have been priced and incorporated
in the contract through contract change order or supplemental agreement. For a fixed-fee contract, enter the estimated cost negotiated.
Changes to the estimated cost will consist only of amounts for changes
in the contract scope of work, not for cost growth.

DI-F-6000B (Continued)
10. PREPARATION INSTRUCTIONS (Continued)

10.2.2.4 ESTIMATED COST OF AUTHORIZED, UNPRICED WORK: Enter the amount (excluding fee or profit) estimated for that work for which written authorization has been received, but for which definitized contract prices have not been incorporated in the contract through supplemental agreement.

10.2.2.5 TARGET PROFIT/FEE %: Enter the fee or percentage of profit which will apply if the negotiated cost of the contract (paragraph 10.2.2.3, above) is met.

10.2.2.6 TARGET PRICE: Enter the target price (negotiated contract cost plus profit/fee) applicable to the definitized contract effort.

10.2.2.7 ESTIMATED PRICE: Based on the latest revised estimate of cost at completion for all authorized contract work and the appropriate profit/fee, incentive, and cost sharing provisions, enter the estimated final contract price (total estimated cost to the Government). This number normally will change whenever the estimated cost at completion is revised.

10.2.2.8 SHARE RATIO: Enter the cost sharing ratio(s) applicable to costs over/under the negotiated contract cost.

10.2.2.9 CONTRACT CEILING: Enter the contract ceiling price applicable to the definitized effort.

10.2.2.10 ESTIMATED CONTRACT CEILING: Enter the estimated ceiling price applicable to all authorized contract effort including both definitized and undefinitized effort.

10.2.2.11 COLUMN (1) - ITEM

10.2.2.11.1 WORK BREAKDOWN STRUCTURE: Enter the noun description of the WBS item for which cost information is being reported. WBS items or levels reported will be those specified in the contract.

10.2.2.11.2 COST OF MONEY: Enter in Columns (2) through (16) the Cost of Money associated with the Cost of Facilities Capital applicable to the contract (see Cost Accounting Standard 414 for guidance).

10.2.2.11.3 GENERAL AND ADMINISTRATIVE (G&A): Enter in Columns (2) through (16) the appropriate G&A costs. If G&A has been included in the total costs reported above, G&A will be shown as a nonadd entry on this line with an appropriate notation. If a G&A classification is not used, no entry will be made other than an appropriate notation to that effect.

DI-F-6000B (Continued)
10. PREPARATION INSTRUCTIONS (Continued)

10.2.2.11.4 UNDISTRIBUTED BUDGET: Enter in Columns (14) and (15) the amount of budget applicable to contract effort which has not yet been identified to WBS elements at or below the reporting level. For example, contract changes which were authorized late in the reporting period should have received a total budget; however, assignment of work and allocation of budgets to individual WBS elements may not have been accomplished as of the end of the period. Budgets which can be identified to WBS elements at or below the specified reporting level will be included in the total budgets shown for the WBS elements in the body of the report and will not be shown as undistributed budget. All undistributed budget will be fully explained in the narrative analysis section of the report (Format 5).

NOTE: The provisions made in this report for undistributed budget are primarily to accommodate temporary situations where time constraints prevent adequate budget planning or where contract effort can only be defined in very general terms. Undistributed budget should not be used as a substitute for adequate contract planning. Formal budgets should be allocated to contract effort and functional organizations at the earliest possible time, normally within the next reporting period.

10.2.2.11.5 SUBTOTALS: Enter the sum of the direct, indirect, Cost of Money, and G&A costs and budgets in Columns (2) through (16). In Columns (14) and (15) also add the undistributed budget.

10.2.2.11.6 MANAGEMENT RESERVE: An amount of the overall contract budget withheld for management control purposes rather than for the accomplishment of a specific task or set of tasks. In Column (14) enter the total amount of budget identified as management reserve as of the end of the current reporting period. In Column (15) enter the amount of management reserve expected to be consumed before the end of the contract. In Column (16) enter the difference between Columns (14) and (15). Amounts of management reserve applied to WBS elements during the reporting period and the rationale for the figure in Column (15) will be explained in the narrative analysis on Format 5. (The entry in Column (15) is discretionary and may be zero if the contractor does not wish to make an estimate.)

NOTE: Negative entries will not be made in Column (14). There is no such thing as "negative management reserve." If the contract is budgeted in excess of the Contract Budget Base (the negotiated contract cost plus the estimated cost for authorized-unpriced work), the provisions applicable to formal reprograming and the instructions in paragraphs 10.2.2.11.8, 10.2.2.12.6 and 10.2.2.12.7 apply.

DI-F-6000B (Continued)
10. PREPARATION INSTRUCTIONS (Continued)

10.2.2.11.7 TOTAL: Enter the sum of all direct, indirect, Cost of Money, G&A costs, undistributed budgets and management reserves in Columns (2) through (16).

10.2.2.11.8 VARIANCE ADJUSTMENT: In exceptional cases, the procuring agency may authorize the contractor to establish baseline budgets which in total exceed the Contract Budget Base. If the contractor uses a portion of the additional budget to eliminate variances applicable to completed work, the total adjustments made to the schedule and cost variances will be shown on this line. The total cost variance adjustment entered on this line in Column (11) will be the sum of the individual cost variance adjustments listed in Column (12).

10.2.2.11.9 TOTAL CONTRACT VARIANCE: In Columns (10) and (11), enter on this line the sum of the cost and schedule variances shown on the TOTAL line and on the VARIANCE ADJUSTMENT line. In Column (14) enter the sum of the negotiated contract cost plus the estimated cost for authorized, unpriced work. In Column (15) enter the latest revised estimate of cost at completion. In Column (16) enter the difference between Columns (14) and (15).

10.2.2.12 Cols (2) through (16): If compliance with the C/SCSC is contractually required, Columns (2) through (16) will contain information developed by the contractor's system implemented in accordance with the definitions and criteria contained in DoD Instruction 7000.2. If compliance with C/SCSC is not contractually required, the data elements in these columns will be negotiated using the definitions of DoD Instruction 7000.2 for guidance.

10.2.2.12.1 Col (2) and Col (7) - BUDGETED COST-WORK SCHEDULED: For the time period indicated, enter the Budgeted Cost for Work Scheduled (BCWS) in these columns.

10.2.2.12.2 Col (3) and Col (8) - BUDGETED COST-WORK PERFORMED: For the time period indicated, enter the Budgeted Cost for Work Performed (BCWP) in these columns.

10.2.2.12.3 Col (4) and Col (9) - ACTUAL COST-WORK PERFORMED (ACWP): For the time period indicated, enter the actual direct and indirect costs for work performed without regard to ceiling. In all cases, costs and budgets will be reported on a comparable basis.

10.2.2.12.4 Col (5) and Col (10) - VARIANCE - SCHEDULE: For the time period indicated, these columns reflect the differences between BCWS and BCWP. For the current period, Col (5), schedule variance is derived by subtracting Col (2) (BCWS) from Col (3) (BCWP). For the cumulative to date, Col (10), schedule variance is derived by subtracting Col (7) (BCWS) from Col (8) (BCWP). A positive figure

DI-F-6000B (Continued)
10. <u>PREPARATION INSTRUCTIONS</u> (Continued)

indicates a favorable variance. A negative figure (indicated by parentheses) indicates an unfavorable variance. Significant variances will be fully explained in the problem analysis on Format 5.

10.2.2.12.5 <u>Col (6) and Col (11) - VARIANCE - COST</u>: For the time period indicated, these columns reflect the differences between BCWP and ACWP. For the current period, Col (6), cost variance is derived by subtracting Col (4) (ACWP) from Col (3) (BCWP). For cumulative to date, Col (11), cost variance is derived by subtracting Col (9) (ACWP) from Col (8) (BCWP). A positive figure indicates a favorable variance. A negative figure (indicated by parentheses) indicates an unfavorable variance. Significant variances will be fully explained in the problem analysis on Format 5.

10.2.2.12.6 <u>Col (12) REPROGRAMING ADJUSTMENTS - COST VARIANCE</u>: Formal reprograming results in budget allocations in excess of the Contract Budget Base and, in some instances, adjustments to previously reported variances. If such variance adjustments have been made, the adjustment applicable to each reporting line item affected will be entered in Col (12). The Total of Col (12) will equal the amount shown on the Variance Adjustment line in Col (11).

10.2.2.12.7 <u>Col (13) REPROGRAMING ADJUSTMENTS - BUDGET</u>: Enter the total amounts added to the budget for each reporting line item as the result of formal reprograming. The amounts shown will consist of the sum of the budgets used to adjust cost variances (Col (12)) plus the additional budget added to the WBS element for remaining work. Enter the amount of budget added to management reserve in the space provided on the Management Reserve line. The Total of Col (13) will equal the amount the contract has been budgeted in excess of the Contract Budget Base. An explanation of the reprograming will be provided in the Problem Analysis Report.

NOTE: Cols (12) and (13) are intended for use only in situations involving formal reprograming (over-target baselines). Internal replanning actions within the Contract Budget Base do not require entries in these columns. Where contractors are submitting CPR data directly from mechanized systems, the addition of Cols (12) and (13) as shown may not be practical due to computer reprograming problems or space limitations. In such cases, the information may be provided on a separate sheet and attached as Format 1a to each subsequent report. Contractors will not be required to abandon or modify existing mechanized reporting systems to include Cols (12) and (13) if significant costs will be associated with such change. Nor will contractors be required to prepare the report manually solely to include this information.

DI-F-6000B (Continued)
10. PREPARATION INSTRUCTIONS (Continued)

10.2.2.12.8 Col (14) - AT COMPLETION - BUDGETED: Enter the budgeted cost at completion for the WBS items listed in Col (1). This entry will consist of the sum of the original budgets plus or minus budget changes resulting from contract changes, internal replanning, and application of management reserves. The total should be equal to the negotiated contract cost plus the estimated cost of authorized but unpriced work except where special exception has been made resulting in formal reprograming.

10.2.2.12.9 Col (15) - AT COMPLETION - LATEST REVISED ESTIMATE: Enter the latest revised estimate of cost at completion including estimated overrun/underrun for all authorized work.

10.2.2.12.10 Col (16) - AT COMPLETION - VARIANCE: Enter the difference between the Budgeted - At Completion (Col 14) and the Latest Revised Estimate at Completion (Col 15) by subtracting Col (15) from Col (14). A negative figure (indicated by parentheses) reflects an unfavorable variance. Significant variances will be fully explained on Format 5.

10.2.3 FORMAT 2 - FUNCTIONAL CATEGORIES:

10.2.3.1 Col (1) - ORGANIZATIONAL OR FUNCTIONAL CATEGORY: Under this item list the organizational units or functional categories which reflect the contractor's internal management structure in accordance with Contractor/Government agreement. This format will be used to collect organizational or functional cost information at the total contract level rather than for individual WBS elements. The level of detail to be reported will normally be limited to the organizational level immediately under the operating head of the facility except when there is a significant variance. If a problem area is indicated at a lower level of the organization, more detailed data will be provided until the problem is resolved.

10.2.3.2 COST OF MONEY: Enter in Columns (2) through (16) Cost of Money applicable to the contract (CAS 414).

10.2.3.3 GENERAL AND ADMINISTRATIVE: Enter in Columns (2) through (16) applicable G&A costs. (See paragraph 10.2.2.11.3).

10.2.3.4 UNDISTRIBUTED BUDGET: Enter in Cols (14) and (15) the budget applicable to contract effort which cannot be planned in sufficient detail to be assigned to a responsible organization or functional area at the reporting level. The amounts shown on this format may exceed the amounts shown as undistributed budget on Format 1 if budget is identified to a task at or below the WBS reporting level

DI-F-6000B (Continued)
10. PREPARATION INSTRUCTIONS (Continued)

but organizational identification has not been made; or may be less than the amount on Format 1 where budgets have been assigned to functional organizations but not to WBS elements.

10.2.3.5 SUBTOTAL: Enter the sum of the direct, indirect, Cost of Money, and G&A costs and budgets in Cols (2) through (16). In Cols (14) and (15) also add the undistributed budget.

10.2.3.6 MANAGEMENT RESERVE: In Col (14) enter the amount of budget identified as management reserve. In Col (15) enter the amount of management reserve forecasted to be consumed before the end of the contract. In Col (16) enter the difference between Cols (14) and (15). The MANAGEMENT RESERVE entries will be identical to those shown on Format 1. (The entry in Col (15) is discretionary and may be zero if the contractor does not wish to make an estimate.)

10.2.3.7 TOTAL: Enter the sum of all direct, indirect, Cost of Money, and G&A costs and budgets, undistributed budgets and management reserves in Cols (2) through (16). The totals on this page should equal the TOTAL line on page 1.

10.2.3.8 COLS (2) THROUGH (16): The instructions applicable to these columns are the same as the instructions for corresponding columns on Format 1 (see paragraphs 10.2.2.12.1 through 10.2.2.12.10). All significant variances will be fully explained in the problem analysis on Format 5.

10.2.4 FORMAT 3 - BASELINE:

10.2.4.1 BLOCK (1) - ORIGINAL CONTRACT TARGET COST: Enter the dollar value (excluding fee or profit) negotiated in the original contract. For a cost plus fixed-fee contract, enter the estimated cost negotiated. For an incentive contract, enter the definitized contract target cost.

10.2.4.2 BLOCK (2) - NEGOTIATED CONTRACT CHANGES: Enter the cumulative cost (excluding fee or profit) applicable to definitized contract changes which have occurred since the beginning of the contract.

10.2.4.3 BLOCK (3) - CURRENT TARGET COST: Enter the sum of Blocks (1) and (2). The amount shown should equal the current dollar value (excluding fee or profit) on which contractual agreement has been reached and should be the same as the amount shown as NEGOTIATED COST on Format 1.

10.2.4.4 BLOCK (4) - ESTIMATED COST OF AUTHORIZED, UNPRICED WORK: Enter the estimated cost (excluding fee or profit) for contract

238

DI-F-6000B (Continued)
10. PREPARATION INSTRUCTIONS (Continued)

changes for which written authorizations have been received, but for
which contract prices have not been negotiated, as shown on Format 1.

10.2.4.5 BLOCK (5) - CONTRACT BUDGET BASE: Enter the sum of Blocks
(3) and (4).

10.2.4.6 BLOCK (6) - TOTAL ALLOCATED BUDGET: Enter the sum of all
budgets allocated to the performance of the contractual effort. The
amount shown will include all management reserves and undistributed
budgets. This amount will be the same as that shown on the TOTAL
line in Col (14) on Format 1.

10.2.4.7 BLOCK (7) - DIFFERENCE: In most cases, the amounts shown
in Blocks (5) and (6) will be identical. If the amount shown in
Block (6) exceeds that shown in Block (5), the difference should be
reflected as a negative value and explained in the narrative analysis
on Format 5 at the time the negative value appears and subsequently
for any change in the value.

10.2.4.8 BLOCK (8) - CONTRACT START DATE: Enter the date the contractor was authorized to start work on the contract, regardless
of the date of contract definitization. (Long lead procurement
efforts authorized under prior contracts are not to be considered.)

10.2.4.9 BLOCK (9) - CONTRACT DEFINITIZATION DATE: Enter the date
the contract was definitized.

10.2.4.10 BLOCK (10) - LAST ITEM DELIVERY DATE: Enter the date the
last major item of equipment is scheduled to be delivered to the
government as specified in the contract. The date shown should
represent the completion of the significant effort on the contract
(approximately 95% of the total contractual effort in most cases).

10.2.4.11 BLOCK (11) - CONTRACT COMPLETION DATE: Enter the contract
scheduled completion date in accordance with the latest contract
modification.

10.2.4.12 BLOCK (12) - ESTIMATED COMPLETION DATE: Enter the latest
revised estimate of contract completion.

10.2.4.13 COL (1) - ITEM:

10.2.4.13.1 PM BASELINE (BEGINNING OF PERIOD): The time-phased
performance measurement baseline (including G&A) which existed at
the beginning of the current reporting period. Most of the entries

DI-F-6000B (Continued)
10. PREPARATION INSTRUCTIONS (Continued)

on this line are taken directly from the PM BASELINE (END OF PERIOD)
line on the previous report. For example, the number in Col (4) on
the PM BASELINE (END OF PERIOD) line from last month's report becomes
the number in Col (3) on the PM BASELINE (BEGINNING OF PERIOD) line
on this report. The number in Col (5) (end of period) last report
becomes Col (4) (beginning of period) this report, etc. This rule
pertains through Col (9) where the time increments change from monthly
to some other periods of time. At this point, a portion of Col (10)
(end of period) would go into Col (9) (beginning of period) and the
remainder of Col (10) (end of period) would go into Col (10) (beginning
of period). Cols (11) through (16) simply move directly up to the
(beginning of period) line without changing columns.

10.2.4.13.2 BASELINE CHANGES: List by number, the contract changes
and supplemental agreements authorized during the reporting period.
All authorized baseline changes should be listed whether priced or
unpriced. The amount of management reserve applied during the period
should also be listed.

10.2.4.13.3 PM BASELINE (END OF PERIOD): The time-phased performance
measurement baseline as it exists at the end of the reporting period.
The difference between this line and the PM BASELINE (BEGINNING OF
PERIOD) should represent the effects of the authorized changes and
allocations of management reserves made during the period. Significant differences should be explained in Format 5 - Problem Analysis
Report, in terms of reasons for necessary changes to time-phasing
due to replanning, and reasons for the application of Management
Reserve.

10.2.4.13.4 MANAGEMENT RESERVE: Enter the total amount of management
reserve remaining as of the end of the reporting period.

10.2.4.13.5 TOTAL: Enter the sum of the PM BASELINE (END OF PERIOD)
and the management reserve in Col (16). This amount should be the
same as that shown on the TOTAL line in Col (14) on Format 1.

10.2.4.14 COL (2) - BCWS - CUM TO DATE: Enter the cumulative BCWS
for the periods indicated. The entry on the PM BASELINE (BEGINNING OF
PERIOD) line should be the same number reported as BCWS - CUM TO DATE
(Col (7)) on the TOTAL line of Format 1 of the previous month's CPR.
On the PM BASELINE (END OF PERIOD) line, enter the cumulative BCWS
as of the last day of the reporting period. (This should be the
same number which appears on the TOTAL line in Col (7) of Format 1 for
this reporting period.)

DI-F-6000B (Continued)
10. PREPARATION INSTRUCTIONS (Continued)

10.2.4.15 COL (3) - BCWS FOR REPORT PERIOD: On the PM BASELINE
(BEGINNING OF PERIOD) line, enter the BCWS planned for the reporting
period. (This should be the number in Col (4) on the PM BASELINE
(END OF PERIOD) line on the preceding month's report.)

10.2.4.16 Cols (4) through (14): In the Blocks above Columns (4)
through (9), enter the appropriate months for the next six report
periods. Enter the projected BCWS (by month for six months and by
other specified periods, or as negotiated with the procuring activity)
for the remainder of the contract.

10.2.4.17 COL (15) - UNDISTRIBUTED BUDGET: On the PM BASELINE
(BEGINNING OF PERIOD) line, enter the number from Col (15) on the PM
BASELINE (END OF PERIOD) line from the preceding report. On the PM
BASELINE (END OF PERIOD) line, enter the Undistributed Budget shown
in Col (14) on Format 1 of this report.

10.2.4.18 COL (16) - TOTAL BUDGET: On the PM BASELINE (BEGINNING
OF PERIOD) line enter the number from Col (16) on the PM BASELINE (END
OF PERIOD) line from the preceding report. In the section where baseline changes (priced and unpriced contract changes and changes in
management reserve) which occurred during the period are listed in
Col (1), enter the amount of each of the changes listed, (negotiated cost for priced changes not previously reported as authorized,
unpriced changes; difference between estimated cost and negotiated
cost for priced changes previously reported as authorized, unpriced
changes; and estimated cost for authorized, unpriced changes). On
the PM BASELINE (END OF PERIOD) line, enter the sum of the amount in
the preceding columns on this line. On the MANAGEMENT RESERVE line,
enter the amount of management reserve available at the end of the
period. On the TOTAL line enter the sum of the amounts in this column
on the PM BASELINE (END OF PERIOD) line and the MANAGEMENT RESERVE
line. (This should equal the amount in Block (6) on this Format and
also the amount of the TOTAL line in Col (14) of Format 1.)

10.2.5 Format 4 - Manpower Loading:

10.2.5.1 General: For those organizational or functional categories
shown in Col (1) equivalent man-months will be indicated for the
current reporting period, cumulative through the current period, and
forecast to completion. Direct man-months will be shown for each
organizational unit or major functional category for the contract.
An equivalent man-month is defined as the effort equal to that of one

DI-F-6000B (Continued)
10. PREPARATION INSTRUCTIONS (Continued)

person for one month. Figures should be reported in whole numbers.
(Partial man-months, .5 and above, will be rounded to 1; below .5 to
0.) When mutually agreed by the contractor and the Government, manpower loading may be reported in terms of man-days or man-hours.

10.2.5.1.1 ORGANIZATIONAL OR FUNCTIONAL CATEGORY: List the organizational or functional categories which reflect the contractor's
internal management structure in accordance with Contractor/Government
agreement. Categories shown should coincide with those shown on
Format 2 of the report.

10.2.5.1.2 TOTAL DIRECT: The sum of all direct man-months for the
organizational or functional categories shown in Col (1).

10.2.5.2 COL (2) - ACTUAL - CURRENT PERIOD: Enter the actual equivalent man-months incurred during the current reporting period.

10.2.5.3 COL (3) - ACTUAL END OF CURRENT PERIOD (CUM): Enter the
actual equivalent man-months incurred to date (cumulative) as of the
end of the report period.

10.2.5.4 COLS (4) THROUGH (14) - FORECAST (NONCUMULATIVE): Enter a
forecast of manpower requirements by month for a six-month period
following the current period and by periodic increment thereafter,
such increment to be negotiated with the procuring activity. The
forecast will be updated at least quarterly unless a major revision
to the plan or schedule has taken place, in which case forecasts will
be changed for all periods involved in the report submitted at the
end of the month in which the change occurred.

10.2.5.5 COL (15) - FORECAST AT COMPLETION: Enter the estimate of
equivalent man-months necessary for the total contract in Col (15)
by organizational or functional category. Any significant change in
the total number of man-months at completion of the contract (i.e.,
Col (14) Total) should be explained in Format 5 - Problem Analysis.

10.2.6 FORMAT 5 - PROBLEM ANALYSIS REPORT: The Problem Analysis
Report is a narrative report prepared to supplement the other pages
of the Cost Performance Report as well as other reports which identify
significant problems. The report should be prepared as specified on
Format 5.

242

Page 14 of 18 Page

CLASSIFICATION

COST PERFORMANCE REPORT — WORK BREAKDOWN STRUCTURE

PAGE ___ OF ___

FORM APPROVED OMB NUMBER 22R0280

CONTRACTOR:
LOCATION:
RDT&E ☐   PRODUCTION ☐

CONTRACT TYPE/NO.:   PROGRAM NAME/NUMBER   REPORT PERIOD   SIGNATURE, TITLE & DATE

| QUANTITY | NEGOTIATED COST | EST COST AUTH, UNPRICED WORK | TGT PROFIT/FEE % | TGT PRICE | EST PRICE | SHARE RATIO | CONTRACT CEILING | EST CONTRACT CEILING |

ITEM	CURRENT PERIOD						CUMULATIVE TO DATE						REPROGRAMING ADJUSTMENTS		AT COMPLETION		
	BUDGETED COST		ACTUAL COST WORK PERFORMED	VARIANCE			BUDGETED COST		ACTUAL COST WORK PERFORMED	VARIANCE		COST VARIANCE	BUDGET	BUDGETED	LATEST REVISED ESTIMATE	VARIANCE
	WORK SCHEDULED	WORK PERFORMED		SCHEDULE	COST		WORK SCHEDULED	WORK PERFORMED		SCHEDULE	COST					
(1)	(2)	(3)	(4)	(5)	(6)		(7)	(8)	(9)	(10)	(11)	(12)	(13)	(14)	(15)	(16)

WORK BREAKDOWN STRUCTURE

COST OF MONEY
GEN AND ADMIN
UNDISTRIBUTED BUDGET
SUBTOTAL
MANAGEMENT RESERVE
TOTAL

RECONCILIATION TO CONTRACT BUDGET BASE

VARIANCE ADJUSTMENT
TOTAL CONTRACT VARIANCE

(DOLLARS IN ___)

CLASSIFICATION

FORMAT 1

Figure 1

Dec 3, 79
7000.10 (Encl 2)

CLASSIFICATION

PAGE _____ OF _____

COST PERFORMANCE REPORT — FUNCTIONAL CATEGORIES

CONTRACTOR:	CONTRACT TYPE/NO.	PROGRAM NAME/NUMBER	REPORT PERIOD	SIGNATURE, TITLE & DATE	FORM APPROVED OMB NUMBER 22R0280
LOCATION:					
RDT&E ☐ PRODUCTION ☐					

| QUANTITY | NEGOTIATED COST | EST COST AUTH. UNPRICED WORK | TGT PROFIT/FEE % | TGT PRICE | EST PRICE | SHARE RATIO | CONTRACT CEILING | EST CONTRACT CEILING |

ORGANIZATIONAL OR FUNCTIONAL CATEGORY	CURRENT PERIOD						CUMULATIVE TO DATE						REPROGRAMMING ADJUSTMENTS			AT COMPLETION	
	BUDGETED COST		ACTUAL COST WORK PERFORMED	VARIANCE			BUDGETED COST		ACTUAL COST WORK PERFORMED	VARIANCE			COST VARIANCE	BUDGET	CONTRACT CEILING / BUDGETED	LATEST REVISED ESTIMATE	VARIANCE
	WORK SCHEDULED	WORK PERFORMED		SCHEDULE	COST		WORK SCHEDULED	WORK PERFORMED		SCHEDULE	COST						
(1)	(2)	(3)	(4)	(5)	(6)		(7)	(8)	(9)	(10)	(11)		(12)	(13)	(14)	(15)	(16)
COST OF MONEY																	
GEN AND ADMIN																	
UNDISTRIBUTED BUDGET																	
SUBTOTAL																	
MANAGEMENT RESERVE																	
TOTAL																	

FORMAT 2

CLASSIFICATION

Figure 2

Page 15 of 18 Pages

CLASSIFICATION

PAGE OF

COST PERFORMANCE REPORT — BASELINE

CONTRACTOR: LOCATION: RDT&E [ ] PRODUCTION [ ]	CONTRACT TYPE/NO.:	PROGRAM NAME/NUMBER	REPORT PERIOD:	FORM APPROVED OMB NUMBER 22R0280

(1) ORIGINAL CONTRACT TARGET COST	(2) NEGOTIATED CONTRACT CHANGES	(3) CURRENT TARGET COST (1) + (2)	(4) ESTIMATED COST OF AUTHORIZED, UNPRICED WORK	(5) CONTRACT BUDGET BASE (3) + (4)	(6) TOTAL ALLOCATED BUDGET	(7) DIFFERENCE (5) — (6) (SEE PAGE 5)

(8) CONTRACT START DATE	(9) CONTRACT DEFINITIZATION DATE	(10) LAST ITEM DELIVERY DATE	(11) CONTRACT COMPLETION DATE	(12) ESTIMATED COMPLETION DATE

ITEM	BCWS CUM TO DATE	BCWS FOR REPORT PERIOD	BUDGETED COST FOR WORK SCHEDULED (NON-CUMULATIVE)											UNDIST BUDGET	TOTAL BUDGET
			SIX MONTH FORECAST						(ENTER SPECIFIED PERIODS)						
			+ 1	+ 2	+ 3	+ 4	+ 5	+ 6							
(1)	(2)	(3)	(4)	(5)	(6)	(7)	(8)	(9)	(10)	(11)	(12)	(13)	(14)	(15)	(16)
PM BASELINE (BEGINNING OF PERIOD)															
(LIST BASELINE CHANGES AUTHORIZED DURING REPORT PERIOD)															
PM BASELINE (END OF PERIOD)															
MANAGEMENT RESERVE															
TOTAL															

FORMAT 3

CLASSIFICATION

Figure 3

Dec 3, 79
7000.10 (Encl 2)

CLASSIFICATION

PAGE _____ OF _____

COST PERFORMANCE REPORT — MANPOWER LOADING

CONTRACTOR:	CONTRACT TYPE/NO.:	PROGRAM NAME/NUMBER:	FORM APPROVED OMB NUMBER 22R0280
LOCATION:			REPORT PERIOD:
RDT&E ☐ PRODUCTION ☐			

ORGANIZATIONAL OR FUNCTIONAL CATEGORY	ACTUAL CURRENT PERIOD	ACTUAL END OF CURRENT PERIOD (CUM)	FORECAST (NON-CUMULATIVE)											AT COMPLETION
			SIX MONTH FORECAST BY MONTH (ENTER NAMES OF MONTHS)						(ENTER SPECIFIED PERIODS)					
(1)	(2)	(3)	(4)	(5)	(6)	(7)	(8)	(9)	(10)	(11)	(12)	(13)	(14)	(15)
TOTAL DIRECT														

(ALL FIGURES IN WHOLE NUMBERS)

CLASSIFICATION

Format 4

Figure 4

246

COST PERFORMANCE REPORT — PROBLEM ANALYSIS

CONTRACTOR:	CONTRACT TYPE/NO.:	PROGRAM NAME/NUMBER:	REPORT PERIOD:	FORM APPROVED OMB NUMBER 22R0280
LOCATION				
RDT&E ☐ PRODUCTION ☐				

EVALUATION

Section 1 — Total Contract: Provide a summary analysis, identifying significant problems affecting performance. Indicate corrective actions required, including Government action where applicable.

Section 2 — Cost and Schedule Variances: Explain all variances which exceed specified variance thresholds. Explanations of variances must clearly identify the nature of the problem, the reasons for cost or schedule variance, impact on the immediate task, impact on the total program, and the corrective action taken. Explanations of cost variances should identify amounts attributable to rate changes separately from amounts applicable to manhours used; amounts attributable to material price changes separately from amounts applicable to material usage; and amounts attributable to overhead rate changes separately from amounts applicable to overhead base changes and amounts applicable to changes in the overhead allocation basis.

Within this section, the following specific variances must be explained:

    a. Schedule variances (Budgeted Cost for Work Scheduled vs Budgeted Cost for Work Performed)

    b. Cost variances (Budgeted Cost for Work Performed vs Actual Cost of Work Performed)

    c. Cost variances at completion (Budgeted at Completion vs Latest Revised Estimate at Completion)

Section 3 — Other Analysis: In addition to the variance explanations above, the following analyses are mandatory:

    a. Identify the effort to which the undistributed budget applies.

    b. Identify the amount of management reserve applied during the reporting period, the WBS and organizational elements to which applied, and the reasons for application.

    c. Explain reasons for significant shifts in time-phasing of the PM Baseline shown on Format 3.

    d. Explain significant changes in total man-months at completion shown on Format 4.

    e. Explain reasons for significant shifts in time-phasing of planned or actual manpower usage shown on Format 4.

Section 4 — Over-Target Baseline: If the difference shown in block (7) on Format 3 becomes a negative value or changes in value, provide:

    a. Procuring activity authorization for the baseline change which resulted in negative value or change.

    b. Reasons for the additional budget in the following terms:

        (1) In-scope engineering changes

        (2) In-scope support effort changes

        (3) In-scope schedule changes

        (4) Economic change

        (5) Other (specify)

    c. The amount (by WBS element) for added in-scope effort not previously identified or budgeted.

FORMAT 5

Figure 5

Dec 3, 79
7000.10 (Encl 3)

DATA ITEM DESCRIPTION	2. IDENTIFICATION NO(S).	
	AGENCY	NUMBER

1. TITLE		
CONTRACT FUNDS STATUS REPORT (CFSR)	DOD	DI-F-6004B

3. DESCRIPTION/PURPOSE

3.1 The Contract Funds Status Report (CFSR), DD Form 1586, Figure 1, is designed to supply funding data about Defense contracts to system managers for: (a) updating and forecasting contract fund requirements, (b) planning and decision-making on funding changes in contracts, (c) developing fund requirements and budget estimates in support of approved programs, and (d) determining funds in excess of contract needs and available for deobligation, and (e) obtaining rough estimates of termination costs.

4. APPROVAL DATE
1 November 1979

5. OFFICE OF PRIMARY RESPONSIBILITY
ASD(C)

6. DDC REQUIRED

8. APPROVAL LIMITATION

7. APPLICATION/INTERRELATIONSHIP

7.1 The CFSR is applicable to contracts over $100,000 in value and 6 months in duration. It is not normally applicable to firm-fixed price contracts (as defined in DAR 3-404.2) except for unpriced portions of such contracts that are estimated to be at least twenty (20) percent of the initial contract value, and except for firm-fixed price contracts which represent a major system acquisition or a major component thereof.

7.2 Contractual Application. ONLY THOSE PARTS OF THE CFSR ESSENTIAL TO THE MANAGEMENT OF EACH ACQUISITION WILL BE REQUIRED. The DoD system manager will determine the need for contract funds information and apply only those portions of the CFSR deemed appropriate. (Continued on pages 2 and 3)

9. REFERENCES (Mandatory as cited in block 10)

DAR 3-404.2
DAR 7-104.35
DAR 7-108.3
DAR 7-203.4
DAR 15-205.42
DAR Section III, Part 4
DoD 5000.12M, 1 Mar 70

MCSL NUMBER(S)
70934

10. PREPARATION INSTRUCTIONS

10.1 Specific Instructions

10.1.1 Item 1 - CONTRACT NUMBER. Enter the assigned contract number and the latest modification number on which contractual agreement has been reached.

10.1.2 Item 2 - CONTRACT TYPE*. Enter the type of contract as identified in DAR, Section III, Part 4; e.g.,

  Cost Plus Fixed Fee (CPFF)
  Fixed Price Incentive (FPI), etc.

10.1.3 Item 3 - CONTRACT FUNDING FOR*. Enter the applicable type as follows:

  Multi-Year Procurement (MYP)
  Incrementally Funded Contract (INC)
  Contract for a Single Year (SYC)

10.1.3.1 For FY. For contracts which are financed with funds appropriated in more than one fiscal year, a report is required for each fiscal year's funds where the separate year's funds in the contract are associated with specific quantities of hardware or services to be furnished. The fiscal year(s) being reported will be shown in this block and that year's share of the total target prices (initial and adjusted) will be shown in Items 9 and 10.

*Items marked with an asterisk (*) have been registered in the DoD Data Element Dictionary.
(Continued on pages 4 through 10)

DD FORM 1 JUN 68 1664

DI-F-6004B (Continued)
7.   APPLICATION/INTERRELATIONSHIP (Continued)

7.2.1 Level of Reporting. If a contract is funded with a single
appropriation, a single line entry at the total contract level should
be considered for CFSR reporting. Reporting by line item or WBS
element will be limited to only those items or elements needed to
suppport funds management requirements and will normally not include
items funded for less than $500,000 or elements below level two of the
contract WBS. Contracts which have a dollar value between $100,000
and $500,000 will require reporting at the total contract level only.

7.2.2 Multiple Appropriations. Where two or more appropriation
sources are used for funding a single contract, contractors will
segregate funds data by appropriation accounting reference. The procuring agency will supply the appropriation numbers applicable to individual line items or WBS elements. If a single line item or WBS
element is funded by more than one appropriation, methods for segregat-
ing and reporting such information will be negotiated and specified
in the contract.

7.2.3 Mechanized Data Submissions. Computer products may be substituted for the DD Form 1586 provided all data elements are available
in a form suitable for DoD management use. Otherwise data should be
submitted in the attached form. Where data are furnished which require
mechanized processing, narrative remarks should accompany tapes or
cards and identify pertinent items to which they apply, and a listing
identifying tape or card data should be included to expedite processing.
In the event that more than one procuring agency desires mechanized
data processing from a single contractor, the procuring agencies will
provide the contractor with a uniform and mutually agreed upon set of
data processing instructions.

7.3 Frequency and Submission. The Contract Funds Status Report, DD
Form 1586 (Figure 1), will be a contractual requirement as set forth in
the DD 1423, Contract Data Requirements List (CDRL) and DD 1660, Management System Summary List. Unless otherwise provided for in the
contract, the CFSR will be prepared as of the end of each calendar
quarter or contractor accounting period nearest the end of each quarter. The required number of copies of the CFSR will be forwarded
to the Administrative Contracting Officer (ACO) within 25 calendar
days after the "as of" date of the report, or as otherwise specified
in the contract. In the event of exceptional circumstances which
call for increased frequency in reporting, such frequency will not be
more often than monthly and will be specified in the contract or will
be mutually agreed upon.

DI-F-6004B (Continued)
7. APPLICATION/INTERRELATIONSHIP (Continued)

7.4 Explanations of Terms

7.4.1 Open Commitments. For this report, a commitment represents the estimated obligation of the contractor (excluding accrued expenditures) to vendors or subcontractors (based on the assumption that the contract will continue to completion).

7.4.2 Accrued Expenditures. For this report, include recorded or incurred costs as defined within the Allowable Cost, Fee and Payments Clause (DAR 7-203.4) for cost type contracts or the Progress Payments Clause (DAR 7-104.35) for fixed price type contracts, plus the estimated fee or profit earned. Such costs include:

7.4.2.1 Actual payments for services or items purchased directly for the contract.

7.4.2.2 Costs incurred, but not necessarily paid, for storeroom issues, direct labor, direct travel, direct other in-house costs and allocated indirect costs.

7.4.2.3 Progress payments made to subcontractors.

7.4.2.4 Pension costs provided they are paid at least quarterly.

7.4.3 Termination Costs. Although this report is prepared on the basis that the contract will continue to completion, it is necessary to report estimated termination cost by Government fiscal year and generally more frequently on incrementally funded contracts. The frequency will be dependent on the funding need dates (i.e., quarterly) and should be compatible with the contract funding clauses, Limitation of Funds clause (cost type contracts) or Limitation of Obligation clause (fixed price type contracts). Termination costs include such items as loss of useful life of special tooling, special machinery and equipment; rental cost of unexpired leases; and settlement expenses. The definition of termination costs is included in DAR 15-205.42. In the event the Special Termination Costs clause (DAR 7-108.3) is authorized, then costs defined in this clause will be eliminated from the estimated termination costs.

7.5 This Data Item Description (DID) implements requirements of DoD Instruction 7000.10 for contract funds status reporting.

7.6 This DID supersedes DI-F-6004A.

DI-F-6004B (Continued)
10. PREPARATION INSTRUCTIONS (Continued)

10.1.4 Item 4 - APPROPRIATION. Enter the appropriation and Service source in this block.

10.1.5 Item 5 - PREVIOUS REPORT DATE. Enter the cut-off date of the previous report. (Year, Month, Day)

10.1.6 Item 6 - CURRENT REPORT DATE. Enter the cut-off date applicable to this report. (Year, Month, Day)

10.1.7 Item 7 - CONTRACTOR. Enter the name, division (if applicable), and mailing address of the reporting contractor.

10.1.8 Item 8 - PROGRAM. Identify the program (if known) by name or enter the type, model and series or other military designation of the prime item or items purchased on the contract. If the contract is for services or a level-of-effort (research, flight test, etc.), the title of the service should be shown.

10.1.9 Item 9 - INITIAL CONTRACT PRICE. Enter the dollar amounts for the initial negotiated contract target price and contract ceiling price when appropriate. For contracts which are financed with funds appropriated in more than one fiscal year, only the share of the total initial target and ceiling associated with the fiscal year shown in Item 3 will be entered.

10.1.10 Item 10 - ADJUSTED CONTRACT PRICE. Enter the dollar amounts for the adjusted contract target price (initial negotiated contract plus supplemental agreements) and adjusted contract ceiling price or estimated ceiling price where appropriate. For contracts which are financed with funds appropriated in more than one fiscal year, only the share of the total adjusted target and ceiling associated with the fiscal year shown in Item 3 will be entered.

10.1.11 Item 11 - FUNDING INFORMATION

10.1.11.1 Col. a. - LINE ITEM/WORK BREAKDOWN STRUCTURE (WBS) ELEMENT. Enter the line item or WBS elements specified for CFSR coverage in the contract.

10.1.11.2 Col. b. - APPROPRIATION IDENTIFICATION. Enter the appropriation number supplied by the DoD for the contract or, if applicable, each line item or WBS element.

10.1.11.3 Col. c. - FUNDING AUTHORIZED TO DATE. Enter dollar amounts of contract funding authorized under the contract from the beginning through the report date shown in Item 6. This entry should contain funds applicable to the fiscal year(s) shown in Item 3.

DI-F-6004B (Continued)
10. <u>PREPARATION INSTRUCTIONS</u> (Continued)

10.1.11.4 <u>Col. d. - ACCRUED EXPENDITURES PLUS OPEN COMMITMENTS TOTAL</u>.
For contract work authorized, enter the total of (a) the cumulative
accrued expenditures incurred through the end of the reporting period,
and (b) the open commitments on the "as of" date of the report. Enter
the total applicable to funds for the fiscal year(s) covered by this
report as shown in Item 3.

  <u>Note a.</u>: On selected contracts, the separation of open commitments and accrued expenditures by line item or WBS element may be a
negotiated requirement in the contract. Utilization of this provision
should be held to the minimum essential to support information needs
of the procuring agency. In the event this separation of data is not
available in the contractor's accounting system or cannot be derived
without significant effort, provision should be made to permit use of
estimates. The procedures used by the contractor in developing estimates should be explained in the Remarks section of the report.

  <u>Note b.</u>: When a Notice of Termination has been issued, potential
termination liability costs will be entered in this column. They will
be identified to the extent possible with the source of liability
(prime or subcontract).

10.1.11.5 <u>Col. e. - CONTRACT WORK AUTHORIZED - DEFINITIZED</u>. For the
fiscal year(s) shown in Item 3, enter the <u>estimated price</u> for the
authorized work on which contractual agreement has been reached, including profit/fee, incentive and cost sharing associated with projected
over/underruns. Amounts for contract changes will not be included in
this item unless they have been priced and incorporated in the contract
through a supplemental agreement to the contract.

10.1.11.6 <u>Col. f. - CONTRACT WORK AUTHORIZED - NOT DEFINITIZED</u>. Enter
the contractor's estimate of the fund requirements for performing
required work (e.g., additional agreements or changes) for which firm
contract prices have not yet been agreed to in writing by the parties
to the contract. Report values only for items for which written orders
have been received. For incentive type contracts, show total cost to
the Government (recognizing contractor participation). Enter in Narrative Remarks a brief but complete explanation of the reason for the
change in funds.

10.1.11.7 <u>Col. g. - SUBTOTAL</u>. Enter the total estimated price for
all work authorized on the contract (Col. e. plus Col. f.).

DI-F-6004B   (Continued)
10. PREPARATION INSTRUCTIONS   (Continued)

10.1.11.8 Col. h. - FORECAST - NOT YET AUTHORIZED. Enter an estimate of fund requirements, including the estimated amount for fee or profit, for changes proposed by the Government or by the contractor, but not yet directed by the contracting officer. In the Narrative Remarks state each change document number and estimated value of each change.

10.1.11.9 Col. i. - FORECAST - ALL OTHER WORK. Enter an estimate of fund requirements for additional work anticipated to be performed (not included in a firm proposal) which the contractor, based on his knowledge and experience, expects to submit to the Government within a reasonable period of time.

10.1.11.10 Col. j. - SUBTOTAL. Enter an estimate of total requirements for forecast funding (the sum of Col. h. plus Col. i.). Specific limitations on the use of the forecast funding section may be a part of the contract.

10.1.11.11 Col. k. - TOTAL REQUIREMENTS. Enter an estimate of total fund requirements for contract work authorized and forecast (the sum of Col. g. plus Col. j.).

10.1.11.12 Col. l. - FUNDS CARRYOVER. For incrementally funded contracts only, report the amount by which the prior Federal fiscal year funding was in excess of the prior year's requirement. If there is no carryover, report zero. Specific instructions for the use of this item may be made a part of the contract.

10.1.11.13 Col. m. - NET FUNDS REQUIRED. Enter an estimate of net funds required, subtracting funds carryover in Col. l. from total requirements in Col. k.

10.1.11.14 Column Totals. Totals should be provided for Columns c. through m. for all line items or WBS elements reported.

10.1.12 Item 12 - CONTRACT WORK AUTHORIZED (WITH FEE/PROFIT) - ACTUAL OR PROJECTED. Data entries will be as follows: In the first column, actuals cumulative to date; in all other columns except the last, projected cumulative from the start of the contract to the end of the period indicated in the column heading; in the last column, the projected cumulative from the start to the end of the contract.

DI-F-6004B   (Continued)
10. PREPARATION INSTRUCTIONS   (Continued)

Columns 2 through 10 will be headed to indicate periods covering the
life of the contract and may be headed to show months, quarters, half
years and/or fiscal years as prescribed by the procuring agency.
Projected data should include all planned obligations, anticipated
accruals, anticipated over/under targets (total cost to the Government
recognizing contractor participation), G&A, and fee/profit.

10.1.12.1 OPEN COMMITMENTS. In the first column enter commitments
open as of the date of the report. In subsequent columns enter the
projected commitments which will be open as of the end of each period
indicated by the column headings. The amount entered will be the
projected cumulative commitments less the planned cumulative expenditures as of the end of time period indicated. At the end of the contract, the amount will be zero.

10.1.12.2 ACCRUED EXPENDITURES. In the first column enter actuals
to date. In subsequent columns enter the projected cumulative accrued
expenditures as of the end of each period indicated by the column
headings.

10.1.12.3 TOTAL (12.a. & 12.b.). In the columns provided, enter the
total contract work authorized - actuals to date (column 1) or projected (columns 2 through 10). This total is the sum of open commitments and accrued expenditures through the periods indicated by the
column headings.

10.1.13 Item 13 - FORECAST OF BILLINGS TO THE GOVERNMENT. In the
first column enter the cumulative amount billed to the Government
through the current report date, including amounts applicable to
progress or advance payments. In succeeding columns enter the amount
expected to be billed the Government during each period reported
(assuming the contract will continue to completion). Amounts will
not be cumulative.

10.1.14 Item 14 - ESTIMATED TERMINATION COSTS. In the columns provided, enter the estimated costs that would be necessary to liquidate
all Government obligations if the contract were to be terminated in
that period. Applicable fee/profit should be included. These entries
may consist of "rough order of magnitude" estimates and will not be
construed as providing formal notification having contractual significance. This estimate will be used to assist the Government in
budgeting for the potential incurrence of such cost. On contracts
with Limitation of Funds/Obligation clauses, where termination costs
are included as part of the funding line, enter the amounts required
for termination reserve on this line.

DI-F-6004B (Continued)
10. PREPARATION INSTRUCTIONS (Continued)

10.2 Narrative Remarks

10.2.1 A separate sheet will be used to submit any additional information or remarks which support or explain data submitted in this report. Information on changes, as specified in the next two paragraphs, will also be reported in the remarks section.

10.2.2 General. The contractor will use the Remarks section of the Contract Funds Status Report to submit information regarding changes, as indicated below. A change in a line item will be reported when the dollar amount reported in Item 11, Col. k. of this submission differs from that reported in the preceding submission. The movement of dollar amounts from one column to another (Item 11, Cols. e. through j.), indicating a change in the firmness of fund requirements, need not be reported in this section. Change reporting should include the following:

10.2.2.1 The location of the changed entry (page, line, and column);

10.2.2.2 The dollar amount of the change;

10.2.2.3 The coded identification of the cause (see classification below); and

10.2.2.4 A narrative explanation of the cause of each change.

10.2.3 Change Categories. The contractor will use the categories shown in this paragraph for identifying the reasons for changing fund requirements. The System Manager will assist the contractor in assigning change categories to assure the assignment of the proper category in relation to the total program. These categories identify two basic causes for changes in funds requirements - change in the scope of the contract (identified simply as "Scope" changes) and changes in the price with no change in the scope ("Price" changes). Categories will be used as shown unless the contractor is advised of specific alternatives through contractual channels. While the general intent in providing categories for use is that one category will describe one change, it is recognized that more than one category may be required in selected cases of changes in estimates of fund requirements. In such cases reporting contractors should identify changes using more than one change category and utilize the Remarks section to describe the circumstances of overlap or duplication. The reasons for change are broken down as follows:

DI-F-6004B   (Continued)
10.   PREPARATION INSTRUCTIONS   (Continued)

10.2.3.1   "Scope" Changes.   There are four categories for this class
of reasons for change in estimates. Report Total Funds Requirements
changes (Item 11, Col. k.) due to:

10.2.3.1.1   Engineering Change*.   An alteration in the physical
or functional characteristics of a system or item delivered, to be
delivered, or under development, after establishment of such characteristics. Specific changes must be separately identified and
quantified. Code A1.

10.2.3.1.2   Quantity Change*.   A change in quantity to be procured,
the cost of which is computed using the original cost-quantity relationships, thereby excluding that portion of the current price
attributable to changes in any other category. Code A2.

10.2.3.1.3   Support Change*.   A change in support item requirements
(e.g., spare parts, training, ancillary equipment, warranty provisions,
Government-furnished property/equipment, etc.). Code A3.

10.2.3.1.4   Schedule Change*.   A change in a delivery schedule,
completion date or intermediate milestone. Each change must separately
be identified as Government responsibility or contractor responsibility
and quantified as to amount. Code A4.

10.2.3.2   Price Changes.   There are three categories for this class.
Report Total Funds Requirements changes (Item 11, Col. k.) due to:

10.2.3.2.1   Economic Change*.   A change due to the operation of one
or more factors of the economy. This includes specific contract changes
related to economic escalation and the economic impact portion of quantity changes not accounted for by the original cost-quantity relationships used to calculate quantity change variance. This category also
includes changing constant or current dollar amounts in program estimates to reflect (1) altered price levels, or (2) definitized contract
amounts. Code B2.

10.2.3.2.2   Estimating Change*.   A change in cost due to correction
of error or refinements of the base estimate. These include mathematical or other errors in estimating, revised estimating relationships, etc. Excluded from this category should be revisions of cost
estimates that occur because of other change categories, i.e.,
engineering, support, schedule, etc. For example, a cost change which
occurs because of the addition of a new warhead is an engineering

DI-F-6004B (Continued)
10. <u>PREPARATION INSTRUCTIONS</u> (Continued)

change, and not an estimating change; a revised production schedule
is a schedule change, not an estimating change. Code B3.

10.2.3.2.3. <u>Other Changes</u>*. A change in contractual amount for
reasons not provided for in other change categories. The reason for
the change should be stated. Code B4.

10.3 General note for ADP personnel processing this report:

10.3.1 Coding must be as indicated in the instructions. In cases
where specific coding instructions are not provided, reference must
be made to the Department of Defense Manual for Standard Data
Elements, DoD 5000.12M. Failure to comply with either the coding
instructions contained herein or those published in referenced
manual will make the noncomplier responsible for required concessions
in data base communication.

Dec 3, 79
7000.10 (Encl 3)

CLASSIFICATION _____

CONTRACT FUNDS STATUS REPORT

(DOLLARS IN _____)

FORM APPROVED
OMB NUMBER 22-RO180

| 1. CONTRACT NUMBER | 3. CONTRACT FUNDING FOR FOR FY | 5. PREVIOUS REPORT DATE | 7. CONTRACTOR (Name, Address and ZIP Code) | 9. INITIAL CONTRACT PRICE TARGET _____ CEILING _____ |
| 2. CONTRACT TYPE | 4. APPROPRIATION | 6. CURRENT REPORT DATE | 8. PROGRAM | 10. ADJUSTED CONTRACT PRICE TARGET _____ CEILING _____ |

11. FUNDING INFORMATION

LINE ITEM/WBS ELEMENT	APPROPRIATION IDENT-IFICATION	FUNDING AUTHORIZED TO DATE	ACCRUED EXPENDITURES PLUS OPEN COMMITMENTS TOTAL	CONTRACT WORK AUTHORIZED			FORECAST			TOTAL REQUIRE-MENTS	FUNDS CARRY-OVER	NET FUNDS REQUIRED
				DEFINITIZED	NOT DEFINITIZED	SUBTOTAL	NOT YET AUTHORIZED	ALL OTHER WORK	SUBTOTAL			
a	b	c	d	e	f	g	h	i	j	k	l	m

12. CONTRACT WORK AUTHORIZED (WITH FEE/PROFIT) - ACTUAL OR PROJECTED

	ACTUAL TO DATE								AT COMPLETION
a. OPEN COMMITMENTS									
b. ACCRUED EXPENDITURES									
c. TOTAL (12a + 12b)									
13. FORECAST OF BILLINGS TO THE GOVERNMENT									
14. ESTIMATED TERMINATION COSTS									

REMARKS

DD FORM 1586
1 OCT 79

PAGE _____ OF _____ PAGES

CLASSIFICATION _____

Figure 1

Dec 3, 79
7000.10 (Encl 4)

DATA ITEM DESCRIPTION	2. IDENTIFICATION NO(S).	
	AGENCY	NUMBER

1. TITLE

COST/SCHEDULE STATUS REPORT (C/SSR)

OSD DI-F-6010A

3. DESCRIPTION/PURPOSE

3.1 This report is prepared by contractors and provides summarized cost and schedule performance information for program management purposes.

4. APPROVAL DATE

1 November 1979

5. OFFICE OF PRIMARY RESPONSIBILITY

ASD(C)

6. DDC REQUIRED

8. APPROVAL LIMITATION

7. APPLICATION/INTERRELATIONSHIP

7.1 The Cost/Schedule Status Report (C/SSR), Figure 1, is applicable to contracts of $2,000,000 or over and 12 months' duration or more which do not use the Cost Performance Report (DI-F-6000). It will be established as a contractual requirement as set forth in the Contract Data Requirements List, DD Form 1423, and Management System Summary List, DD Form 1660.

7.2 Data reported on the C/SSR will pertain to all authorized contract work, including both priced and unpriced effort. Data reported will be limited to level 3 of the contract work breakdown structure or higher. However, if a problem area is indicated at a lower level, more detailed data will be provided on an exception basis until the problem is resolved.
(Continued on page 2)

9. REFERENCES (Mandatory as cited in block 10)

DoD 4120.3M, Aug 78
MIL STD 881A, 25 Apr 75
DoDI 7000.2, 10 Jun 77

MCSL NUMBER(S)
71559

10. PREPARATION INSTRUCTIONS

10.1 Unless otherwise stated in the solicitation, the effective issue of the document(s) cited in the referenced document(s) in this block shall be that listed in the issue of the DoD Index of Specifications and Standards (reference DoD 4120.3M) and the supplements thereto specified in the solicitation and will form a part of this data item description to the extent defined within.

10.2 Heading Information

    10.2.1 CONTRACTOR: Enter the name and division (if applicable) of the reporting contractor.

    10.2.2 LOCATION: Enter the plant location and mailing address.

    10.2.3 RDT&E ☐ PRODUCTION ☐: Check appropriate box. Separate reports are required for each type of contract.

    10.2.4 CONTRACT TYPE AND NUMBER: Enter the contract type, contract number and the number of the latest contract change order or supplemental agreement applicable to the contract.

    10.2.5 PROGRAM NAME/NUMBER: Enter the name, number, acronym and/or the type, model and series, or other designation of the prime items purchased under the contract.

(Continued on pages 2 through 5)

DD FORM 1664
1 JUN 68

DI-F-6010A (Continued)
7.   APPLICATION/INTERRELATIONSHIP (Continued)

7.3 Frequency of reporting will be specified in the contract but will
not exceed a monthly requirement. Reports will be submitted to the
procurement activity no later than 25 calendar days following the
reporting cut-off date. Reports may reflect data as of the end of the
calendar month or as of the contractor's accounting period cut-off date.

7.4 The definitions of terms contained in the Cost/Schedule Control
Systems Criteria (C/SCSC) of DoD Instruction 7000.2, "Performance
Measurement for Selected Acquisitions," may be used as guidance in
completing Columns (2) through (9) of the C/SSR with the exception of
the definitions for Budgeted Cost for Work Scheduled and Budgeted
Cost for Work Performed (see paragraphs 10.4.2 and 10.4.3, below).
However, application of the C/SSR does not in any way invoke unique
requirements or disciplines of the C/SCSC, such as applied direct
costs or use of work packages for determining Budgeted Cost for Work
Performed, unless these methods constitute the contractor's normal
way of doing business. The derivation of Budgeted Cost for Work Performed to satisfy C/SSR requirements will be left to the discretion
of the reporting contractor and subject to negotiation and inclusion
as a part of the contract. While the contractor must be in a position
to explain the method used for determining Budgeted Cost for Work Performed, the in-depth demonstration review referred to in DoD Instruction
7000.2 is not a requirement of C/SSR. If compliance with C/SCSC is
required, the provisions of DAR 3-501 and 7-104.87 must be used.

7.5 The variance thresholds which, if exceeded, require problem analysis
and narrative explanations, will be as specified in the contract or as
otherwise mutually agreed to by the contracting parties.

7.6 This Data Item Description supersedes DI-F-6010.

---

10. PREPARATION INSTRUCTIONS (Continued)

10.2.6 REPORT PERIOD: Enter the beginning and ending dates of the period
covered by the report.

10.2.7 SIGNATURE, TITLE AND DATE: The contractor's authorized representative will sign the report and enter his title and the date of
signature.

10.3 Contract Data:

10.3.1 Item (1) - ORIGINAL CONTRACT TARGET COST: Enter the dollar value
(excluding fee or profit) negotiated in the original contract. For a

DI-F-6010A (Continued)
10. PREPARATION INSTRUCTIONS (Continued)

cost plus fixed-fee contract, enter the estimated cost negotiated. For an incentive contract, enter the definitized contract target cost.

10.3.2 Item (2) - NEGOTIATED CONTRACT CHANGES: Enter the cumulative cost (excluding fee or profit) applicable to definitized contract changes which have occurred since the beginning of the contract.

10.3.3 Item (3) - CURRENT TARGET COST: Enter the sum of Items (1) and (2). The amount shown should equal the current dollar value (excluding fee or profit) on which contractual agreement has been reached.

10.3.4 Item (4) - ESTIMATED COST OF AUTHORIZED, UNPRICED WORK: Enter the estimated cost (excluding fee or profit) for contract changes for which written authorization has been received but for which contract prices have not been negotiated.

10.3.5 Item (5) - CONTRACT BUDGET BASE: Enter the sum of Items (3) and (4).

10.4 Performance Data:

10.4.1 Col. (1) - WORK BREAKDOWN STRUCTURE: Enter the noun description of the work breakdown structure (WBS) elements for which cost information is being reported. WBS elements or levels required will be those specified in the contract.

10.4.2 Col. (2) - BUDGETED COST - WORK SCHEDULED: Enter the numerical representation of the value of all work scheduled to be accomplished as of the reporting cut-off date.

10.4.3 Col. (3) - BUDGETED COST - WORK PERFORMED: Enter the numerical representation of the value of all work accomplished as of the reporting cut-off date.

NOTE: Specific methods used to derive the Budgeted Cost for Work Scheduled and the Budgeted Cost for Work Performed will be delineated in the proposal and explained on the initial report. If methods used should change during the contract, explain the new method and the reason for the change in procedure.

10.4.4 Col. (4) - ACTUAL COST WORK PERFORMED: Enter the cumulative actual costs (direct and indirect) applicable to work accomplished as of the reporting cut-off date. Actual costs and budgeted costs will be reported on a comparable basis.

DI-F-6010A (Continued)
10. PREPARATION INSTRUCTIONS (Continued)

10.4.5 Col. (5) - SCHEDULE VARIANCE: Enter the difference between the Budgeted Cost for Work Scheduled and the Budgeted Cost for Work Performed by subtracting Col. (2) from Col. (3). A negative figure indicates an unfavorable variance and should be shown in parentheses. Variances exceeding established thresholds must be fully explained.

10.4.6 Col. (6) - COST VARIANCE: Enter the difference between the Budgeted Cost for Work Performed and the Actual Cost for Work Performed by subtracting Col. (4) from Col. (3). A negative figure indicates an unfavorable variance and should be shown in parentheses. Variances exceeding established thresholds must be fully explained.

10.4.7 Col. (7) - AT COMPLETION - BUDGETED: Enter the total budget identified to each WBS element listed in Col. (1). Assigned budgets will consist of the original budgets plus or minus budget adjustments resulting from contract changes, internal replanning, and application of management reserves.

10.4.8 Col. (8) - AT COMPLETION - LATEST REVISED ESTIMATE: Enter the latest revised estimate of cost at completion including estimated overrun/ underrun for all authorized work. The estimated cost at completion consists of the sum of the actual cost to date plus the latest estimate of cost for work remaining.

10.4.9 Col. (9) - AT COMPLETION - VARIANCE: Enter the difference between the Budgeted Cost at Completion, Col. (7), and the Estimated Cost at Completion, Col. (8), by subtracting Col. (8) from Col. (7). A negative figure indicates an unfavorable variance and should be shown in parentheses. Variances exceeding established thresholds must be fully explained.

10.4.10 GENERAL AND ADMINISTRATIVE (G&A): Enter in Columns (2) through (9) the appropriate G&A costs. If G&A has been included in the costs reported above, G&A will be shown as a non-add entry on this line with an appropriate notation. If a G&A classification is not used, no entry will be made other than an appropriate notation to that effect.

10.4.11 UNDISTRIBUTED BUDGET: Enter in Cols. (7) and (8) the amount of budget applicable to authorized contract effort which has not been identified to WBS elements at or below the reporting level. All undistributed budget will be fully explained.

10.4.12 MANAGEMENT RESERVE: Enter in Col. (7) the amount of budget identified as management reserve as of the end of the reporting period. Enter in Col. (8) the amount of management reserve expected to be consumed before the end of the contract. Enter in Col. (9) the difference

DI-F-6010A   (Continued)
10. PREPARATION INSTRUCTIONS   (Continued)

between Cols. (7) and (8). Amounts of management reserve applied during the reporting period and the rationale for the figure in Col. (8) will be explained in the Narrative Analysis. (The entry in Col. (8) is discretionary and may be zero if the contractor does not wish to make an estimate.) Application of management reserve during the reporting period will be explained in terms of amounts applied, WBS elements to which applied, and reasons for application.

10.4.13 TOTAL: Enter the sum of the direct, indirect and G&A budgets and costs in Cols. (2) through (9). In Cols. (7), (8) and (9), also add the Undistributed Budget and Management Reserve.

10.5 Narrative Explanations:

10.5.1 Provide a summary analysis of overall contract performance, including significant existing or potential problems and identify corrective actions taken or required, including Government action where required.

10.5.2 Explanations of significant variances must be explicit and comprehensive. They must clearly identify the nature of the problems being experienced, the impact on the total contract, and the corrective actions taken or required.

10.5.3 Normally, the amount shown on the Total line in Col. (7), Budgeted at Completion, will equal the amount shown in Item (5), Contract Budget Base. This relationship is necessary to insure that the Budgeted Cost for Work Scheduled and the Budgeted Cost for Work Performed provide meaningful indicators of contractual progress. Therefore, if the amount shown on the Total line in Col. (7), Budgeted at Completion, exceeds the amount shown in Item (5), Contract Budget Base, fully explain the reasons for the additional budget allocation and identify by WBS element the specific amounts added to each element.

COST/SCHEDULE STATUS REPORT

FORM APPROVED
OMB NUMBER 22R0027

CONTRACTOR:

LOCATION:

RDT&E ☐ PRODUCTION ☐

CONTRACT TYPE/NO.

PROGRAM NAME/NUMBER

REPORT PERIOD:

SIGNATURE, TITLE & DATE

Contract Data

(1) ORIGINAL CONTRACT TARGET COST	(2) NEGOTIATED CONTRACT CHANGES	(3) CURRENT TARGET COST (1) + (2)	(4) ESTIMATED COST OF AUTHORIZED, UNPRICED WORK	(5) CONTRACT BUDGET BASE (3) + (4)

Performance Data

WORK BREAKDOWN STRUCTURE (1)	CUMULATIVE TO DATE					AT COMPLETION		
	BUDGETED COST		ACTUAL COST WORK PERFORMED (4)	VARIANCE		BUDGETED (7)	LATEST REVISED ESTIMATE (8)	VARIANCE (9)
	Work Scheduled (2)	Work Performed (3)		Schedule (5)	Cost (6)			
GENERAL AND ADMINISTRATIVE								
UNDISTRIBUTED BUDGET								
MANAGEMENT RESERVE								
TOTAL								

Figure 1

APPENDIX D
DODI 7000.11
CCDR

NUMBER 7000.11

DATE September 5, 1973

Department of Defense Instruction

ASD(C)
ASD(I&L)
DDPA&E

SUBJECT   Contractor Cost Data Reporting (CCDR)

Refs.: (a) through (h), see enclosure 1

I. PURPOSE

This Instruction provides guidance for collecting projected and actual cost data on acquisition programs from contractors and in-house government plants through a single integrated system for DoD cost analysis and procurement management purposes. The word "contractor" in this Instruction is used herein to apply to both industrial contractors and in-house government facilities.

II. APPLICABILITY

The provisions of this Instruction apply to the Military Departments and Defense Agencies (hereinafter referred to as DoD Components) having acquisition programs covered by the criteria established herein.

III. CANCELLATIONS

The following issuances and forms are hereby cancelled and superseded for use on all new acquisition programs: References (d) and (e), Report Control Symbol DD Comp (AR) 739, and Cost Information Reports (CIR) for Aircraft, Missile and Space Systems, April 21, 1966. See paragraph IV.D. of this Instruction concerning the use of CIR and Procurement Information Reporting (PIR) on existing programs.

IV. SCOPE AND POLICY

A. The Contractor Cost Data Reporting Plan (reference (f)) and forms will be used as the basis for contractor responses to applicable Requests for Proposals (RFPs), and will be included in all resulting contracts meeting the CCDR criteria in subsection IV.B. (below). CCDR will also be included in equivalent documents where the supplier is an in-house government facility.

B. For purposes of CCDR, two categories of procedures are established. Category I procedures apply to all acquisition programs which are estimated to require RDT&E Total Obligational Authority (TOA) in excess of $50 million or cumulative production TOA in excess of $200 million (based on the five year defense program as defined in DoD Instruction 7045.7 reference (a)). Category II procedures apply to selected contracts or specific line items within Category I requirements; generally the data will not be required on contracts of less than $2 million.

C. All aircraft, electronic, missile, ordnance, ship, space and surface vehicle acquisition programs and their related components which meet the criteria of Category I, above, will be covered by CCDR requirements. This coverage will be in accordance with the procedures described herein from the point of Defense Systems Acquisition Review Council (DSARC) milestone II approval for full-scale development through the completion of production DoD Directive 5000.1 (reference (b)), unless specifically waived by the OSD Cost Analysis Improvement Group (CAIG) DoD Directive 5000.4 (reference (h)). In some instances, CCDR may be required on large advanced development prototype programs.

1. Acquisition programs not meeting the criteria of Category I may be covered by Category I procedures (including appropriate review and approval procedures) at the discretion of the DoD Component or the OSD CAIG.

2. Other acquisition programs not covered by Category I procedures may collect cost data using the Category II procedures described herein at the discretion of the DoD Component. This determination shall consider contract type, complexity and/or criticality of the item as it pertains to the overall structure of the national defense, future procurement plans (i.e., multi-procurements of the item versus a single procurement), contract value, and the need for a historical data base to support cost analysis and procurement management objectives.

D. CIR and PIR reporting currently in use on existing programs shall be continued on these programs unless it is considered mutually advantageous to the Government and the contractor(s) to substitute CCDR for the above reports. Whenever CIR reporting requirements remain on applicable programs, the CIR reports shall be forwarded to the OSD CAIG under the procedures established for Category I reporting in subsection V.I. of this Instruction.

E. The criteria for CCDR reporting are applicable to the selection of prime contractors as well as subcontractors. The identification of prime and subcontractors who are required to report will be determined during the CCDR Plan review process by the selection of those elements of the contract work on which data are required.

F. For Category I contracts, reporting will be required on only a few firm fixed-price prime or subcontracts when those contracts represent the development or production of a major acquisition program or component thereof. For Category II contracts, it is expected that CCDR generally will not be required on firm fixed-price contracts.

V.   PROCEDURES

    A.   CCDR requirements are contained in DD Form 1921 (Cost Data
Summary Report), DD Form 1921-1 (Functional Cost Hour Report),
DD Form 1921-2 (Progress Curve Report), and DD Form 1921-3
(Plant-Wide Data Report) (see enclosures 2 through 5). A com-
patible form(s) to CCDR will be included in the Armed Services
Procurement Regulation (ASPR) to be used in contractor cost
proposals. All of the CCDR forms will normally be utilized
for Category I reporting. For Category II reporting, only
DD Forms 1921-1 and 1921-2 will normally be utilized; however,
in those instances where the financing for a Category II contract is substantial enough to require the application of a
WBS in accordance with Military Standard 881 (reference (g)),
DD Form 1921 may be used at the discretion of the contracting
DoD Component. Each CCDR form will be used to provide contract
actuals and estimates. DD Forms 1921 and 1921-1 will also be
used in contractor responses to solicitations as well as to provide contractor program estimates. Additional procedures, including instructions for the preparation and submission of the
forms, are specified in Contractor Cost Data Reporting System
(reference (f)) and will be followed by all DoD Components in
the implementation of this Instruction.

    B.   For systems falling under the criteria of Category I procedures,
the appropriate DoD Component is responsible for preparing the
proposed CCDR Plan (including the WBS level of detail for reporting and report frequency) at least 60 days prior to issuance
of its RFP to industry for full-scale development or, in some
instances, large advanced development prototype programs.

        1.   The WBS utilized in preparing the CCDR Plan will be in con-
formance with Military Standard 881 (reference (g)).

        2.   The CCDR Plan will be distributed to the officially
designated organizational entities in the other materiel
commands, Military Departments' headquarters and the OSD
CAIG at least 10 days prior to a meeting convened at the
procuring materiel command headquarters to which the
above representatives will be invited.

        3.   The CCDR Plan recommended at the meeting will be provided
to the designated representatives following the meeting.
Unless one of these representatives objects within
10 days after the date of the distribution of the recommended CCDR Plan, it will be considered approved.

        4.   Objections not resolved at the materiel command head-
quarters review meeting will be made in writing to the

materiel command responsible for preparing the CCDR Plan under consideration, with an information copy to the Chairman of the OSD CAIG. Objections will be referred to the OSD CAIG for resolution. The OSD CAIG will have 15 days from within receipt of the objection to determine whether the recommended CCDR Plan should be modified as a result of the objection.

C. Whenever any DoD Component wishes to prepare a change to a Category I CCDR Plan, it shall notify all the representatives who participated in the original review of that plan of the proposed change. If no written objection is received within 15 days, the change will be considered approved. If any objection is raised, a meeting will be convened at the procuring materiel command headquarters as described in subsection V.B. above. Subsequent steps will be as described in that subsection.

D. For systems covered under Category II procedures, DoD Components will assure that implementation plans are reviewed and approved in time for the data requirements to be included in the RFP for the contract on which they will be implemented. The review of the plans for implementing Category II requirements will take place at the procuring materiel command headquarters. This review shall insure data requirements are not excessive to actual needs and are consistent and comparable for similar types of weapon systems.

E. Contractually, each CCDR form will be identified as a single line entry on the DD Form 1423, Contract Data Requirements List (CDRL), with the detailed requirements listed in the DD Forms 1664, the Data Item Descriptions for each CCDR report.

F. CCDR submissions will be made by the contractor or in-house Government activity within 45 days after the end of the reporting period, as specified by the CCDR Plan. When subcontractors report to the prime contractor, the prime contrator will be given an additional 15 days to consolidate the appropriate reports.

G. Application of the DD Form 1921-3, Plant-Wide Data Report, will be controlled in accordance with the review procedures and reporting frequencies described elsewhere in this Instruction. The report should be submitted on an annual basis. Implementation of the report is limited to Category I contracts only. When required, this report will be covered in appropriate contracts. In the event that a DD Form 1921-3 is already being furnished on another contract within an applicable contractor facility, copies of that report will satisfy this requirement.

H. Reporting frequency for recurring reports shall be as specified
    in the CCDR Plan.

    1. Generally, reports for Category I contracts should be sub-
        mitted upon completion of major contract milestones or at
        least annually, except for DD Form 1921-2, the Progress
        Curve Report, where reporting will be upon completion of a
        unit/lot but at least annually. However, Category I re-
        porting frequencies may be adjusted during the CCDR Plan
        review procedures.

    2. Reports for Category II contracts normally will be sub-
        mitted at completion of the contracts. In selected in-
        stances, DoD requirements for data may justify more
        frequent reporting; however, this increased frequency may
        not exceed quarterly reporting. Contract type and contract
        value should be determining factors in the DoD Component
        decision prescribing this increased frequency. Justifica-
        tion for Category II reporting frequency will be provided
        during the review described in subsection V.D.

    3. Provision may also be included in the CCDR Plan to specify
        the number of special submissions that may be requested
        during the life of the program, e.g., requirements for up-
        dated cost projections to support a scheduled DSARC review.

I. Contractor submitted CCDR reports and related material will be
    handled and distributed as follows:

    1. In the case of Category I reports, all such reports, except
        those used as contractor responses in support of RFPs, will
        be forwarded within one week after receipt from the con-
        tractor to the Director of Defense Program Analysis and
        Evaluation, acting as the executive agent of the OSD CAIG.
        When CCDR formats are used to collect information in re-
        sponse to RFPs, the completed formats for the winning con-
        tractor will be forwarded to the OSD CAIG as soon as
        possible following the completion of source selection, con-
        sistent with the policy established in DoD Directive 4105.62
        (reference (c)). Category II reports will only be forwarded
        to the OSD CAIG upon request.

    2. Other DoD Components desiring to receive CCDR reports on a
        specific system or contract, may notify the appropriate
        Military Department at the meeting at the procuring materiel
        command headquarters described in subsection V.B. above or
        by subsequent notification in writing.

    3. Requests from other Federal Agencies for CCDR information
        will be processed through the OSD CAIG.

4. If a DoD Component has compelling reasons for not making CCDR information available, it will promptly refer the matter to the OSD CAIG for resolution.

5. Reports prepared by DoD Components on the accuracy or validity of CCDR information will be promptly forwarded to all offices receiving the completed reports on which the evaluation was made. This does not include audit reviews discussed in section VII. of this Instruction. Requests from higher headquarters for clarification of information in the CCDR reports will be addressed to the appropriate materiel command.

6. Copies of all CCDR data will be stored at one central location at each materiel command.

J. Each DoD Component will designate an official who will be responsible for assuring that DoD Component policies and procedures are established for the implementation of CCDR in accordance with the provisions of this Instruction, including the storage of CCDR data and their submission to appropriate DoD officials. He will also be responsible for assuring the forwarding to the OSD CAIG of all CCDR Plans (including any changes thereto) for both Category I and II systems within 15 days after they are approved for implementation. This official will also advise the OSD CAIG, on a quarterly basis, of all acquisition programs for which CCDR Plans are currently approved for implementation (including the status of implementation and changes thereto during the previous quarter).

VI. RESPONSIBILITIES

A. The OSD CAIG will establish policy guidance pertaining to the CCDR system and will monitor its implementation to insure consistent and appropriate application throughout the DoD.

B. The Secretaries of the Military Departments (or Directors in the case of Defense Agencies) will be responsible for the overall administration and implementation of the CCDR system. This will include assuring that an appropriate official is designated to monitor the application of the CCDR program.

C. The Military Departments, on a triservice basis, will develop and issue a joint implementing manual which outlines the procedures to be used in the implementation, collection, maintenance, storage and retrieval of data collected through the CCDR system. The joint implementing manual and any revisions thereto will be coordinated among the responsible DoD Components and submitted to the OSD CAIG for review for

conformance to policy prior to publication. These procedures
will include a CCDR Plan format which will be used by each DoD
Component to identify its specific CCDR requirements for contractor responses to RFPs and to be included in contracts.
The CCDR Plan format will be included in reference (f) upon
publication of the document.

1. The CCDR Plan will identify:

   a. Coverage of prime, associate and subcontractors.

   b. Reporting elements (including WBS level).

   c. CCDR forms to be used for each reporting WBS element
       for submission by the appropriate contractors.

   d. Reporting frequencies for each format and each re-
       porting element.

   e. Estimated cost and quantities for each reporting item
       for both RDT&E and procurement.1/

   f. Whether Category I or II procedures are applicable.

   g. Whether the CCDR formats will be used as a means to
       collect contractor data in support of RFPs or be
       placed on contract.

   h. The number of special CCDR submissions which will be
       requested during the life of the program.

2. These procedures will also describe requirements for:

   a. Submission of the CCDR Plan (reference (f)) including
       changes to an approved CCDR Plan.

   b. Preparation, review and approval of the CCDR Plan.

   c. Implementation of an approved CCDR Plan.

3. Procedures for approval of CCDR Plans for Category I and
    II contracts will be in accordance with the policy stated
    in section V. of this Instruction.

4. A copy of the procedures and forms to implement the CCDR
    Plan will be submitted to the Chairman of the OSD CAIG
    prior to use.

1/ The estimated cost and quantities are for internal DoD use only in
order to illustrate the significance of each WBS element for which
CCDR reporting is proposed. Costs and quantities should not be placed
in CCDR Plans included in solicitations.

VII.   FIELD/AUDIT REVIEWS

    A. Requirements for field reviews of contractor implementation of CCDR, including audits, will be made through the cognizant Administrative Contracting Officer (ACO).

    B. Audit reviews of CCDR data will be performed by the Defense Contract Audit Agency. The scope and extent of such reviews will consist of (1) an evaluation of the effectiveness of the contractor's policies and procedures to produce data compatible with the objectives of this Instruction and its supporting implementing guidance, and (2) selective tests of the reported data. Any exceptions will be included with appropriate comment in the audit reports, which shall be issued to the cognizant ACO, with a copy to the OSD CAIG.

VIII. REPORTING REQUIREMENTS

The CCDR forms have the Office of Management and Budget approval number 22R0322. A Data Item Description (DD Form 1664) for each CCDR form is contained in reference (f).

IX.   EFFECTIVE DATE AND IMPLEMENTATION

This Instruction is effective immediately. The official designated position (by title) required by subsection V.J. of this Instruction will be provided to the OSD CAIG within 30 days. Implementing instructions shall be issued by the responsible DoD Components within 60 days after issuance of this Instruction. Two copies of all implementing instructions shall be forwarded to the Assistant Secretaries of the Defense (Comptroller), (Installations and Logistics) and the Director of Defense Program Analysis and Evaluation.

Assistant Secretary of Defense   Assistant Secretary of Defense
(Comptroller)   (Installations & Logistics)

Director of Defense Program
Analysis and Evaluation

Enclosures - 5
1. References
2. DD Form 1921, Cost Data Summary Report
3. DD Form 1921-1, Functional Cost-Hour Report
4. DD Form 1921-2, Progress Curve Report
5. DD Form 1921-3, Plant-Wide Data Report

7000.11 (Encl 1)
Sept 5,73

REFERENCES

(a) DoD Instruction 7045.7, "Planning, Programming and Budgeting System," October 29, 1969
(b) DoD Directive 5000.1, "Acquisition of Major Defense Systems," July 13, 1971
(c) DoD Directive 4105.62, "Selection of Contractual Sources for Major Defense Systems" (to be issued)
(d) DoD Instruction 7041.2, "Cost Information Reports (CIR)," June 13, 1966 (hereby cancelled)
(e) DoD Instruction 7000.9, "Procurement Information Reporting (PIR)," April 30, 1970 (hereby cancelled)
(f) Contractor Cost Data Reporting System, AMCP 715-8, NAVMAT-5241, AFSCP/AFLCP 800-15 (to be issued)
(g) Military Standard 881, "Work Breakdown Structures for Defense Materiel Items," November 1, 1968
(h) DoD Directive 5000.4, "OSD Cost Analysis Improvement Group (CAIG)," June 13, 1973

7000. 11 (Encl 2)
Sept 5, 73

CLASSIFICATION

Form Approved
OMB No. 22R0322

COST DATA SUMMARY REPORT
(Dollars in _____)

1. PROGRAM	
2. ☐ CONTRACT ☐ RFP ☐ PROGRAM ESTIMATE	3. ☐ RDT&E ☐ PROCUREMENT
	4. MULTIPLE YEAR CONTRACT ☐ YES ☐ NO
	5. REPORT AS OF
	6. FY FUNDED:

7. CONTRACT TYPE	8. CONTRACT PRICE	9. CONTRACT CEILING	10. ☐ PRIME/ASSOCIATE ☐ SUBCONTRACTOR *(Name and Address, Include ZIP Code)*	11. NAME OF CUSTOMER *(Subcontractor use only)*

REPORTING ELEMENTS	ELEMENT CODE	TO DATE — COSTS INCURRED			AT COMPLETION — COSTS INCURRED			
		NON-RECURRING	RECURRING	TOTAL	UNITS	NON-RECURRING	RECURRING	TOTAL
b	c	d	e	f	g	h	i	j

CONTRACT LINE ITEM
a

REMARKS

NAME OF PERSON TO BE CONTACTED

SIGNATURE

DATE

DD FORM 1921
1 AUG 73

CLASSIFICATION

7000.11 (Encl 3)
Sept 5, 73

Form Approved
OMB No. 22R0322

SECURITY CLASSIFICATION

FUNCTIONAL COST - HOUR REPORT

1. PROGRAM	**2. REPORT AS OF**

5. ☐ CONTRACT ☐ RFP

☐ PROGRAM ESTIMATE

3. DOLLARS IN **4. HOURS IN**

6. ☐ NON-RECURRING ☐ RECURRING ☐ TOTAL **7.** ☐ RDT&E ☐ PROCUREMENT ☐ OTHER

SECTION A

8. MULTIPLE YEAR CONTRACT ☐ YES ☐ NO **10.** ☐ PRIME/ASSOCIATE ☐ SUBCONTRACTOR *(Name and address; Include ZIP Code)* **11. NAME OF CUSTOMER** *(Subcontractor use only)*

9. FY FUNDED:

12. REPORTING ELEMENT(S)

SECTION B

FUNCTIONAL CATEGORIES	ADJUSTMENTS TO PREVIOUS REPORTS a	CONTRACTOR		SUBCONTRACT OR OUTSIDE PROD. & SERV.		TOTAL	
		TO DATE b	AT COMPL. c	TO DATE d	AT COMPL. e	TO DATE f	AT COMPL. g
ENGINEERING							
1. DIRECT LABOR HOURS							
2. DIRECT LABOR DOLLARS	$	$	$	$	$	$	$
3. OVERHEAD	$	$	$	$	$	$	$
4. MATERIAL	$	$	$	$	$	$	$
5. OTHER DIRECT CHARGES *(Specify)*	$	$	$	$	$	$	$
6. TOTAL ENGINEERING DOLLARS	$	$	$	$	$	$	$
TOOLING							
7. DIRECT LABOR HOURS							
8. DIRECT LABOR DOLLARS	$	$	$	$	$	$	$
9. OVERHEAD	$	$	$	$	$	$	$
10. MATERIALS AND PURCHASED TOOLS	$	$	$	$	$	$	$
11. OTHER DIRECT CHARGES *(Specify)*	$	$	$	$	$	$	$
12. TOTAL TOOLING DOLLARS	$	$	$	$	$	$	$
QUALITY CONTROL							
13. DIRECT LABOR HOURS							
14. DIRECT LABOR DOLLARS	$	$	$	$	$	$	$
15. OVERHEAD	$	$	$	$	$	$	$
16. OTHER DIRECT CHARGES *(Specify)*	$	$	$	$	$	$	$
17. TOTAL QUALITY CONTROL DOLLARS	$	$	$	$	$	$	$
MANUFACTURING							
18. DIRECT LABOR HOURS							
19. DIRECT LABOR DOLLARS	$	$	$	$	$	$	$
20. OVERHEAD	$	$	$	$	$	$	$
21. MATERIALS AND PURCHASED PARTS	$	$	$	$	$	$	$
22. OTHER DIRECT CHARGES *(Specify)*	$	$	$	$	$	$	$
23. TOTAL MANUFACTURING DOLLARS	$	$	$	$	$	$	$
24. PURCHASED EQUIPMENT	$	$	$	$	$	$	$
25. MATERIAL OVERHEAD	$	$	$	$	$	$	$
26. OTHER COSTS NOT SHOWN ELSEWHERE *(Specify)*	$	$	$	$	$	$	$
27. TOTAL COST LESS G&A	$	$	$	$	$	$	$
28. G&A	$			$	$	$	$
29. TOTAL COST PLUS G&A	$			$	$	$	$
30. FEE OR PROFIT	$			$	$	$	$
31. TOTAL OF LINES 29 & 30	$			$	$	$	$

SECTION C (CAT II ONLY)

DIRECT LABOR MAN-HOURS INCURRED THIS REPORT PERIOD

	ENGINEERING a	TOOLING b	QUALITY CONTROL c	MANUFACTURING d
1. TOTAL BEGINNING OF REPORT PERIOD				
2.				
3.				
4.				
5.				
6. TOTAL END OF REPORT PERIOD				

FORM CONTINUED ON REVERSE

DD FORM 1921-1
1 AUG 73

SECURITY CLASSIFICATION

7000.11 (Encl 3)
Sept 5, 73

SECURITY CLASSIFICATION

PLANT-WIDE LABOR AND OVERHEAD INFORMATION

SECTION D (CAT II ONLY)		1. DIRECT LABOR			2. PLTWIDE OH		1. DIRECT LABOR			2. PLTWIDE OH		1. DIRECT LABOR			2. PLTWIDE OH	
		WORK	BASIC RATE	EFF RATE	IND WORK	RATE	WORK	BASIC RATE	EFF RATE	IND WORK	RATE	WORK	BASIC RATE	EFF RATE	IND WORK	RATE
		a	b	c	d	e	f	g	h	i	k	l	m	n	p	q
	1. ENGINEERING															
	2. TOOLING															
	a. DESIGN															
	b. FABRICATION															
	3. QUALITY CONTROL															
	4. MANUFACTURING															
	5. MATERIAL	▓	▓	▓			▓	▓	▓			▓	▓	▓		
	6. G & A	▓	▓	▓			▓	▓	▓			▓	▓	▓		

		1. DIRECT LABOR			2. PLTWIDE OH		1. DIRECT LABOR			2. PLTWIDE OH		1. DIRECT LABOR			2. PLTWIDE OH	
		WORK	BASIC RATE	EFF RATE	IND WORK	RATE	WORK	BASIC RATE	EFF RATE	IND WORK	RATE	WORK	BASIC RATE	EFF RATE	IND WORK	RATE
		a	b	c	d	e	f	g	h	i	k	l	m	n	p	q
	1. ENGINEERING															
	2. TOOLING															
	a. DESIGN															
	b. FABRICATION															
	3. QUALITY CONTROL															
	4. MANUFACTURING															
	5. MATERIAL	▓	▓	▓			▓	▓	▓			▓	▓	▓		
	6. G & A	▓	▓	▓			▓	▓	▓			▓	▓	▓		

REMARKS

NAME OF PERSON TO BE CONTACTED	SIGNATURE	DATE

SECURITY CLASSIFICATION

7000.11 (Encl 4)
Sept 5, 73

PROGRESS CURVE REPORT (Recurring Cost Only)	1. PROGRAM	Form Approved OMB No. 22R0322

SECTION A

2. DOLLARS IN	3. HOURS IN	5. CONTRACT	6. REPORT FOR _____ MONTHS
4. TOTAL UNITS ACCEPTED PRIOR TO THIS REPORT			ENDING: _____

7. MULTIPLE YEAR CONTRACT ☐ YES ☐ NO	9. ☐ PRIME/ASSOCIATE ☐ SUBCONTRACTOR (Name and address; Include ZIP Code)	10. NAME OF CUSTOMER (Subcontractor use only)
8. FY FUNDED:		

11. REPORTING ELEMENT(S)

SECTION B

ITEM	UNITS/LOTS ACCEPTED					ESTIMATE OF NEXT UNIT/LOT TO BE ACCEPTED	TO COMPLETE CONTRACT
	a	b	c	d	e	f	g
1. MODEL AND SERIES							
2. FIRST UNIT OF LOT							
3. LAST UNIT OF LOT							
4. CONCURRENT UNITS							
CHARACTERISTICS 5.							
6.							
7.							
CONTRACTOR DATA (PER UNIT/LOT)							
8. DIRECT QUALITY CONTROL MAN-HOURS							
9. DIRECT MANUFACTURING MAN-HOURS							
10. QUALITY CONTROL DIRECT LABOR DOLLARS	$	$	$	$	$	$	$
11. MANUFACTURING DIRECT LABOR DOLLARS	$	$	$	$	$	$	$
12. RAW MATERIAL & PURCHASED PARTS DOLLARS	$	$	$	$	$	$	$
13. PURCHASED EQUIPMENT DOLLARS	$	$	$	$	$	$	$
14. TOTAL DOLLARS	$	$	$	$	$	$	$
SUBCONTRACT/OUTSIDE PROD. & SERV.							
15. DIRECT QUALITY CONTROL MAN-HOURS							
16. DIRECT MANUFACTURING MAN-HOURS							
17. TOTAL MAN-HOURS							
18. QUALITY CONTROL DIRECT LABOR DOLLARS	$	$	$	$	$	$	$
19. MANUFACTURING DIRECT LABOR DOLLARS	$	$	$	$	$	$	$
20. RAW MATERIAL & PURCHASED PARTS DOLLARS	$	$	$	$	$	$	$
21. PURCHASED EQUIPMENT DOLLARS	$	$	$	$	$	$	$
22. TOTAL DOLLARS	$	$	$	$	$	$	$
UNIT TOTAL ☐ AVERAGE ☐							
23. DIRECT QUALITY CONTROL MAN-HOURS							
24. DIRECT MANUFACTURING MAN-HOURS							
25. TOTAL MAN-HOURS							
26. QUALITY CONTROL DIRECT LABOR DOLLARS	$	$	$	$	$	$	$
27. MANUFACTURING DIRECT LABOR DOLLARS	$	$	$	$	$	$	$
28. RAW MATERIAL & PURCHASED PARTS DOLLARS	$	$	$	$	$	$	$
29. PURCHASED EQUIPMENT DOLLARS	$	$	$	$	$	$	$
30. TOTAL DOLLARS	$	$	$	$	$	$	$
31. % SUBCONTRACT OR OUTSIDE PROD. & SERV.							
MFG FLOW TIME							
32. START							
33. FINISH							
34.							
35.							
36.							
37.							
38.							
39							

(MOS OR QTRS)

DD FORM 1 AUG 73 1921-2

280

7000. 11 (Encl 4)
Sept 5, 73

ITEM	UNITS/LOTS ACCEPTED					ESTIMATE OF NEXT UNIT/LOT TO BE ACCEPTED	TO COMPLETE CONTRACT
	a	b	c	d	e	f	g
PERFORMANCE DATA (PER UNIT/LOT)							
40. STANDARD HOURS							
41. VARIANCE							

SCHEDULE OF RELEASE DATES	ENGINEERING a	MATERIAL b	TOOLING c	MANUFACTURING d
1. PLANNED				
2. ACTUAL				

REMARKS

SECTION C (CAT II ONLY)

NAME OF PERSON TO BE CONTACTED	SIGNATURE	DATE

7000.11 (Encl 5)
Sept 5, 73

SECURITY CLASSIFICATION

SECURITY CLASSIFICATION

PLANT-WIDE DATA REPORT

1. CONTRACTOR

2. PLANT LOCATION

3. REPORT PERIOD ENDING

4. DATE SUBMITTED

OVERHEAD ACCUMULATION, DISTRIBUTION AND APPLICATION

☐ ACTUAL   ☐ ESTIMATE

SECTION A

TIME PERIOD			PROGRAM/ PROJECT a	QTY. b	BUYER c	① FROM TO DIRECT COST					② FROM TO DIRECT COST					③ FROM TC DIRECT COST					④ FROM TO DIRECT COST					⑤ FROM TO DIRECT COST				
						ENG. d	MFG. e	MAT'L f	OTHER g		ENG. d	MFG. e	MAT'L f	OTHER g		ENG. d	MFG. e	MAT'L f	OTHER g		ENG. d	MFG. e	MAT'L f	OTHER g		ENG. d	MFG. e	MAT'L f	OTHER g	
1.																														
2.																														
3.																														
4.																														
5.																														
6.																														
7.																														
8.																														
9.																														
10.																														
11.																														
12. OTHER GOVT. EFFORT																														
13. COMMERCIAL EFFORT																														
14. TOTAL DIRECT COST BASE																														

SECTION B

INDIRECT COST CATEGORY	① INDIRECT COST				② INDIRECT COST				③ INDIRECT COST				④ INDIRECT COST				⑤ INDIRECT COST			
	ENG. h	MFG. i	MAT'L j	OTHER k	G&A	ENG. h	MFG. i	MAT'L j	OTHER k	G&A	ENG. h	MFG. i	MAT'L j	OTHER k	G&A	ENG. h	MFG. i	MAT'L j	OTHER k	G&A
15. INDIRECT LABOR																				
16. EMPLOYEE BENEFITS																				
17. PAYROLL TAXES																				
18. EMPLOYMENT																				
19. COMMUNICATION/TRAVEL																				
20. PRODUCTION RELATED																				
21. FACILITIES-BUILDING/LAND																				
22. FACILITIES-FURNITURE/EQUIPMENT																				
23. ADMINISTRATION																				
24. FUTURE BUSINESS																				
25. OTHER MISCELLANEOUS																				
26. CREDITS																				
27. TOTAL OVERHEAD COST																				
28. TOTAL G&A COST																				
29. OVERHEAD/G&A RATE																				
EMPLOYMENT – INDIRECT																				
30. WORKERS																				

DD FORM 1 AUG 73 1921-3

282

SECURITY CLASSIFICATION

SECTION C	DIRECT LABOR RATES																	
	1ST QUARTER			2ND QUARTER			3RD QUARTER			4TH QUARTER			PAST YEAR	YEAR:	YEAR:
	WORKERS a	BASIC RATE b	EFF. RATE c	WORKERS a	BASIC RATE b	EFF. RATE c	WORKERS a	BASIC RATE b	EFF. RATE c	WORKERS a	BASIC RATE b	EFF. RATE c	BASIC RATE b	BASIC RATE b	BASIC RATE b
1. ENGINEERING															
2. TOOLING															
a. DESIGN															
b. FABRICATION															
3. QUALITY CONTROL															
4. MANUFACTURING															

REMARKS:

NAME OF PERSON TO BE CONTACTED

SIGNATURE

DATE

SECURITY CLASSIFICATION

APPENDIX E
JOINT IMPLEMENTATION GUIDE
JIG
FOR C/SCSC

HQ AIR FORCE SYSTEMS COMMAND PAMPHLET	AFSCP 173-5
HQ AIR FORCE LOGISTICS COMMAND PAMPHLET	AFLCP 173-5
HQ US ARMY MATERIEL DEVELOPMENT AND READINESS COMMAND PAMPHLET	DARCOM-P 715-5
HQ NAVAL MATERIAL COMMAND PAMPHLET	NAVMAT P5240
DEFENSE LOGISTICS AGENCY HANDBOOK	DLAH 8315.2

COST ANALYSIS

COST/SCHEDULE CONTROL SYSTEMS CRITERIA JOINT IMPLEMENTATION GUIDE

1 OCTOBER 1980

DEPARTMENTS OF THE AIR FORCE, THE ARMY, THE NAVY, AND THE DEFENSE LOGISTICS AGENCY

DEPARTMENTS OF THE AIR FORCE, THE ARMY, THE NAVY, AND THE DEFENSE LOGISTICS AGENCY

Headquarters Air Force Systems Command
    Andrews Air Force Base, DC 20334

AFSC PAMPHLET 173-5

Headquarters Air Force Logistics Command
    Wright-Patterson Air Force Base, OH 45433

AFLC PAMPHLET 173-5

Headquarters US Army Materiel Development and Readiness Command
    Alexandria VA 22333

DARCOM PAMPHLET 715-5

Headquarters Naval Material Command
    Crystal Plaza, Washington DC 20360

NAVMAT PAMPHLET 5240

Headquarters Defense Logistics Agency
    Cameron Station, Alexandria VA 22314

DLA HANDBOOK 8315.2
1 October 1980

Cost Analysis

COST/SCHEDULE CONTROL SYSTEMS CRITERIA
JOINT IMPLEMENTATION GUIDE

This guide provides procedures which have been approved by AFSC, AFLC, DARCOM, NMC, and DLA commanders for use during planning and implementation of cost/schedule control systems criteria (C/SCSC) and for surveillance of contractor compliance. Users of this guide are encouraged to submit recommendations for refined procedures, through command channels, to appropriate focal points within their respective command headquarters.

Table of Contents

Supersedes AFSCP/AFLCP 173-5, DARCOM-P 715-5, NAVMAT P5240, DSAH 8315.2, 1 Oct 76. (See signature page for summary of changes.)
OPR: AFSC/ACC
        AFLC/ACM
        DARCOM/DRCPP-K
        NMC/MAT 08C32
        DLA-AE

Distribution: (see page 71)

288

Chapter 1

INTRODUCTION

1-1. Purpose:

a. **Uniform Guidance.** This guide provides uniform guidance for the military departments and other Defense agencies (hereafter referred to as DOD components) responsible for implementation of the Cost/Schedule Control Systems Criteria (C/SCSC) consistent with the provisions of DOD Instruction 7000.2, Performance Measurement for Selected Acquisitions. Contents were developed jointly by AFSC, AFLC, DARCOM, NMC, DCAA, and DLA. For the purpose of this guide the term "criteria" is synonymous with "C/SCSC." The term "performance" is intended to mean "cost/schedule performance." Procedural guidance for surveillance of Cost/Schedule Control Systems is provided in the C/SCSC Joint Surveillance Guide (AFSCP/AFLCP 173-6, DARCOM-P 715-10, NAVMAT P5243, DLAH 8315.1, DCAAP 7641.46).

b. **Implementation:**

(1) Uniform implementation of the criteria consistent with guidance described herein will avoid imposition of separate duplicative cost and schedule systems on contractors. When management control systems, acceptable to both the contractor and DOD components, are applied to Defense contracts within a given contractor's facility, the systems will provide a common source of information required by all management levels of the Government and the contractor. Where supplemental instructions issued by individual commands to provide additional guidance to their operations, instructions will be consistent with the contents of this pamphlet.

(2) The criteria are intended to be sufficiently general in nature so as to permit their use in evaluating proposals for both development and production programs. Since the two types of programs tend to differ significantly, it is impossible to provide detailed guidance which will apply specifically in all cases. The reader should be on the alert for areas in which distinctions in detailed interpretations seem appropriate or reasonable, whether or not they are specifically identified. Use of the criteria must be based on common sense, which means being practical but also mindful of the overall requirement for performance measurement.

c. **Assistance to Users.** These procedures provide a basis to assist:

(1) DOD managers in assessing the acceptability of contractors' systems in response to the criteria.

(2) Contractors in understanding and responding to the criteria for cost and schedule control systems.

1-2. Background:

a. **Management Needs.** A fundamental responsibility in the acquisition and modification of major system acquisitions is to ensure that visibility of contractors' progress is sufficient to reliably indicate the results being obtained. In carrying out this responsibility in selected contracts within applicable Defense programs, DOD receives and reviews cost and schedule performance data. To be meaningful these data must: (1) portray budgets allocated over time to specific contract tasks; (2) indicate work progress; (3) properly relate cost, schedule and technical accomplishment; (4) be valid, timely, and auditable; and (5) supply DOD managers with information at a

practicable level of summarization. Such data should be derived from the same internal management control systems as used by the contractor to manage the contract.

b. **Criteria Concept.** No single common set of management control systems will meet every DOD and contractor management data need for performance measurement. Due to variations in organizations, products, and working relationships, it is not feasible to prescribe a universal system for cost and schedule controls. DOD has adopted an approach which simply defines the criteria that contractors' management control systems must meet. The criteria provide the basis for determining whether contractor management control systems are acceptable.

(1) The responsibility for developing and applying the specific procedures for complying with these criteria is vested in the contractors, but the specific management control systems they propose is subject to DOD acceptance. In instances where the contractor's systems do not meet the criteria, necessary adjustments to achieve compliance will be required.

(2) By applying criteria, rather than specific DOD prescribed management control systems, contractors have the latitude and flexibility for meeting their unique management needs. This approach allows contractors to use existing management control systems or other systems of their choice, provided they meet the criteria.

(3) When the solicitation document (request for proposal, request for quotation, and the like) specifies application of the criteria, an element in the evaluation of proposals will be the prospective contractor's proposed systems for planning and controlling contract performance. The prospective contractor will describe the systems to be used in sufficient detail to permit their evaluation for compliance with the criteria (appendix A).

(4) If awarded the contract, the contractor will be required to have a comprehensive description of the management control systems and demonstrate to a Government C/SCSC review team their effective application in planning and controlling the work under the contract. DOD relies on the contractor's systems when they are accepted and does not superimpose duplicative planning and control systems (appendix B).

(5) Contractors having systems previously accepted are encouraged to maintain the essential elements and disciplines of the systems, if they intend to remain in the competitive environment for future defense contracts involving large acquisition programs.

c. **Typical Actions.** This guide contains general procedures which may be adapted to specific situations as they arise. Details concerning each implementation will be developed by the procuring activity responsible for the contracts and be consistent with the guidance contained here and in DODI 7000.2. A matrix of the overall process is provided in figure 1-1.

1-3. Joint Participation:

a. **DOD Components.** Successful application of the criteria requires the participation and coordinated efforts of various

3

AFSCP 173-5 AFLCP 173-5 DARCOM-P 715-5 NAVMAT P5240 DLAH 8315.2

Typical C/SCSC Action Items (See Chapter 5)	ACTION AGENCY	
	DOD	Contractor
1. Criteria specified in solicitation (DAR Clause).	X	
2. Description of system submitted in proposals.		X
3. Evaluation review of system description in proposals.	X	
4. Source Selection Evaluation Board (SSEB) considers findings of evaluation review.	X	
5. Criteria requirement in contract (DAR Clause).	X	
6. C/SCSC Review Team is organized.	X	
7. Implementation visit/readiness assessment.	X	X
8. Demonstrates management control systems.		X
9. Determines compliance.[1]	X	
10. Official acceptance.[2]	X	
11. Continuous surveillance.[2]	X	
12. Continuous operation of systems meeting criteria		X

NOTES: 1. After contractor corrects any deficiencies the DOD team reexamines those areas.
2. Demonstration may be required for major changes after acceptance.

Figure 1-1. Typical Actions for C/SCSC Implementation.

DOD components. Generally, the procuring activity is responsible for ensuring implementation of the criteria with the contractors concerned. It is mutually advantageous, however, for representatives of other interested DOD components to participate in C/SCSC reviews.

b. **Liaison.** The principal points of contact among DOD components for implementation of the criteria are identified in chapter 4. The primary functions of the representatives participating are also described. These contact points have been established to coordinate functions and monitor the activities responsible for these functions.

1-4. Appeals. Differences in interpretation of criteria application between Government personnel and the contractor, which cannot be resolved, may be appealed to the focal point (figure 4-1) for resolution. If the difference involves contractor system applications concerning more than one DOD component, the appeal may be directed to the Performance Measurement Joint Executive Group (figure 4-1) for resolu-

tion. While either a Government or contractor representative may initiate an appeal, participants in the appeal have the opportunity to provide appropriate rationale, exhibits, discussion, etc., as required to support the positions. Pending resolution of appeals, the C/SCSC review team should continue to complete assessment of the contractor's compliance with the criteria or the contractor's system description as appropriate.

1-5. Revisions and Additions. Persons using this guide are encouraged to submit suggestions for improvements to appropriate focal points identified in figure 4-1. When proposed revisions are coordinated and jointly approved, send to HQ AFSC/ACC, Andrews AFB DC 20334. Any conflict between the C/SCSC Joint Implementation and Surveillance Guides should be brought to the attention of the Performance Measurement Joint Executive Group (figure 4-1) for resolution.

Chapter 2

CRITERIA

2-1. General Information. When required by the contract, the systems used by the contractor in planning and controlling the performance of the contract must meet the criteria set forth in paragraph 2-4. The contractor's internal systems need not be changed if they satisfy these criteria. Information required by DOD must be produced from the same system used by the contractor for internal management. DOD reporting requirements are specified separately in DD Form 1423, Contract Data Requirements List, accompanying each solicitation and in the contract (chapter 7).

2-2. Scope:

a. **DOD Requirements.** Implementation of the criteria is prescribed by DODI 7000.2 for selected contracts within major systems acquisitions. DODD 5000.1, Major System Acquisitions, and DODI 5000.2, Major System Acquisitions Procedures, set forth the policies and guidelines for designating major systems. Major system acquisitions are designated by the Secretary of Defense at the time the Mission Element Need Statement (MENS) is approved. The Executive Secretary of the Defense System Acquisition Review Council (DSARC) will maintain the list of major system acquisitions.

b. **Major Command Thresholds.** The contract value for mandatory application of the C/SCSC will be identified in the policies of the major commands, as identified in figure 4-1. Application of the C/SCSC to contracts below the mandatory levels established is optional subject to the policies of the cognizant major command.

c. **Subcontracts.** Subcontracts will be selected for application of C/SCSC in accordance with the policies of the cognizant major command by mutual agreement between the prime contractor and the procuring authority, according to the criticality of the subcontract to the program (appendix B).

d. **Exceptions:**

(1) Firm-fixed-price or firm-fixed-price-with-economic-price-adjustment contracts or subcontracts will not be selected for application of C/SCSC. All other types of contracts, including fixed-price incentive, may have C/SCSC applied. Exceptions to this policy will be fully justified on an individual basis by the program manager and submitted to the cognizant major command for approval.

(2) There are other situations involving major contracts where the application of C/SCSC may not be necessary. In such cases, the procuring activity will forward requests for waivers, prior to releasing the request for proposal (RFP) to the major command focal point (figure 4-1) for approval. When waivers are granted, C/SCSC review activities will not be performed. However, contract cost performance reporting will still be required. This reporting will normally be provided via the Cost/Schedule Status Report (C/SSR) or Cost Performance Report (CPR), tailored if necessary. Examples of contractual situations where waivers will be considered are:

(a) Follow-on contracts within mature production programs which are not experiencing significant cost or schedule problems and where no significant changes to the product are anticipated.

(b) Contracts to acquire items directly from produc-

tion lines which currently manufacture predominently commerical products.

e. **Contractor Systems.** As a minimum, contractors' management control systems are expected to provide a framework for defining work, assigning work responsibility, establishing budgets, controlling costs, and summarizing, with respect to planned versus actual accomplishments, the detailed cost, schedule and related technical achievement information for appropriate management levels. Such systems must provide for—

(1) Realistic budgets for work scheduled within responsibility assignments.

(2) Accurate accumulation of costs related to progress of the planned work.

(3) Comparison between the actual resources applied and the estimated resources planned for specific work assignments.

(4) Preparation of reliable estimates of costs to complete remaining work.

(5) Support of an overall capability for managers to analyze available information to identify problem areas in sufficient time to take remedial action.

f. **Payments.** Implementation of these criteria is not intended to affect the basis on which program payments or cost reimbursements are made.

2-3. Terms Explained:

a. **Actual Cost of Work Performed (ACWP).** The costs actually incurred and recorded in accomplishing the work performed within a given time period.

b. **Actual Direct Costs.** Those costs identified specifically with a contract, based upon the contractor's cost identification and accumulation system as accepted by the cognizant Defense Contract Audit Agency (DCAA) representatives. (See Direct Costs.)

c. **Allocated Budget.** (See Total Allocated Budget.)

d. **Applied Direct Costs.** The amounts recognized in the time period associated with the consumption of labor, material, and other direct resources, without regard to the date of commitment or the date of payment. These amounts are to be charged to work-in-process when any of the following takes place:

(1) Labor, material, and other direct resources are actually consumed.

(2) Material resources are withdrawn from inventory for use.

(3) Material resources are received that are uniquely identified to the contract and scheduled for use within 60 days.

(4) Major components or assemblies are received on a line flow basis that are specifically and uniquely identified to a single serially numbered end item.

e. **Apportioned Effort.** Effort that by itself is not readily divisible into short-span work packages but which is related in direct proportion to measured effort.

f. **Authorized Work.** That effort which has been definitized and is on contract plus that effort for which definitized contract costs have not been agreed to but for which written authorization has been received.

g. Baseline. (See Performance Measurement Baseline.)

h. Budgeted Cost for Work Performed (BCWP). The sum of the budgets for completed work packages and completed portions of open work packages, plus the appropriate portion of the budgets for level of effort and apportioned effort.

i. Budgeted Cost for Work Scheduled (BCWS). The sum of the budgets for all work packages, planning packages, etc., scheduled to be accomplished (including in-process work packages), plus the amount of level of effort and apportioned effort scheduled to be accomplished within a given time period.

j. Budgets for Work Packages. (See Work Package Budgets.)

k. Contract Budget Base. The negotiated contract cost plus the estimated cost of authorized unpriced work.

l. Contractor. An entity in private industry which enters into contracts with the Government. In this guide, the word also applies to Government-owned, Government-operated activities which perform work on major defense programs.

m. Cost Account. A management control point at which actual costs can be accumulated and compared to budgeted cost for work performed. A cost account is a natural control point for cost/schedule planning and control since it represents the work assigned to one responsible organizational element or one contract work breakdown structure (CWBS) element.

n. Direct Costs. Any costs which can be identified specifically with a particular final cost objective. This term is explained in DAR 15-202.

o. Estimated Cost at Completion or Estimate at Completion (EAC). Actual direct costs, plus indirect costs allocable to the contract, plus the estimate of costs (direct and indirect) for authorized work remaining.

p. Indirect costs. Costs which, because of their incurrence for common or joint objectives, are not readily subject to treatment as direct costs. This term is further defined in DAR 3-701.3 and DAR 15-203.

q. Initial Budget. (See Original Budget.)

r. Internal Replanning. Replanning actions performed by the contractor for remaining effort within the recognized total allocated budget.

s. Level of Effort (LOE). Effort of a general or supportive nature which does not produce definite end products or results.

t. Management Reserve (Synonymous with Management Reserve Budget). An amount of the total allocated budget withheld for management control purposes rather than designated for the accomplishment of a specific task or set of tasks. It is not a part of the Performance Measurement Baseline.

u. Negotiated Contract Cost. The estimated cost negotiated in a cost-plus-fixed-fee contract or the negotiated contract target cost in either a fixed-price-incentive contract or a cost-plus-incentive-fee contract.

v. Original Budget. The budget established at, or near, the time the contract was signed, based on the negotiated contract cost.

w. Overhead. (See Indirect Costs.)

x. Performance Measurement Baseline. The time-phased budget plan against which contract performance is measured. It is formed by the budgets assigned to scheduled cost accounts and the applicable indirect budgets. For future effort, not planned to the cost account level, the performance measurement baseline also includes budgets assigned to higher level CWBS elements, and undistributed budgets. It equals the total allocated budget less management reserve.

y. Performing Organization. A defined unit within the contractor's organization structure, which applies the resources to perform the work.

z. Planning Package. A logical aggregation of work within a cost account, normally the far term effort, that can be identified and budgeted in early baseline planning, but is not yet defined into work packages.

aa. Procuring Activity. The subordinate command in which the Procuring Contracting Office (PCO) is located. It may include the program office, related functional support offices, and procurement offices. Examples of procuring activities are AFSC/ESD, AFLC/OC-ALC, DARCOM/MICOM, and NMC/NAVAIRSYSCOM.

ab. Replanning. (See Internal Replanning.)

ac. Reprogramming. Replanning of the effort remaining in the contract, resulting in a new budget allocation which exceeds the contract budget base.

ad. Responsible Organization. A defined unit within the contractor's organization structure which is assigned responsibility for accomplishing specific tasks.

ae. Significant Variances. Those differences between planned and actual performance which require further review, analysis, or action. Appropriate thresholds should be established as to the magnitude of variances which will require variance analysis.

af. Total Allocated Budget. The sum of all budgets allocated to the contract. Total allocated budget consists of the performance measurement baseline and all management reserve. The total allocated budget will reconcile directly to the contract budget base. Any differences will be documented as to quantity and cause.

ag. Undistributed Budget. Budget applicable to contract effort which has not yet been identified to CWBS elements at or below the lowest level of reporting to the Government.

ah. Variances. (See Significant Variances.)

ai. Work Breakdown Structure. A product-oriented family tree division of hardware, software, services, and other work tasks which organizes, defines, and graphically displays the product to be produced as well as the work to be accomplished to achieve the specified product.

(1) **Project Summary Work Breakdown Structure.** A summary work breakdown structure (WBS) tailored to a specific defense material item by selecting applicable elements from one or more summary WBSs or by adding equivalent elements unique to the project (MIL-STD-881 (latest revision)).

(2) **Contract Work Breakdown Structure (CWBS).** The complete WBS for a contract, developed and used by a contractor within the guidelines of MIL-STD-881 (latest revision) and according to the contract work statement.

aj. Work Package Budgets. Resources which are formally assigned by the contractor to accomplish a work package, expressed in dollars, hours, standards, or other definitive units.

ak. Work Packages. Detailed short-span jobs, or material items, identified by the contractor for accomplishing work required to complete the contract. A work package has the following characteristics:

(1) It represents units of work at levels where work is performed.

(2) It is clearly distinguished from all other work packages.

(3) It is assignable to a single organizational element.

(4) It has scheduled start and completion dates and, as applicable, interim milestones, all of which are representative of physical accomplishment.

(5) It has a budget or assigned value expressed in terms of dollars, man-hours, or other measurable units.

(6) Its duration is limited to a relatively short span of time or it is subdivided by discrete value milestones to facilitate the objective measurement of work performed.

(7) It is integrated with detailed engineering, manufacturing, or other schedules.

2-4. Criteria. The contractor's management control systems will include policies, procedures, and methods designed to ensure that they will accomplish the following:

a. **Organization:**

(1) Define all authorized work and related resources to meet the requirements of the contract, using the framework of the CWBS.

(2) Identify the internal organizational elements and the major subcontractors responsible for accomplishing the authorized work.

(3) Provide for the integration of the contractor's planning, scheduling, budgeting, work authorization and cost accumulation systems with each other, the CWBS, and the organizational structure.

(4) Identify the managerial positions responsible for controlling overhead (indirect costs).

(5) Provide for integration of the CWBS with the contractor's functional organizational structure in a manner that permits cost and schedule performance measurement for CWBS and organizational elements.

b. **Planning and Budgeting:**

(1) Schedule the authorized work in a manner which describes the sequence of work and identifies the significant task interdependencies required to meet the development, production, and delivery requirements of the contract.

(2) Identify physical products, milestones, technical performance goals, or other indicators that will be used to measure output.

(3) Establish and maintain a time-phased budget baseline at the cost account level against which contract performance can be measured. Initial budgets established for this purpose will be based on the negotiated target cost. Any other amount used for performance measurement purposes must be formally recognized by both the contractor and the Government.

(4) Establish budgets for all authorized work with separate identification of cost elements (labor, material, etc.).

(5) To the extent the authorized work can be identified in discrete, short-span work packages, establish budgets for this work in terms of dollars, hours, or other measurable units. Where the entire cost account cannot be subdivided into detailed work packages, identify the far-term effort in larger planning packages for budget and scheduling purposes.

(6) Provide that the sum of all work package budgets plus planning packages within a cost account equals the cost account budget.

(7) Identify relationships of budgets or standards in underlying work authorization systems to budgets for work packages.

(8) Identify and control LOE activity by time-phased budgets established for this purpose. Only that effort which cannot be identified as discrete, short-span work packages or as apportioned effort will be classed as level of effort.

(9) Establish overhead budgets for the total costs of each significant organizational component whose expenses will become indirect costs. Reflect in the contract budgets, at the appropriate level, the amounts in overhead pools that will be allocated to the contract as indirect costs.

(10) Identify management reserves and undistributed budget.

(11) Provide that the contract target cost plus the estimated cost of authorized but unpriced work is reconciled with the sum of all internal contract budgets and management reserves.

c. **Accounting:**

(1) Record direct costs on an applied or other acceptable basis in a formal system that is controlled by the general books of account.

(2) Summarize direct costs from cost accounts into the WBS without allocation of a single cost account to two or more WBS elements.

(3) Summarize direct costs from the cost accounts into the contractor's functional organizational elements without allocation of a single cost account to two or more organizational elements.

(4) Record all indirect costs which will be allocated to the contract.

(5) Identify the basis for allocating the cost of apportioned effort.

(6) Identify unit costs, equivalent unit costs, or lot costs, as applicable.

(7) The contractor's material accounting system will provide for:

(a) Accurate cost accumulation and assignment of costs to cost accounts in a manner consistent with the budgets using recognized, acceptable costing techniques.

(b) Determination of price variances by comparing planned versus actual commitments.

(c) Cost performance measurement at the point in time most suitable for the category of material involved, but no earlier than the time of actual receipt of material.

(d) Determination of cost variances attributable to the excess usage of material.

(e) Determination of unit or lot costs when applicable.

(f) Full accountability for all material purchased for the contract, including the residual inventory.

d. **Analysis:**

(1) Identify at the cost account level on a monthly basis using data from, or reconcilable with, the accounting system:

(a) Budgeted cost for work scheduled and budgeted cost for work performed.

(b) Budgeted cost for work performed and applied (actual where appropriate) direct costs for the same work.

(c) Variances resulting from the above comparisons classified in terms of labor, material, or other appropriate elements together with the reasons for significant variances.

(2) Identify on a monthly basis, in the detail needed by

management for effective control, budgeted indirect costs, actual indirect costs, and variances along with the reasons.

(3) Summarize the data elements and associated variances listed in (1) and (2) above, through the contractor organization and WBS to the reporting level specified in the contract.

(4) Identify significant differences on a monthly basis between planned and actual schedule accomplishment and the reasons.

(5) Identify managerial actions taken as a result of criteria items (1) through (4) above.

(6) Based on performance to date and on estimates of future conditions, develop revised estimates of cost at completion for WBS elements identified in the contract and compare these with the contract budget base and the latest statement of funds requirements reported to the Government.

e. **Revisions and Access to Data:**

(1) Incorporate contractual changes in a timely manner, recording the effects of such changes in budgets and schedules. In the directed effort before negotiation of a change, base such revisions on the amount estimated and budgeted to the functional organizations.

(2) Reconcile original budgets for those elements of the WBS identified as priced line items in the contract, and for those elements at the lowest level of the DOD Project Summary WBS, with current performance measurement budgets in terms of (a) changes to the authorized work and (b) internal replanning in the detail needed by management for effective control.

(3) Prohibit retroactive changes to records pertaining to work performed that will change previously reported amounts for direct costs, indirect costs, or budgets, except for correction of errors and routine accounting adjustments.

(4) Prevent revisions to the contract budget base (paragraph 2-3k) except for Government-directed changes to contractual effort.

(5) Document, internally, changes to the performance measurement baseline (paragraph 2-3x) and, on a timely basis, notify the procuring activity through prescribed procedures.

(6) Provide the contracting officer and duly authorized representatives access to all of the foregoing information and supporting documents.

Chapter 3

CRITERIA DISCUSSION

3-1. General Information. This chapter is devoted to a discussion of C/SCSC. The explanations and interpretations in this guide are intended to ensure a uniform and consistent implementation of performance measurement requirements. This chapter is intended to clarify DOD requirements and objectives for defense and contractor organizations which must operate cost/schedule control systems which satisfy the criteria.

3-2. Organization. The organization section of the C/SCSC is concerned principally with definition of work required to be performed by the contractor and the assignment of tasks to organizations responsible for performing the work. It requires that all authorized work be defined within the framework of a CWBS. MIL-STD-881 (latest revision), Work Breakdown Structures for Defense Material Items, establishes guidelines governing the preparation and employment of WBS.

a. **Contract Work Breakdown Structure (CWBS).** The contractor's extension of the WBS should reflect what contract work is to be done and the way it is to be managed and performed. It must include the levels at which required reports are to be submitted to the Government, contract line items (if in consonance with MIL-STD-881 (latest revision)), major subcontractors, intermediate levels, and cost accounts. Lower level elements should be meaningful products or task-oriented subdivisions of a higher level element.

(1) A WBS serves many purposes and facilitates planning by providing a formal structure for identifying the work. It simplifies the problems of summarizing contract or project-oriented data, and it establishes the reporting structure for Government-required management information. CWBS planning should take into consideration C/SCSC data elements, summation characteristics, scheduling systems, technical performance parameters, configuration items, and actual cost history. Below the levels contained in MIL-STD-881 (latest revision), the CWBS should recognize and accommodate the differences in the way work is organized and performed in the development and production phases.

(2) There is need for contractor flexibility in CWBS extension. Contractors may recommend and negotiate alteration of the preliminary contract WBS, particularly below the levels contained in MIL-STD-881 (latest revision). The contractor has complete flexibility in extending the negotiated CWBS to reflect its approach to accomplishing the work. It is not necessary to extend all elements of the CWBS to the same level. A basic objective is to subdivide the total contractual effort into manageable units of work. Large or complex tasks may require numerous subdivisions. Other tasks of lesser complexity or size may require substantially fewer levels. There is no need to use "dummy" levels to force all segments of the CWBS to a common level. However, if this enables the contractor to use a particular data accumulation coding system more effectively, dummy levels are acceptable.

(3) In the establishment of the lower levels of a CWBS, it is essential to recognize and accommodate the differences between the organization, performance, and management control of work in the development and production phases. System design and development normally is organized and performed along the lines of the major subsystems of the overall system. The design is normally developed in progressively greater detail until it is established at the component level. In the production or manufacturing phase, components first are fabricated or purchased and then joined together in progressively larger subassemblies and assemblies until a complete system is produced. In addition, the production sequence normally follows a physical parts breakdown rather than the subsystem breakdown characteristic of design. It may, therefore, be impractical to use the same lower levels of the CWBS in the production phase as were used during the development phase. Extension of production WBS requirements beyond those contained in MIL-STD 881 (latest revision) should be reviewed with the contractor to verify compatibility with the hardware manufacturing breakdown and should be limited to those levels absolutely essential to the satisfaction of DOD management needs.

b. **Interrelation of WBS and Organization.** The CWBS defines and organizes the work to be performed. The contractor's organizational structure reflects the way the contractor has organized the people who will accomplish the work. To assign work responsibility to appropriate organization elements, the CWBS and organizational structure must be interrelated with each other; that is, functional responsibility must be established for identified units of work. This interrelationship may occur at any level, but the criteria require that the integration exist at least at the level where performance of work is managed. Other natural points of integration may occur as a result of the manner in which the contractor's work authorization, budgeting, and scheduling functions interface with each other and the CWBS.

c. **Establishment of Cost Accounts.** The assignment of lower level CWBS elements to responsible lower level functional managers provides a key point for management control purposes and cost collection. The lowest level at which functional responsibility for individual CWBS elements exists, actual costs are accumulated, and performance measurement is conducted, is referred to as the cost account level. While they are usually located immediately above the work package level, cost accounts may be located at higher levels when in consonance with the contractor's method of management. In addition to its function as a focal point for collecting costs, the cost account in a performance measurement system is also the lowest level in the structure at which comparisons of actual (applied) direct costs to budgeted costs are required. This should not be construed to imply that actual costs cannot be collected at a level below the cost account. Some contractors also collect costs and make comparisons at the work package level. Data elements BCWS, BCWP, ACWP, and variances determined at the cost account level should be summarized through both the WBS and the organizational structure for reporting to higher levels of contractor management and to the Government.

(1) The cost account is the main action point for planning and control of contractual effort, since virtually all aspects of the system come together at this point including budgets, schedules, work assignments, cost collection, progress assessment, problem identification, and corrective actions.

Most management actions taken at higher levels are on an exception basis based on significant problems identified at the cost account level. For these reasons, the levels selected for establishment of cost accounts should be carefully considered at the outset of a new contract to ensure that the work will be properly defined into manageable units and that functional responsibilities are clearly and reasonably established. The quality and amount of visibility available during the performance of the contract will largely depend upon the level and makeup of the cost accounts.

(2) Integration of the CWBS and organizational structure at the cost account level may be visualized as a matrix with the functional organizations listed on one axis and the applicable CWBS elements listed on the other axis (figure 3-1). Each organization may then be clearly identified with the work for which it is responsible. Further subdivision of the effort into work packages may be accomplished by the appropriate organization managers by assigning work to operating units. Critical subcontractors (as determined by the prime contractor and DOD program manager) must also be separately measured and integrated into the CWBS. Figure 3-1 illustrates integration of the CWBS and organizational structure for a development contract.

(3) As stated in paragraph 3-2a(3), care should be taken to allow the contractor the flexibility to structure a production CWBS which is compatible with the manufacturing breakdown of the production hardware and accommodates any differences in the management required for the development phase and the management required for the production phase. This same need for compatibility with the manufacturing process and recognition of differences in the management of development and production, applies to the points of interface between the CWBS and the organization levels of the contractor which are selected to be the cost account and performance measurement (planning and control) baseline levels for production work. In general, it is more economical and effective to establish cost accounts for production at higher levels of both the CWBS and the organization structure than would be the case for comparable development effort. During the production phase, it is important for the Government to allow the contractor flexibility in the points of interface between the CWBS and the manufacturing organization levels. Cost accounts should not be established at such a low level of the CWBS that repetitive reporting of detailed performance data would have questionable utility.

(a) The lowest echelons of production management are primarily concerned with sustaining the required manufacturing through-put as defined by work orders and schedules issued to them. Cost and schedule management by contract or product is normally the responsibility of higher echelons of management within the contractor's production organizations. These are typically supported by one or more production planning and control organizations which develop integrated schedules for the performance of all production work and prepare appropriate work orders. The planning and control of production typically is in terms of the major functional organizations responsible for material procurement and handling, component fabrications, and product assembly. Tooling, production engineering, quality, inspection, and testing are assigned appropriate supporting roles. Within the major functional organizations, work orders usually cover a manufacturing lot of like items and are likely to cross the boundaries

of lower level organizations as the manufacturing lot is moved through the various manufacturing processes.

(b) The selection of a low organizational level for the production cost account is likely to result in the assignment of cost and schedule management and analysis responsibilities at a level which is inappropriate for two reasons. First, it will be below the level at which cost and schedule management capability and responsibility actually exist in the organization. Secondly, it is likely to result in the generation of a substantial number of additional plans, documents, and performance reports without significantly improving management control. A similar condition can arise if cost accounts are established at very low levels of the WBS. If the two are combined (cost accounts located at low levels of both WBS and organization), the result may be increased costs for control system operation without additional benefits. Tracing of cost and schedule data to very low levels of detail (that is, part number and performing organization) is normally not a problem in production. A satisfactory production planning and control system should have this capability, but cost accounts need not be established at that level. The establishment of cost accounts at the level of major functional departments (or comparable organizations) within the overall manufacturing organization usually results in the proper level of management.

(c) The levels of the work breakdown which define appropriate production cost accounts in conjunction with the organization breakdown level are to a significant extent related to the hardware involved. The level of CWBS appropriate for cost accounts in an electronics production contract is likely to be unsuited to an aircraft production contract. The contractor typically will have a breakdown of the hardware by assembly, subassembly, component, and part number. This breakdown will normally be aligned with the sequence of manufacturing operations followed in building the hardware. It can be of considerable use in determining the appropriate level for establishing cost accounts for production contracts. However, the lowest level of a hardware manufacturing breakdown, the individual part, is almost never the appropriate level for the cost account. Typically, the hardware subsystem, sub-subsystem, or major assembly may be suitable levels for the cost accounts, depending on the product being produced.

(4) While all direct costs are accumulated in cost accounts, the criteria do not require the recording of indirect costs (overhead) at this level. Contractors must, however, be able to identify the organizational managers responsible for controlling the indirect costs that are allocated to Government contracts. Indirect budgets should be established and assigned to the organization managers responsible for controlling such costs. Further, overhead pools and corresponding budgets must be designated and the methods used for allocation clearly defined and documented.

(5) At the lower levels, all work should be categorized into one of three different types of effort: (a) discrete tasks which have a specific end product or end result; (b) work which does not result in a final product; for example, sustaining engineering, liaison, coordination, followup, or other support type activities; and (c) factored effort which can be directly related to other identified discrete tasks; for example, portions of quality control or inspection. In the C/SCSC, discrete tasks are referred to as "work packages," support type effort as "level-of-effort (LOE)," and factored effort as "Apportioned effort." All work under the contract must eventually

296

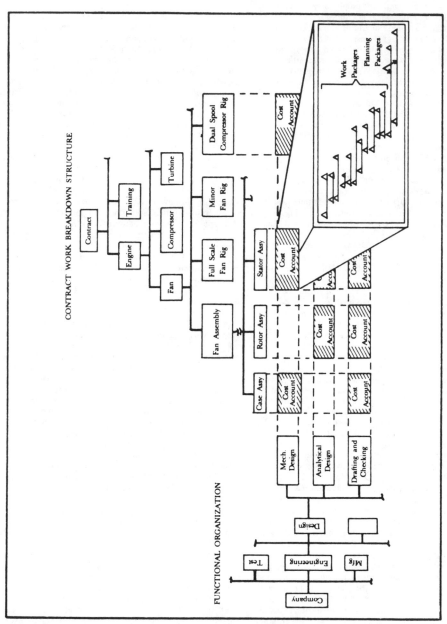

Figure 3-1. Integration of CWBS and Organizational Structure.

11

be planned as and placed in one of these categories during the performance of the contract.

d. **Work Packages.** Work packages constitute the basic building blocks used by the contractor in planning, controlling, and measuring contract performance. A work package is simply a low level task or job assignment. It describes the work to be accomplished by a specific performing organization and serves as a vehicle for monitoring and reporting progress of work. Documents which authorize and assign work to a performing organization are designated by various names throughout industry. "Work package" is the generic term used in the criteria to identify discrete tasks which have definable end results. Consequently, there may be no need for a contractor to establish a new procedure or introduce new documentation to meet the work package requirement. To be effective for planning and controlling work, work packages should have the characteristics defined in chapter 2, paragraph 2-3ak.

(1) A key feature from the standpoint of evaluating accomplishment is the desirability of having short-term work packages. This requirement is not intended to force contractors to make arbitrary cutoff points simply to have short-term work packages. Work packages should be natural subdivisions of effort planned according to the way the work will be done. However, when work packages are relatively short, little or no assessment of work-in-process is required and the evaluation of contract status is possible mainly on the basis of work package completions. The longer the work packages, the more difficult and subjective the work-in-process assessment becomes unless they are subdivided by objective indicators such as discrete milestones with preassigned budget values or completion percentages.

(2) It is recognized that work packages will vary significantly between functions. For example, manufacturing work packages tend to be quite short and discrete as a natural product of the fabrication and assembly operations. Engineering work package planning may be somewhat more difficult since the work is more dynamic in nature throughout the development phase, making it more difficult to define in discrete terms. For these reasons, the criteria do not attempt to impose specific limitations on work package duration. It should be recognized, however, that reports of contract status, such as the Cost Performance Report, are normally provided to the Government on a monthly basis. Although reporting normally is done only for summary level items, accomplishment should be based on completed work packages plus a determination of the amount of work completed in open work packages. Work packages which extend over several reporting periods may require special evaluations to determine the amount and value of in-process work completed as of the reporting cutoff date, and an undesirable amount of subjective judgment may be used in making the determination. On the other hand, work packages which start during one reporting period and end during that period or the next, provide a more objective basis for determining status of contract work. This does not mean that the criteria require work packages to be limited to 2 months in duration, but it does mean that objective devices for evaluating completed work in-process should exist for longer work packages. The use of objective indicators or milestones within such work packages is a desirable technique which should reduce the subjectivity of the work-in-process evaluation.

(3) A manufacturing work package is derived from the relationship between the work breakdown structure and the manufacturing organizational structure and represents a logical subdivision of this relationship. A manufacturing work package may be: a combination of several part numbers; a single part number; a combination of several shop traveler packets; a group of sequences on a shop traveler packet; a single purchase order; a purchase order item number; a subdivision of purchase order elements; or other logical product structure/manufacturing subdivisions.

(a) A combination of part numbers may be grouped in one work package (that is, all parts going into one assembly may be a logical grouping for a work package of this type). Each part number, shop release, or sequence, or combinations thereof may be considered work package milestones.

(b) A part number may be a work package consisting of one or more shop releases. Each shop release or sequence or combination thereof may be considered work package milestones.

(c) A shop release may be a work package. Each sequence or combination of sequences may be considered work package milestones.

(d) Individual sequences may be work packages.

(e) Predetermined combinations of sequences may be work packages.

(f) A combination of purchase orders may be grouped into one work package (that is, several related purchase orders going to one vendor may be a logical grouping for a work package of this type). Each purchase order, purchase order item number, part number, or delivery date, or combination thereof may be considered work package milestones.

(g) A purchase order consisting of one or more part numbers may be a work package. Each purchase order item number, part number, or delivery date, or combination thereof may be considered work package milestones.

(h) A purchase order item number may be a work package. Each part number, or delivery date, or combination thereof may be considered work package milestones.

(i) A part number (purchased) may be a work package. Delivery dates may be considered work package milestones.

(j) A subdivision or grouping of purchase order elements such as "purchase order-part number-delivery date" may be a work package.

(4) In the definition and establishment of manufacturing work packages proper recognition should be given to the characteristics of the production process as opposed to those of design and development. The most significant of these is the relative ease of measurement of most manufacturing work. Manufacturing typically produces a finite output in accordance with a detailed schedule. There are many reasonably accurate and objective techniques for measuring manufacturing performance. The normal production planning and control system usually includes several subdivisions of the manufacturing work which provide a basis for acceptable performance measurement. The objective is to select as the "work package" the work subdivision which best satisfies the requirement for performance measurement.

(a) Since accurate measurement of in-process manufacturing is not usually a problem, the most compelling reason for the selection of the smallest (shortest duration, least value) work subdivision as the production work package is to

298

minimize the need to make changes to the schedules or budgets of open (in-process) work packages or packages scheduled to be started in the current accounting period, both of which are restricted by the C/SCSC in the interests of preserving a stable near-term planning and measurement baseline. However, the smallest formally-defined subdivisions of manufacturing work are, in many production control systems, scheduled with definitive dates only a short interval in advance of their start, which creates problems in satisfying the normal C/SCSC requirement for advance work package planning.

(b) In many production control systems, longer term planning of the lowest work levels is done only in terms of "schedule windows"; that is, time periods of a month or more in which the actual work performance of the "package" will consume only a fraction of the total time, or of "complete by" dates. In some control systems, the formal scheduling of the lowest level of work subdivision may not exceed this degree of precision at any point. Where systems do provide for the establishment of start and completion dates for smaller subdivisions of manufacturing work, these dates are frequently subject to in-process revision to achieve efficient day-to-day workloading of the performing organizations, and to reflect current schedule priorities.

(c) The use of large work subdivisions to satisfy the C/SCSC work package requirement does not avoid this problem, since the type of schedule changes described are still internal changes to the package when it is in-process. Further, the cancellation (closing) and reissue of a new work package for each change generally does not constitute a practical or economical approach in manufacturing, particularly for contractors who have automated their production scheduling and manpower planning (and in some cases also work order preparation and issue).

(d) Under these conditions, a certain amount of rescheduling of manufacturing work packages is appropriate and acceptable providing procedures are in existence which prevent the inadvertent invalidation of baseline schedules and budgets through these detail-level changes. The substance of such procedures should be to limit the range of rescheduling so as to maintain consistency with key production schedule dates. Key production schedule dates define the required completion dates for key elements of the manufacturing plan, are normally found on internal production schedules, and normally should not be more than 3 months apart.

(5) It is emphasized that "work packages" is a generic term used to identify discrete work tasks. In some production control systems involving repetitive manufacturing operations, objective indicators reflecting groups of tasks, may be used and viewed as work packages. For example, when objective indicators are used, values should be established each month based on the tasks in the group. The monthly value established for the group of tasks becomes BCWS for the month. It must be stressed that the measurement of performance of manufacturing work through the use of objective indicators does not eliminate the requirement for detailed planning and control of manufacturing work. The breakdown of manufacturing work into work/shop orders which specify the processes or assembly steps, materials, and organizations necessary to fabricate or assemble a manufacturing lot, and which have assigned schedules and budgets or values, is an accepted general practice in the management of manufacturing effort. This is essential if

schedules and efficient performance are to be maintained.

(a) Examples of the use of objective indicators for measuring accomplishment of repetitive manufacturing operations may include:

<u>1</u>. The use of milestones with assigned or readily determinable budget values.

<u>2</u>. Direct measurement of accomplishment in terms of units of work; that is, some form of an earned or equivalent unit measurement system.

<u>3</u>. An input-output measurement system which compares planned levels and actual performance.

These indicate the principal types of manufacturing measurement systems and reflect the fact that a contractor who already has an effective means of measuring manufacturing performance should be able to satisfy the C/SCSC, providing that this means of measurement is integrated with the contractor's baseline plan for the performance of the manufacturing work.

(b) The contractor must still have a baseline plan for manufacturing work which includes time-phased budgets that are consistent with the schedules for the performance of the work. The performance measurement indicators (milestones, earned units, scheduled output, etc.) must be clearly identified and directly related to cost accounts. They must be scheduled in a sequence which supports the achievement of higher level schedules including those specified for cost accounts. These indicators (milestones, units, etc.) must clearly represent the accomplishment of an identifiable quantity of work within the cost account and be assigned a value reflecting the planned cost of that work. These values must summarize or reconcile to the total budget for the cost account. The use of a measurement base which is only generally indicative of some progress (for example, equal value milestones not related to specific work) is not acceptable.

(c) The performance measurement indicators (milestones, etc.) must be scheduled with sufficient frequency to provide a basis for accurate performance measurement. This entails provision for measurement which supports monthly reports of cost and schedule performance status at the cost account level. To do this, it is normally necessary to measure performance of tasks below the cost account in a way which accurately indicates the performance in each report period. For example, this can be done by scheduling performance measurement indicators with at least bimonthly frequency (2 months) or by providing for a means of accurately assessing "in-process" work when indicators are scheduled at greater than bimonthly intervals.

(d) The restrictions on changes to schedules for manufacturing performance measurement indicators are equivalent to those regarding changes to manufacturing work packages specified in paragraph 3-2d(4)(d). Rescheduling must be constrained so as to maintain consistency with key production schedule dates. Procedures should be established which provide the necessary constraints. There should not be changes to the budgets or values assigned to performance measurement indicators which are scheduled to occur in the current monthly accounting period. This is required in order to maintain baseline stability.

e. **Level of Effort (LOE)**. LOE activity is treated differently from work packaged effort. While work packages are discrete and accomplishment can be measured based on the

13

completed pieces of work, LOE is "measured" through the passage of time. LOE activity must be separately identified from work packaged effort to avoid distorting that which is measurable. The amount of LOE activity will vary among performing organizations, but within each should be held to the lowest practical minimum. The criteria do not establish guidelines as to how much LOE is acceptable, but require that only work which cannot be work packaged or apportioned be designated LOE. This activity should be budgeted on a time-phased basis for control and reporting purposes.

f. Apportioned Effort. Apportioned effort is dependent on or related in direct proportion to the performance of other effort. For example, quality assurance and other inspection functions are frequently treated as apportioned effort based on the amount of manufacturing effort. Apportioned effort may be included and budgeted as a part of the work package or cost account to which it relates or may be established as a separate work package with its own budget which is based on a percentage of the related work package or cost account budget. Factors established for the application of apportioned effort must be documented and applied in a formal, consistent manner. Apportioned effort should be limited to that which is genuinely related to discrete effort.

g. Detailed Planning. While all contractual effort eventually is planned and controlled through work packages, LOE, or apportioned effort, it may not be practicable or possible to do such detailed planning for an entire contract at the outset. A "rolling wave" planning concept may be used. Using this concept, work is planned in finite but sizable increments at the outset of a contract. These planning increments (that is, cost accounts) form the basis for work authorization, budgeting, and master scheduling. As the contract work is defined and planned in more detail, tasks suitable for job assignment evolve naturally, and at least the near term work is segregated into work packages. Thus, the contractual effort is progressively divided into smaller segments as work on the contract proceeds and as responsibility is assigned to successively lower levels of management. However, such work package definition must be accomplished in sufficient time for budgets to be developed and detailed plans for work accomplishment to be completed. Detailed planning approximately 6 months in the future should provide for adequate planning and control. The extent of the detailed planning is determined by the nature of the work. Production effort is normally planned considerably longer than 6 months in the future. However, some development projects are less readily defined and consequently detailed planning may be less than 6 months in advance. Once work packages have been defined and budgeted, controls should be established to minimize further changes to budgets, schedule, or scope of work, particularly in the near time frame (approximately 30 days) (paragraphs 3-2d(4)(d) and 3-2d (5)(d)).

3-3. Planning and Budgeting. The organization criteria establish the basic framework for defining and organizing the work to be performed. This section of the criteria deals with the requirements for program scheduling and budgeting. Generally, it requires that all authorized work be scheduled and that budgets be assigned to identified manageable units of effort.

a. Planning. The assignment of budgets to scheduled segments of work produces a time-phased plan against which actual performance can be compared. The establishment, maintenance, and use of this plan are extremely important aspects of performance measurement. Good planning demands thoroughness and discipline at the outset with continuing discipline required in the maintenance and operation of the plan. This does not mean that the system must be totally inflexible but that changes to the time-phased budget plan must be rigorously controlled and documented.

(1) While planning is required at all levels of management, it becomes progressively more detailed and finite at lower levels of the organizational structure and the CWBS.

(2) Usually, all of the work for a given contract cannot be planned in detail at the outset, but it can and should be initially divided into larger segments so that the entire contract requirement may be viewed as a sum of identified parts.

(3) When it is clearly impractical to plan authorized work in cost accounts, budget should be identified to effort at higher CWBS levels for further subdivision at the earliest opportunity. The budget for this effort must be identified specifically to the work for which it is intended, be time-phased, and have controls established to ensure that it is not used in performance of other work. Eventually, all the work to be performed will be planned by specific organizational elements to the appropriate level of detail. The key point pertaining to summary level planning is that it is no substitute for early and definitive planning. Without timely and adequate work definition and budget allocation, the validity of the entire performance measurement baseline is questionable.

(4) For authorized unpriced work, it is acceptable for the contractor to plan and budget near-term effort in cost accounts while the remaining effort and budget should be planned at a higher level. After negotiation, the remaining effort will be planned and budgeted within cost accounts as soon as practicable to ensure disciplined baseline planning.

b. Work Authorization. Before work actually begins, the work authorization system should define and identify the work to be done and the organizational elements responsible. Schedules and budgets should be established for all work at appropriate levels within the framework of the CWBS. Task authorizations, work orders, or other appropriate operational sheets may be used for this purpose.

c. Scheduling. The scheduling system should provide for all specified work to the lowest defined element of the CWBS in a way compatible with contract milestones and meaningful in terms of the technical requirements of the contract. It should provide schedules so actual progress can be related. Such schedules should identify key milestones and activities which recognize significant constraints and relationships. Scheduling should interface with other planning and control systems to the extent necessary for measurement and evaluation of contract status. The scheduling system should provide current status and forecasts of completion dates for scheduled work. The contractor's summary and detailed schedules should enable a comparison of planned and actual status of program accomplishment based on milestones or other indicators used by the contractor for control purposes.

(1) The criteria do not require the use of any specific scheduling system or methodology. Various scheduling techniques are available which will satisfy these requirements.

(2) Basically, the criteria require the scheduling system to be formal, complete, and consistent. The scheduling system

300

should contain a summary or master schedule and related subordinate schedules which provide a logical sequence and show interdependencies from the summary to the detailed work package levels.

(3) Networking or critical path techniques may be used at summary levels supported by bar charts or other techniques at the detailed levels, if desired, provided that adequate and clear relationships exist between the two.

d. Budgeting. The planning and scheduling procedures serve as the basis for developing budgets and work authorizations. As the work is progressively defined in greater detail, budgets for the planned work should be concurrently assigned. Budgets may be stated either in dollars, man-hours, or other measurable units; although budgets for cost accounts and higher levels are normally expressed in dollars. In general, the budget systems should provide for the following:

(1) Direct budgets allocated to organizations performing the planned work identified to elements in the CWBS.

(2) Indirect budgets allocated to specific organizations having responsibility for controlling indirect costs.

(3) Identification of any management reserves and undistributed budget.

(4) Normally, the total of direct and indirect budgets, and management reserves equals the negotiated contract cost plus the estimated cost of authorized unpriced work. Since primary budget assignments may be made to functional organizations rather than to pieces of hardware or tasks, the level at which the organizational and CWBS elements are integrated may be the first point at which budgets are specifically assigned to CWBS elements. This is not always the case. Certain elements of the CWBS may be priced line items with budgets assigned at the summary level, and then subdivided as the work is broken down into manageable units of effort. Regardless of the budgeting technique used, all work eventually receives a budget.

e. Management Reserve.

(1) In most major acquisition contracts, particularly in the development phase, there is considerable uncertainty regarding the timing, CWBS element involved, or magnitude of future difficulties. The C/SCSC permit the use of a management reserve provided that adequate identification and controls are maintained. Management reserve budget and its use must always be accounted for at the total contract level. Normally, it is retained and controlled at this level, although in some cases it might be distributed to and controlled at lower management levels. In any event, management reserve budget is maintained separately from undistributed budget. There is no such thing as "negative management reserve." If the contract is budgeted in excess of the contract budget base (the negotiated contract cost plus the estimated cost for authorized-unpriced work), the provisions applicable to formal reprogramming should apply.

(2) Management reserve is not a contingency which can either be eliminated from contract prices during subsequent negotiations or used to absorb the cost of contract changes. The contractor should not be required to use existing management reserve to provide funds for authorized but undefinitized work or other modifications to authorized contractual efforts. The contractor may, if the documented management system permits, use management reserve to provide temporary budgets for authorized undefinitized effort; however, it must remain clear to both parties that the management reserve budget was derived from the funding previously negotiated for the contractual effort authorized prior to the change in process. Definitization of contract changes may result in establishing a new level of management reserve reflecting the revised effort. This new level may exceed prior reserves.

f. Undistributed Budgets. Budgets applicable to contract effort, which cannot be specifically identified to CWBS elements at or below the level specified for reporting to the Government, are referred to as undistributed budgets.

(1) The establishment of an undistributed budget may be necessary when contract changes are authorized. For example, reporting deadlines may preclude the planning of newly authorized work prior to report preparation. However, since budgets for all authorized contract work must be accounted for, some provision for the budget applicable to contract changes must be made. In such cases, undistributed budgets identified to the specific contract changes may be established. Except as provided in (2) below, the budget should be distributed to appropriate CWBS elements and cost accounts by the end of the next reporting period.

(2) For authorized work which has not been negotiated, the contractor may maintain budgets in an undistributed budget account until negotiations have been concluded, allocating budget only to that work which will start in the interim. After negotiations, the remaining budget will be allocated appropriately.

g. Contract Budget Base. The original budget established for those elements of the CWBS identified as priced line items in the contract should constitute a traceable basis against which contract growth can be measured. The starting point or base on which these original budgets are built is the negotiated contract cost (paragraph 2-3u). For C/SCSC purposes, this is called the contract budget base. The contract budget base increases or decreases only as a result of changes authorized by the contracting officer. For definitized changes, the contract budget base increases or decreases by the amount negotiated for those changes. For authorized work which has not been negotiated, the contract budget base increases or decreases by the amount of cost estimated by the contractor for that effort. After negotiations, the contract budget base is adjusted to reflect any change resulting from the negotiations. The contract budget base, therefore, is a dynamic amount, changing as the authorized work under the contract changes; but it is a controlled amount, since it cannot be changed by the contractor except as a result of contracting officer actions.

h. Economic Price Adjustment (EPA). For those contracts which recognize abnormal escalation by use of price adjustment clauses, the amounts related to these clauses can be treated in essentially the same manner as undefinitized changes (paragraph 3-6a). If it can be foreseen that economic conditions will apparently result in contract cost revision under the economic price adjustment clause, the contractor may estimate the amount of the adjustment anticipated at the end of the specified economic price adjustment period or other period agreed to by the contracting parties and may include that amount in the contract budget base. Distribution of the estimate should be made to management reserve and the performance measurement baseline or both. As the contract proceeds, and amounts applicable to EPA are definitized, the contract budget base is adjusted to reflect these changes and also to reflect the contractor's latest estimated cost adjustment for the next period. At all times, the economic price adjustment estimate should be identified to contract specified periods and reflect actual experience, current trends, and a reevaluation of future conditions. Thus, the performance measurement baseline can reflect the economic price adjustment conditions contained in the contract, and performance can be measured against a more realistic plan. At the contract level, estimates for economic price adjustment will be identified and reported separately from estimates for unnegotiated changes. No matter what period is chosen for inclusion of the estimate in the contract budget base, the estimated and definitized values should be specifically identifed and reported by the time periods specified in the economic price adjustment clause. The purpose is to properly identify what was definitized versus what was estimated. This is necessary for estimate tracking and for tracing adjustments to management reserve and to the budget for remaining work.

i. **Performance Measurement Baseline.** As the contract effort is defined within the CWBS and identified to responsible organizational elements, the basis for budget assignments to identified tasks is provided. Eventually, each work package will have a budget. Since all work packages cannot normally be planned at the beginning of a contract, initial planning may consist of larger segments of work assigned to designated organizational elements. These functional work assignments frequently serve as cost accounts in addition to their role in the planning function. Budgets assigned to cost accounts are time-phased according to the schedule for performing that work, thus forming the major portion of the time-phased budget baseline; that is, the performance measurement baseline which is used in the measurement of both task and organizational performance. Further budget assignments to work packages are made as detailed planning proceeds. When all work packages are planned within a cost account, the sum of their assigned budgets should equal the total cost account budget (paragraph 3-4b).

(1) All cost accounts must contain a budget, schedule, and scope of work and should realistically represent the manner in which work is assigned and budgeted to the organizational units. The cost account budget should include all direct costs for the total of work with separate identification of cost elements (labor, material, other direct costs). Establishing and maintaining control at the cost account level permits flexibility in the management of resources at the lower detail levels through work package replanning. However, since cost account budgets and schedules also establish the constraints required for baseline control, cost accounts should not be exorbitantly long, or additional controls are needed. When cost accounts average about a year in length, replanning within cost accounts can be accommodated without the need for rigid constraints. It is not intended to limit cost accounts to one year in length, but to ensure that budgeting procedures prohibit budget planned for far-term work from being used in the near term. Therefore, cost accounts which exceed a year in length must be disciplined by budget allocation constraints and/or procedures that prohibit the premature use of budget planned and required for far-term effort within these accounts.

(2) Replanning of work packages within cost accounts is sometimes necessary to compensate for internal conditions which affect the planning and scheduling of remaining work. Such replanning should, however, be accomplished within the constraints of the previously established cost account schedule and budget. When more extensive replanning of future work is necessary and the total cost account budget must be changed, management reserves may be used to increase or decrease the cost account budgets if done in a formal, documented manner. If replanning requires that work and associated budget be transferred between cost accounts, this transfer must also be documented. Except for correction of errors and accounting adjustments, no retroactive changes will be made to budgets for completed work. Replanning actions designed to reduce costs, improve or reflect improved efficiency of operations, or otherwise enhance the completion of the contract, are encouraged. Replanning actions which significantly affect the time phasing of the performance measurement baseline should be clearly auditable by review of contractor records and should be shown in applicable reports to the DOD procuring activity. Maintenance of a performance measurement baseline is required to ensure that deviations from plan are visible and can be examined to determine their causes (paragraph 3-6c). Reschedule of manufacturing work packages is discussed in paragraph 3-2d(4).

(3) The total allocated budget used to report contract performance to the DOD must always represent an amount which is formally recognized by both parties. This is to force recognition of contractual requirements and to preclude undisciplined changes that could result from the use of an administratively established base. The initial establishment of the performance measurement baseline should be tied to the negotiated contract cost. As new work is authorized on the contract, the negotiated contract cost and the performance measurement baseline are increased accordingly. Normally, the total allocated budget (that is, the performance measurement baseline plus management reserve) should not exceed the negotiated contract cost plus the estimated cost of authorized but unpriced work (that is, the contract budget base).

(4) Nothing in the criteria prevents the contractor from establishing an internal operating budget which is less than or more than the total allocated budget. Operating budgets are sometimes used to establish internal targets for rework or added in-scope effort which is not significant enough to warrant formal reprogramming. Such budgets do not become a substitute for the cost account budgets in the performance measurement baseline, but should be visible to all levels of management as appropriate. Cost account managers should be able to evaluate performance in terms of both operating budgets and cost account budgets to meet the requirements of internal management and reporting to the Government. Establishment and use of operating budgets should be done with caution. Working against one plan and reporting progress against another is undesirable and the operating budget should not differ significantly from the cost account budget in the performance measurement baseline. Operating budgets are intended to provide targets for specific elements of work where otherwise the targets would be unrealistic. They are not intended to serve as a completely separate work measurement plan for the contract as a whole.

(5) Any increase which results in a total allocated budget in excess of the contract budget base constitutes formal reprogramming and must be formally submitted by the contractor and formally recognized by the procuring activity. This includes documented reconciliation from the old baseline. It should be clearly understood that such changes are not

302

acceptable on a frequent basis, such as quarterly or semiannually, but may be expected to occur only once or twice during the life of a multiyear contract. One would not expect such an adjustment, for instance, on a contract that covers a single year.

(6) When a contractor formally notifies the procuring agency of a total allocated budget in excess of the contract budget base and the revised plan is accepted for reporting performance to the Government, then it should also be recognized that this condition may be an indicator to the Administrative Contracting Officer (ACO) that progress payments, liquidation rates, or cost reimbursement fee vouchers may require review for appropriate adjustment.

3-4. Accounting. The contractor's accounting system must provide for adequately recording all direct and indirect costs applicable to the contract. Such costs must be directly summarized from the level at which they are applied to the contract through both the WBS and functional organization structures according to procedures acceptable to DCAA.

a. Direct Costs. The criteria require the contractor to record direct costs on an applied or other acceptable basis for performance measurement and unit costing purposes. Direct labor costs are normally applied to work in-process on an as-used (applied) basis. Direct material costs should also be recorded in the same manner; however, there may be cases where it is not logical to make this a uniform requirement. In these cases, if existing contractor systems provide the fundamental elements for cost and schedule performance measurement and for determining unit or lot cost as appropriate, they may be accepted even though they do not record material as a direct cost at the point of usage.

(1) To be acceptable, contractor material accounting systems should have the following characteristics:

(a) An accurate cost accumulation system which assigns material cost to appropriate cost accounts in a manner consistent with the budget.

(b) Recognized costing techniques acceptable to DCAA.

(c) Capability to establish price variances and cost variances attributed to usage where appropriare.

(2) Little need be said of the first two characteristics since these are the province of the DCAA in their normal activities, and they are participants in the review.

(3) With regard to material accounting, the contractor should be able to account for all subcontract material and purchased parts which, by their value and significance, warrant such attention. It is not cost effective to require individual identification of such things as small hardware, miscellaneous wiring materials, and other items of a similar nature.

(4) Material price variance is an essential element of material cost control. This can be determined early in the cycle of ordering materials, at which point the price of the materials can be compared with the amount budgeted for that material. Accumulation of these differences represents the total material price variance. Various routines can be used to calculate this variance, but the system should readily provide such data. When it becomes known that material costs will vary from the amounts planned, the contractor should show these differences in the estimates of final costs.

(5) Material usage variance is an important cost factor on repetitive volume, production type jobs, but may be of marginal significance on single copy R&D equipment. Final material usage variances are not available until the work is completed. However, acceptable cost accounting techniques for analyzing and determining current and projected usage variances should be expected to provide continuing internal measurement when the value and nature of the material warrant. The criteria contain a requirement that contractors' systems be capable of formally planning and tracking the cost of material usage. For most contractors, purchases of material in excess of bill of material requirements are standard practice for many categories of material. Planning for material usage allowance to cover scrap, test rejections, unanticipated test quantities, and the like, is a practical necessity and the contractor should have records of such provisions. The more uncertain the expected usage, the more important it is to have a good plan and to keep track of performance against it particularly for contract peculiar materials or materials which require long procurement leadtimes.

(6) In those instances where the contractor maintains separate stores inventory areas, actual or applied direct cost of "store" material or components will be relieved from the inventory account and charged as actual direct cost on the contract when issued. Normally, all unused material should be returned to stores for disposition. Actual direct material cost includes the materials in the final product, scrap, damaged materials, and so forth, plus any material purchased for the contract but not used, for which an alternate use cannot be found. However, unit cost projections for follow-on procurements would be expected to include material consumed plus material requirements for schedule assurance based on waste and spoilage trends determined from an appropriate phase of the contract performance.

(7) Work progress is determined on the basis of completion of individual segments of work or the attainment of specific milestones. Each such segment of work or milestone is assigned a budget for the resources estimated as necessary to perform that work. Actual resources expended must be recorded on the same basis as resource budgets were assigned if meaningful comparisons are to be made. The definition of applied direct costs takes into consideration the different types of material involved in a contract. Not all material items are processed through inventory accounts. High-dollar value items such as major components or assemblies are frequently scheduled for delivery in accordance with the assembly line schedule. Items of this type are not usually scrapped if found defective, but are returned to the supplier for rework or repair. Under the applied direct cost approach, the costs of such items may be considered as applied direct material costs at the time they are received provided they are either scheduled for use within 60 days or are specifically identified to a unique, serially-numbered end item. If a contractor's system is qualified on other than an "applied cost" basis, actual direct costs may be recorded upon receipt of material, or upon payment, as appropriate under the system.

(8) Neither the applied direct cost approach nor any acceptable alternate should be interpreted to relieve the contractor of the need to maintain records of contract commitments for material.

(9) To avoid distortion of cost variances, costs of material should be reported as incurred in the same period as that in which BCWP is earned for the material. In situations

where BCWP is earned and the associated invoice has not been paid, estimated actual cost may be incorporated into ACWP from purchase order information.

b. **Cost Accounts.** Ordinarily cost accounts are established by the contractor at the lowest level in the CWBS at which actual costs are recorded and compared with budgeted costs. As the natural control point for cost/schedule planning and control, the cost account provides a logical point for cost collection and evaluation (paragraphs 3-2c and 3-3i(1)).

c. **Indirect Costs.** The contractor should charge indirect costs to appropriate overhead pools by methods acceptable to DCAA.

(1) Controls of indirect costs are required and should include:

(a) Establishment of realistic time-phased budgets or forecasts by organization; for example, department or cost center.

(b) Placement of responsibility for indirect costs in a manner commensurate with a person's authority.

(c) Variance analyses and appropriate action to eliminate or reduce costs where feasible.

(d) Review of budgets at least annually and when major unforeseen variations in workload or other factors affecting indirect costs become known.

(2) After indirect costs are accumulated and allocated to contracts, they are applied at the level selected by the contractor. There is no requirement in the criteria to apply indirect costs at either the work package or the cost account levels, although some contractors may choose to do so. However, it must be possible to summarize indirect costs from the applied level to the contract level without the need for further divisions.

d. **Level of Effort.** LOE costs are normally segregated from costs of discrete effort at the cost account level to permit an evaluation of the measurable effort before it is combined with the support effort. This segregation is intended to prevent distortion of measurable activity until at least one comparison of BCWP versus ACWP has been made.

e. **Apportioned Effort.** Cost should be directly related to the discrete work packages or cost accounts to which the cost pertains. Factors and methods used to apply apportioned effort should be formally defined in established procedures with such costs accumulated on the same basis as budgets are allocated.

3-5. Analysis. The C/SCSC do not require the submission of data or reports from the contractor to the Government. The criteria only set forth characteristics which contractors' systems must possess, and specify the type of data which should be derived from the systems. Five basic data elements are identified in the criteria: ACWP, BCWS, BCWP, Budget at Completion (BAC) and Estimated Cost at Completion (EAC). ACWP (direct and indirect) was discussed previously under accounting (paragraph 3-4). BAC was discussed in paragraph 3-3i. This section discusses BCWS, BCWP, EAC, and analyses of variances resulting from comparisons of these five basic elements.

a. **Budgeted Cost for Work Scheduled.** BCWS represents the time-phased budget plan against which performance is measured. For the total contract, BCWS is normally the negotiated contract cost plus the estimated cost of authorized but unpriced work (less any management reserve). It is time-phased by the assignment of budgets to scheduled increments of work. For any given time period, BCWS is determined at the cost account level by totaling the budgets for all work packages scheduled to be completed, plus the budget for the portion of in-process work (open work packages) scheduled to be accomplished, plus the budgets for LOE and apportioned effort scheduled to be completed during the period. In developing BCWS, consideration should be given to the methods planned for taking credit for BCWP (b below).

b. **Budgeted Cost for Work Performed.** BCWP consists of the budgeted costs for all work actually accomplished during a given time period. At the cost account level, BCWP is determined by totaling the budgets for work packages actually completed, plus the budget applicable to the completed in-process work within open work packages, plus the budgets for LOE scheduled for the period and the appropriate value for apportioned effort associated with completed work. The major difficulty encountered in the determination of BCWP is the evaluation of in-process work (work packages which have been started but have not been completed at the time of cutoff for the report). As discussed previously in paragraphs on the organization criteria, the use of short-span work packages or establishment of discrete value milestones within work packages will significantly reduce the work-in-process evaluation problem and procedures used will vary depending on work package length. For example, some contractors prefer to take no BCWP credit for a work package until it is completed, others take credit for 50 percent of the work package budget when it starts and the remaining 50 percent at completion. Some contractors use formulae which approximate the time phasing of the effort, others use earned standards, while still others prefer to make physical assessments of work completed to determine the applicable budget earned. For longer work packages many contractors use discrete milestones with preestablished budget or progress values to measure work performance. The criteria do not specify any particular method as the technique used will largely depend on work package content, size, and duration. The use of arbitrary formulae, as described above, should be limited to very short work packages (paragraph 3-2d(2)).

c. **Data Analyses:**

(1) Comparisons of BCWS with BCWP relate work completed to work scheduled during a given period of time. While this provides a valuable indication of schedule status, in terms of dollars worth of work accomplished, it may not clearly indicate whether or not scheduled milestones are being met since some work may have been performed out of sequence or ahead of schedule. A formal time-phased scheduling system must, therefore, provide the means of determining the status of specific activities and milestones.

(2) Comparisons of BAC with EAC are required internally at the cost account level and provide estimated variances expected at the completion of the contract. Cost account managers need to be constantly alert to circumstances which will cause the estimate at completion and, therefore, the variance at completion, to change. Such changes must be reported monthly (paragraph 3-5f).

(3) Comparisons of BCWP and ACWP will clearly show whether completed work has cost more or less than was planned for that work. Analyses of these differences should reveal the factors contributing to the variances, such as poor initial estimate for the task, technical difficulties requiring

application of additional resources, the cost of labor or materials different than planned, personnel efficiency different than planned, or a combination of these or other reasons.

(4) Comparisons of BCWP with BCWS and with ACWP are required at the cost account level. Cost accounts consist of an aggregation of work packages which are the responsibility of a single organization. Managerial authority and responsibility for corrective action should exist at this point making the cost account a key management control point in the system. It is important that the performance measurement baseline be maintained at this level since comparisons of planned versus actual performance are of little value if the measurement base is subject to uncontrolled fluctuation and change. Since higher level management information consists of direct summaries of the results of such comparisons, there is less need for further calculations at high levels to determine program status.

(5) When a subcontractor is required to comply with the C/SCSC and provide a Cost Performance Report (CPR), subcontractor data will be provided to the prime contractor for performance measurement purposes. If a subcontractor is not required to comply with the criteria, the prime contractor should establish procedures which tie the planned and actual accomplishment of the subcontractor to valid indicators, such as the proposed payment schedule or completion of identified work segments. The Cost/Schedule Status Report (C/SSR) may be used for obtaining the data from a subcontractor when the CPR is not needed.

(6) The analysis of every cost and schedule variance is usually unnecessary and unproductive. Therefore the contractor should establish internal cost and schedule variance thresholds and analyze only those variances which are significant; that is, those which exceed the thresholds. These thresholds may vary with respect to the level of the WBS element, the level of the organizational element, the amount of work remaining, etc. It is essential that these internal variance thresholds be so established that all significant variances will be analyzed while at the same time avoiding an excessive number of variance analyses.

d. **Summarization.** BCWS, BCWP, ACWP, and associated variances should be summarized directly into both the WBS and organizational structure from the cost account level to provide both contract status and organizational performance at all levels of management. Because favorable variances in some areas are offset by unfavorable variances in other areas, higher level managers will normally see only the most significant variances at their own level. However, the accumulation of many small variances which may be adding up to a large overall cost problem not attributable to any single major difficulty will also be evident. The same is true of the information to be reported to the Government.

(1) If required by the contract, the Cost Performance Report (OMB: 22-R0280) provides data to the Government at a summary level, normally the third level of the contract WBS or higher. Functional cost information will be reported at the total contract level for major functional categories which reflect the contractor's organizational structure, such as engineering, manufacturing, tooling, material, subcontract, etc. While only problems having significant cost or schedule impact on the contract will appear on this report due to the wash-out effect of favorable and unfavorable variances, all significant variances should be explained in the problem analyses portion of the report. The reason for reporting only summary level information to the Government is that as long as contract performance is proceeding according to plan, there should be no need to report additional detail. If actual performance begins to deviate from the plan, the contractor's system should provide the capability for tracing the variances to their source to isolate the causes of the deviations.

(2) It should be recognized that this method of performance measurement is only one of the management tools available to contractors and DOD project managers. Many major problems are disclosed through methods other than monthly cost reports. For example, failure to meet closely monitored schedule, manpower, or technical achievement plans and requirements should promptly alert contractor management that a problem exists. However, the Cost Performance Reports should indicate the overall cost impact of such problems on the contractor.

(3) It is important to establish reasonable variance thresholds that will cause problem analyses and narrative reports to be prepared. Careful selection of these thresholds is necessary to prevent unnecessary work associated with preparing an excessive number of written analyses.

(a) Generally, thresholds are established requiring a variance analysis for any cost or schedule variance that exceeds a certain percentage of BCWS or BCWP and/or exceeds an established dollar minimum (for example, $\pm$ _____ % of cum BCWS, or $ _____ , whichever is greater). When initially establishing the thresholds, it may be advisable to provide for tightening these thresholds as the contract progresses, in view of the increased cumulative values of BCWS, BCWP, and ACWP.

(b) Another approach is to establish the thresholds as a percentage of the Budget at Completion (BAC) rather than as a percentage of BCWS and BCWP (for example, 100(BCWP-ACWP)/BAC for cost variance threshold; 100(BCWP-BCWS)/BAC for schedule variance threshold). This results in a threshold which becomes a progressively smaller percentage of cumulative BCWS and BCWP as the contract progresses. Since this type of variance threshold may be relatively loose early in the contract, the threshold for early variances may be limited by adding a threshold based on a percentage of cumulative BCWS (for example, $\pm$ _____ % of BAC, or $\pm$ _____ % of cumulative BCWS, whichever is less).

(c) Whenever a variance exceeds the prescribed threshold, an analysis and explanation are required. Consideration should be given to establishing higher thresholds for underrun or ahead-of-schedule conditions to minimize the generation of analyses and explanations of variances that do not have potential for adverse impact.

(d) The selection of thresholds should avoid, on the one hand, the explanation of variances that are unimportant, while not missing variances that are significant. It should be recognized that no particular approach or set of thresholds is "best" for all circumstances. It may be appropriate to use different thresholds for different levels of management, for different organizational elements, and for reporting to the customer. Whenever, during the performance of a contract, it becomes apparent that the thresholds are no longer appropriate, they should be revised. Too few or too many variance analyses in relation to the performance status of the contract may indicate improperly set thresholds which require adjustment.

e. **Technical Achievement.**

(1) The key to meaningful correlation of technical achievement with cost and schedule control is the proper organization and supervision of effort. If a CWBS matches the specification tree and also reflects the manner in which the contractor actually does the work, the problem of correlation is greatly simplified. In correlating cost, schedule, and technical achievement, it is apparent that unfavorable cost or schedule conditions are usually caused by technical difficulties. Therefore, quantitative information as to technical status is desirable and should be supplemented by narrative reports.

(2) As work on a contract progresses, the contractor determines the adequacy and quality of the work performed by making inspections, tests, or other types of technical measurements. If the results are satisfactory and no corrective action is required, the work is then allowed to proceed further. If, on the other hand, deficiencies are found, the contractor considers various alternatives for corrective action; for example, redesign, scrap and remake, rework, etc. When considering these alternatives, the impact on cost and schedule must be weighed in addition to the technical considerations. After one of the alternatives is selected as the desired course of action to correct the deficiencies, it becomes necessary to plan the additional work in terms of new work packages or additions to existing unopened work packages and to change the schedules affected. In some cases the contractor may choose to provide additional budget to the responsible organization. Thus, there is a close relationship between technical achievement (that is, inspection and test) and its impact on cost and schedule.

f. **Estimated Cost at Completion.** C/SCSC also requires the contractor to periodically develop comprehensive estimates of costs at contract completion. In developing this estimate at completion, the contractor should use all available information to arrive at the best possible estimate of costs for all authorized contract effort. The procedure should be systematically and consistently used from period to period, with adequate consideration given to performance to date. The EAC procedures should provide for the formulation or updating of an estimate of cost to completion, time-phased to the extent necessary to reflect projected rates. This is necessary to ensure that resource requirements are realistic and phased in accordance with projected performance. In addition, the estimate at completion should be examined monthly for accuracy as a routine cost management function, and should be updated, as warranted. Such an examination is required to ensure reliable and timely EAC status reporting consistent with contractor reporting requirements. Both the comprehensive EACs and the monthly updates are essential as a basis for management decisionmaking by both the contractor and DOD managers. While no specific time period for developing the comprehensive EAC is established by the criteria, it is expected that a comprehensive estimate will be prepared on an annual basis as a minimum, usually in support of the business plan update, or more frequently when performance indicates that the current estimate is invalid. The estimated cost at completion submitted to the Government on the Cost Performance Report should be reconcilable with internal cost reports and the contractor's latest statement of funds requirements reported on DD Form 1586, Contract Funds Status Report (CFSR) (OMB: 22-R0180), or its equivalent.

EACs should be established without regard for contract ceilings.

3-6. Revisions. The final section of the criteria pertains to revisions to planning which are necessitated either by contractual change or by internal conditions which require replanning within the scope of the contract. It also deals with maintaining the validity of the performance measurement baseline.

a. **Contract Changes.** Government-directed changes to the contract can impact virtually all aspects of the contractor's internal planning and control system, such as work authorizations, budgets, schedules, and estimated final costs. Revisions required to incorporate authorized changes to contractual effort should be made in a timely manner.

(1) Where the change has been negotiated and priced, budget revisions are based on the negotiated cost of the change. Where work is authorized before negotiations, appropriate change order planning will be accomplished and budgets will be established based on the contractor's cost estimate for the change.

(a) The adjustment of budgets to reflect negotiations is normally accomplished by revising undistributed budgets, management reserves, budgets established for work not yet started, or a combination of these. The use of undistributed budgets or management reserve generally has the least impact since it does not change budgets already issued and agreed to by the responsible organization.

(b) Because budgets associated with near term work should be well planned, retroactive changes to budgets for completed work associated with the change should not be necessary.

(2) Adequate records of all budgeting changes should be maintained to provide the basis for reconciliation with original budgets at the priced line item level and for subsidiary budgets at the lowest level of the DOD project summary WBS as a minimum.

b. **Internal Replanning.** It may be necessary to perform other replanning actions within the scope of the authorized contract to compensate for cost, schedule, or technical problems which have caused the original plan to become unrealistic; require a reorganization of work or people to increase efficiency of operations; or require different engineering or manufacturing approaches than originally contemplated.

(1) Due to the importance of maintaining a valid baseline for performance measurement, such changes should be accomplished in a systematic and timely manner and must be carefully controlled. Many such changes can be handled within the budget and schedule constraints of cost accounts. Other changes may require the application of management reserves to cost accounts to cover additional costs anticipated as a result of the changes. All changes which affect cost account budgets or include significant schedule revisions, which impact on the time-phasing of the performance measurement baseline, should be brought to the attention of the DOD procuring activity in applicable contractually required reports. This requirement is not intended to reduce contractor flexibility in the management of their resources, but is intended to assist all users of the data produced from the management systems in understanding and interpreting it correctly.

(2) If the contractor proposes a change to budgets for completed or in-process work, the contract administration office (CAO), in conjunction with the procuring activity, should promptly and thoroughly evaluate the proposed change and its effect on performance measurement. This review should occur before the procuring activity approves the change. The agreement with the contractor should address the specific adjustments to be made and the time period during which the change will be implemented (paragraph 3-6d(7)).

c. **Formal Reprogramming:**

(1) During the life of a contract, situations may arise whereby available contract budgets for the remaining work are decidedly insufficient. Consequently, performance measurement against the available budgets becomes unrealistic. Under these circumstances, a requirement may exist for the total allocated budget to exceed the contract budget base, and formal reprogramming may be necessary. As appropriate, formal reprogramming by the contractor may entail: replanning future work; replanning in-process work; or adjusting variances (that is, cost or schedule or both). Such reprogramming allows the contractor to increase the amount of budget for the remaining work to a more realistic amount, adequate to provide reasonable budget objectives, work control, and performance measurement.

(2) A thorough analysis of contract status requiring full coordination between the Government program manager and the contractor is necessary before the implementation and recognition of a total allocated budget in excess of the contract budget base. The contractor must perform a detailed estimate of all costs necessary to complete the contract. Factors to consider in developing the estimate are: the amount of authorized work remaining, the estimated cost of the resources required to accomplish the remaining work, and the budget (including management reserve, if any) available for reallocation to the remaining work. If the difference between the estimated cost to complete and the remaining budget is a significant amount, the contractor will notify the procuring activity of the need to increase the remaining budgets and measure subsequent performance against a total contract goal higher than the contract budget base.

(3) Before making a decision as to whether to recognize a baseline over the contract budget base, the procuring activity should consider the following:

(a) The primary consideration should be an analysis of the work remaining and the budget remaining. The fact that a contract is overrun to date and is projecting an overrun at completion is not the most important factor in the decision. Changing a baseline merely to compensate for variances already experienced is inappropriate.

(b) The contract should have at least six months of substantial work remaining after reprogramming.

(c) Reprogramming should not be done more frequently than annually and preferably no more frequently than once during the life of the contract.

(4) If the procuring activity is satisfied that the new baseline represents a reasonable plan for completing the contract, the new goal may be accepted as a basis for future performance measurement. Timeliness is essential in making this determination. Therefore, the procuring activity should take immediate action to evaluate the—

(a) Impact on contract status reporting, such as the effect on cost and schedule variances and the change in the relationship of BCWP to the contract value.

(b) Method to be employed by the contractor in implementing the change; for example, adjustments to variances applicable to completed work, and/or adjustments to work-in-process.

(c) Estimated amount of time required to accomplish the reprogramming and the guidelines for performance measurement during that time.

(d) Effect on other contractual requirements; for example, the status of contractually specified program milestones, the contract share ratio, and the liquidation rates for progress payments.

(5) In formal reprogramming, the changes to baseline budgets must be fully documented and traceable. Internal records and reports should be revised expeditiously and provide appropriate visibility to account for the manner in which contract budgets were changed. If variances are adjusted, the BCWS and BCWP values before adjustment will be retained to ensure traceability. Establishment of management reserve for the reprogrammed effort is acceptable in most circumstances. If deemed necessary, guidance may be obtained from the appropriate focal points identified in figure 4-1.

d. **Baseline Maintenance.** To maintain the validity of the performance measurement baseline, contractor discipline is mandatory throughout the organization, particularly in regard to budgetary control. Contractors' written internal procedures should clearly delineate acceptable and unacceptable budget practices. These should include the following:

(1) Budgets are assigned to specific segments of work (CWBS elements, cost accounts, planning packages, and work packages).

(2) Work responsibility should not be transferred from one cognizant organization to another, or from one cost account to another without transferring the associated budget.

(3) A budget assigned to future specific tasks should not be used to perform another task, regardless of the CWBS level involved.

(4) When management reserves are used, records should clearly indicate when and where they were applied.

(5) When undistributed budgets exist, records should clearly identify their amount, purpose, and level at which held.

(6) Budgets which are assigned to work packages should not be changed once they are started unless the scope of work is affected by contractual change, or other reasons agreed to by the contracting parties.

(7) Retroactive changes to budgets or costs for completed work or to schedules are not made except for correction of errors or normal accounting adjustments.

Chapter 4

DOD COMPONENT RELATIONSHIPS

4-1. General Information. As noted in paragraph 1-3, representatives of various DOD components participate in C/SCSC implementation. Besides major commands within the military departments, DCAA and DLA/DCAS are included. This chapter explains responsibilities of various representatives concerned with implementation of the criteria contained in chapter 2 and discussed in chapter 3. Implementation procedures are explained in chapter 5. Chapter 6 describes contract administration and audit functions.

4-2. Terms Explained. Several terms are used with reference to various activities responsible for criteria implementations. When applied to specific efforts, these terms are intended to describe functions rather than organizations. Each command may assign different designations consistent with internal operations to accomplish responsibilities associated with these terms. For example, figure 4-1 indicates which organizations usually perform functions described in this publication. Significant terms used for this purpose are described below:

a. Major Command. The overall responsibility for implementation of the criteria within each military service is assigned to the major command headquarters which is responsible for selected acquisitions; for example, DARCOM, NMC, AFSC, or AFLC. When two or more commands have collateral interest in application of criteria by a specific contractor facility, one is designated as the lead command to organize C/SCSC review activities. The lead command provides liaison with DCAA and DCAS as well as other major commands through focal points described in c below. Various factors considered in designation of the lead command are—

(1) When a new contractual requirement involving criteria implementation exists or is imminent, the command responsible for the applicable procuring activity is the lead command. As such, it will organize C/SCSC review teams (paragraph 4-3).

(2) When no new contractual requirement exists or is imminent, the major command having cognizance for contract administration will function as the lead command. If the DCAS has cognizance, then the lead command will be the major command with the predominant dollar interest, based upon a computation of the contractor's unliquidated obligations with each major command.

(3) When there is any question about designation of the lead command regarding a specific contractor facility, the designation will be accomplished by mutual agreement through established focal points.

b. Procuring Activity. This term usually identifies the subordinate command where the program contracting office is located. It includes the program office and related functional support offices as well as procurement offices. Examples of procuring activities are AFSC/ASD, AFLC/OC-ALC, DARCOM/MICOM, and NMC/NAVAIRSYSCOM.

c. Focal Points. Major command headquarters have established focal points to serve as the principal points of contact for coordination and exchange of information on implementation of the criteria. There may be more than one focal point depending on the circumstances described by supplemental instructions published by applicable commands. Usually, focal points within the lead command are responsible for the following functions:

(1) The focal point for coordination directs the organization of teams, schedules reviews, and maintains liaison with the focal point for procurement support and with other focal points as designated by other commands or DOD components. The focal point is also responsible for review and approval of major changes (that is, those requiring interpretation of the criteria) to accepted systems. Such changes should be referred to it by procuring activities.

(2) The focal point for procurement support is concerned with contractual activities regarding establishment of initial contract provisions, memorandum of understanding, and surveillance policy guidance.

d. Executive Group. The Performance Measurement Joint Executive Group provides a forum to arbitrate any matters concerning C/SCSC reviews and other C/SCSC matters that cannot be resolved amicably through focal points established in the headquarters of applicable commands. This group is expected to solve problems before they reach such magnitude that they would be referred to the Joint Logistics Commanders individually or collectively. Officials designated to serve on the group represent the following:

(1) Associate Director for Cost Performance Reporting, Directorate for Procurement and Production, HQ DARCOM.

(2) Head, Acquisition Management Controls Branch, Systems Contracting Division, Office of the Assistant Deputy Chief of Naval Material for Contracts and Business Management, HQ NMC.

(3) Director of Cost and Management Analysis (ACC), DCS/Comptroller, HQ AFSC.

(4) Appropriate command system or program representative when a program is involved which is not under the staff supervision of NMC, DARCOM, or AFSC.

(5) HQ DCAA and DLA/DCAS as appropriate.

e. Contract Administration Office. This is the cognizant office within a military command or DLA which is assigned to administer contractual activities at a specific facility. It is a general term and includes AFPROs, NAVPROs, SUPSHIPs, Army Plant Representatives, DCASRs, DCASMAs, and DCASPROs. The cognizant CAO may be part of the procuring activity or it may be part of DLA when DCAS is assigned responsibilities for plant cognizance. The focal point in DLA concerning criteria implementation is the Production Engineering Division (DLA-HE). Additional guidance regarding CAO functions is provided in paragraph 6-2.

f. Contract Auditor. This is the representative of the cognizant audit office designated by the DCAA for conducting audit reviews of the contractor's accounting system policies and procedures for compliance with the criteria. As mentioned in paragraph 6-3, the auditor participates in demonstration reviews as well as subsequent surveillance.

4-3. Demonstration Review Teams. The procuring activity of the lead command will organize a team of qualified individuals to conduct in-plant reviews of the contractor's management control systems. The purpose of these reviews is to verify that the contractor is operating systems which meet the criteria.

AFSCP 173-5   AFLCP 173-5   DARCOM-P 715-5   NAVMAT P5240   DLAH 8315.2

Function	Army	Navy	Air Force
Major Commands*	DARCOM	NMC	AFSC AFLC***
Procuring Activity	Major subordinate commands	NAVSYSCOMS	Major subordinate commands
Focal point for:** (1) Coordination/liaison	DRCPP-K[1]	MAT-08C32[2]	ACC[3] ACM***[4]
(2) Procurement Support	DRCPP-K[1]	MAT-08C32[2]	ACC[3] PMM***[5]
Performance Measurement Joint Executive Group	DRCPP-K[1]	MAT-08C32[2]	ACC[3]
Contract Administration Office (CAO)	DCAS/Army Plant Rep/NAVPRO/SUPSHIPS/ AFPRO/AFCMC		

* One Command will serve as lead command during a C/SCSC review.
** In DLA the focal point is DLA-AE. The cognizant audit office maintains liaison for DCAA.
***AFLC only. Overall Air Force liaison is provided by HQ AFSC/ACC.

[1] Associate Director for Cost Performance Reporting, Directorate for Procurement and Production, HQ DARCOM.
[2] Branch Head, Acquisition Management Controls Branch, Systems Contracting Division, Asst. Deputy Chief of Naval Material (Contracts and Business Management) HQ NMC.
[3] Directorate of Cost and Management Analysis, HQ AFSC.
[4] Directorate of Management and Cost Analysis, HQ AFLC.
[5] Directorate of Contract Management/Maintenance, HQ AFLC.

Figure 4-1. **Functional Responsibilities of Selected Organizations.**

a. **Team Composition.** The focal point for coordination within the headquarters of the lead command will approve the review director and team chief. It will inform focal points designated by other commands, DCAA, and DCAS regarding those appointments and request them to identify representatives with pertinent qualifications to serve as team members. As soon as a review schedule is developed, the lead command will apprise all participants. The team functions are—

(1) Review Director. The director is usually located in the lead command headquarters. The director will organize and monitor team efforts in collaboration with representatives from field commands and other DOD components selected to work with each C/SCSC review team. The director may be concerned with more than one team simultaneously, and will furnish policy guidance and interpretation of the criteria to the team chief and team members.

(2) Team Chief. The team chief may be selected or designated from within the lead command headquarters or subordinate command (for example, MICOM for DARCOM, NAVSEASYSCOM or NAVAIRSYSCOM for NMC, ASD or SD for AFSC, etc.). The chief will organize the team and lead team members in reviewing the application of the criteria by a specific contractor. The chief reports to the review director who maintains liaison with other DOD component focal points.

(3) Team Members. Teams will be composed of qualified representatives from major command headquarters and subordinate commands, the office of the program manager, applicable functional offices, cognizant CAO, and the cognizant resident or branch audit office. The team chief supervises assigned members during the course of the C/SCSC reviews. The assigned auditor will obtain technical advice from the audit supervisor as necessary.

b. **Operation of Team.** The team is responsible for a rigorous assessment of the contractor's compliance with the criteria. Such assessment should include review of management control techniques used by contractor organizational elements which perform work on the contract. Additional guidance is contained in chapter 5.

(1) Members will be responsible to the team chief for the completion of their assignments. To the extent possible, the chief assigns tasks consistent with background qualifications of team members. However, the chief will retain the prerogative to select and use any professional skills and methods considered necessary to adequately accomplish an assignment.

(2) Members should be full-time participants during C/SCSC reviews. However, the team may be augmented with functional specialists to assist in specific aspects of a review.

(3) Team size and types of expertise of members will be determined by the requirements; for example, the type of review, contract size, contractor characteristics, program characteristics, etc.

c. **Qualifications of Members.** Normally, members should

AFSCP 173-5   AFLCP 173-5   DARCOM-P 715-5   NAVMAT P5240   DLAH 8315.2

possess one or more of the following qualifications:

(1) Knowledge of the technical content of the program or contract.

(2) Knowledge of the principal engineering design and test requirements of the activity under review.

(3) General industrial engineering/production control background.

(4) Accounting/auditing knowledge.

(5) Program planning and control experience.

(6) Management analysis/cost/price analysis experience.

(7) Contract negotiation or administration experience.

d. **Training.** All members should receive specialized training, dealing with management control systems concepts and performance requirements and interpretations, before participating as team members. Formal training, such as that given in the Air Force Institute of Technology (AFIT) Course 360, Evaluation of Cost/Schedule Control Systems, is a requirement that normally will not be waived. Such training should be supplemented by additional instruction to ensure the fullest comprehension of the task to be performed during the demonstration review. On-the-job training will be provided, when feasible, to enlarge upon background experience and classroom training for members without prior demonstration review participation.

4-4. Review Techniques:

a. **Checklist.** Appendix E provides a checklist for use by the team members in the examination of the contractor's management control systems to ensure conformance. The checklist includes a restatement of criteria followed by specific questions or areas to be addressed by the review team.

b. **Formats.** To clarify checklist items, formats should be developed as illustrations during the review. Appendix F provides typical formats for displaying team findings and for supporting conclusions drawn.

4-5. Coordination:

a. **Advance Planning.** The focal point for coordination in the lead command will inform focal points of other commands, DCAA, and DCAS as far in advance as possible concerning the starting date and estimate of the duration of the review. Applicable focal points will then inform the lead command focal point for coordination as to whether they intend to participate in the review. If so, they will identify their representatives for the review team.

b. **Administration:**

(1) The team chief will make all necessary arrangements ensuring availability of team members for the time required for preliminary indoctrination and each review for which the team member is needed. Members will be administratively responsible to the team chief during the period of the review.

(2) If another review is necessary to determine the correction of observed deficiencies, or to cover another phase of the program, the same members should be reassembled, if practicable.

310

Chapter 5
COST/SCHEDULE CONTROL SYSTEMS CRITERIA
IMPLEMENTATION PROCEDURES

5-1. General Information:

a. Policy. It is the general policy of DOD procuring activities to require—

(1) Application of the C/SCSC to programs that are within the scope outlined in paragraph 2-2.

(2) No changes to contractors' existing management control systems except those necessary to meet the criteria.

(3) The contractor to use data from its own management control system(s) in reports to the Government.

b. Circumstances. When it has been determined that the criteria will be applied to a specific major system acquisition, generally it will be as—

(1) A requirement within a new contract(s), usually first expressed in a solicitation document (paragraph 5-2a), or

(2) A requirement of an existing contract(s), subject to bilateral agreement between the contractor and the Government.

c. Phasing. Since the contractor's management control systems utilized during development and during production are usually significantly different from each other, normally separate demonstration reviews will be required for the development phase and production phase. The contractor may request a simultaneous review of the systems used for both development and production contracts, thus obviating the necessity for successive reviews. However, the production system demonstrated to gain acceptance should be of such extent that its review will demonstrate its applicability to production contracts that warrant the imposition of the C/SCSC.

d. Review Cycle. The checklist and guidance in this guide will be used by DOD representatives for evaluation of contractors' proposals concerning C/SCSC implementation and for conducting an in-plant demonstration review of a contractor's management control systems after a contract is awarded. They may also serve as a reference for the contractor in preparing descriptions of its management control systems. Contractors are encouraged to follow the criteria and checklist when preparing descriptions so as to provide for more effective assessment by DOD representatives. The phases of a typical review cycle include evaluations preliminary to contract award (paragraph 5-2c), an implementation visit after contract award (paragraph 5-4a), readiness assessment after the implementation visit (paragraph 5-4b), and the in-plant demonstration review leading to official acceptance (paragraph 5-5a). A redemonstration review may also be scheduled when it is necessary to examine any changes made by the contractor after deficiencies are identified (paragraph 5-5c). After acceptance, the review process continues as a surveillance function (paragraph 6-1c(2), 6-2b, and 6-3b). Figure 5-1 shows typical phases of C/SCSC implementation.

5-2. Preaward actions. Preaward acquisition documents should be reviewed to ensure that C/SCSC and related reporting are properly included when appropriate.

a. Solicitation. When it is determined that the criteria will be implemented on a new contract, they will be included as a requirement in the solicitation document. The DAR clause used for this purpose is in appendix A.

b. Proposal. In response to the solicitation, each contractor's proposal should include a description of the management control systems to be used to meet the requirements of the criteria under contract. The contractor may propose to use the existing systems which in the contractor's judgment meet the criteria.

(1) The description of the contractor's management control system must be presented in sufficient detail to effectively describe compliance with the criteria, and to permit adequate surveillance of the operational systems by the cognizant DOD components. The contractor must also clearly show how the systems meet each of the criteria in chapter 2. While the contractors system description is not expected to follow the evaluation/demonstration review checklist (appendix E) the description should address all items in the checklist. The contractor should correlate checklist items with applicable portions of the system description to ensure adequate coverage (appendix A).

(2) A contractor proposing to use management control systems previously accepted may satisfy the criteria requirement in the solicitation document by citing in the proposal the memorandum of understanding (paragraph 5-8) or notification of acceptance.

c. Evaluation. Normally, for a new program the evaluation review is accomplished as a part of precontract award procedures. It is the process of evaluating proposed or existing systems and methods by which the contractor plans to comply with the criteria. The review is basically an analysis of the contractor's management control systems proposed in response to the criteria prescribed in the solicitation. The review will include use of applicable parts of the checklist (appendix E). If a contractor has proposed to use a previously accepted system, the cognizant CAO and resident auditor will furnish a report stating whether or not the contractor's system still meets the criteria.

d. Onsite Examination. Normally, an onsite examination of the contractor's systems in operation will not be required during the evaluation review. However, when any part of the system is not clearly understood, an onsite examination of that part may be necessary to clarify the contractor's intent. If an onsite review is necessary, approval of the activity responsible for source selection will be obtained. The focal point for coordination in the lead command will formally notify the cognizant CAO and the resident auditor of the requirement as far in advance as possible. The CAO and DCAA will each provide a representative to assist in the onsite review. Care should be exercised during the entire evaluation review process to ensure that the contractor and DOD have the same understanding of the system described in the contractor's proposal. Data examples using actual data in the case of existing systems, should be provided to illustrate systems procedures and data flow.

e. Coordination. During an onsite evaluation, if it is found that the contractor's proposed system is in use under a contract with another command, coordination with the other command should be maintained during the evaluation review process. If it becomes necessary to review actual plans and reports of the other command's contract, concurrence of the

25

AFSCP 173-5 AFLCP 173-5 DARCOM-P 715-5 NAVMAT P5240 DLAH 8315.2

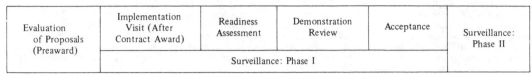

Evaluation of Proposals (Preaward)	Implementation Visit (After Contract Award)	Readiness Assessment	Demonstration Review	Acceptance	Surveillance: Phase II
	Surveillance: Phase I				

Figure 5-1. Typical Phases of C/SCSC Implementation.

other command should be obtained.

f. **Proprietary Information.** Care must be exercised to avoid improper disclosure of information obtained from contractors, especially in competitive situations, when an onsite evaluation is being made in which the degree of compliance with performance measurement criteria is a factor in contract award.

g. **Evaluation Report.** Following the evaluation review, a written report will be prepared by the evaluation review team which will attest whether or not the contractor's systems description in the proposal adequately describes compliance with the criteria. If not, the report will identify specific deficiencies. The reports will be provided to the Source Selection Evaluation Board.

5-3. Contracts:

a. **Provisions.** The contract will require that the contractor's systems comply with the criteria throughout performance of the contract. The applicable DAR clause is in appendix B. It covers the requirements of the criteria and other conditions as follows:

(1) Requires the contractor to establish, demonstrate, and use management control systems which meet the criteria.

(2) Requires the contractor to obtain approval of changes affecting the accepted management system description before their implementation.

(3) Provides for Government access to pertinent records and data associated with the management control systems.

(4) When mutually agreed to by the procuring activity and the prime contractor, the criteria will be applied to selected subcontractors, based upon such factors as criticality to program. In these cases, the prime contractor will contractually require subcontractors to comply with the criteria. Subcontracts selected for application of the criteria should be identified in the prime contract.

(a) After a prime contractor has reviewed and accepted a subcontractor's management control system, the prime contractor should provide the subcontractor a written statement that documents the acceptance. Such acceptance does not constitute DOD acceptance and does not apply to DOD contracts or subcontracts from prime contractors on other DOD programs.

(b) Review and acceptance of these selected subcontractors' management control systems may be performed by the procuring activity in coordination with the prime contractor when requested by either the prime contractor or subcontractor. Such reviews and acceptances will be accomplished in accordance with paragraph 5-4 through 5-8.

b. **Prior Acceptance.** Contractors whose management control systems were accepted for application to another contract of the same type (for example, development, production) at the same facility will not be required to undergo a demonstration review on a new contract unless significant modifications have been made to the previously accepted systems, or surveillance reveals that the accepted systems have not been operated as contractually agreed to in the prior contract. Prior acceptance will be withdrawn if deficiencies are not corrected. This applies to all accepted systems, whether or not covered by a memorandum of understanding (paragraph 5-8).

c. **Subsequent Application Review.** When a contractor has a previously accepted system, a subsequent application review should be conducted in conjunction with a newly awarded contract with a C/SCSC requirement in the same facility. This review is normally conducted within 90 days after contract award to determine that the contractor has properly applied the previously accepted management control system to the new contract. The team composition and duration for the subsequent application review should be minimized. See appendix G for specific guidance.

5-4. Preliminary Actions:

a. **Implementation Visit.** As soon as possible after contract award, preferably within 30 days, representatives of the C/SCSC review team should visit the contractor's plant and review the contractor's plans for implementing the C/SCSC. Areas of noncompliance or potential problems will be identified. This visit provides an early dialogue between the lead command the contractor relative to the C/SCSC review process. During this preliminary review the contractor will usually make presentations to reflect the systems design and operation and explain applicable reports. The team will examine selected documents and procedures proposed by the contractor. During the visit, a schedule will be developed for the readiness assessment and full-scale demonstration review.

b. **Readiness Assessment.** The readiness assessment is a meeting or series of meetings, usually 3 to 5 days duration, held by representatives of the team with the contractor before the full-scale demonstration review. Without involving the time and expense of the full Government and contractor teams, it provides an opportunity to review contractor progress toward implementing the criteria, to clear up misunderstandings, and to assess the contractor's readiness to demonstrate a fully integrated management control system. It assists in the Government's preparation for the full-scale demonstration review by familiarizing key team members with the fundamentals of the contractor's systems. Any discrepancies should be identified to the contractor for correction. Team members should not design or recommend changes to systems to meet the criteria. The contractor will be afforded an opportunity to correct deficiencies.

5-5. Demonstration Review:

a. **Demonstration by the Contractor.** When a demonstration review is required, it will begin as soon as practicable following the contractor's implementation of its management

312

AFSCP 173-5   AFLCP 173-5   DARCOM-P 715-5   NAVMAT P5240   DLAH 8315.2

systems pertinent to the contractual effort. The C/SCSC review team will examine the contractor's working papers and documents to ascertain compliance and document their findings. For this purpose, the contractor will be required to make available to the team the documents used in the contractor's management control systems; for example, budgeting, work authorization, accounting, and other functional documents which apply to the specific contracts being reviewed. The documentation must be current and accurate.

(1) The contractor will demonstrate to the team how the management control systems are structured and used in actual operation. The contractor will make available all appropriate internal planning and control documentation required for an indepth analysis of the adequacy of the systems in relation to the criteria and the work under contract.

(2) The contractor should have current written descriptions available which describe the management control systems. Applicable portions of the systems descriptions and operating procedures must also be available at the contractor's operating levels. Detailed operating procedures should delineate the following:

(a) Responsibilities of operating personnel.
(b) Limitations on action.
(c) Internal authorization required.

b. **Compliance with Criteria.** The burden of proof for demonstrating compliance with the criteria necessarily rests with the contractor. The C/SCSC review team will assess compliance with the criteria.

c. **Corrective actions.** If the contractor's systems are not acceptable, corrective actions to achieve compliance with criteria must be initiated by the contractor. Areas to be reexamined will be clearly identified to the contractor. A schedule for developing solutions and for a subsequent demonstration review to determine acceptability will be agreed upon by the contractor and review director.

d. **Review Process:**

(1) The team will follow the evaluation/demonstration review checklist (appendix E) to assist members in completing an orderly, comprehensive and conclusive review. The team may employ sampling techniques when it is not practical to review entire systems. Generally, the team will proceed in any given area until conclusive findings are reached. Based upon the best judgment and counsel available, the team chief will identify the cutoff points in any test after sufficient evidence has been obtained on which to base conclusive findings.

(2) The evaluation of a contractor's indirect cost control system is within the purview of the cognizant plant representative and the DCAA; the responsibility for ensuring that these systems are in compliance with the C/SCSC is normally assigned to their representatives on the demonstration review team. If the DCAA auditor has accomplished a recent evaluation of the indirect cost control system that verifies compliance with the criteria, a second investigation during the demonstration review is normally not required.

5-6. Acceptance:

a. **Formal Report.** At the conclusion of the demonstration review, a formal C/SCSC review report will be prepared and submitted to the review director. Appendix C discusses in detail the format and content of the report.

(1) Preparation of the demonstration review report is the responsibility of the team chief.

(2) The report will state whether the contractor's system complies with the criteria. If it does not comply, the report will identify the areas of noncompliance in detail.

(3) Requirements and deadlines for preparing drafts of various sections of the report may be delegated to individual team members. A draft of the report should be made available for review by team members.

(4) Any significant disagreements on the final wording or content of the report will be referred through appropriate channels for resolution, as described in paragraphs 4-2c and d.

b. **Procedures.** The demonstration review report will be the basis for acceptance of the contractor's management control systems by the DOD components.

(1) All demonstration review reports will be subject to review by the lead command focal point for coordination and approval at the major command headquarters responsible for conducting the demonstration review. C/SCSC review reports will be offered by the lead command to the other military service focal points for coordination before release.

(2) The appropriate contracting officer will inform the contractor regarding acceptance or nonacceptance of its systems and provide the contractor with copies of the report when released by the review director.

(3) The contractor will provide a description of the accepted management systems according to appendix B, paragraph (b). A memorandum of understanding (paragraph 5-8a) may be used to satisfy the requirement of describing accepted systems.

c. **Report Distribution.** The lead command focal point for coordination will control the issuance and distribution of the reports. When applicable, the cover page of each report will contain a statement indicating that the report contains contractor proprietary data, and that distribution of copies will be limited. Contents will not be disseminated outside DOD, (and NASA), in whole or in part, without the express permission of the cognizant service focal point and the contractor.

5-7. Compliance After Acceptance. Acceptance of a Contractor's management control systems as meeting the criteria is not intended to inhibit continuing innovations and improvement of its systems. However, contractors are contractually obligated to maintain their systems in a state which satisfies the criteria.

a. Surveillance to ensure that contractors do so is a DOD management responsibility which will be accomplished by the cognizant CAO and contract auditor. Indications that a contractor's system is failing to comply with any part of the criteria can be cause for scheduling another demonstration review and may result in revocation of prior acceptance. Specific discrepancies discovered as a result of the demonstration review or normal surveillance procedures should be corrected immediately. Surveillance responsibilities are described in chapter 6 and in more detail in the C/SCSC Joint Surveillance Guide.

b. Contractor-proposed changes to accepted management control systems will be submitted to the cognizant CAO in accordance with the C/SCSC Joint Surveillance Guide.

5-8. Memorandum of Understanding:

a. **General.** After demonstration and acceptance of a contractor's management control systems, the contractor's

27

system descriptions should be updated as necessary to accurately describe the system as accepted. Since complete descriptions may be voluminous, consideration should be given to preparing them in a format which may be referenced or summarized for use in related documents. A memorandum of understanding (referencing the description of the accepted systems) may then be executed relative to the application of those accepted systems to contracts which require compliance with the C/SCSC. Pertinent features of the Memorandum of Understanding (appendix D) are described below:

(1) The memorandum of understanding is not a contract clause, but it may be incorporated in any contract by appropriate reference when the contract includes a requirement for compliance with the criteria.

(2) This document serves to clarify intent of the contractor and DOD components relative to implementation of the criteria. It contains reference to a description of accepted systems and subsystems and provides for Government access to pertinent contractor records and data for surveillance purposes. Provision is also made to permit changes to accepted systems.

(3) A memorandum of understanding may be executed after the contractor's management control systems are applied to a single contract containing the criteria requirement or it may be developed without an existing or pending contractual requirement when requested by the contractor or DOD, provided that demonstration review is accomplished through mutual agreement.

(4) If a request for a memorandum of understanding is processed without an existing or pending contractural requirement, it will be necessary to designate the lead command (paragraph 4-2a). Applicable demonstration reviews may involve any contract in the facility where performance measurement systems are applied, provided that the contracts selected will ensure that a representative appraisal of the contractor's system is made.

(5) When a Memorandum of Understanding is to be consummated between the DOD components and the contractor, such a memorandum will be prepared and executed by the appropriate ACO, based upon the demonstration review report and letter of acceptance.

(6) A memorandum of understanding will normally be limited for application to a single contractor facility as defined for the purpose of contract administration and may be limited as to application to development or production contracts.

(7) A contractor may respond to solicitations for potential contracts by citing the Memorandum of Understanding in the proposal. Procuring activities may evaluate the current status of implementation of criteria by the contractor to ensure themselves that applicable systems are acceptable without requesting a full-scale demonstration review (paragraph 5-3c).

b. **Procedures.** In the execution of a memorandum of understanding, the following procedures will apply:

(1) A contractor desiring a memorandum of understanding will direct a written request to the cognizant CAO.

(2) The CAO will forward the request to the lead command focal point for coordination.

(3) A contractor requesting a memorandum of understanding subsequent to acceptance under an existing or previous DOD contract will make this known to the CAO. The CAO will coordinate the request with the lead command focal point. The other military departments will be asked to review the contractor's system either through review of the lead command C/SCSC review report or a joint service subsequent application review. Following agreement, a memorandum of understanding will be executed as set forth above.

(4) The Memorandum of Understanding should be distributed to each military department, CAO, DCAA, contractor, and other appropriate addressees.

Chapter 6

CONTRACT ADMINISTRATION AND AUDIT

6-1. General Information:

a. **Scope.** This chapter describes the responsibilities of the cognizant CAO and the resident DCAA auditor for the review and surveillance of C/SCSC management control systems (paragraphs 6-2 and 6-3). With the commencement of contract performance, contractors are expected to operate management systems which have been proposed and evaluated, prior to contract award. Surveillance is a DOD management responsibility to be carried out at each contractor's facility to ensure the contractor complies with the requirements of the executed contract. Uniform guidance for the DOD components performing this surveillance is contained in the C/SCSC Joint Surveillance Guide.

b. **Time Span.** Following award of the contract, the contractor's management control systems may be in various stages of implementation. The surveillance function will begin immediately following contract award. Continuing surveillance will be directed toward the procedures and functions of the contractor's management control systems. During surveillance, if the description of the systems identified in the contract is found to differ from the contractor's practices, the procuring activity must be promptly informed.

c. **Phases of Surveillance.** Surveillance consists of two phases. The first is applicable immediately after contract award, the second following the demonstration review (figure 5-1).

(1) Phase I. This phase is directed to assisting the procuring activity and monitoring the progress of the contractor to ensure satisfactory implementation of the contractor's management control systems. The cognizant CAO and contract auditor will provide team members for the C/SCSC reviews and assist the DOD procuring activity in monitoring remedial actions to meet the criteria. During this period, even though the contractor's systems have not yet been accepted, it is necessary that the procuring activity make decisions based upon contractor reports derived from the currently operating management control systems. Thus, it is necessary to verify that the data contained in the reports submitted are in accordance with contractual requirements and are valid and complete.

(2) Phase II. Immediately following acceptance of the contractor's management control systems, surveillance should be formalized to include a comprehensive program covering the complete scope of the criteria. Such a program should provide for verifying, tracing, and evaluating the information contained in the reports submitted to DOD procuring components. It also should ensure that the contractor's management control system continues to operate as accepted and that any proposed or actual changes comply with the criteria and are reflected in the contractor's system description.

6-2. CAO Functions and Responsibilities. The cognizant CAO will—

a. During Phase I—

(1) Provide a C/SCSC review team member to assist the DOD procuring activity by monitoring contractor progress during the implementation process.

(2) Consummate a memorandum of agreement with the Government program office to ensure all participants understand their surveillance responsibilities.

(3) Prepare a surveillance plan, using the written description of the systems provided by the contractor and referenced in the contract. The assistance of the contract auditor should be obtained in respect to that part of the program concerning financial data. The written surveillance program plan will be submitted by the cognizant CAO to the DOD procuring activity for concurrence.

b. During Phase II—

(1) Implement the surveillance plan which will assess continuity and consistency in the operation of the contractor's systems.

(2) Evaluate any formal or informal changes in the management systems to determine whether such systems continue to comply with the criteria and contract provisions. The purpose is to detect and appraise alterations which are not in accord with the criteria.

(3) Perform recurring evaluations of the effectiveness of the contractor's policies and procedures, selective tests of the contractor's internal data flow, and validations of external reports submitted to the Government.

(4) Forward to the contract auditor a list of all reports submitted in response to DD Form 1423, Contract Data Requirements List, which requires audit verification of financial data.

(5) Verify that the contractor's systems continue to comply with the criteria and contract provisions.

(6) Apprise the contractor and DOD components of any deficiencies in the contractor's management control systems. Determine whether corrective actions taken have remedied such deficiencies.

(7) Advise the contractor and the concerned DOD procuring activity of any uncorrected deficiencies which affect the overall acceptability of contractor's systems.

6-3. DCAA Functions and Responsibilities. The cognizant DCAA audit office will provide an auditor who will—

a. During Phase I—

(1) Serve as a C/SCSC review team member for the review of the accounting system and related financial areas, including budgeting, direct and indirect costs, variance analysis, and forecasting.

(2) Participate in monitoring contractor progress in assigned areas during C/SCSC implementation.

b. During Phase II—

(1) Perform reviews of the contractor's accounting system policies and procedures for compliance with performance measurement criteria and contract provisions.

(2) Perform periodic reviews, on a selective basis, of the financial data contained in the various reports prepared by the contractor to determine whether they accurately reflect the information in the contractor's books and records.

(3) Perform periodic evaluations of the contractor's financial policies and procedures.

(4) Prepare audit reports incorporating deficiencies, disclosed during surveillance reviews, that cannot be resolved with the contractor. Such reports should be addressed to the procuring activity through the cognizant CAO.

AFSCP 173-5   AFLCP 173-5   DARCOM-P 715-5   NAVMAT P5240   DLAH 8315.2

Chapter 7

DATA REQUIREMENTS

7-1. General Information.

a. **Specification.** The contractor is required to use data from the operative management control systems in making reports to DOD components. The inclusion of the criteria in a solicitation document or contract is not of itself a requirement for delivery of data. Data requirements must be specified on DD Form 1423. Management control systems can be applied to a contract only according to either of the following:

(1) DD Form 1660, Management Systems Summary List, identifying appropriate systems from the DOD Acquisition Management Systems and Data Requirements Control List (AMSDL).

(2) The Defense Acquisition Regulation (DAR), formerly the Armed Services Procurement Regulation (ASPR).

b. **Performance Measurement.** Normally the Cost Performance Report (CPR), latest revision of data item DI-F-6000, will be required. Regardless of the reporting formats required, all reported performance measurement information must be derived from the contractor's internal systems. To provide a sound basis for responsible decisionmaking by both contractor management and DOD managers, contractors' management control systems must provide timely data which effectively relate cost, schedule, and technical accomplishment within the framework of the CWBS. As a minimum, a contractor's systems must be capable of providing, at least monthly, such information as—

(1) BCWS, BCWP, and ACWP.

(2) Actual indirect costs and budgeted indirect costs.

(3) Budgeted cost at completion and estimated cost at completion.

(4) Significant variances resulting from the analysis of these data. These variances should be identified in terms of labor rate and efficiency variances, material price and usage variances, and deviations from overhead budgets, together with the reasons for the CWBS and organizational elements to which resources have been allocated.

(5) Actual and planned schedule, and significant differences between the planned and actual achievements together with the reasons.

(6) Appropriate managerial actions taken or proposed as a result of variances and differences reported.

(7) Baseline changes and reasons.

(8) Management reserve changes and reasons.

7-2. Data Elements. A CWBS which has been prepared in accordance with guidance provided in MIL-STD-881 (latest revision), constitutes the basic framework against which the data elements selected are to be reported. Even though reported cost and schedule data may be required only at summary levels, all such data must consist of traceable accumulations which account for work performed and resources expended at appropriate lower levels.

7-3. Cost Performance Report. When required by the contracting activity, the Cost Performance Report will be obtained from the contractor by specifying data item DI-F-6000 (latest revision) on DD Form 1423. DI-F-6000 (latest revision) is listed in the DOD 5000.19L, Volume II, Authorized Management Systems and Data Requirements Control List. It may be requisitioned from the Naval Publications and Forms Center, 5801 Tabor Avenue, Philadelphia PA 19120.

AFSCP 173-5	AFLCP 173-5	DARCOM-P 715-5	NAVMAT P5240	DLAH 8315.2

APPENDIX A

DEFENSE ACQUISITION REGULATIONS

SOLICITATION PROVISION

7-2003.43 Notice of Cost/Schedule Control Systems. In accordance with 1-331(h), insert the following provision.

NOTICE OF COST/SCHEDULE CONTROL SYSTEMS (1974 APR)

(a) The offeror shall submit a comprehensive plan for compliance with the attached criteria (DODI 7000.2 Performance Measurement for Selected Acquisitions) for the internal Cost/Schedule Control Systems which are or will be operational for any contract resulting from this solicitation, and which includes the C/SCSC clause set forth in ASPR 7-104.87. The offeror shall identify existing management systems separately from proposed modifications to meet the criteria. The plan shall:

  (i) describe the management systems and their application in all major functional cost areas such as engineering, manufacturing and tooling, as related to development of the work breakdown structure, planning, budgeting, scheduling, work authorization, cost accumulation, measurement and reporting of cost and schedule performance, variance analysis, and baseline control;

  (ii) describe compliance with each of the criteria, preferably by cross-referencing appropriate elements in the description of systems with the items in the checklist for C/SCSC contained in AFSCP/AFLCP 173-5, DARCOM-P 715-5, NAVMAT P-5240, *Cost/Schedule Control Systems Criteria Joint Implementation Guide;

  (iii) identify the major subcontractors, or major subcontracted effort in the event major subcontractors have not been selected, planned for application of the criteria;

  (iv) describe the proposed procedure for administration of the criteria as applied to subcontractors.

(b) If the contractor is utilizing Cost/Schedule Control Systems which have been previously accepted, or is operating such systems under a current Memorandum of Understanding, evidence of such may be submitted in lieu of the comprehensive plan mentioned above. In such event, the Contracting Officer will determine the extent to which such systems shall be reviewed to assure continued compliance with the criteria.

(c) The offeror shall provide information and assistance as requested by the Contracting Officer for evaluation of compliance with the cited criteria.

(d) The offeror's plan for Cost/Schedule Control Systems will be evaluated prior to contract award. Upon acceptance of the Cost/Schedule Control Systems, a description of the accepted systems will be referenced in the contract.

(e) Subcontractor selection for application of the C/SCSC will be by agreement between the prime contractor and the Government. The prime contractor will contractually require the selected subcontractors to comply with the criteria. However, demonstrations and reviews of these selected subcontractors' management systems may be performed by the procuring authority when requested by either the prime or subcontractor.

(End of provision)

*Add DLA 8315.2.

AFSCP 173-5   AFLCP 173-5   DARCOM-P 715-5   NAVMAT P5240   DLAH 8315.2

APPENDIX B

DEFENSE ACQUISITION REGULATIONS

CONTRACT CLAUSE

7-104.87 Cost/Schedule Control Systems. In accordance with 1-331(h), insert the following clause:

COST/SCHEDULE CONTROL SYSTEMS (1979 MAR)

(a) The Contractor shall establish, maintain and use in the performance of this contract Cost/Schedule Control Systems meeting the attached criteria (DODI 7000.2 Performance Measurement for Selected Acquisitions). Prior to acceptance by the Contracting Officer and within ninety* (90) (*or as otherwise agreed to by the parties) calendar days after contract award, the Contractor shall be prepared to demonstrate the operation of its systems to the Government to verify that the proposed systems meet the established criteria set forth above. As a part of the demonstration, review and acceptance procedure, the Contractor shall furnish the Government a description of the Cost/Schedule Control Systems applicable to this contract in such form and detail as indicated by the AFSCP/AFLCP 173-5, DARCOM-P 715-5, NAVMAT P-5240 *Cost/Schedule Control Systems Criteria Joint Implementation Guide hereinafter referred to as the guide, or required by the Contracting Officer. The Contractor agrees to provide access to all pertinent records, data and plans as requested by representatives of the Government for the conduct of the review.

(b) The description of the management systems accepted by the Contracting Officer, identified by title and date, shall be referenced in the contract. Such systems shall be maintained and used by the Contractor in the performance of this contract.

(c) Contractor changes to the accepted systems shall be submitted to the Contracting Officer for review and approval The Contracting Officer shall advise the Contractor of the acceptability of such changes within sixty (60) days after receipt from the Contractor. When systems existing at time of contract award do not comply with the criteria, adjustments necessary to assure compliance will be effected at no change in contract price or fee.

(d) The Contractor agrees to provide access to all pertinent records and data requested by the Contracting Officer or a duly authorized representative for the purpose of permitting Government surveillance to ensure continuing application of the accepted systems to this contract. Deviations from accepted systems discovered during contract performance shall be corrected as directed by the Contracting Officer.

(e) The Contractor shall require that each selected subcontractor, as mutually agreed to between the Government and the Contractor and as set forth in the schedule of this contract, shall meet the Cost/Schedule Control Systems criteria as set forth in the guide and shall incorporate in all such subcontracts adequate provisions for demonstration, review, acceptance and surveillance of subcontractors' systems, to be carried out by the Government when requested by either the prime or subcontractor.

(f) If the Contractor or subcontractor is utilizing Cost/Schedule Control Systems which have been previously accepted or is operating such systems under a current Memorandum of Understanding, the Contracting Officer may waive all or part of the provisions hereof concerning demonstration and review.

(End of Clause)

*Add DLAH 8315.2.

318

APPENDIX C

C/SCSC REVIEW REPORT FORMAT

Primary consideration must be given to the fact that reports (particularly the findings) must provide a basis for effective review by others with limited or no knowledge of the specific management system. The quality of the report is usually taken as a direct reflection of the nature and quality of the review and as such is the vehicle for obtaining acceptance on a Triservice basis. The following is a format for a typical C/SCSC review report:

1. **Table of Contents.**

2. **Index to Exhibits.**

3. **General.** Introductory comment:

   a. **Background.** Briefly describe the events relating to the contractor's implementation of C/SCSC and the Government's reviews relating thereto. Also, identify the contract purpose, type, duration, amounts (total, ceiling price, target cost, etc.), the program being supported, and the cognizant DOD component.

   b. **Contractual Requirement.** Identify the specific contract requirement for the C/SCSC.

4. **Purpose.** Identify the purpose of the review. Normally, it will be for the demonstration review (and redemonstration review(s) if applicable) of the performance measurement system operated in a specific contract effort. For a Subsequent Application Review, when a system has been previously accepted, the report need consist only of an abbreviated or summary report with few, if any, exhibits.

5. **Scope.** This section should identify the specific contractual entity which is the subject of this review; for example, division, company, plant, and the functional organizations such as engineering, manufacturing, quality assurance, etc., included in the review. Also, discuss whether the review is related to development or production contracts and if the system is restricted to the specific contract or is used throughout the facility.

6. **Review Process.** Describe the extent of the review, indicate the approach taken; that is, "criteria category," "functional," or other. Areas not investigated should be discussed and reasons provided; for example, when review of the method of implementing contract changes could not be done because no contract changes had been executed. Identify the methodology used in conducting the review indicating such items as range of interviews, depth of review, etc. Team members and their associated responsibilities should be identified in this section.

7. **Findings.** Organize this section according to the major categories of the criteria; for example, organization, planning and budgeting, accounting, analysis, and revisions. Address each of the five basic areas reviewed in narrative of sufficient depth to explain system compliance. It should state each criterion, describe how the management system complies with that criterion, and be supported by exhibits to illustrate and prove the compliance.

   a. State each checklist question, followed by the findings of the team. Findings must explain how the system satisfies or does not satisfy the checklist question by going into sufficient depth to clearly establish compliance or noncompliance. When practicable, reference the contractor's system description paragraph numbers.

   b. The narrative may be supported by or relate to exhibits. However, the narrative must explain the exhibits so that it would not be necessary for the reviewer to turn to the exhibit to understand why it is there and what it portrays. The narrative should be able to stand by itself, but exhibits cannot stand alone. The narrative in the Findings Section should state explicitly what the reader should look for on each exhibit and how the exhibit proves that the requirement is met.

8. **Conclusions.** This section should include the overall evaluation of the systems reviewed as to their compliance with the criteria. Reference should be made, when applicable, to the supporting evidence in the Findings Section. This portion of the report must contain a conclusion concerning the acceptability of the contractor's system as to its compliance with the C/SCSC. The acceptance statement should specifically identify the system demonstrated and whether it is used for development or production.

9. **Recommendations.** This section should recommend necessary corrective actions to achieve acceptability or compliance. The recommendations should not delineate specific corrective methods to correct deficiencies but should identify areas requiring improvement. Suggested improvements to enhance the system can be noted here but should be identified separately from corrective actions necessary to comply with the criteria. If applicable, include a recommendation of the necessity for a redemonstration review.

10. **Redemonstration Reviews.** When it is necessary to conduct redemonstration reviews because of deficiencies found and not corrected during the demonstration review, the following guidance applies:

    a. The deficiencies existing at the conclusion of the demonstration review are to be cited in the findings associated with the specific criteria items. These deficiencies then become the basis for the redemonstration review and are addressed in this section of the report. The report will have separate sections to address the findings of each redemonstration review.

    b. The redemonstration review section will be presented in the same format as the demonstration review section. Only those events applicable to the redemonstration will be addressed. However, do not restate the deficiency in the Findings Section unless necessary for understanding the new findings.

11. **Exhibits:**

    a. The exhibits will include as a minimum those exhibits, formats, and procedures called for in the Evaluation/Demonstration Review Checklist for C/SCSC. Exhibit 1 will be a

AFSCP 173-5   AFLCP 173-5   DARCOM-P 715-5   NAVMAT P5240   DLAH 8315.2

reproduced checklist marked to show, for each question, the compliance or noncompliance of the management system. The criterion block will be left blank and all NAs will be placed in the "No" column. ("No" answers should be explained in the Findings.)

b. The remarks column of the checklist may be used to show the page and paragraph where the question is discussed, exhibit numbers as applicable, or contractor's system description paragraph number.

c. In preparing exhibits, it is important that—

(1) Exhibits be completely legible. Do not reduce them merely to avoid foldouts. Foldouts are entirely acceptable when they provide clearer, more legible exhibits.

(2) Exhibits be annotated and marked to highlight the specific element(s) of information and to identify the trail in support of the related narrative.

(3) Exhibits be placed at the end of the report and numbered consecutively without regard to the category of criteria to which they relate.

(4) Exhibits be placed in the lower outside corner.

(5) Exhibits be from the same time frame and, where feasible, from the same leg of the WDS.

(6) Exhibits supporting the Analysis Section of the Findings be provided for both direct and indirect cost variances. Indirect cost variances must be analyzed from the standpoint of the manager responsible for their control; that is, the point at which they were incurred.

NOTE: The following precautions should be observed in report preparation:

a. The narrative content must adequately explain how the system complies with the related criteria. There is a strong tendency to refer to contractor documents without an adequate description of the nature and function of the document.

b. Elements elected for trace should be stated in the narrative. Selected trace elements should be consistently used in reporting on the various categories of the criteria.

c. Exhibits must be legible and complete. In many cases, handwritten exhibits cannot be deciphered. Required reconciliations, such as reconciliation of internal to external reports, are frequently omitted.

d. Exhibits must identify the specific areas to which attention is directed; that is, they must be marked to highlight the items of interest.

e. Exhibits must portray "live data," except when used to reproduce a part of directives, procedures, etc.

AFSCP 173-5   AFLCP 173-5   DARCOM-P 715-5   NAVMAT P5240   DLAH 8315.2

APPENDIX D

EXAMPLE OF MEMORANDUM OF UNDERSTANDING FOR C/SCSC

This Memorandum of Understanding entered into as of _____ establishes a mutual agreement between the Department(s) of the (Army-Navy-Air Force, as appropriate) and (insert contractor's full name, including facility and location) regarding the implementation and maintenance of management control systems conforming to the criteria established by Department of Defense Instruction 7000.2, Performance Measurement for Selected Acquisitions, and as implemented by DARCOM-P 715-5, NAVMAT P5240, and AFSCP/AFLCP 173-5.

WHEREAS, the contractor has demonstrated certain management control systems and subsystems as identified and defined in (contractor's system description dated _____ _____), and

WHEREAS, the Department(s) of the (Army-Navy-Air Force, as appropriate), by letter dated _____ _____ , based on demonstration review report dated _____ , did validate such systems and subsystems; then.

BE IT UNDERSTOOD AND AGREED that such systems and subsystems which have been validated as indicated above, together with approved changes thereto, shall apply to future (specify type of contract; for example, RDT&E, production, or both) contracts entered into between the contractor and the Department(s) of the (Army-Navy-Air Force, as appropriate) which require compliance with the C/SCSC; and

BE IT FURTHER UNDERSTOOD AND AGREED THAT:
(1) Contractor-proposed changes to those validated systems and subsystems will be submitted to the cognizant CAO for review and approval or disapproval by the ACO.
(2) The contractor agrees to provide access to pertinent records and data in order to permit adequate surveillance of the validated systems and subsystems.

This Memorandum of Understanding will remain in force indefinitely, subject to modification by mutual agreement or termination by either party.

_____   _____
(Administrative Contracting Officer)   (Contractor)

35

AFSCP 173-5   AFLCP 173-5   DARCOM-P 715-5   NAVMAT P5240   DLAH 8315.2

APPENDIX E

EVALUATION/DEMONSTRATION REVIEW CHECKLIST FOR C/SCSC			
CHECKLIST ITEMS	YES	NO	REMARKS
I. ORGANIZATION			
1. DEFINE ALL THE AUTHORIZED WORK AND RELATED RESOURCES TO MEET THE REQUIREMENTS OF THE CONTRACT, USING THE FRAMEWORK OF THE CWBS.			
a. Is only one CWBS used for the contract (attach copy of CWBS)?			
b. Is all contract work included in the CWBS?			
c. Are the following items included in the CWBS (annotate copy of CWBS to show elements below)?			
(1) Contract line items and end items (if in consonance with MIL-STD 881A).			
(2) All CWBS elements specified for external reporting.			
(3) CWBS elements to be subcontracted, with identification of subcontractors.			
(4) Cost account levels.			
2. IDENTIFY THE INTERNAL ORGANIZATIONAL ELEMENTS AND THE MAJOR SUBCONTRACTORS RESPONSIBILE FOR ACCOMPLISHING THE AUTHORIZED WORK.			
a. Are all authorized tasks assigned to identified organizational elements? (This must occur at the cost account level as a minimum. Prepare exhibit showing relationships.)			
b. Is subcontracted work defined and identified to the appropriate subcontractor within the proper WBS element? (Provide representative example.)			
3. PROVIDE FOR THE INTEGRATION OF THE CONTRACTOR'S PLANNING, SCHEDULING, BUDGETING, WORK AUTHORIZATION, AND COST ACCUMULATION SYSTEMS WITH EACH OTHER, THE CWBS, AND THE ORGANIZATIONAL STRUCTURE. (Reference format 1.)			
a. Are the contractor's management control systems listed above integrated with each other, the CWBS, and the organizational structure at the following levels: (Use matrix to illustrate the relationships.)			
(1) Total contract?			
(2) Cost account?			
4. IDENTIFY THE MANAGERIAL POSITIONS RESPONSIBLE FOR CONTROLLING OVERHEAD (INDIRECT COSTS).			
a. Are the following organizational elements and managers clearly identified?			
(1) Those responsible for the establishment of budgets and assignment of resources for overhead performance?			

36

322

Appendix E—continued

CHECKLIST ITEMS	YES	NO	REMARKS
(2) Those responsible for overhead performance control of related costs.			
b. Are the responsibilities and authorities of each of the above organizational elements or managers clearly defined?			
5. PROVIDE FOR INTEGRATION OF THE CWBS WITH THE CONTRACTOR'S FUNCTIONAL ORGANIZATIONAL STRUCTURE IN A MANNER THAT PERMITS COST AND SCHEDULE PERFORMANCE MEASUREMENT FOR CWBS AND ORGANIZATIONAL ELEMENTS. (Provide matrix showing integration.)			
a. Is each cost account assigned to a single organizational element directly responsible for the work and identifiable to a single element of the CWBS?			
b. Are the following elements for measuring performance available at the levels selected for control and analysis:			
(1) Budgeted cost for work scheduled?			
(2) Budgeted cost for work performed?			
(3) Actual costs of work performed?			
II. PLANNING AND BUDGETING			
1. SCHEDULE THE AUTHORIZED WORK IN A MANNER WHICH DESCRIBES THE SEQUENCE OF WORK AND IDENTIFIES THE SIGNIFICANT TASK INTER-DEPENDENCIES REQUIRED TO MEET THE DEVELOPMENT, PRODUCTION, AND DELIVERY REQUIREMENTS OF THE CONTRACT.			
a. Does the scheduling system contain (Prepare exhibit showing traceability from contract task level to work package schedules.)—			
(1) A master program schedule?			
(2) Intermediate schedules, as required, which provide a logical sequence from the master schedule to the cost account level?			
(3) Detailed schedules which support cost account and work package start and completion dates/events?			
b. Are significant decision points, constraints, and interfaces identified as key milestones?			
c. Does the scheduling system provide for the identification of work progress against technical and other milestones, and also provide for forecasts of completion dates of scheduled work?			
d. Are work packages formally scheduled in terms of physical accomplishment by calendar dates (Gregorian, Julian, or manufacturing day)?			
2. IDENTIFY PHYSICAL PRODUCTS, MILESTONES, TECHNICAL PERFORMANCE GOALS, OR OTHER INDICATORS THAT WILL BE USED TO MEASURE OUTPUT.			

AFSCP 173-5   AFLCP 173-5   DARCOM-P 715-5   NAVMAT P5240   DLAH 8315.2

Appendix E—continued

CHECKLIST ITEMS	YES	NO	REMARKS
a. Are meaningful indicators identified for use in measuring the status of cost and schedule performance? (Provide representative samples.)			
b. Does the contractor's system identify work accomplishment against the schedule plan? (Provide representative examples.)			
c. Are current work performance indicators and goals relatable to original goals as modified by contractual changes, replanning, and reprogramming actions? (Provide exhibit showing incorporation of changes to original indicators and goals.)			
3. ESTABLISH AND MAINTAIN A TIME-PHASE BUDGET BASELINE AT THE COST ACCOUNT LEVEL AGAINST WHICH CONTRACT PERFORMANCE CAN BE MEASURED. INITIAL BUDGETS ESTABLISHED FOR THIS PURPOSE WILL BE BASED ON THE NEGOTIATED TARGET COST. ANY OTHER AMOUNT USED FOR PERFORMANCE MEASUREMENT PURPOSES MUST BE FORMALLY RECOGNIZED BY BOTH THE CONTRACTOR AND THE GOVERNMENT. (Reference formats 2 and 8.)			
a. Does the performance measurement baseline consist of the following?			
(1) Time-phase cost account budgets.			
(2) Higher level CWBS element budgets (where not yet broken down into cost account budgets).			
(3) Undistributed budget, if any.			
(4) Indirect budgets, if not included in the above.			
b. Is the entire contract planned in time-phased cost accounts to the extent practicable?			
c. In the event that future contract effort cannot be defined in sufficient detail to allow the establishment of cost accounts, is the remaining budget assigned to the lowest practicable CWBS level elements for subsequent distribution to cost accounts.			
d. Does the contractor require sufficient detailed planning of cost accounts to constrain the application of budget initially allocated for future effort to current effort? (Explain constraints.)			
e. Are cost accounts opened and closed based on the start and completion of work contained therein?			
4. ESTABLISH BUDGETS FOR ALL AUTHORIZED WORK WITH SEPARATE IDENTIFICATION OF COST ELEMENTS (LABOR, MATERIAL, ETC.). (Reference formats 2, 3, and 4.)			
a. Does the budgeting system contain: (Provide exhibit.)			
(1) The total budget for the contract (including estimates for authorized but unpriced work)?			

324

Appendix E—continued

CHECKLIST ITEMS	YES	NO	REMARKS
(2) Budgets assigned to major functional organizations? (See checklist Item II, 9ab.)			
(3) Budgets assigned to cost accounts?			
b. Are the budgets assigned to cost accounts planned and identified in terms of the following cost elements? (Reference Formats 3 and 4.)			
(1) Direct labor dollars and/or hours.			
(2) Material and/or subcontract dollars.			
(3) Other direct dollars.			
c. Does the work authorization system contain: (Prepare sample exhibit.)			
(1) Authorization to proceed with all authorized work?			
(2) Appropriate work authorization documents which subdivide the contractual effort and responsibilities within functional organizations.			
5. TO THE EXTENT THE AUTHORIZED WORK CAN BE IDENTIFIED IN DISCRETE, SHORT-SPAN WORK PACKAGES, ESTABLISH BUDGETS FOR THIS WORK IN TERMS OF DOLLARS, HOURS, OR OTHER MEASURABLE UNITS. WHERE THE ENTIRE COST ACCOUNT CANNOT BE SUBDIVIDED INTO DETAILED WORK PACKAGES, IDENTIFY THE FAR TERM EFFORT IN LARGER PLANNING PACKAGES FOR BUDGET AND SCHEDULING PURPOSES: (Reference formats 6, 6a, and 6b.)			
a. Do work packages reflect the actual way in which the work will be done and are they meaningful products or management-oriented subdivisions of a higher level element of work? (Provide representative sample.)			
b. Are detailed work packages planned as far in advance as practicable?			
c. Is work progressively subdivided into detailed work packages as requirements are defined?			
d. Is future work which cannot be planned in detail subdivided to the extent practicable for budgeting and schedule purposes. (Provide sample.)			
e. Are work packages reasonably short in time duration or do they have adequate objective indicators/milestones to minimize the in-process work evaluation?			
f. Do work packages consist of discrete tasks which are adequately described? (Provide representative sample.)			
g. Can the contractor substantiate work package and planning package budgets?			
h. Are budgets or values assigned to work packages and planning packages in terms of dollars, hours, or other measurable units?			

AFSCP 173-5   AFLCP 173-5   DARCOM-P 715-5   NAVMAT P5240   DLAH 8315.2

Appendix E—continued

CHECKLIST ITEMS	YES	NO	REMARKS
i. Are work packages assigned to performing organizations?			
6. PROVIDE THAT THE SUM OF ALL WORK PACKAGE BUDGETS PLUS PLANNING PACKAGES WITHIN A COST ACCOUNT EQUALS THE COST ACCOUNT BUDGET. (Reference format 2.)			
a. Does the sum of all work package budgets plus planning packages within cost accounts equal the budgets assigned to those cost accounts?			
7. IDENTIFY RELATIONSHIPS OF BUDGETS OR STANDARDS IN UNDERLYING WORK AUTHORIZATION SYSTEMS TO BUDGETS FOR WORK PACKAGES.			
a. Where engineered standards or other internal work measurement systems are used, is there a formal relationship between these values and work package budgets? (Provide samples showing relationships.)			
8. IDENTIFY AND CONTROL LEVEL OF EFFORT ACTIVITY BY TIME-PHASE BUDGETS ESTABLISHED FOR THIS PURPOSE. ONLY THAT EFFORT WHICH CANNOT BE IDENTIFIED AS DISCRETE, SHORTSPAN WORK PACKAGES OR AS APPORTIONED EFFORT WILL BE CLASSED AS LOE. (Reference format 6.)			
a. Are time-phase budgets established for planning and control of level of effort activity by category of resource; for example, type of manpower and/or material? (Explain method of control and analysis.)			
b. Is work properly classified as measured effort, LOE, or apportioned effort and appropriately separated?			
9. ESTABLISH OVERHEAD BUDGETS FOR THE TOTAL COSTS OF EACH SIGNIFICANT ORGANIZATIONAL COMPONENT WHOSE EXPENSES WILL BECOME INDIRECT COSTS. REFLECT IN THE CONTRACT BUDGETS AT THE APPROPRIATE LEVEL, THE AMOUNTS IN OVERHEAD POOLS THAT WILL BE ALLOCATED TO THE CONTRACT AS INDIRECT COSTS. (Reference DCAA Audit Manual and DAR 15-203.) (Reference format 7.)			
a. Are overhead cost budgets (or projections) established on a facility-wide basis at least annually for the life of the contract?			
b. Are overhead cost budgets established for each organization which has authority to incur overhead costs?			
c. Are all elements of expense identified to overhead cost budgets or projections?			
d. Are overhead budgets and costs being handled according to the disclosure statement when applicable, or otherwise properly classified (for example, engineering overhead, IR&D)?			
e. Is the anticipated (firm and potential) business base projected in a rational, consistent manner? (Explain.)			
f. Are overhead costs budgets established on a basis consistent with the anticipated direct business base?			
g. Are the requirements for all items of overhead established by rational, traceable processes?			

AFSCP 173-5   AFLCP 173-5   DARCOM-P 715-5   NAVMAT P5240   DLAH 8315.2

Appendix E—continued

CHECKLIST ITEMS	YES	NO	REMARKS
h. Are the overhead pools formally and adequately identified? (Provide a list of the pools.)			
i. Are the organizations and items of cost assigned to each pool identified?			
j. Are projected overhead costs in each pool and the associated direct costs used as the basis for establishing interim rates for allocating overhead to contracts?			
k. Are projected overhead rates applied to the contract beyond the current year based on—			
(1) Contractor financial periods; for example, annual?			
(2) The projected business base for each period?			
(3) Contemplated overhead expenditure for each period based on the best information currently available?			
l. Are overhead projections adjusted in a timely manner to reflect—			
(1) Changes in the current direct and projected base?			
(2) Changes in the nature of the overhead requirements?			
(3) Changes in the overhead pool and/or organization structures?			
m. Are the WBS and organizational levels for application of the projected overhead costs identified?			
10. IDENTIFY MANAGEMENT RESERVES AND UNDISTRIBUTED BUDGET.			
a. Is all budget available as management reserve identified and excluded from the performance measurement baseline?			
b. Are records maintained to show how management reserves are used? (Provide exhibit.)			
c. Is undistributed budget limited to contract effort which cannot yet be planned to CWBS elements at or below the level specified for reporting to the Government?			
d. Are records maintained to show how undistributed budgets are controlled? (Provide exhibit.)			
11. PROVIDE THAT THE CONTRACT TARGET COST PLUS THE ESTIMATED COST OF AUTHORIZED BUT UNPRICED WORK IS RECONCILED WITH THE SUM OF ALL INTERNAL CONTRACT BUDGETS AND MANAGEMENT RESERVES. (Reference formats 3, 4, and 5.)			
a. Does the contractor's system description or procedures require that the performance measurement baseline plus management reserve equal the contract budget base?			

Appendix E—continued

CHECKLIST ITEMS	YES	NO	REMARKS
b. Do the sum of the cost account budgets for higher level CWBS elements, undistributed budget, and management reserves reconcile with the contract target cost plus the estimated cost for authorized unpriced work? (Provide exhibit.)			

III. ACCOUNTING

1. RECORD DIRECT COSTS ON AN APPLIED OR OTHER ACCEPTABLE BASIS CONSISTENT WITH THE BUDGETS IN A FORMAL SYSTEM THAT IS CONTROLLED BY THE GENERAL BOOKS OF ACCOUNT.

CHECKLIST ITEMS	YES	NO	REMARKS
a. Does the accounting system provide a basis for auditing records of direct costs chargeable to the contract?			
b. Are elements of direct cost (labor, material, and so forth) accumulated within cost accounts in a manner consistent with budgets using recognized acceptable costing techniques and controlled by the general books of account?			

2. SUMMARIZE DIRECT COSTS FROM THE COST ACCOUNTS INTO THE WBS WITHOUT ALLOCATION OF A SINGLE COST ACCOUNT TO TWO OR MORE WBS ELEMENTS. (Reference format 3.)

CHECKLIST ITEMS	YES	NO	REMARKS
a. Is it possible to summarize direct costs from the cost account level through the CWBS to the total contract level without allocation of a lower level CWBS element to two or more higher level CWBS elements? (This does not preclude the allocation of costs from a cost account containing common items to appropriate using cost accounts.)			

3. SUMMARIZE DIRECT COSTS FROM THE COST ACCOUNTS INTO THE CONTRACTOR'S FUNCTIONAL ORGANIZATIONAL ELEMENTS WITHOUT ALLOCATION OF A SINGLE COST ACCOUNT TO TWO OR MORE ORGANIZATIONAL ELEMENTS. (Reference format 4.)

CHECKLIST ITEMS	YES	NO	REMARKS
a. Is it possible to summarize direct costs from the cost account level to the highest functional organizational level without allocation of a lower level organization's cost to two or more higher level organizations?			

4. RECORD ALL INDIRECT COSTS WHICH WILL BE ALLOCATED TO THE CONTRACT.

CHECKLIST ITEMS	YES	NO	REMARKS
a. Does the cost accumulation system provide for summarization of indirect costs from the point of allocation to the contract total?			
b. Are indirect costs accumulated for comparison with the corresponding budgets?			
c. Do the lines of authority for incurring indirect costs correspond to the lines of responsibility for management control of the same components of costs? (Explain controls for fixed and variable indirect costs.)			
d. Are indirect costs charged to the appropriate indirect pools and incurring organization?			
e. Are the bases and rates for allocating costs from each indirect pool consistently applied?			

328

Appendix E—continued

CHECKLIST ITEMS	YES	NO	REMARKS
f. Are the bases and rates for allocating costs from each indirect pool to commercial work consistent with those used to allocate such costs to Government contracts?			
g. Are the rates for allocating costs from each indirect cost pool to contracts updated as necessary to ensure a realistic monthly allocation of indirect costs without significant year-end adjustments?			
h. Are the procedures for identifying indirect costs to incurring organizations, indirect cost pools, and allocating the costs from the pools to the contracts formally documented?			
5. IDENTIFY THE BASES FOR ALLOCATING THE COST OF APPORTIONED EFFORT.			
a. Is effort which is planned and controlled in direct relationship to cost accounts or work packages identified as apportioned effort?			
b. Are methods used for applying apportioned effort costs to cost accounts applied consistently and documented in an established procedure?			
6. IDENTIFY UNIT COSTS, EQUIVALENT UNIT COSTS, OR LOT COSTS AS APPLICABLE.			
a. Does the contractor's system provide unit costs, equivalent unit or lot costs in terms of labor, material, other direct, and indirect costs? (Describe procedure.)			
b. Does the contractor have procedures which permit identification of recurring or nonrecurring costs as necessary?			
7. THE CONTRACTOR'S MATERIAL ACCOUNTING SYSTEM WILL PROVIDE FOR: ACCURATE COST ACCUMULATION AND ASSIGNMENT OF COSTS TO COST ACCOUNTS IN A MANNER CONSISTENT WITH THE BUDGETS USING RECOGNIZED, ACCEPTABLE COSTING TECHNIQUES; DETERMINATION OF PRICE VARIANCES BY COMPARING PLANNED VERSUS ACTUAL COMMITMENTS; COST PERFORMANCE MEASUREMENT AT THE POINT IN THE MOST SUITABLE FOR THE CATEGORY OF MATERIAL INVOLVED, BUT NO EARLIER THAN THE TIME OF ACTUAL RECEIPT OF MATERIAL; DETERMINATION OF COST VARIANCES ATTRIBUTABLE TO THE EXCESS USAGE OF MATERIAL; DETERMINATION OF UNIT OR LOT COSTS WHEN APPLICABLE; AND FULL ACCOUNTABILITY FOR ALL MATERIAL PURCHASED FOR THE CONTRACT INCLUDING THE RESIDUAL INVENTORY.			
a. Does the contractor's system provide for accurate cost accumulation and assignment to cost accounts in a manner consistent with the budgets using recognized acceptable costing techniques?			
b. Are material costs reported within the same period as that in which BCWP is earned for that material?			
c. Does the contractor's system provide for determination of price variances by comparing planned vs actual commitments?			
d. Is cost performance measurement at the point in time most suitable for the category of material involved, but no earlier than the time of actual receipt of material?			

43

AFSCP 173-5   AFLCP 173-5   DARCOM-P 715-5   NAVMAT P5240   DLAH 8315.2

Appendix E—continued

CHECKLIST ITEMS	YES	NO	REMARKS
e. Does the contractor's system provide for the determination of cost variances attributable to the excess usage of material?			
f. Does the contractor's system provide unit or lot costs when applicable?			
g. Are records maintained to show full accountability for all material purchased for the contract, including the residual inventory?			

IV. ANALYSIS

1. IDENTIFY AT THE COST ACCOUNT LEVEL ON A MONTHLY BASIS USING DATA FROM, OR RECONCILABLE WITH, THE ACCOUNTING SYSTEM; BCWS AND BCWP; BCWP AND APPLIED (ACTUAL WHERE APPROPRIATE) DIRECT COSTS FOR THE SAME WORK; VARIANCES RESULTING FROM THE ABOVE COMPARISONS CLASSIFIED IN TERMS OF LABOR, MATERIAL, OR OTHER APPROPRIATE ELEMENTS, TOGETHER WITH THE REASONS FOR SIGNIFICANT VARIANCES.

CHECKLIST ITEMS	YES	NO	REMARKS
a. Does the contractor's system include procedures for measuring performance of the lowest level organization responsible for the cost account? (Provide typical example.)			
b. Does the contractor's system include procedures for measuring the performance of critical subcontractors?			
c. Is cost and schedule performance measurement done in a consistent, systematic manner?			
d. Are the actual costs used for variance analysis reconcilable with data from the accounting system?			
e. Is budgeted cost for work performed calculated in a manner consistent with the way work is planned? (For example, if work is planned on a measured basis, budgeted cost for work performed is calculated on a measured basis.)			
f. Does the contractor have variance analysis procedures and a demonstrated capability for identifying (at the cost account and other appropriate levels) cost and schedule variances resulting from the system (provide examples) which—			
(1) Identify and isolate problems causing unfavorable cost variances?			
(2) Evaluate the impact of schedule changes, work-around, etc?			
(3) Evaluate the performance of operating organizations?			
(4) Identify potential or actual overruns and underruns?			

2. IDENTIFY ON A MONTHLY BASIS, IN THE DETAIL NEEDED BY MANAGEMENT FOR EFFECTIVE CONTROL, BUDGETED INDIRECT COSTS, ACTUAL INDIRECT COSTS, AND VARIANCES, ALONG WITH THE REASONS. (Reference format 7.)

330

Appendix E—continued

CHECKLIST ITEMS	YES	NO	REMARKS
a. Are variances between budgeted and actual indirect costs identified and analyzed at the level of assigned responsibility for their control (indirect pool, department, etc.)?			
b. Does the contractor's cost control system provide for capability to identify the existence and causes of cost variances resulting from—			
(1) Incurrence of actual indirect costs in excess of budgets, by element of expense?			
(2) Changes in the direct base to which overhead costs are allocated?			
c. Are management actions taken to reduce indirect costs when there are significant adverse variances?			
3. SUMMARIZE THE DATA ELEMENTS AND ASSOCIATED VARIANCES LISTED IN ITEMS 1 AND 2 ABOVE THROUGH THE CONTRACTOR ORGANIZATION AND WBS TO THE REPORTING LEVEL SPECIFIED IN THE CONTRACT. (Reference formats 2, 3, 4, 5, 10, and 11.)			
a. Are data elements (BCWS, BCWP, and ACWP) progressively summarized from the detail level to the contract level through the CWBS? (Provide exhibit.)			
b. Are data elements summarized through the functional organizational structure for progressively higher levels of management? (Provide exhibit.)			
c. Are data elements reconcilable between internal summary reports and reports forwarded to the Government?			
d. Are procedures for variance analysis documented and consistently applied at the cost account level and selected WBS and organizational levels at least monthly as a routine task? (Provide examples.)			
4. IDENTIFY ON A MONTHLY BASIS SIGNIFICANT DIFFERENCES BETWEEN PLANNED AND ACTUAL SCHEDULE ACCOMPLISHMENT TOGETHER WITH THE REASONS.			
a. Does the scheduling system identify in a timely manner the status of work? (Provide representative examples.)			
b. Does the contractor use objective results, design reviews, and tests to trace schedule performance? (Provide examples.)			
5. IDENTIFY MANAGERIAL ACTIONS TAKEN AS A RESULT OF CRITERIA ITEMS 1 THROUGH 4 ABOVE.			
a. Is data disseminated to the contractor's managers timely, accurate, and usable? (Provide examples.)			
b. Are data being used by managers in an effective manner to ascertain program or functional status, to identify reasons for significant variance, and to initiate appropriate corrective action? (Provide examples.)			

AFSCP 173-5   AFLCP 173-5   DARCOM-P 715-5   NAVMAT P5240   DLAH 8315.2

Appendix E—continued

CHECKLIST ITEMS	YES	NO	REMARKS
c. Are there procedures for monitoring action items and corrective actions to the point of resolution and are these procedures being followed?			
6. BASED ON PERFORMANCE TO DATE AND ON ESTIMATES OF FUTURE CONDITIONS, DEVELOP REVISED ESTIMATES OF COST AT COMPLETION FOR WBS ELEMENTS IDENTIFIED IN THE CONTRACT AND COMPARE THESE WITH THE CONTRACT BUDGET BASE AND THE LATEST STATEMENT OF FUNDS REQUIREMENTS REPORT TO THE GOVERNMENT. (Reference formats 12, 13, and 14.)			
a. Are estimates of costs at completion based on—			
(1) Performance to date?			
(2) Actual costs to date?			
(3) Knowledgeable projections of future performance?			
(4) Estimates of the cost for contract work remaining to be accomplished considering economic escalation?			
b. Are the overhead rates used to develop the contract cost estimate to complete based on—			
(1) Historical experience?			
(2) Contemplated management improvements?			
(3) Projected economic escalation?			
(4) The anticipated business volume?			
c. Are estimates of cost at completion generated with sufficient frequency to provide identification of future cost problems in time for possible corrective or preventive actions by both the contractor and the Government program manager?			
d. Are estimates developed by program personnel coordinated with those responsible for overall plant management to determine whether required resources will be available according to revised planning?			
e. Are estimates of cost at completion generated by knowledgeable personnel for the following levels:			
(1) Cost accounts?			
(2) Major functional areas of contract effort?			
(3) Major subcontracts?			
(4) WBS elements contractually specified for reporting of status to the Government (lowest level only)?			
(5) Total contract (all authorized work)?			
f. Are the latest revised estimates of costs at completion compared with the established budgets at appropriate levels and causes of variances identified?			

46

AFSCP 173-5   AFLCP 173-5   DARCOM-P 715-5   NAVMAT P5240   DLAH 8315.2

Appendix E—continued

CHECKLIST ITEMS	YES	NO	REMARKS
g. Are estimates of cost at completion generated in a rational, consistent manner? Are procedures established for appropriate aspects of generating estimates of costs at completion?			
h. Are estimates of costs at completion utilized in determining contract funding requirements and reporting them to the Government?			
i. Are the contractor's estimates of costs at completion reconcilable with cost data reported to the Government?			
V. REVISIONS AND ACCESS TO DATA			
1. INCORPORATE CONTRACTUAL CHANGES IN A TIMELY MANNER, RECORDING THE EFFECTS OF SUCH CHANGES IN BUDGETS AND SCHEDULES. IN THE DIRECTED EFFORT BEFORE NEGOTIATION OF A CHANGE, BASE SUCH REVISIONS ON THE AMOUNT ESTIMATED AND BUDGETED TO THE FUNCTIONAL ORGANIZATIONS.			
a. Are authorized changes being incorporated in a timely manner?			
b. Are all affected work authorizations, budgeting, and scheduling documents amended to properly reflect the effects of authorized changes? (Provide examples.)			
c. Are internal budgets for authorized, but not priced changes based on the contractor's resource plan for accomplishing the work?			
d. If current budgets for authorized changes do not sum to the negotiated cost for the changes, does the contractor compensate for the differences by revising the undistributed budgets, management reserves, budgets established for work not yet started, or by a combination of these?			
2. RECONCILE ORIGINAL BUDGETS FOR THOSE ELEMENTS OF THE WBS IDENTIFIED AS PRICE LINE ITEMS IN THE CONTRACT, AND FOR THOSE ELEMENTS AT THE LOWEST LEVEL OF THE DOD PROJECT SUMMARY WBS, WITH CURRENT PERFORMANCE MEASUREMENT BUDGETS IN TERMS OF CHANGES TO THE AUTHORIZED WORK AND INTERNAL REPLANNING IN THE DETAIL NEEDED BY MANAGEMENT FOR EFFECTIVE CONTROL. (Reference formats 8 and 9.)			
a. Are current budgets resulting from changes to the authorized work and/or internal replanning, reconcilable to original budgets for specified reporting items?			
3. PROHIBIT RETROACTIVE CHANGES TO RECORDS PERTAINING TO WORK PERFORMED THAT WILL CHANGE PREVIOUSLY REPORTED AMOUNTS FOR DIRECT COSTS, INDIRECT COSTS, OR BUDGETS, EXCEPT FOR CORRECTION OF ERRORS AND ROUTINE ACCOUNTING ADJUSTMENTS.			
a. Are retroactive changes to direct costs and indirect costs prohibited except for the correction of errors and routine accounting adjustments?			
b. Are direct or indirect cost adjustments being accomplished according to accounting procedures acceptable to DCAA?			

AFSCP 173-5　　　　AFLCP 173-5　　　　DARCOM-P 715-5　　　　NAVMAT P5240　　　　DLAH 8315.2

Appendix E—continued

CHECKLIST ITEMS	YES	NO	REMARKS
c. Are retroactive changes to BCWS and BCWP prohibited except for correction of errors or for normal accounting adjustments?			
4. PREVENT REVISIONS TO THE CONTRACT BUDGET BASE EXCEPT FOR GOVERNMENT-DIRECTED CHANGES TO CONTRACTUAL EFFORT.			
a. Are procedures established to prevent changes to the contract budget base (see definition) other than those authorized by contractual action?			
b. Is authorization of budgets in excess of the contract budget base controlled formally and done with the full knowledge and recognition of the procuring activity? Are the procedures adequate?			
5. DOCUMENT, INTERNALLY, CHANGES TO THE PERFORMANCE MEASUREMENT BASELINE AND, ON A TIMELY BASIS, NOTIFY THE PROCURING ACTIVITY THROUGH PRESCRIBED PROCEDURES.			
a. Are changes to the performance measurement baseline made as a result of contractual redirection, formal reprogramming, internal replanning, application of undistributed budget, or the use of management reserve, properly documented and reflected in the Cost Performance Report?			
b. Are procedures in existence that restrict changes to budgets for open work packages, and are these procedures adhered to?			
c. Are retroactive changes to budgets for completed work specifically prohibited in an established procedure, and is this procedure adhered to?			
d. Are procedures in existence that control replanning of unopened work packages, and are these procedures adhered to?			
6. PROVIDE THE CONTRACTING OFFICER AND DULY AUTHORIZED REPRESENTATIVES ACCESS TO ALL OF THE FOREGOING INFORMATION AND SUPPORTING DOCUMENTS.			
a. Does the contractor provide access to all pertinent records to the C/SCSC Review Team and surveillance personnel?			

334

APPENDIX F

C/SCSC REVIEW WORKSHEETS AND EXHIBITS

1. The following are typical formats for performing data reconciliations and evaluating cost account and work package characteristics. It is recognized that the formats may require modification to meet the requirements of different organizations and contract work breakdown structures. The team members assigned responsibilities applicable to these formats should include them as exhibits in the review report. Worksheets needed to develop the data arrayed on the formats should be developed by the responsible team member.

2. In accomplishing the formats, the following must be considered:

a. Formats should include effort which has significant portions of measured effort (including material work packages, if separate), apportioned (factored) effort, and LOE.

b. Data must be evaluated for consistent application of standards or targets, planned ratios and bases, factors, rates, and methods.

c. Accomplishment indicators (for example, realization factors, milestones) must be consistent for computing BCWP.

d. Derivation of the data elements used in the sample formats must be substantiated.

e. Formats listed below should be accomplished using applicable instructions and definitions:

(1) Subsystem Integration Major Organization (for example, Engineering) and Associated Documentation.

(2) Reconciliation of Internal Data—Cost Account Data.

(3) Reconciliation of Internal Data—CWBS Data.

(4) Reconciliation of Internal Data—Organization Data.

(5) Reconciliation of Internal Data—Summary Level Data.

(6) Evaluation of Cost Accounts/Work Packages Organization—(For Example, Manufacturing).

(a) Length of Cost Accounts/Work Packages (Cont'd).

(b) Value of Cost Accounts/Work Packages (Cont'd).

(7) Contract Indirect Cost Evaluation.

(8) Performance Measurement Baseline Change Traceability—Cost Account Level.

(9) Reconciliation of Internal Data (Budget Revision)—Reporting Level CWBS Elements.

(10) Reconciliation of External Reports to Internal Data (CWBS).

(11) Reconciliation of External Reports to Internal Data (Organization).

(12) Reconciliation of External Reports.

(13) Reconciliation of Internal Data (Estimated Cost at Completion)—Contract Work Breakdown Structure.

(14) Reconciliation of Internal Data (Estimated Cost at Completion).

AFSCP 173-5   AFLCP 173-5   DARCOM-P 715-5   NAVMAT P5240   DLAH 8315.2

Appendix F—continued

SUBSYSTEM INTEGRATION
MAJOR ORGANIZATION (FOR EXAMPLE: ENGINEERING) AND
ASSOCIATED DOCUMENTATION
SAMPLE FORMAT 1

CWBS LEVEL (1)	ORGANIZATION LEVEL (2)	SCHEDULING (3)	BUDGETING (4)	WORK AUTHORIZATION (5)	PERFORMANCE MEASUREMENT (6)
Contract					
Cost Account					
Work Package					

NOTES:

1. Column 1—Identify a representative element for each level of the CWBS from the total contract level to the cost account and work package level.

2. Column 2—Where applicable, identify suborganization responsible for various CWBS levels.

3. Columns 3, 4, 5, and 6—Identify the appropriate document title associated with the column heading for each CWBS level (column 1) and internal organization level (column 2).

4. Prepare format for each major organization.

5. There need not be a different type of document used for each CWBS and organization level.

6. Integration of internal documents with the organization and WBS should occur, as a minimum, at the cost account/work package level and the total contract.

7. Reference criteria checklist item I-3.

Appendix F—continued

RECONCILIATION OF INTERNAL DATA
COST ACCOUNT DATA
SAMPLE FORMAT 2

Cost Account Organization Work Package/Planning Package	Total Budget	As Applicable (To Date Data)																
		Labor-Hrs			Labor $			Mat'l $			ODC $			Overhead $			Total $		
		BCWS	BCWP	ACWP	BCWS	BCWP	ACWP	BCWS	BCWP	ACWP	BCWS	BCWP	ACWP	BCWS	BCWP	ACWP	BCWS	BCWP	ACWP
CA No. Org. No. WP/PPN.																			
Cost Account Subtotal																			
CA No. Org. No. WP/PPN.																			
Cost Account Subtotal																			
Other																			
Selected CWBS Element Total																			

NOTES:
1. Overhead $ need not be at work package or cost account level. Include these $ at the level where contractor allocates them.
2. Summarization to contract level continues on sample formats 3, 4, 5, 13, 14.
3. Reference criteria checklist items II-3, II-4, II-6, and IV-3.

AFSCP 173-5   AFLCP 173-5   DARCOM-P 715-5   NAVMAT P5240   DLAH 8315.2

Appendix F—continued

RECONCILIATION OF INTERNAL DATA
CWBS DATA
SAMPLE FORMAT 3

Selected Reporting Level CWBS Element (For Example: Level 3)

COST ELEMENT	TOTAL BUDGET	TO DATE		
		BCWS	BCWP	ACWP
Labor–Hrs.				
Labor $				
Mat' $				
ODC $				
OH $				
Total $				

Selected Level 4 CWBS Element

All Other Level 4 CWBS Elements

All Other Level X CWBS Element

Selected Level X CWBS Element

All Other Cost Account

Selected Cost Account From Sample Format 2

As Applicable

COST ELEMENTS	TOTAL BUDGET	TO DATE		
		BCWS	BCWP	ACWP
Labor–Hrs.				
Labor $				
Mat'l $				
ODC $				
OH $				
Total $				

NOTES:

1. Reconcile total budget, BCWS, BCWP, and ACWP for data sample cost accounts to successively higher CWBS levels.

2. In summarizing to higher levels, various cost elements may need to be added. Overhead costs need not be at the cost account level. Include these costs at the level where the contractor allocates them to the CWBS.

3. Selected cost accounts should be the same as selected for the organizational summarization.

4. Reference criteria checklist items II-4, II-11, III-2, and I/-3.

Appendix F—continued

RECONCILIATION OF INTERNAL DATA
ORGANIZATION DATA
SAMPLE FORMAT 4

NOTES:

1. Reconcile total budget, BCWS, BCWP, and ACWP for data sample cost account to successively higher organizational levels.
2. In summarizing to higher levels, various levels may need to be added. Overhead costs need not be at the cost account level. Include these costs at the level where the contractor allocates them to organizations.
3. Selected cost accounts should be the same as selected for WBS summarization.
4. Reference criteria checklist items II-4, II-11, III-3, and IV-3.

53

Appendix F—continued

RECONCILIATION OF INTERNAL DATA
SUMMARY LEVEL DATA
SAMPLE FORMAT 5

REPORTING LEVEL CWBS ELEMENTS	DATA ELEMENT	MAJOR INTERNAL ORGANIZATIONS									
		ENGINEERING				MANUFACTURING				PROCUREMENT	OTHER	TOTAL
		LABOR	MAT'L	ODC	OH	LABOR	MAT'L	ODC	OH	SUBCONTRACTS		
	Budget (Total)											
	BCWS To Date											
	BCWP To Date											
	ACWP To Date											
	Budget (Total)											
	BCWS To Date											
	BCWP To Date											
Subtotal of Reported Elements	Budget (Total)											
	BCWS To Date											
	BCWP To Date											
	ACWP To Date											
Undistributed Budget												
Management Reserve												
Overhead not included above												
Total Budget												

NOTES:

1. Accomplish at summary WBS levels, and Undistributed Budget.
2. Management Reserve—Identify and add to internal budgets to reconcile to negotiated contract cost.
3. Discrepancies—Document, identify levels where occurred, and dollar amount; include cause if known.
4. Reference criteria checklist items III-11 and IV-3.

AFSCP 173-5   AFLCP 173-5   DARCOM-P 715-5   NAVMAT P5240   DLAH 8315.2

Appendix F —continued

EVALUATION OF COST ACCOUNTS/WORK PACKAGES
ORGANIZATION—(FOR EXAMPLE, MANUFACTURING)
SAMPLE FORMAT 6

| COST ACCT NO. WORK PACKAGE PLANNING PACKAGE | CLASSIFICATION OF WORK EFFORT (LOE, DISCRETE APPORTIONED) (1) | START DATE | | COMPLETE DATE | | DURATION (6) | BUDGET (7) | REMARKS: COMMENTS ON WORK CLASSIFICATION DURATION (8) |
		SCHED (2)	ACTUAL (3)	SCHED (4)	ACTUAL (5)			
CA No. ___ WP/PP No. ___ ___ ___								
CA No. ___ WP/PP No. ___ ___ ___								

NOTES:

1. Column 1—Selected cost accounts and associated work packages/planning packages from sample format 2.
2. Column 7—State if work is properly classified (Column 2) and identify work-in-process BCWP formulas.
3. Graphically display measured effort data on formats 6a and 6b.
4. If work packages are subdivided by milestones, identify this in Column 1 and complete the format with milestone information.
5. Reference criteria checklist items II-5 and II-8.

Appendix F –continued

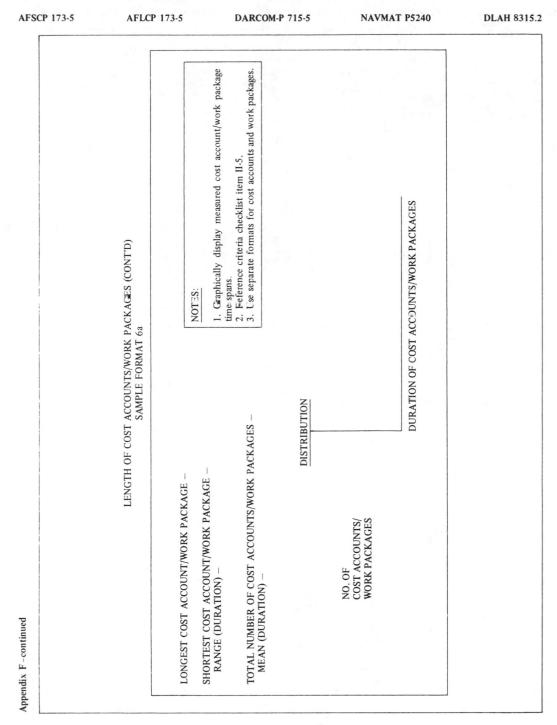

LENGTH OF COST ACCOUNTS/WORK PACKAGES (CONT'D)
SAMPLE FORMAT 6a

NOTES:

1. Graphically display measured cost account/work package time spans.
2. Reference criteria checklist item II-5.
3. Use separate formats for cost accounts and work packages.

LONGEST COST ACCOUNT/WORK PACKAGE –

SHORTEST COST ACCOUNT/WORK PACKAGE –
RANGE (DURATION) –

TOTAL NUMBER OF COST ACCOUNTS/WORK PACKAGES –
MEAN (DURATION) –

DISTRIBUTION

NO. OF
COST ACCOUNTS/
WORK PACKAGES

DURATION OF COST ACCOUNTS/WORK PACKAGES

342

Appendix F—continued

VALUE OF COST ACCOUNTS/WORK PACKAGES (CONT'D)
SAMPLE FORMAT 6b

LARGEST COST ACCOUNT/WORK PACKAGE –

SMALLEST COST ACCOUNT/WORK PACKAGE –
RANGE (VALUE) –

TOTAL NUMBER OF MEASURED COST ACCOUNT/WORK PACKAGES –
MEAN (VALUE) –

DISTRIBUTION

NO. OF
COST ACCOUNTS/
WORK PACKAGES

VALUE OF COST ACCOUNTS/WORK PACKAGES (HOURS OR DOLLARS)

NOTICES:

1. Graphically display measured cost account/work package values.
2. Reference criteria checklist item II-5.
3. Use separate formats for cost accounts and work packages.

57

Appendix F—continued

CONTRACT INDIRECT COST EVALUATION
SAMPLE FORMAT 7

TYPE OF OVERHEAD POOL	DATA ELEMENT	MAJOR ORGANIZATIONS					
		ENGINEERING	FACTORY	TOOLING	LOGISTICS	ETC.	SUBTOTAL
Manufacturing	Budget (Total) Budget to Date Actuals to Date Difference						
Engineering	Budget (Total) Budget to Date Actuals to Date Difference						
Material	Budget (Total) Budget to Date Actuals to Date Difference						
ETC.							
Total	Budget (Total) Budget to Date Actuals to Date Difference						

NOTES:

1. Format illustrates overhead planning budget to date, and actuals to date, by overhead pool and associated organization allocation base.
2. Data to accomplish this format should be derived from the lowest level at which contract indirect costs are planned and allocated to organizations.
3. Analyze differences on supporting worksheets.
4. Reference criteria checklist items II-9 and IV-2.

AFSCP 173-5   AFLCP 173-5   DARCOM-P 715-5   NAVMAT P5240   DLAH 8315.2

Appendix F—continued

PERFORMANCE MEASUREMENT BASELINE CHANGE TRACEABILITY
COST ACCOUNT LEVEL
SAMPLE FORMAT 8

COST ACCOUNT No. (1)	ORIGINAL BUDGET (2)	CHANGES CONTRACT (3)	CHANGES MGT RESERVE (4)	HIGHER CWBS ELEMENT (5)	SUB-TOTAL (2, 3, 4, & 5) (6)	CURRENT BUDGET (7)	DIFFERENCE (7-6) (8)	EXPLANATION OF DIFFERENCES (9)
No. _____ _____ _____ _____								
Element CWBS Subtotal								
No. _____ _____ _____ _____								
Element CWBS Subtotal								
No. _____ _____ _____ _____								
Element CWBS Subtotal								
No. _____ _____ _____ _____								
Element CWBS Subtotal								

NOTES:

1. Format reconciles current cost account budget to original budgets for baseline control.
2. Analyze differences on supporting worksheets.
3. Reference criteria checklist items II-3 and V-2.

Appendix F—continued

RECONCILIATION OF INTERNAL DATA (BUDGET REVISION)
REPORTING LEVEL CWBS ELEMENTS
SAMPLE FORMAT 9

CWBS ELEMENTS	ORIGINAL BUDGET	CHANGES		SUBTOTAL (2, 3, AND 4)	CURRENT BUDGET	DIFFERENCE (6-5)	EXPLANATION OF DIFFERENCE
		CONTRACT	MGT. RESERVE				
(1)	(2)	(3)	(4)	(5)	(6)	(7)	(8)
							NOTES:
							1. Reconcile current reporting level CWBS element budget to original budgets and compare values to contract target cost.
							2. Analyze differences on supporting work-sheets.
							3. Reference criteria checklist item V-2.
Total Internal Budgets							
Undistributed Budget							
Management Reserve							
Overhead not Included Above							
Total Contract Negotiated Cost							

Appendix F—continued

AFSCP 173-5   AFLCP 173-5   DARCOM-P 715-5   NAVMAT P5240   DLAH 8315.2

RECONCILIATION OF EXTERNAL REPORTS TO INTERNAL DATA (CWBS)
SAMPLE FORMAT 10

CWBS	DATA ELEMENTS							
	CURRENT PERIOD				CUMULATIVE TO DATE			
	BCWS	BCWP	ACWP		BCWS	BCWP	ACWP	
AIR VEHICLE Cost Performance Report								
Contractor's Internal Report								
Difference								
TEST Cost Performance Report								
Contractor's Internal Report								
Difference								
SYSTEMS ENGINEERING Cost Performance Report								
Contractor's Internal Report								
Difference								
SUPPORT EQUIPMENT Cost Performance Report								
TOTAL Cost Performance Report								
Contractor's Internal Report								
Difference								

NOTES:

1. Reports to be compared should cover identical periods.
2. Items shown in the first column are for illustrative purposes. Use applicable WBS reporting level items.
3. Analyze difference on a separate worksheet, trace each difference to its origin, and explain.
4. Reference criteria checklist item IV-3.

61

AFSCP 173-5   AFLCP 173-5   DARCOM-P 715-5   NAVMAT P5240   DLAH 8315.2

Appendix F—continued

RECONCILIATION OF EXTERNAL REPORTS TO INTERNAL DATA
(ORGANIZATION)
SAMPLE FORMAT 11

ORGANIZATION	DATA ELEMENTS					
	CURRENT PERIOD			CUMULATIVE TO DATE		
	BCWS	BCWP	ACWP	BCWS	BCWP	ACWP
ENGINEERING						
Cost Performance Report						
Contractor Internal Report						
Difference						
TOOLING						
Cost Performance Report						
Contractor Internal Report						
Difference						
QUALITY CONTROL						
Cost Performance Report						
Contractor Internal Report						
Difference						
MANUFACTURING						
Cost Performance						
Contractor Internal Report						
Difference						
TOTAL						
Cost Performance Report						
Contractor Internal Report						
Difference						

NOTES:

1. Reports to be compared should cover identical periods.
2. Items shown in the first column are illustrative. Use applicable contractor organizational structure.
3. Analyze differences on a separate worksheet, trace each difference to its origin, and explain.
4. Reference criteria checklist item IV-3.

AFSCP 173-5   AFLCP 173-5   DARCOM-P 715-5   NAVMAT P5240   DLAH 8315.2

Appendix F—continued

RECONCILIATION OF EXTERNAL REPORTS
SAMPLE FORMAT 12

REPORT	NEGOTIATED CONTRACT COST	CUMULATIVE ACTUAL COST	ESTIMATED COST AT COMPLETION	EXPLANATION OF DIFFERENCES
Cost Performance Report				
DD Form 1586, Contract Funds Status Report				
Difference				

NOTES:

1. Ascertain that reports conform to current contractual requirements.
2. Reports to be compared should cover identical periods.
3. Reconcile for variation in report requirements (for example, applicable FY funds in CFSR vs total contract authorized funds in CPR).
4. Analyze differences remaining after reconciliation on separate worksheet, trace to origin, and explain.
5. Reference criteria checklist item IV-6.

AFSCP 173-5   AFLCP 173-5   DARCOM-P 715-5   NAVMAT P5240   DLAH 8315.2

Appendix F—continued

RECONCILIATION OF INTERNAL DATA
(ESTIMATED COST AT COMPLETION)
CONTRACT WORK BREAKDOWN STRUCTURE
SAMPLE FORMAT 13

CWBS ELEMENT, REPORTING LEVEL	CONTRACTOR INTERNAL ESTIMATED COST AT COMPLETION	ESTIMATED COST AT COMPLETION COST PERF. REPORT	DIFFERENCE (3-2)	EXPLANATION OF DIFFERENCE
(1)	(2)	(3)	(4)	(5)
Subtotal				
Undistributed Budget				
Overhead not included above				
Total				

NOTES:
1. Show reconciliation from lowest level CWBS element where EAC is calculated to reporting level on sample format 14.
2. Reference criteria checklist item IV-6.

350

Appendix F—continued

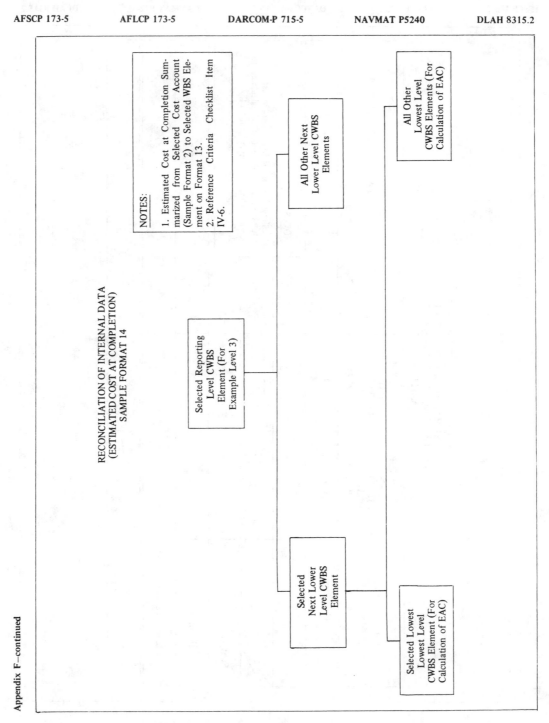

RECONCILIATION OF INTERNAL DATA
(ESTIMATED COST AT COMPLETION)
SAMPLE FORMAT 14

NOTES:

1. Estimated Cost at Completion Summarized from Selected Cost Account (Sample Format 2) to Selected WBS Element on Format 13.
2. Reference Criteria Checklist Item IV-6.

Selected Reporting Level CWBS Element (For Example Level 3)

All Other Next Lower Level CWBS Elements

All Other Lowest Level CWBS Elements (For Calculation of EAC)

Selected Next Lower Level CWBS Element

Selected Lowest Lowest Level CWBS Element (For Calculation of EAC)

AFSCP 173-5   AFLCP 173-5   DARCOM-P 715-5   NAVMAT P5240   DLAH 8315.2

APPENDIX G

C/SCSC SUBSEQUENT APPLICATION REVIEWS
POLICY AND GUIDANCE

1. Purpose of Guidance. The following guidance is to assist in the proper performance of subsequent application review activities in order to achieve a greater degree of uniformity in the conduct of such reviews and to ensure understanding of review responsibilities and requirements.

2. Definition. A C/SCSC subsequent application review is a formal review performed in lieu of a C/SCSC demonstration review when compliance with the DOD Cost/Schedule Control Systems Criteria (C/SCSC) is a requirement in a contract (DAR 7-104.87) at a facility where the management control system has been accepted previously as meeting the C/SCSC. The contractor's system must have been accepted for the same type of contract (that is, development or production). Because the intent of conducting a subsequent application review is to minimize unnecessary repetition of work previously performed in the demonstration review, the length and scope of a subsequent application review are limited.

3. Objective. The objective of a subsequent application review is to ensure that, on a new contract, the contractor is properly and effectively using the accepted system, revised in accordance with approved changes. It is not the purpose of the review to reassess the contractor's previously accepted system.

4. Importance of the Subsequent Application Review. The C/SCSC subsequent application reviews are a major function of a command's C/SCSC program. Although not as comprehensive as initial C/SCSC demonstration reviews, subsequent application reviews are of equal importance to a continued successful implementation of a command's C/SCSC program and its credibility. Subsequent application review findings and recommendations are of consequence to all Army, Navy, and Air Force program offices that may be doing business with a particular contractor. Uniformity of application and consistency of interpretation are advantageous to both DOD and the contractors.

5. Basis for Application.
   a. **Same Facility.** Subsequent application reviews will normally be required in connection with new contracts which require C/SCSC where the work is to be performed at a facility whose management control system has previously been accepted on another contract of the same type (that is, development, production). Where there is a production option on a development contract, a subsequent application review (or a demonstration review if there is no accepted production system) will normally be required when work on the production option begins. Where the contract is a follow-on contract for the same (or almost the same) item at the same facility, the subsequent application review requirement may be waived on recommendation by the focal point to the contracting officer on request of the procuring activity.
   b. **New Facility.** A subsequent application review may be held in lieu of a demonstration review when a contractor proposes to extend the application of an accepted management control system to a facility within the corporate or division structure other than the facility for which the management system was originally accepted, provided the facility is in the same geographical area and is under the cognizance of the same CAO.
   c. **Contractual Requirement.** DAR Clause 7-104.87, Cost/Schedule Control Systems, requires that the contractor be prepared to demonstrate that its management control system meets the criteria, that is, C/SCSC. The clause also provides that "If the contractor . . . is utilizing Cost/Schedule Control Systems which have previously been accepted, . . . the Contracting Officer may waive all or part of the provisions concerning . . . demonstration and review." (See DAR clause.)
   d. **Policy.**
      (1) A subsequent application review will be performed in lieu of a complete C/SCSC demonstration review when:
         (a) A contractor or subcontractor is contractually required to apply C/SCSC and is using a management control system which has been previously accepted.
         (b) The C/SCSC surveillance monitor in the contract administration office (CAO) confirms that the accepted system has been or is being operated as contractually agreed to in the prior or current contract.
      (2) When a contractor has an accepted system for the proper acquisition phase, a demonstration review will be required only when determined necessary by the service focal point.
   e. **Determination.** The major command will make the final recommendation to the contracting officer as to whether a subsequent application review or a demonstration review will be required of the contractor, considering such relevant factors as:
      (1) Assessment of CAO and DCAA surveillance findings.
      (2) Current and prior experience of other Government program offices requiring C/SCSC application by the contractor.
      (3) The extent to which the current system description document materially varies from the originally approved document, as a result of major revisions and/or cumulative revisions which have been made to the system after acceptance.
   f. **Triservice.** If the contractor, using a previously accepted management control system, desires a Triservice acceptance of a new facility, the choice of a subsequent application review in lieu of a demonstration review must be coordinated among the services.

6. Responsibilities. The major command (figure 4-1) has the authority and responsibility for—
   a. Selection of the subsequent application review director.
   b. Approval of the scope and extent of the subsequent application review.
   c. Final approval of review team recommendations.

7. Selection and Composition of Team. Subsequent Application Review team members must meet the same standards as Demonstration Review team members (chapter 4). The members should be experienced and understand the C/SCSC.

Appendix G—continued

Knowledge of the program is desirable. Formal training, such as that given in AFIT courses 360 and/or 361 (Evaluation and/or Surveillance of Cost/Schedule Control Systems Criteria), is a requirement that normally will not be waived. The review director, team chief, and members will be formally assigned to the team. The team composition will normally be as indicated for demonstration review teams (chapter 4, paragraph 4-3a), although the number of team members will normally be fewer. The C/SCSC surveillance monitor in the CAO may be selected as team chief, or as an assistant team chief (paragraph 4-3).

8. Pre-Award Process:

a. A contractor proposing to apply a management control system previously accepted may satisfy the C/SCSC requirements of the solicitation document by citing in its proposal the formal notice of prior acceptance of the management system and/or the Memorandum of Understanding by which the contractor has agreed to apply the accepted system to all contracts requiring C/SCSC.

b. Upon receipt of notification in the proposal that the contractor will apply the accepted system to a pending contract, the procuring activity will inform the major command focal point (through subordinate command channels) of the contractor's C/SCSC proposal response.

c. Based upon information available from the contractor's proposal, from the CAO and DCAA surveillance findings from other procuring activities, and from other services' C/SCSC experience with the given contractor, a determination will be made as to the nature and extent of the subsequent application review. The procuring activity will be responsible for this appraisal and will forward its recommendation to the major command focal point. The focal point will review the recommendation, and will notify the procuring activity of its approval or disapproval.

9. Conduct of the Subsequent Application Review:

a. **Team Preparation.** After contract award and prior to formal review activities with the contractor, the subsequent application review team chief should ensure that the team reviews the findings of the CAO and DCAA C/SCSC surveillance activities. The team should also review the contractor's management control system description, demonstration review report upon which the current acceptance was based, and/or reports of prior subsequent application reviews.

b. **Implementation Visit.** When the review director and/or team chief consider it to be necessary, an implementation visit should be made to the contractor's plant to discuss plans and actions associated with the subsequent application review and to ensure that the anticipated scope of the review is understood. Coordination by telephone or correspondence may be used in lieu of an implementation visit, whenever practicable.

c. **Contractor Preparation.** Prior to the start of the subsequent application review, it is desirable (but not mandatory) that—

(1) The principal contract tasks be definitized.

(2) The contractor has developed schedules and a complete set of performance measurement baseline budgets for the definitized work under the contract.

(3) The contractor has completed at least two complete

monthly accounting periods of performance against baseline budgets and schedules, and has submitted Cost Performance Reports (CPR) for these two periods.

(4) Each subcontractor required to comply with the C/SCSC or to provide Cost/Schedule Status Reports (C/SSR), has submitted at least one CPR or C/SSR to the prime contractor.

(5) Obvious significant deficiencies in the contractor's management control system operation on the new contract (possibly evident from the quality of the reports, on-site progress reviews, or C/SCSC surveillance) have been identified to the contractor and corrected.

d. **Review conduct.** The review is normally conducted within 90 days after contract award to determine that the contractor is properly using the previously accepted management control system on the new contract. The team composition and the duration of the review should be the minimum necessary to complete the task. Usually a 3-5 day visit to the contractor's facility by a team composed of fewer members than a demonstration review team will suffice. The review is normally conducted by the office which conducts demonstration reviews and includes participation by the cognizant CAO and Defense Contract Audit Agency (DCAA) representative. The review director assigned by the major command focal point is expected to provide consistency of C/SCSC interpretation, and maintain the depth of review at a reasonable level.

e. **Review Procedure:**

(1) The basic review routine is similar to that of a C/SCSC demonstration review. The direct use of the Evaluation/Demonstration review checklist for C/SCSC, appendix E to the C/SCSC Joint Implementation Guide, is not appropriate unless used on an exception basis and in abbreviated form. The level of detail resulting from strict application would otherwise be too great and would result in a full reevaluation of the contractor's management control system.

(2) The review will consist of five basic activities. These are:

(a) An overview briefing by the contractor to familiarize the review team with the accepted management control system identifying any changes which have occurred since the management system was last subjected to a demonstration or subsequent application review.

(b) A review, on a sample basis, of the documentation which establishes and records changes to the contractor's baseline plan for the contract. This will include work authorization, schedules, budgets, resource plans, and change records. The purpose is to verify that the contractor has established and is maintaining a valid, comprehensive integrated baseline plan for the contract.

(c) A review, on a sample basis, of the reporting of cost and schedule performance against the baseline plan, along with appropriate analyses of problems and projection of future costs. Also, a tracing of the summarization of cost/schedule performance data from the lowest level of formal reporting to the CPR. The purpose of this activity is to verify the accuracy of reported information.

(d) Interviews with a selected sample of contractor managers to verify that the contractor's previously accepted control systems are fully implemented and are being used in

AFSCP 173-5   AFLCP 173-5   DARCOM-P 715-5   NAVMAT P5240   DLAH 8315.2

Appendix G—continued

the management of the contract.

(e) An exit briefing by the review team covering the review team's draft findings.

NOTE: In all of the foregoing activities, the sample actually reviewed should be relatively small so as to limit the duration of the review. However, samples should be carefully selected to focus on the areas of greatest cost, activity, and, if possible, risk. If significant problems are found, the sample size and, if necessary, the duration of the review should be extended sufficiently to determine their extent.

10. Results of the Subsequent Application Review.

a. Conclusion of the Review. It is expected that the subsequent application review will result in approval after one review. However, there can be no approval until all discrepancies have been corrected. Significant discrepancies should be brought to the attention of the contractor by the review director or team chief. If possible, corrective actions and/or a schedule for correction of deficiencies should be agreed upon during the review.

b. Uncorrected Discrepancies. Outstanding discrepancies resulting from a subsequent application review, will be corrected within a reasonable time period (normally 30 days) as specified by the procuring activity performing the review. Failure to do so can result in termination of the Memorandum of Understanding (if any) and withdrawal of prior acceptance of the contractor's system.

c. Further Review. Where it is necessary to verify that deficiencies have been corrected, the review director should determine whether this can be accomplished by the CAO or whether it will be necessary to reassemble all or part of the review team for a follow-up review. This determination should be based upon an evaluation of the nature of the corrective action required and the contractor's plan and schedule for corrective action. Follow-on reviews must be approved by the major command focal point and will be scheduled by the team chief. The contractor's corrective actions prior to the follow-up review will be monitored by the C/SCSC surveillance monitor and reported to the team chief.

11. Deficiencies in the Previously Accepted System. At the time of the subsequent application review, there is a mutual presumption that the contractor's management system is in compliance with the C/SCSC as accepted by DOD. In those instances when the subsequent application review team determines that the contractor's accepted management system does not meet C/SCSC requirements, the contractor and ACO should be promptly notified. The information provided must detail the specific areas of deviation. The procuring activity and the focal point should be notified of major discrepancies

and advice should be obtained from all parties regarding items of major disagreement including the lead service involved in acceptance of the system. In those cases where problems cannot be resolved by the team, the discrepancy will be elevated to the focal point. In exceptional cases, particularly when more than one military department is involved, the Performance Measurement Joint Executive Group should be convened to adjudicate outstanding issues.

12. Review Report:

a. A formal report of the subsequent application review will be prepared by the team chief and forwarded to the major command focal point within 10 workdays after the completion of the review. It should document overall findings, problems, conclusions, and recommendations (see attached outline). Specifically, it should identify the contractor facility and contract reviewed, the dates of the review, and the review team members. It should state the significant findings including any significant discrepancies and any agreements with the contractor regarding their correction. Also, it should specify what further review is required, if any, and recommend responsible activities (CAO, review team, etc.).

b. Abbreviated reports will be prepared for any follow up reviews required to assess corrective action. They will be forwarded to the major command focal point within 7 workdays after completion of the follow-up review.

c. Upon review and approval of the report and its recommendations, the procuring activity will be advised of action to be taken.

13. Action on the Subsequent Application Review Report:

a. Upon major command focal point approval of a recommendation that the contractor's application of C/SCSC to the new contract be approved, the major command focal point will so notify the procuring activity. The Procuring Contracting Officer (PCO) will then advise the CAO that the contractor should be informed formally of the approval.

b. If discrepancies are reported by the team, the PCO will notify the contractor in writing through the CAO of these discrepancies requiring a reply from the contractor within 30 days attesting to the correction of deficiencies. A copy of the PCO letter will be furnished to the major command focal point.

c. If the team chief recommends that a follow-up review be conducted and the major command focal point agrees with this recommendation, the contractor will be so notified through the procuring activity and the CAO, with a copy furnished the major command focal point. The team chief will coordinate plans for the follow-up review with the review director and the contractor.

AFSCP 173-5   AFLCP 173-5   DARCOM-P 715-5   NAVMAT P5240   DLAH 8315.2

Appendix G—continued

SUBSEQUENT APPLICATION REVIEW REPORT OUTLINE

1. **Introduction**:

a. Summarize type and scope of contract.

b. Give basis of acceptance of contractor's system as C/SCSC compliant.

c. Identify any other in-plant contracts requiring C/SCSC compliance.

d. Identify team members and their organizations.

2. **Scope of Review**. Identify contractor organizations and data samples reviewed.

3. **Findings**.

a. Organize findings in paragraph form under each of the major criteria groups; that is, Organization, Planning and Budgeting, Accounting, Analysis, and Revisions.

b. Each criterion need not be addressed. Determine data samples and manager interviews by the critical aspects of the contractual statements of work. As a minimum, the findings should address:

(1) WBS subdivision and integration with the contractor's organizational structure.

(2) Schedule subdivision and integration with cost account/work package schedules.

(3) Work package identification.

(4) Baseline establishment and maintenance.

(5) BCWP determination.

(6) Identification of management reserves and undistributed budgets.

(7) Establishment of internal budgets which add up to the contract budget base.

(8) Material measurement.

(9) Estimated cost at completion determination and reasonableness.

(10) Identification of variance analysis thresholds and quality of analysis.

(11) Contractor manager knowledge and use of the system.

(12) Contractual change incorporation.

4. **Conclusions and Recommendations**.

a. The contractor has (or has not) properly implemented the system.

b. Deficiencies found and corrective action taken and planned to be taken.

c. Recommendation for a second review if necessary.

d. Recommended items for CAO surveillance.

| AFSCP 173-5 | AFLCP 173-5 | DARCOM-P 715-5 | NAVMAT P5240 | DLAH 8315.2 |

OFFICIAL

ALTON D. SLAY, General, USAF
Commander
Air Force Systems Command

JAMES L. WYATT, JR., Colonel, USAF
Director of Administration

JAMES H. RIX, Colonel, USAF
Director of Administration

BRYCE POE, II, General, USAF
Commander
Air Force Logistics Command

JUDITH L. TILT
MAJ, GS
Adjutant General

JOHN R. GUTHRIE
General, USA
Commanding
US Army Materiel Development
    and Readiness Command

J. R. LEWIS
Rear Admiral, USN
Deputy Chief of Naval Material
    for Acquisition

R. F. McCORMACK, Colonel, USA
Staff Director, Administration
Defense Logistics Agency

SUMMARY OF CHANGES

This revision achieves consistency with the current DODI 7000.2, amplifies procedures for conducting subsequent application reviews, and clarifies criteria interpretation for application for C/SCSC to production contracts.

356

| AFSCP 173-5 | AFLCP 173-5 | DARCOM-P 715-5 | NAVMAT P5240 | DLAH 8315.2 |

DISTRIBUTION: SPECIAL

DEPARTMENT OF THE AIR FORCE: F; X 2615
   HQ AFSC 1600
   PDO 4015, Andrews AFB DC 20334

   AD, ASD, ESD, BMO, SD (AC) . . . 100 cy ea 500
   AFCMD/TM 100

   HQ AFLC 415
   PDO 4000
   2750 ABW/DAPR, Wright-Patterson AFB OH 45433

DEPARTMENT OF THE ARMY 600
   HQ DARCOM/DRXAM-ABS (for stock only) 200
   5001 Eisenhower Avenue, Alexandria VA 22333
     (DRXAM-ABE . . . 10 cy)
     (DRCPP-K . . . . 200 cy)

   Letterkenny Army Depot/SDSLE-AJD (for stock only) 400
     Chambersburg PA 17201

DEPARTMENT OF THE NAVY 1000
   Defense Printing Service, Distribution Section
   Rm BD 831, Pentagon, Washington DC 20350

   (For DPS distribution only)
   A1 (MRAL, FM, RES only) (2 cy ea) 6
   A2A (NAVCOMPT NCB 43 only) 2
   A4A (CNM MAT 08C32) 100
   FKA1A (NAVAIR 5243) 100
   FKA1B (NAVELEX 504B) 100
   FKA1G (NAVSEA 903) 100
   C4K (JCMPO only) 50
   Stock:
   Navy Publications and Forms Center
   5801 Tabor Ave, Phila PA 19120 550

DEFENSE LOGISTICS AGENCY: 62 1000
   HQ DLA (DASC-EPD)
   Building 6, Door 26
   Cameron Station, Alexandria VA 22314

OFFICE OF THE SECRETARY OF DEFENSE 118
   OASD/Comp MS . . . 100; OASD (PA&E . . . 6;
   OASD/I&L . . . 6; ODDR&E . . . 6)

DEFENSE SYSTEMS MANAGEMENT COLLEGE 200
   Bldg 202, Fort Belvoir VA 22060

DEPARTMENT OF THE AIR FORCE 45
   HQ USAF (AC . . . 12; RDM . . . 12; LGP . . . 12);
   SAF (FM . . . 3; RD . . . 3; IL . . . 3)

AFIT/SLCT, Wright-Patterson AFB OH 45433 500

*U.S. GOVERNMENT PRINTING OFFICE: 1981-0-724-924/992

APPENDIX F
C/SSR CLAUSES

Appendix C

SAMPLE SOLICITATION CLAUSE
(When C/SSR is in the CDRL)

1. **Notice of Cost/Schedule Status Report (C/SSR) Requirements.**

   a.   The offeror will explain the methods to be used to generate the C/SSR data elements; in particular, how Budgeted Cost for Work Performed (BCWP) is determined, including explanation of Budgeted Cost for Work Scheduled (BCWS) and budget baseline control as necessary to support the BCWP discussion. The method for establishing variances from planned performance and making variance analyses will be explained.

   b.   In the event that the offeror has a cost/schedule control system that has been accepted by a DoD component as complying with the DoD Cost/Schedule Control Systems Criteria (C/SCSC) on a contract of the same nature (e.g., development, production, etc.), and plans to use the accepted system on this contract, the offeror may submit a copy of the acceptance letter or Memorandum of Understanding in lieu of the explanation required above.

   c.   After contract award, the Government manager or designated representative(s) will visit the contractor's facility for familiarization with the cost and schedule information being generated in satisfaction of the C/SSR contractual requirements. For the purpose of this visit, the contractor shall provide briefings and documents as necessary to explain and describe the methods of data generation in actual operation.

   d.   Should the contractor choose to modify or change procedures after contract award in such a way as to affect C/SSR data or reporting, the contractor will inform the Administrative Contracting Officer of such changes according to provisions of the contract. Such notification shall be given before submission of any contractually required reports involving the modified procedures.

   e.   The contractor shall require a subcontractor to furnish Cost/Schedule Status Reports (C/SSR) in each case where such a sub-contract is other than firm-fixed-price, and is 12 months or more in duration, and either (a) has a dollar amount which exceeds $2 million, or (b) has critical tasks relative to this contract. Critical tasks will be defined by mutual agreement between the Government and the prime contractor. Each such subcontractor's reported cost and sche-dule information will be incorporated into the prime contractor's C/SSR.

Appendix C -- (Cont.)

2. Preliminary Contract Work Breakdown Structure (CWBS).

a.   Upon award of a contract, the contractor may extend the preliminary Contract Work Breakdown Structure (CWBS) contained in this solicitation in as much detail as necessary to identify and structure the work effort to successfully achieve the end objective(s) of the contract work scope. The CWBS will serve as a framework for contract planning, budgeting, and reporting status of costs and schedule to the Government. The offeror shall develop the detailed levels of the CWBS in a manner which will assure compatibility with internal organizations and management systems and which will identify the major elements of work to be subcontracted.

b.   Any changes that the offeror wishes to make to the preliminary CWBS included in this solicitation shall be identified appropriately, and the proposed revision will be evaluated prior to contract award. The offeror shall provide information and assistance as requested, if needed, for evaluation of any proposed revision to the preliminary CWBS. Any changes thereafter proposed by the contractor to the specified reporting level elements of the approved CWBS will require prior written approval of the Procuring Contracting Officer.

Appendix D

SAMPLE CONTRACT CLAUSE
(When C/SSR is in the CDRL)

1. Cost/Schedule Status Report (C/SSR) Requirements.

a.   The Government manager or designated representative(s) will visit the contractor's facility to observe and understand how cost and schedule information is being generated in accordance with C/SSR contractual requirements.   During the visit the contractor will provide briefings and documents necessary to explain and describe the internal procedures used on the contract.

b.   If the contractor elects to change procedures during contract performance in a way which will affect C/SSR data or reporting the contractor shall submit notification and description of such change, with an explanation of the reasons, to the Administrative Contracting Officer, prior to submission of any contractually-required reports that contain information derived from the modified procedures.

c.   On request by the Government manager or designated representative, the contractor agrees to provide, during performance of the contract, access to pertinent records and data which underlie and support the cost and schedule data reported.

d.   If the contractor uses on this contract a cost/schedule control system which previously has been accepted by a DoD component as meeting the requirements of the DoD Cost/Schedule Control Systems Criteria (C/SCSC) on a contract of the same nature (e.g., development, production, etc.,) this system may be used to satisfy all aspects of the cost/schedule control systems requirements of this contract.

2. Contract Work Breakdown Structure (CWBS).

a.   The contractor shall develop the Contract Work Breakdown Structure (CWBS) from the summary CWBS set forth herein.   The summary CWBS will provide the basis for any further extension by the contractor to lower levels during the performance of the contract.

b.   The contractor shall use the CWBS as a framework for contract planning, budgeting, and reporting status of costs and schedule to the government.   Major elements of work that are subcontracted will be identified in the CWBS.

3. Subcontract Reporting Requirements.

The contractor shall require a subcontractor to furnish Cost/Schedule Status Reports (C/SSR) in each case where such a sub-contract is other than firm-fixed-price, and is 12 months or more in duration, and either (a) has a dollar amount which exceeds $2 million, or (b) has critical tasks relative to this contract. Critical tasks will be defined by mutual agreement between the Government and the prime contractor. Each such subcontractor's reported cost and sche-dule information will be incorporated into the prime contractor's C/SSR.

APPENDIX G
DOE CLAUSES

APPENDIX 2

SAMPLE

CSCSC SOLICITATION CLAUSE

NOTICE OF COST AND SCHEDULE CONTROL SYSTEMS

(a)   The offeror shall submit a plan for compliance with the Criteria for the internal cost and schedule control systems (management control systems) which are and/or will be operational for any contract resulting from this solicitation which includes the Cost and Schedule Control Systems Contract Clause. The Criteria for contractors' cost and schedule control systems are set forth in   DOE/CR-0015, Contract Performance Measurement Implementation Guide. The offeror shall identify his existing management control systems separately from proposed modifications to meet the Criteria. The plan shall:

(i)   describe the management control systems and their application in all major functional cost areas such as engineering, manufacturing, construction, etc., including their relationships to the Contract Work Breakdown Structure (CWBS);

(ii)   describe the procedures for planning, budgeting, scheduling, work authorization, cost accumulation, measurement and reporting of cost and schedule performance, estimating of costs at completion, variance analyses, and baseline control, including their relationships to the major functional cost areas and the CWBS;

(iii)   describe compliance with each of the Criteria*, preferably by cross-referencing the description of the management control systems with the items in the Criteria Checklist contained in DOE/CR-0015.

(iv)   identify the major subcontractors or major subcontracted effort in the event major subcontractors have not been selected, to whose management systems the Criteria will be applied;

(v)   describe the proposed procedures for administration of the Criteria when applied to subcontractors.

(b)   If the contractor is utilizing management control systems which have been previously accepted by the Department of Energy (DOE) or by the Department of Defense, or is operating such systems under a current Memorandum of Understanding with DOE, or the Department of Defense, evidence of such may be submitted in lieu of the plan mentioned above. In such an event, the Contracting Officer will determine the extent to which such systems shall be reviewed to assure continued compliance with the Criteria.

(c)   The offeror shall provide information and assistance as requested by the Contracting Officer for evaluation of compliance with the cited Criteria.

(d)   The offeror's plan for compliance with the Criteria for cost and schedule control systems will be evaluated prior to contract award. Upon validation or acceptance of the cost and schedule control systems, a description of these systems will be referenced in the contract. Subsequent changes to validated systems will require prior approval of the Contracting Officer. Subsequent changes to accepted systems will require notification to the Contracting Officer.

(e)   Subcontractor selection for application of the Criteria will be by agreement between the prime contractor and the Government. The prime contractor will contractually require the selected subcontractors to comply with the Criteria. However, demonstration and reviews of these selected subcontractors' management systems may be performed by DOE when requested by either the prime or subcontractor.

(f)   Changes to contractor management control systems required to meet the cited Criteria shall be made at no direct cost to DOE.

---

*Note: DOE will identify any Criteria and/or Criteria checklist items which may be waived.

U S GOVERNMENT PRINTING OFFICE 1980 -311-119/81

ATTACHMENT 4

SAMPLE CSCSC CONTRACT CLAUSE

COST AND SCHEDULE CONTROL SYSTEMS

(a)   In the performance of this contract, the contractor shall establish, maintain, and use cost and schedule control systems (management control systems) meeting the Criteria* set forth in DOE/CR-0015 , Cost and Schedule Control Systems Criteria for Contract Performance Measurement - Implementation Guide, annexed hereto and hereinafter referred to as the "Guide". Prior to acceptance by the Contracting Officer and within ____ calendar days after contract award, the contractor shall be prepared to demonstrate systems operation to the government to verify that the proposed systems meet the designated Criteria.   As a part of the review procedures, the Contractor shall furnish the government a description of the cost and schedule control systems applicable to this contract in such form and detail as indicated by the Guide, or as required by the Contracting Officer. The Contractor agrees to provide access to all pertinent records, data, and plans as requested by representatives of the government for the conduct of systems review.

(b)   The description of the management control systems accepted by the Contracting Officer, identified by title and date, shall be referenced in the contract.   Such systems shall be maintained and used by the contractor in the performance of this contract.

(c)   Contractor changes to the reviewed systems shall be submitted for review and approval as required by the Contracting Officer.   When Contracting Officer approval is required, the Contracting Officer shall advise the contractor of the acceptability of such changes within sixty (60) days after receipt from the contractor.   When systems existing at the time of contract award do not comply with the designated Criteria, adjustments necessary to assure compliance will be made at no change in contract price or fee.

(d)   The contractor agrees to provide access to all pertinent records and data requested by the Contracting Officer, or duly authorized representative, for the purpose of permitting government surveillance to insure continuing application of the accepted systems to this contract.   Deviations from the systems description identified during contract performance shall be corrected as directed by the Contracting Officer.

(e)   The contractor shall require that each selected subcontractor, as mutually agreed to between the government and the contractor and as set forth in the schedule of this contract, meet the Criteria for cost and schedule control systems as set forth in the subcontract and shall incorporate in all such subcontracts adequate provisions for review and surveillance of subcontractors' systems to be carried out by the prime contractor, or by the government when requested by either the prime or subcontractor.

----

*   Those Criteria and/or Criteria Checklist items which are applicable to the contract will be specifically identified by the Contracting Officer.

ATTACHMENT 5

EXAMPLE OF CSCSC MEMORANDUM OF UNDERSTANDING

This Memorandum of Understanding, entered into as of _____ (date) _____ establishes a mutual agreement between the Department of Energy and (insert contractor's full name, including facility and location) regarding the implementation and maintenance of management control systems conforming to the Department of Energy established Cost and Schedule Control Systems Criteria (CSCSC) and as implemented by the DOE/CR-0015 Cost and Schedule Control Systems Criteria for Contract Performance Measurement-Implementation Guide.

Whereas, the contractor has demonstrated certain management control systems as identified and defined in (contractor's systems description dated _____), and

Whereas, the Department of Energy by letter dated _____, based on Demonstration Review Report dated _____, did validate such systems; then:

Be It Understood and Agreed that such systems which have been validated as indicated above, together with approved changes thereto, shall apply to future (specify type of contract, for example, Architect and Engineering, Construction, etc.) contracts entered into between the contractor and the Department of Energy which require compliance with the CSCSC; and

Be It Further Understood and Agreed that:

(1)   Contractor proposed changes to those validated systems will be submitted to the cognizant contracting office for review and approval or disapproval by the Contracting Officer.

(2)   The contractor agrees to provide access to pertinent records and data in order to permit adequate surveillance of the validated systems.

This Memorandum of Understanding will remain in force indefinitely, subject to modification by mutual agreement or termination by either party.

_____   _____
       (Contractor)   (Contracting Officer)

☆ U.S. GOVERNMENT PRINTING OFFICE: 1980— 311-119:72

APPENDIX H
C/SCSC FORMS

WBS _____

PROJECT/PROGRAM	WORK BREAKDOWN STRUCTURE DICTIONARY (STATEMENT OF CONTENT)	DATE	
CONTRACT NO.		PAGE	OF

WBS LEVEL						ELEMENT TITLE	MPC CODE
1	2	3	4	5	6		

WBS DICTIONARY

EFFORT REQUIRED	FSD				PRODUCTION				ASSOCIATED LOWER LEVEL ELEMENTS		
	NR		R		NR		R		WBS NO.	LEVEL	TITLE
	YES	NO	YES	NO	YES	NO	YES	NO			
ENGR DESIGN											
ENGR TEST											
INTEG LOG SUP											
GRAPHICS											
TOOLING											
MFG ENGR											
MANUFACTURING											
MFG SUPPORT											
QUALITY ASSUR											
MATERIEL											
FACILITIES											
DATA PROCESS											

FSD — FULL-SCALE DEVELOPMENT; NR — NONRECURRING; R — RECURRING

COST ACCOUNT PLAN (CAP)

PAGE 1 OF

PROGRAM	NUMBER	TITLE	TYPE OF CAP	TYPE OF EFFORT
			☐ DISCRETE	☐ RECURRING
SUMMARY COST ELEMENT			☐ LEVEL OF EFFORT	☐ NONRECURRING
			☐ APPORTIONED	☐ PROVISIONING

SALES ORDER			EARNED VALUE CRITERIA (DIRECT ONLY)		
			☐ STANDARDS ☐ % COMPLETION	☐ DIRECT
DEPARTMENT			☐ BAR CHARTS ☐ LEVEL OF EFFORT	☐ INDIRECT
			☐ MILESTONES ☐ APPORTIONED BASE _____	

SCHEDULES START DATE	SCHEDULED COMPLETE DATE	PREPARED BY	DEPT	DATE

BUDGETED COST OF WORK (BCW)	HOURS	DOLLARS

STATEMENT OF WORK

COST ACCOUNT PLAN (S.O.W.)

APPROVALS						
ISSUE	COST ACCOUNT MGR	DATE	CONTROLLER	DATE	PROGRAM OFFICE	DATE
ORIGINAL						
REV						
REV						
REV						
REV						
REV						
REV						

COST ACCOUNT PLAN TASK SCHEDULE

PROGRAM	NUMBER	TITLE	EARNED VALUE CRITERIA	BUDGETED COST OF WORK (BCW)
			[1] APPORTIONED BASE	HOURS:
			[2] PERCENT COMPLETE	DOLLARS:
			[3] LEVEL OF EFFORT	
SUMMARY COST ELEMENT			[4] MILESTONES	PREPARED BY:
SALES ORDER			ISSUE	DEPT: DATE:
DEPARTMENT			ORIG	COST ACCOUT MGR DATE
			REV	CONTROLLER DATE
WORK PACKAGE				PROGRAM OFFICE DATE

EARNED VALUE CRITERIA
[1] APPORTIONED BASE
[2] PERCENT COMPLETE
[3] LEVEL OF EFFORT
[4] MILESTONES

COST ACCOUT MGR   DATE
CONTROLLER   DATE
PROGRAM OFFICE   DATE

BCW HOURS

BCWS MONTHLY
BCWS CUMULATIVE
BCWP MONTHLY
BCWP CUMULATIVE

BUDGET TRANSFER REQUEST

ORIGINATOR		DEPT NO.	ZONE	EXT	DATE
FROM		**TO**			
DEPARTMENT		DEPARTMENT			
SALES ORDER NO.		SALES ORDER NO.			
SUMMARY COST ELEMENT NO.		SUMMARY COST ELEMENT NO.			

MANAGEMENT RESERVE ☐	INTERDEPARTMENT ☐	ECP/CP ☐

DESCRIPTION OF TASK

BUDGET TRANSFER

HOURS (ALLOCATED)	DOLLARS (UNBURDENED)

APPROVAL SIGNATURES	
TRANSFERING MANAGER	PERFORMING MANAGER
PROGRAM CONTROLLER	BASELINE:	REVISED CAP DUE:

C/SCS PROBLEM ANALYSIS REPORT

PROBLEM ANALYSIS

① PROGRAM _____

② CAP _____
③ SO _____
④ WBS _____
⑤ CAP MGR _____
⑥ DEPT _____

⑦ PAR REV NO. _____
⑧ DATE _____
⑨ AS OF _____

D
L

⑩ IMPACT:

	SCHEDULE (HRS/$)	%	COST (HRS/$)	%
CAP CUM VARIANCE TO DATE	x			
CAP EBT VARIANCE AT COMP	x			

	SCH	COST		SCH	COST
RECOVERABLE	□	□	IRRECOVERABLE	□	□

⑬ DEPARTMENTAL PROGRAM IMPACT:

⑪ PROBLEM/REASON: (IDENTIFY SPECIFIC COST/SCHEDULE ITEMS)

⑫ CORRECTIVE ACTION: (WHAT, BY WHOM AND WHEN)

PLAN OF ACTION:

REPORT DATE	CUM TO DATE	CUMULATIVE BY MONTH						
COST BCWP + FORECAST								
ACWP + FORECAST								
VARIANCE								
SCHEDULE BCWS (PER CAP)								
BCWP + FORECAST								
VARIANCE								

⑭ PREPARED BY

⑮ APPROVED BY

376

CSCS PROBLEM ANALYSIS

CONTRACTOR:

LOCATION:

CONTRACT NO.

☐ RDT & E   ☐ PRODUCTION

PROGRAM NAME/NUMBER

AUTHORIZED SIGNATURE/TITLE/DATE

ANALYSIS REPORT (ELEMENT)

WORK BREAKDOWN STRUCTURE ITEM/FUNCTION	CONTRACT BUDGET	ITEMS CREATING CHANGES TO _____ EAC						EAC
		BURDEN RATES	LABOR RATES	LABOR	MATERIAL	PREMIUM	OTHER	SUBTOTAL	

( ) = UNDERRUNS

(ALL ENTRIES IN 000'S OF DOLLARS THRU G & A)

INDEX